Martin Caidin

# THE B-17:
# THE FLYING FORTS

MARTIN CAIDIN was the author of over fifty books and more than a thousand magazine articles and was recognized as one of the outstanding aeronautics and aviation authorities in the world. The National War College, the Air Force's Air University and several other institutions use his books as doctrine and strategy guides, historical references and textbooks. He twice won the Aviation/Space Writers Association award as the outstanding author in the field of aviation. Caidin died in March 1997.

# THE B-17
# THE FLYING
# FORTS

MARTIN CAIDIN

**ibooks**
new york
www.ibooksinc.com

DISTRIBUTED BY SIMON & SCHUSTER, INC.

An Original Publication of ibooks, inc.

Copyright © 1968, 2001 by Martin Caidin
Originally published as *Flying Forts*

Introduction © 2001 by David Ballantine

An ibooks, inc. Book

Distributed by Simon & Schuster, Inc.
1230 Avenue of the Americas, New York, NY 10020

ibooks, inc.
24 West 25th Street
New York, NY 10010

The ibooks World Wide Web Site Address is:
http://www.ibooksinc.com

ISBN 0-7434-3470-6
First ibooks, inc. printing October 2001
10 9 8 7 6 5 4 3 2 1

Cover art by Bob Larkin
Cover design by Mike Rivilis

Printed in the U.S. A.

This book is for

Bill Coleman
Lieutenant Colonel, USAF
*who flew one of the Little Friends*

# Contents

CONTENTS

# Introduction

My own association with the Boeing B-17 was of the briefest nature. The time was very close to V-J Day and I was in East St. Louis on my way back to North Camp Hood, Texas. It occurred to me that I might hitchhike successfully out of the local air field on my way back to my station. And yes, there was a plane, a B-17 bound for Victoria, Kansas. There was a slight delay while we waited for our navigator, delivered by a W.A.C.-driven jeep whose crew carefully loaded him up through the open bomb bay. He was able to retain the unconsciousness exhibited at the inception of the flight all the way to its end.

This was not a problem as our pilot was able to fly an iron compass route by simply following the railway tracks on the ground below that showed up on his hand-held map. This B-17 had seen better days and oil leaked from a couple of its engines, but not in a sufficient volume so as to alarm the pilot. He even let me fly his tired old lady for a while. Needless to say we safely reached Victoria or I would not be writing this.

On August 20, 1935, Boeing had only a single B-17, the prototype Model 299. It was a new type of heavy bomber brought into existence as a speculative venture. The stakes were high for the young airplane manufacturer; top management was literally risking the future of the company on their new bomber. As flight tests of Model 299 progressed, it was discovered that this aircraft was like something from a science-fiction novel. Unlike the bomber prototypes from competing companies that were founded on proven experience or a part of the then-limping present of military bomber design, Boeing's Model 299 was an aircraft that was many years ahead of its time.

Then, it was almost as if the gods of war had been angered by Boeing's dramatic test-flight successes. After another flawless demonstration, Army Air Force Major Pete Hill took Model 299 on a final test flight. The result was a crash that killed everyone on the plane. A board of inquiry subsequently determined that Hill had neglected to perform the most rudimentary preflight test. He had failed to check the control console. If he had, he would have discovered that the elevators and rudder had been locked.

The fortunes of Boeing crashed with Model 299 as well. Proponents of other, lesser, aircraft came quickly forward, questioning the need and practicality of a strategic bomber of such an advanced design. Fortunately, Model 299 had impressed key far-seeing men in the Army Air Force. They managed to get funding for the B-17. Despite the severe setback, Boeing was back in business. Modifications improved performance further, and soon production models were flying off to war. In the aftermath of the attack on Pearl Harbor on December 7, 1941, the B-17 helped provide America with one of its first heroes, Captain Colin Kelly whose B-17, on December 11, was credited with sinking a Japanese battleship off the Philippine coast. Kelly did not survive the attack. Much later it was discovered that Kelly had not attacked a battleship and in fact did not sink anything. But by that time America—and the B-17—was well into the war.

The combat history of the B-17 showed that the initial belief in the ability of the bomber to protect itself against a determined enemy was optimistic. The most tragic example was the second raid on Schweinfurt, Germany in 1943—Black Thursday—where B-17 formations without any fighter escorts fought their way through the full wrath of the Luftwaffe. The result was a massacre. Yet despite the incredibly brutal punishment many of the B-17s suffered, planes that by all rights should have crashed, managed to bring their fearsomely wounded crews home. After Schweinfurt, some questioned if the strategic bomber offensive was a failure. It was not. But clearly, in order to perform its mission of striking deep into enemy territory, the B-17 would need help.

That help came in the form of the Little Friends—the fighters. P-38s, P-47s, and the bestest Little Friend of them all, the P-51 equipped with long-range auxiliary fuel tanks. The skies over Germany and occupied Europe were filled with the warplanes of the U.S. 8th Air Force. Domination of the sky above Normandy during D-Day was so complete that General Eisenhower said to his troops, "If you see fighting aircraft over you, they will be ours."

The B-17's attacks on Germany's industry continued and by the end of February 1945, that nation's major cities were in smoldering ruins from border to border. In writing THE B-17: THE FLYING FORTS, Martin Caidin wrote a stirring tribute to a great warplane and the gallant men who flew it.

David Ballantine
*New York*
July 2001

# Foreword

There is an old saying that the military historian enjoys the invaluable vantage of 20-20 hindsight. Studying past events with impersonal objectivity, he is able to peer through the eyes of a hundred or a thousand combatants of a single great conflict. He is afforded the unique attitudes of both sides and, painstakingly, as much as is possible after the dimming of memory and the obliteration inevitably of certain records, he reweaves the tapestry of what has gone before. Omissions most certainly there will be. Yet the task is immeasurably simpler than if the historian were required to fulfill his role during those moments when the events in issue were being enacted. History is the eagle's view and the perspective of the back room. The historian uses both to solve the mysteries of the past.

Well, almost.

When shortly after the turn of the century men took to the air to wage war, they also baffled and harassed the historian. Until the Great War of 1914–1918 fields of battle might be revisited and the paths of armies walked again. There were maps to consult and points of shredded geography to relearn what had trampled the earth underfoot. Even great battles at sea, with ponderous vessels chained to strategies long established, remained restricted within time and two-dimensional movement.

Not so the arena of aerial conflict. There, as many as thirty thousand men in winged chariots have fought a single terrible duel that covered not simply thousands of square miles, but tens of thousands of *cubic* miles. An arena where, only minutes after unbridled fury, the nature of the skies erased forever the scars of battle.

The only marker of the combat waged in the heavens is the memory of the participants and the statistical hieroglyphics of the survivors. Never is there the opportunity to revisit the scenes where men and machines clashed. The debris and sputum of battle, the contrails and funereal pyres of greasy smoke, the shattered chunks and bits and pieces of metal, the searing lash of flame; gleaming empty shell cases and torn parachutes, gutted behemoths and limb-flailing men.... All these vanish forever with the first sigh of the wind. There is no such thunder in history nor will ever be again, as filled the skies of Europe during World War II. A thunder from a stream of mighty bombers many hundreds of miles in length, ten thousand engines beating sonorously against an earth far below. And the cry, deep-throated and howling, of another three thousand engines—the fighters rising and swooping to do battle. Thunder upon thunder, explosions and racketing thousands of guns, a cacophonous rainfall of millions of spent bullets and cannon shells and debris and bombs.

Then, the gentle sighing of wind. Silence. The air cleansed as it was before the approach of the metallic thunder.

And yet, what was slashed for those moments in the skies turned crimson red and black and sun gleaming off silvery wings, remains. It remains in memory, and it remains in what was committed of that memory to paper. The statistics, of course; the numbers of the combatants. How many bombers, how many fighters, how many bombs and gallons of fuel and engines and shells and rockets and lives and all the other statistical structure-work of the historical ledger. There are so many great airfields to count, so many runways from which the giants trundled faster and faster, finally to grasp precariously with wide wings and throbbing engines the first shuddering moments of flight.

There are so many numbered and colored flares for which men must watch, there are so many radio beacons on which to home; there are specific points over the earth, measured in geographical location, height, speed, and time, where the giants assemble, from where they wheel in stately formation and then, performing slavishly to the hands of the clock, march off through the heavens to meet the enemy who also is a prisoner of the statistical miasma of modern war. Oh, there are the numbers, all right. Long lists of numbers; charts, graphs, tally sheets. Thick reams of them. But they're not enough.

Air war is above all the story of men. As they view what transpires, from an individual, yet interrelated and always multifaceted approach, it is the story of men.

And it is the story of the machines in which they flew to contest the enemy.

This is the story of one such machine, the airplane that became famed the world over as, simply, the *Queen.*

This airplane—the Boeing B-17 Flying Fortress—was invested by the men who flew her, and by those who fought against her, with a personality and a status afforded few machines with wings. If there is a Hall of Fame of great airplanes then unquestionably among its roster we will find the B-17; indeed, even in that hallowed final resting place the B-17 would occupy a niche of especial honor.

What imparts greatness to an aircraft? As swiftly as that question is put to words there will spring up a host of responses. Many bear the same message; they repeat among many different men, pilots and crewmen, the same reactions. Others will not share this repetition. Different men find different reasons for embracing fondly the memories of the craft in which they flew off to war. But always, through the broad spectrum of the explanations and the answers, a single thread of continuity begins to emerge. There is a single factor to cement all the others.

A pilot of the B-17 would say: *"This was an airplane you could trust."*

That alone tells other pilots many things. Immediately they think of a machine minus the vices that in some airplanes kill men. An airplane you can trust means just that—she lets you know what she will do and she will not spring on you, at the worst possible moments of flight, a vicious flight characteristic that can tear control from the hands of its crew. But this, by itself, is not enough. The B-17 was a military airplane, a four-engine, long-range heavy bomber. As such it was created to fulfill a national need and to perform a national mission. How it flew was important, if not vital. But if it flew superbly and fought poorly it could not be an effective weapon. It had to fulfill its roles both as an airplane *and* as a weapon.

And even these characteristics give us but a glimpse into the fiber of the airplane or of the weapon or of both.

There are impersonal, coldly objective points of view that sometimes tell us much. Of the B-17, a noted British air war historian[1] said: "Few other aircraft of the Second World War gained the universal affection of their aircrew over so long an operational period as did the Boeing B-17 Fortress, which formed the spearhead of the American bombing offensive in Europe from beginning to end, as well as serving in every other theater of war. No single aircraft type contributed more to the defeat of the Luftwaffe, both in the air and on the ground, than the Fortress, which enabled tangible expression to be given to the controversial U.S. policy for the strategic assault of Germany by day in the face of formidable political argument as well as desperate enemy opposition."

And this in itself is a paradox. The fact of the matter

was that the Flying Fortress had few single outstanding facets of superiority which might be claimed by its builders or the men who flew it into battle. The B-17 was neither the largest nor the heaviest four-engine bomber of World War II. It did not carry the heaviest bomb load and other large aircraft were faster, and could fly farther, than the Fortress. It was not built in the greatest number. It was "not" a great many things.

But all agree it was the greatest bomber that ever took to the skies. Why? How?

That is this story. Our British air historian comments that the "Fortress achieved fame . . . on the strength of several outstanding attributes. Of these, perhaps the most important were an excellent high-altitude capability, and the ability to absorb an amazing amount of battle damage. To these attributes were added . . . an exceptionally heavy defensive armament. . . ."

An official survey by the Army Air Force, of our leading bomber types in use during World War II, noted simply:[2] "Against the Luftwaffe, the capital enemy, the rugged and steady B-17 remained the natural pick."

Beirne Lay, Jr., one of the outstanding heavy bomber pilots of World War II, who worked with the writer during the compilation of research for my book on the ill-famed raid of October 14, 1943, against Schweinfurt, *Black Thursday*, noted yet another quality of the Flying Fortress. Discussing different bomber types, he concluded that "I have to give the nod to the B-17 from a pilot's standpoint. The 17 was easier to fly in formation at high altitude, its engines were less critical during a long climb under heavy load, the bird was more stable and flew better with one or more engines out at high altitude. And it was less vulnerable to battle damage because of less reliance on hydraulic systems.

"When my group converted from B-24s to B-17s, results improved immediately in every department—crew morale, bombing accuracy, abort rate and formation flying. . . ."

And there are the words that from Lieutenant General Frank A. Armstrong, Jr. former commander of the 97th Bomb Group, establish an extraordinary testimonial:

". . . I recall the many requirements I placed on the B-17, both as a commander and as a pilot. Not once did it falter and many times it accomplished the almost impossible. During my thirty-three-year military career I flew many types of aircraft, from DHs to B-47 jet bombers. My combat flying was done in the B-17 and B-29—the first in Europe and the second off Guam. I must say, in all fairness, that both the ships were excellent aircraft. My being alive today attests to that fact.

"I am personally aware of the fact that a B-17 could absorb three thousand bullets, fly with no rudder and complete its combat mission on two engines. To me the Flying Fortress was, and always will be, the Queen of the Sky. I owe my life to the Queen. God help us had she not been in the being when the war began."

So there was that, too. An airplane ready and available, when the need was there. But again, even the need was not enough. All the other factors had to be there as well. From these initial, brief insights into the B-17, immediately there emerges a sense about the machine—rugged; steady; the ability to take a terrible mauling at the hands of the enemy; stable; reliable; a pilot's airplane. These are the ingredients from which great machines are made.

But we are getting ahead of our story—this is the story of an airplane, and of the men who flew within, and fought against, the B-17. No airplane may speak for itself. It can be given voice only by men, and by a statistical record.

Through the words of the men whom the reader will meet on the pages of this book the B-17 will tell of itself, will assume that personality of which its pilots speak so readily.

There is a further note to be brought to the attention of the reader. This book has been years in the making: not specifically these pages, but in many other of my books the Flying Fortress has dominated the research and the writing, and pointed ultimately in the direction of this one book, for everything that has been accumulated over more than twenty years of writing research has contributed to it.

At the Research Studies Institute of the Air University of the United States Air Force I studied thousands of reports of combat missions flown by B-17 crews. Many of these were the cold and official records of such missions. Others were not; in the original handwriting of crews going through debriefing, they have lost nothing of the personal touch imparted to them at the moment of writing. The personal notes of pilots and copilots and their crewmen—bombardiers, navigators, radiomen, gunners, and observers. I have read thousands of interrogation reports of the intelligence and debriefing officers, spanning in their assembled pages an air war fought across almost every area of the entire world.

The official records comprise a staggering total. From the reports of individual crewmen, they rise through a widening spectrum of organization, like an inverted pyramid of history. Pilots, crews, squadrons, groups, headquarters, wings, higher headquarters, and all of them with branches offshooting into evaluations, intelligence studies, technical reports. Through official records of other air combatants there is always much to be learned—the stories told by escorting fighter pilots, by the enemy pilots who opposed the B-17s, by the enemy who faced them from the ground. These, too, are an integral element of *Flying Forts!*

I have been especially fortunate in reaching back through the years to ascertain the Japanese side of the B-17 ledger. The records of the Japanese, for the great part obliterated in the cyclone of destruction and defeat, survived for me in the form of close personal friends within what was, during the war, the Japanese high command. As well as pilots, such as Saburo Sakai, and others, with whom I spent years amassing the details that enabled me to write such books as *Zero!* and *Samurai!* which told of that air war from the point of view of our former enemy.

Much the same has been done in respect to those pilots who flew German and Italian fighters against the B-17. Personal stories, interwoven with the official record, told against the backdrop of the men within the B-17s. . . . It is from these studies, this research over a period of many years, that this last telling of the story of the B-17 has been drawn.

In some ways the past may be relived. There are, literally, tens of thousands of photographs that have captured moments of history. Each moment, of course, speaks for those preceding and following the instant recorded by the camera. These are invaluable in retaining keys to the past. In addition I studied hundreds of thousands of feet of motion picture film. Some of this footage, such as was taken by automatic gun cameras, is technically poor but historically rich in content. Other camera footage in an instant sweeps us back to moments when the actual events were being created. Black-and-white film and spectacular color footage, taken from within B-17s and from the vantage of the attacking enemy, have left us with a legacy unmatched. There is, as well, the legacy of sound—recordings made of combatants of both sides, carrying through to the present the intensities of those instants when emotion, from fear through exultation, lent special meaning to the sounds to which we listen so carefully today.

There is more. Through the last twenty-five years I have been fortunate in knowing as close friends many who helped carve the final immortality of the B-17. Men who were there to design, to build, to test, to fly and to fight with the Flying Fortress. Men like Colonel Budd J. Peaslee, veteran fighter, bomber and air scout pilot of the 8th Air Force, the Air Commander of the terrible mission of *Black Thursday*. Men like Major General Dale O. Smith, USAF, Ret., who flew more missions than he would like to remember in battle-scarred Forts. Friends such as Lt. Colonel Keith M. Garrison, USAF, who cut his battle teeth as a youngster in the B-17, and who went on to fly Boeing descendants of the Fortress. Attrition, not battle, cut down this brilliant young officer when he died on February 1, 1960, in the flaming crash of a great jet bomber. But Keith Garrison, like so many others, left his legacy with us. It is these men—friend and former foe—who number finally in the hundreds, who helped to create this final chapter of the Flying Fortress.

Then there is one element, last in this listing, but—fortunately—anything but last in its importance to this story. That is personal knowledge, feeling, and a kinship with the Flying Fortress. The writer through the past two decades has had many occasions in which to take to the air with the B-17. As a correspondent I flew in B-17s of many different types. Indeed, as an *after*-war correspondent I had the opportunity to become acquainted in the air with B-17s that were employed for dropping missiles, for missile-range clearance activities, weather and engine research, VIP transports, radiation detection warning aircraft, drones, crop dusting!, carrying cucumbers and rare tropical fish in pressurized containers—to mention only a few of the assorted tasks which have befallen the postwar Fortresses.

But, most of all, there were three ancient B-17s with which twelve of us recreated moments of the past. In 1961, to film the motion picture, "The War Lover," a group of improbable adventurers, under the helm of Gregory R. Board and John Crewdson, flew three B-17s from Tucson, Arizona, to England where the airplanes starred in the film. It was the sort of adventure where we planned on minimum difficulty en route—a three-day flight from Arizona to England which, instead, became a series of wild misadventures and incidents that extended itself to seventeen days of hilarity, hysteria and wonder, both on the ground and in the air. One of the results of that flight was the book, *Everything but the Flak*, in which, with words and, fortunately, many photographs taken by two professional photographers who went along with us, we were able to record permanently a flight and a journey all of us have come to cherish. More to the point, the opportunity was provided at that time to learn, truly, the B-17 inside and out.

The three airplanes, when found, were in deplorable condition. They were abandoned near-wrecks and half-wrecks. Spare parts and materials for their resurrection were in short supply or simply unavailable. Greg Board performed near-miracles with his skilled team in rebuilding the old bombers. Rebuilding them, refitting them, flight-testing them—and effecting their delivery to England.

I flew on that mission as copilot in Blue One, the lead Fortress, with Greg Board (an extraordinarily gifted pilot) in the left seat. The entire affair brought home to me, as nothing else ever could have, the feel and character of the Fortress. After the flight to England, there were flights during which filming took place, and further flights, after Blue One returned to the States, in an airplane which had fast become a friend to all of us involved in our little derring-do. Ours was, at the time, the last formation flight of B-17s across the ocean and, I dare say, likely it will remain the last ever to be flown. This book, then, is more than a compilation of material of others—I feel a personal thread in its writing.

A word of explanation is necessary at this point. First, this is the story of the B-17—*not* of the war it fought, or of the period prior to that war, or the era that followed. This distinction I have had to observe carefully, otherwise there would be no end or limits to this book. So lines had to be drawn. Hopefully, these lines encompass the B-17 which is, after all, our main interest. At the same time, there have been many books in which the Flying Fortress assumed a major, even a dominating role. My own study of Mission 115 of the 8th Bomber Command, *Black Thursday*, is one such book. The problem as to how much of such earlier accounts to include in this book was settled by limiting the material to only that which the writer felt was vital to the telling of the final story of the B-17. Whatever was available readily enough in previous publications has been kept to its minimum in *Flying Forts!* Thus much of the greatest air battle ever fought, the mission of October 14, 1943, against Schweinfurt, Germany, has in these pages a carefully selective representation. The organizational details of B-17 operations alone would fill more pages than are contained in this book; but the reader who desires such details may readily find them in the six-volume history, *The Army Air Forces in World War II*. It is not the province of this book to include in great detail such material.

And never will there be another book comparable to the splendid, tragic story, *Serenade to the Big Bird*, written by Bert Stiles, who flew 35 missions as copilot of a Flying Fortress over Europe. Here in the self-accounting of a young American airman is a glimpse into the lives of the men who flew the great Forts in a manner that could never be told in any other way. It is an incisive, singular, deeply human story, and to that book the reader is directed with urgency.

Because of the need for selectivity of material, inevitably there will be much omitted that some readers feel should have been included; the writer can only trust that what emerges is representative of the Fortress herself.

One last word. Earlier I made reference to the effect that *Flying Forts!* might constitute the final chapter on the Flying Fortress. It cannot, of course, because there remain yet untold many stories still submerged in the history of World War II. As one historian of the Air Force has noted, "fresh fragments of tragedy, pathos, and valor will continue to emerge from the mists of memory so long as the generation which participated walks the face of the earth. Many episodes of the great war were shrouded in mystery. Many strange things happened for which there is no explanation, and the memory of them endures in the minds of those who experienced them."

How true those words. . . .

In bringing to a close this Foreword, I do so with a reminder, not only to the reader, but to myself as well, that there will remain, for many years to come, not only stories that remain untold, but those for which no man has ever provided an answer.

On November 23, 1944, there occurred an incident in Europe which, had it not been documented thoroughly, would not now be included in these pages. Yet, strange may it be, it *did* happen. The writer of the incident following, a former British officer, John V. Crisp, wrote these notes while at The Cottage, West End, Essendon, Hertfordshire, England. They were brought to the attention of officials in this country through the American Embassy in Britain. John V. Crisp writes—

On November 23, 1944, the aircraft-spotters of a British antiaircraft unit, located a few miles southeast of Brussels, were astonished to see a B-17 *Flying Fortress* approaching their gun site with its undercarriage down and losing height rapidly. They called the Troop Commander immediately and almost at once the B-17 landed on the rough plowed field where the guns were dug in, bouncing along to within thirty yards of them. At the last moment one wing tip dipped, catching in the ground and slewing the plane round. The airscrew [propeller] of the outerport engine buckled on impact, but the remaining three engines continued to tick over.

Expecting the crew to jump to the ground, the gunners waited to welcome them, but no one appeared and on walking round the plane no sign of life could be seen. It was at this point that the Troop Commander put through a call to me at my Operations Room at Erps-Querps, near Cortonburg. Within twenty minutes I was examining the B-17, not having had any previous experience of flying machines, and eventually discovered a way into it underneath the fuselage. The whole craft was quite devoid of occupants, although evidence of fairly recent occupation was everywhere.

In order to converse with greater comfort, I climbed into the pilot's seat with a view to switching off the three engines which still continued to run, and managed, with a certain amount of experiment, to find the correct switches. I next looked at the navigator's table. The aircraft log was open and the last words, written some time before, were "Bad Flak." With curiosity, I traced the flight back from the

Ruhr to Letchworth in Hertfordshire, which by coincidence was my home county, and I wondered at what could have happened to the crew.

We now made a thorough search and our most remarkable find in the fuselage was about *a dozen parachutes neatly wrapped and ready for clipping on.* This made the whereabouts of the crew even more mysterious. The Sperry bombsight remained in the perspex nose, quite undamaged, with its cover carefully folded beside it. Back on the navigator's desk was the code book giving the Colours and Letter of the day for identification purposes. Various fur-lined flying jackets lay in the fuselage together with a few bars of chocolate, partly consumed in some cases.

On close inspection of the B-17 itself no damage could be discovered, other than that of the port wing which was the result of the rough landing. I at once drove to the Operations Room of the 83rd Tactical Air Force situated near Everburg to report the landing and handed in the navigator's log, the code book and various maps, but the story behind the arrival of the B-17, unoccupied, remains a mystery to me this day.

Attempts were made, through identification numbers and squadron assignment, to discover what might have happened to the crew that had occupied the B-17 prior to its unmanned landing in the open field.

They have never been found.

Martin Caidin
*Cape Kennedy, Florida*

# I

# IN THE BEGINNING

# CHAPTER I

# MISSION OVER BUKA

FAR BENEATH THE LONE Flying Fortress the islands of the northern Solomons lay rich and green against the backdrop of the Pacific. Scattered clouds imparted a sense of height to the crew of the B-17 cruising more than five miles above the earth. Bundled into heavy fleece-lined flight suits and boots, clumsy in their goggles, leather helmets and oxygen-system hookups, the men in the bomber scanned the skies about them with wary, practiced eyes. Deep as they were within Japanese territory the air had been empty of enemy planes. It was a small miracle; they hoped it would remain. One airplane was an inviting target to Japanese interceptors, and every minute longer without the expected sighting of wings climbing to their altitude was another lease on life.

Several crewmen glanced down again, studying the islands. Beneath the lush jungle growth that stretched inland from the white beaches thousands of Japanese soldiers and construction battalions labored frantically to complete defense systems, to dig in against the American assault they knew was inevitable. The American offensive in the Solomons was shifting into high gear. The months-long struggle for Guadalcanal, shifting precariously in superiority from one combatant to the other, was now safely behind the Americans. We were firmly entrenched on that bloodied patch of jungle island. The early airfields, crude in construction and battered day and night by Japanese artillery, warships and bombers, had become solid staging areas for a growing American air assault. We had new fighters, more than a match for the Zero, and we had them in numbers sufficient to make the Japanese study the future with grim and unhappy thoughts. New bombers, faster and more heavily gunned than the patchwork air fleet the Japanese had ripped apart since the early months of the war, moved out daily against their targets.

We weren't just hitting the Japanese where it hurt. We were cutting them up, bloodying their main forces, setting up the meat grinder that would be hurled against them and that, the Japanese knew, could well dislodge them from their island bases. The enemy had to do more than to build log barricades and dig in artillery.

In April of 1943 the Japanese High Command made its decision. Waiting for the Americans to build up momentum promised only a battering ram of explosives hurled at defending positions. There was a better way and in that decision to move first the Japanese were experienced, skilled and capable. Don't wait—strike first.

None other than Admiral Isoroku Yamamoto, Commander-in-Chief of the Imperial Combined Fleet, assumed command of the massive air assault to be directed against the Americans. Architect of Japan's sweeping victories against the Americans, British and the Dutch from the opening shot of the war, Yamamoto left nothing to his subordinates. This wasn't just another air operation; the experienced Japanese admiral brought in several major air fleets consisting of hundreds of new fighters and bombers. He brought with him his most experienced staff officers and when Yamamoto made his move, it was with staggering effect. The bombers came over in perfect formation under the escorting guns and cannon of Zero fighters. They slammed at air bases, harbor facilities, base camps, shipping—anything and everything that presented a worthwhile target.

Our own fighters—Lightnings, Airacobras, Kittyhawks, Wildcats and Corsairs—took a heavy toll of the enemy. Yamamoto kept up the pressure; his air fleets continued their heavy strikes, accepting their losses, inflicting hammering blows against American installations.

The American fighters weren't enough. If the Japanese were prepared to accept the beatings in the air then they might accomplish their purpose of breaking the back of the American drive before it could gain the momentum necessary to carry it deep into the enemy camp. To stop the Japanese in the air we needed to strike at their home bases, catch the bombers and the fighters on the ground. We needed to chew up the runways, rip the airbase installations, bring the sustained Japanese air offensive to a halt.

No air campaign of the extent waged under Yamamoto's personal direction could be sustained with the air bases of which we knew. There was no question but that the Japanese had extended the runways of existing fields and that they had built new fields. But where were these bases? How many were they in number? How many planes, of what types, were being supported by each field?

Intelligence requested air reconnaissance photos. If we were to smash the Japanese air offensive on the ground, and quickly, we needed detailed information of the enemy where he lived. There was more to it, of course. Stopping the air strikes of the Japanese was only one element of the campaign we waged. Once *we* went to the offensive we would be committing ships at sea and powerful invasion forces. Targets prime for a powerful air strike by the Japanese, who certainly would make every attempt to crush invasion attempts while the thin-skinned troop transports hove to off enemy beaches, and thousands of men lay exposed in their slow landing craft.

The great wheeling motion of our own building offensive snubbed on a lack of precise intelligence. Headquarters issued the requirement—photographic reconnaissance by a single plane coming over its camera targets in daylight at high altitude, the one plane to fly straight down the northern Solomons, its pilot keeping the compass needle glued to the glass, unwavering, so that in the lower nose of the machine a man would stare through an optical eyepiece at the surface far below, and trip his cameras. It would be a long run, over known air bases, attempting to ferret out suspected airfields.

It wasn't a choice mission. It was, in truth, a lousy mission. The odds were that a single plane wouldn't make it. The Japanese Zero pilots would shout to one another when they received orders to scramble against the loner high over their runways. Whatever crew would make this mission couldn't help but know the score. There was a chance, slimmer than a sheet of parchment, that they might just pull it off, get the pictures and run for it before the Japanese fighters swarmed over them. It was a chance but no one believed in it.

At headquarters of the 43rd Bombardment Group on Dobodura, New Guinea, the commanding officer received the orders for the lone reconnaissance mission. He studied the papers and he cursed; he knew the odds as well as any pilot under his command. And he knew he wouldn't *order* any crew out over the northern Solomons. It would have to be a volunteer mission—volunteers for a suicide mission.

The first pilot he ran into was Captain Jay Zeamer, Jr. The CO told him what was needed. Zeamer assembled his crew and again the CO gave them the facts—unvarnished and grim. To a man the entire crew volunteered.

The CO wasn't really too surprised. Jay Zeamer and his crew hadn't even blinked an eye among them when the CO said the mission "is going to be rough; goddamned rough." Zeamer and his closely knit crew had volunteered their B-17 for just about every dirty, rough assignment that came to the 43rd Bombardment Group.

The strange part of it was that this crew could never be described in the official records of the Group as having a long, exceptional record, or of maintaining unusual efficiency, or whatever it was that evaluating officers like to put down on paper to send on to higher headquarters.

The truth of the matter was that Jay Zeamer for years had been a thorn in the side of almost every pilot with whom he flew. Zeamer was described by those pilots, to a man, as being a "tremendous guy." Following this declaration of friendship was almost always a bellowed "But get him outta my goddamned airplane!"

Jay Zeamer, until he showed up at the 43rd, had tried in vain, again and again, to elevate his status from copilot to pilot. His best friends wouldn't check him out, wouldn't say the words to gain for him what he coveted—the left seat of a bomber cockpit.

Jay Zeamer was an oddball. His crew? They were described by their friends as "oddballs and screw-offs, every last one of them." Which, in truth they were. The black sheep of their outfits. Misfits, characters. Nobody wanted them.

Except Jay Zeamer. He turned them into the best crew in the 43rd Bombardment Group. In a beat-up, patchwork, castoff B-17 they carried out missions that the other crews said were impossible. When their CO brought to them the need for the reconnaissance mission over the northern Solomons, they bought the whole pie and to a man they volunteered.

The dice of war are unpredictable.

No other mission in the skies, before or since, would rank with the flight of that lone B-17 over the northern Solomons.

On other flights of battle, before June 16, 1943, when Jay Zeamer and his crew left Dobodura, Americans have fought in such a manner as to be awarded by a grateful nation the Congressional Medal of Honor. On other flights of battle since that date, in that same war and others that followed, other Americans also were so honored.

But only on June 16, 1943, and only to the crew of that one B-17—to two men of that crew—was there so extraordinary a moment in our history.

Two men, Jay Zeamer, pilot, and Joseph R. Sarnoski, bombardier, *each* were awarded the Medal of Honor.

The silvered wings and fuselage of the Martin B-26 Marauder flashed in the early morning sun at Langley Field, Virginia, as the big twin-engined bomber sailed in for a landing. Just before the airplane crossed the end of the runway it seemed to wobble, a precarious wingtip-rolling motion of lost speed and control. Thunder cracked across the field as the pilot slammed forward on the throttles in a desperate measure for power. At the last moment the Marauder straightened, then touched down smoothly on its main gear.

Minutes later the B-26 rolled to a stop on the flight line

of the 22nd Bombardment Group, and the crew deplaned. Lt. Walt Krell, the pilot, waited for the copilot with whom he'd been flying—the copilot he was trying to check out as pilot. Krell turned to the second man.

"Dammit, Jay," he said heatedly, "you're just not paying attention up there. You'll never check out as a pilot unless you get rid of those bad habits. Man, you nearly killed us that time!"

Lt. Jay Zeamer looked blankly at Krell. "What did I do wrong, Walt?"

Krell stared at Zeamer, his mouth working silently. The words wouldn't come. Krell turned on his heel and stalked away, furious.

That was late 1941. Walt Krell and Jay Zeamer had been friends long before they were assigned together in the 22nd Bomb Group, first outfit in the AAF to fly the hot, fast B-26 Marauder. Krell liked Zeamer—despite the fact that Zeamer seemed to have some block built into his system that prevented his checking out in the left seat of the B-26 as pilot.

"I went through flying school with Zeamer," Krell explained, turning back the years. "In fact, I was right behind Jay when we were training in Illinois. Jay was in the class right ahead of me, and he was Captain of Cadets. I took over when he left and we ran into each other again—this was at Maxwell Field in Alabama where he stayed one class ahead of me all through that school. Now, Jay Zeamer as a pilot had the kind of very relaxed attitude that I liked. When you got right down to it he was the most relaxed man in an airplane I ever knew. Nothing ever seemed to bother him. No emergency could shake him. He was the kind of a guy that everyone took to.

"When we got into B-26s, all of us checked out as pilots in the left seat. Except Jay Zeamer, that is. For some strange reason Jay just couldn't hack it. Every one of us tried to check him out. We figured that someone, some-where along the line, would find the monkey that was rid-ing Jay's back. But, whatever it was we couldn't find it. Jay was stuck in the right seat as copilot.

"We kept trying, of course. You just had to do your best to get him into the left seat, where everyone felt he be-longed. But we just couldn't turn him loose because . . . well, the way he'd come into the field would turn your hair white. We'd go out and shoot landings, and slow the air-plane down to about 130 and you'd hear, you would feel it get washy, soft and mushy on the controls; you'd grab it and put it on the ground and turn it back to Zeamer and then you'd say: 'Jay, you know what you did wrong that time?'

"He not only didn't know what he had done—he didn't even know that anything was wrong! None of us could check him out. He kept flying in the copilot's seat with guys that were new pilots—they had all graduated *after* Jay got his wings, class after class after them. They made it into the left seat, but not Jay Zeamer.

"The situation didn't change when the war started. Right after the Japanese raked Pearl Harbor over the coals we took the B-26s out on anti-submarine patrol off the west coast. Jay Zeamer was still in the right seat as copilot. Then we went down to Australia and New Guinea, the first Marauder outfit in combat in the Southwest Pacific. We flew combat missions until they were coming out of our ears. The Japs were beating the hell out of us, casualties were brutal. Day after day we went out on combat mis-sions. We were so short of crews we were using Australian sergeants in the cockpits. And—you guessed it—Jay Zeamer still couldn't check out as pilot!

"We had a new pilot named Seffern, who was coming

along very well, and we upgraded him as quickly as we could into the left seat so that he flew his own Marauder. We assigned Jay Zeamer as his copilot; I think Jay was fast becoming the oldest, most experienced copilot in the business. I took Seffern on his first mission when he flew as pilot. I was always very careful with a new man, I wanted him close to see what he could do and how he handled himself.

"On this mission we went out to hit the Japanese field at Lae, along the northern coast of New Guinea. As we came into the target Seffern sort of fell back from his place in formation. That can be tricky as hell; it messes up your position for crossfire from each bomber and it strings out your bomb drop. Anyway, I had to fool around and nurse the power while he got back where he belonged. He was in fair position when we made our bomb run. The flak was pretty bad and we went into the long shallow dive we always used to pick up speed to get the hell away from the Zeros. We went right down to the water, everything wide open and every airplane hell-bent for leather to get all the speed it could. Sure enough, Seffern was all messed up. I picked him up again and had to baby him just over the water all the way back to Seven-Mile Drome. I was mad as hell because Seffern was erratic all that flight back to our base.

"Right away I put him on the carpet and demanded to know what the hell was wrong in his airplane. Instead of making excuses Seffern blew up. 'I'll tell you what the hell was wrong!' he shouted. 'You gave me Zeamer for a copilot, damn you!'

" 'What's wrong with that?' I asked him.

"Seffern stared at me. 'Wrong? I'll tell you. When you gave me the signal to get ready for the bomb run, I woke Zeamer up and—'

"I broke in right there. 'You what?' I asked him.

" 'That's right,' Seffern snapped. 'I had to wake him up. He was sound asleep. I told him what I wanted him to do. Zeamer woke up but he didn't do anything I asked. He didn't check the cockpit or go on the throttles or anything else. When he woke up he strapped on his Mae West, buckled on his 'chute, and then he takes that goddamned World War I tin helmet of his and sticks it on his head. I haven't got time to watch him any more because I'm looking out the left window holding position on you. I can't see what's going on in the cockpit. When we made the bomb run and you went to 2,400 RPM—I saw you start to pull away—I called for 2,400 RPM from Zeamer. Nothing happened. I'm watching you pull away and I can't look in the cockpit and I'm hollering as loud as I can for 2,400 RPM. Nothing! Finally you're far away from me and I turned to look at Zeamer—maybe the guy got hit by flak or something—and he's fast asleep again! All the way through the flak and the bombing run he's been asleep! I belted him on the chest to wake him up and hollered at him some more. By now you were way ahead of me and I saw you starting to drop back. I glanced again at Zeamer and for Chrissakes, Walt, he was sound asleep all over again!' "[3]

Walt Krell picked up the events of the moment: "That was the kind of guy he was—with flak hitting all around us, the Zeros waiting to come in, dropping bombs, Jay was so bored with the whole thing that he just didn't give a damn. When I spoke to him later he was real sore. Zeamer looked me right in the eye. 'I'm getting out of this outfit,' he told me. 'I'll never get anywhere here; hell, they won't even let me be cook.'

"So we left Zeamer at Iron Range in Australia. Dwight Divine, the 22nd's CO, wangled a transfer for Zeamer to the 43rd Bombardment Group. Zeamer took one look at the B-

17s the 43rd had and, I think, right away, there on the spot, he fell in love with that big airplane. But it didn't do him any good. They knew all about Jay Zeamer and, besides, everyone wanted to fly the Fortress, and copilots were a dime a dozen, and Zeamer was the last of the dozen. He was popular with the crews, you couldn't help liking Zeamer, but nobody wanted him in their airplane.

"When the 43rd went back up to New Guinea from Iron Range for combat operations, they left Zeamer behind. He was stuck at that godawful base in Australia and tagged as general cook, bottle washer and handyman. He got mad as hell and one day he saw his chance. The service squadron had dragged a wrecked B-17 to one end of the field to use for spare parts. The airplane had been banged up and written off by the maintenance officer as junk to be cannibalized for operational planes. Somehow Jay Zeamer wangled the authority to try to patch up the plane, and he did just that. The mechanics said it was impossible but Zeamer didn't care. He drove the ground crews out of their minds, but they screwed together that B-17 with baling wire and all kinds of junk and spare parts from old wrecked ships they had there. Finally the thing was ready to fly and the maintenance chief at Iron Range radioed 43rd headquarters in New Guinea that the plane was ready to go. Headquarters notified them they would send down a crew to get the Fortress.

"Zeamer blew up. He took things in his own hands. He went through the outfit and recruited a crew from a bunch of renegades and screwoffs. They were the worst of the 43rd—men nobody else wanted. But they gravitated toward one another and they made a hell of a crew. The gang of them piled into the B-17, fired it up, and Zeamer and his outcasts flew it on up to New Guinea. When they got there someone tried to take the airplane away from Zeamer. Jay

was so mad he appropriated the Flying Fortress for himself
and his crew. He ordered his men not to give up the airplane and they weren't about to see *that* happen. By now
they would have done anything for Zeamer. They loaded
their fifty calibers and they told everyone to stay the hell
away, and Zeamer and his crew even slept in that damn
airplane for fear someone would try to take it away from
them.

"I know all this from first-hand. I was wounded and
when I came out of the hospital I went back to combat with
Shanty O'Neill's 38th Bombardment Group, up at Seven-
Mile. Zeamer would come over to visit me quite often.
Everyone was talking about him and his renegades. The CO
of the 43rd even overlooked the fact that Jay still hadn't
been checked out as pilot.

"But whenever the 43rd got a real lousy mission—the
worst possible mission of all that nobody else wanted to
fly—they went down to see Jay Zeamer and his gang. They
couldn't keep them on the ground, no matter how bad or
rough that mission might be. They didn't care. They
crawled into that airplane and just flew and what was more
they always carried out their missions. It was the
damnedest thing. They'd fly in the worst possible weather,
the kind of storms that made other pilots grateful they
were on the ground. And Zeamer would always find his
way in. Sometimes the weather would be so bad, in ships
that were shot up, other planes would crash, or the crews
would bail out because it was impossible to get back down
safely. Impossible for everyone except Jay Zeamer, that is.
I used to talk with him about it. I would ask him how the
hell he could bring in that damn airplane and land when
everyone else was getting lost. He'd grin and mumble
something about, 'It's simple. I just do this and I do that
and I bring her in the same old way. No trouble at all.'

"Then, finally, they got orders to carry out a mission that was rougher than rough. A reconnaissance mission that nobody wanted to take. Nobody in his right mind, maybe. So they went to see Jay Zeamer and his crew. . . ."

Mile after mile passed beneath the wings of the Fortress. Photographer William Kendrick worked his cameras from one island base to the other, recording on film the precious information so desperately needed in headquarters. Luck remained with them; the sky was strangely free of flak. Almost six miles high the gunners squinted in the bright sun, searching, always searching for the telltale specks of climbing enemy fighters. Long before they had cleared their guns, making the B-17 tremble and shake from the recoil of the heavy .50 calibers.

Nobody talked over the intercom. No one would talk unless there was a need to use words. Zeamer didn't want the intercom cluttered up with nonsense when they would need silence.

The mission was almost completed. Almost every area assigned for photographic coverage had been passed. The last base to be photographed was Buka airstrip, near Bougainville. It had a nasty reputation; the Zero pilots at Buka were always charged up for a fight. Buka drifted slowly into sight far ahead of the plexiglas nose.

The belly gunner broke intercom silence. Doubled up in his ball turret, almost form-fitting with its two heavy machine guns, he scanned the field far below. And saw the first specks, already growing larger.

"Belly gunner to pilot. Here they come, sir. I make out at least ten fighters in the air. They're climbing for us."

The crewmen strained at their positions to see the Japanese clawing for altitude. No one wanted to be late at his guns. Zeamer and copilot John Britton kept the Fortress flying dead on the compass; Kendrick stayed at his cameras. That's why he was in the airplane—to take pictures.

In the nose, bombardier Lt. Joseph R. Sarnoski peered through the plexiglas, studying Buka airstrip. He saw more fighters tearing down the runway, little toy airplanes with dust streaming from their wheels. Sarnoski began counting.

"Skipper, there's more. I count twelve . . . fifteen . . . at least twenty now."

Jay Zeamer had a decision to make. At this point he *could* swing away from Buka and run for home. No one would criticize his battle judgment. Twenty Zero fighters were simply too much for any one B-17 to tackle by itself. To remain on course and give the Japanese time in which to climb to their altitude and set up their attack wasn't simply begging for trouble. Most pilots would have called it suicide.

The Fortress held its course. There remained just enough time for Zeamer to slam the throttles to full power and to get the hell out from under. But the pictures . . . Zeamer knew their value, he knew that many people would die on the beaches unless he and his men completed their mission.

Steady as a rock the B-17 held course. Kendrick stayed at his cameras. Now it was too late to run.

The Zeros swept up and forward of the Flying Fortress, banking with practiced ease. They knew their adversary well and even with the odds so greatly in their favor, the Japanese pilots were taking no chances. Experience had taught them not to attack the B-17 from astern where they could be brought under the concerted firepower of several turrets and hand-operated .50 calibers. The weakest zone of defense for the B-17, the Japanese had learned, was the nose, against which the fighters could close with a combined speed of 500 miles per hour. The Zeros would have time sufficient in which to utilize to the maximum effect their machine guns and cannon, while the bomber's gunners would be at their greatest disadvantage. Half the Zeros swept ahead of the lone Fortress, turned, and, while the other ten fighters took up positions for simultaneous attacks from the sides and from below, raced head-on for the bomber.

Kendrick stayed glued to his cameras, Zeamer kept the bomber unflinchingly on course. Above and behind the cockpit Sgt. John J. Able in the top turret swung his two fifties around to the front. The ball-turret gunner was busy tracking several fighters making diversionary attacks.

The Zeros rushed in. Bright flame winked along wings and engine cowlings as the Japanese pilots opened fire. The B-17 was big, easy to hit, as the Zeros came in with two fighters teaming up, doubling their firepower. Machine-gun slugs and cannon shells raked the bomber in a storm of fire. Almost at once the Fortress shook violently her entire length as the plexiglas nose smashed open. A long burst of fire tore the metal skin, ripping equipment, slashing through the body of the airplane. The ever-present drone of the four engines dimmed suddenly with the effect of the Japanese fire. Then the .50 calibers answered the attack. Acrid smoke filled the plane. Despite everything Zeamer and Britton could do in the cockpit the Fortress rocked and vibrated from the recoil of her own guns and the punching blows of the enemy cannon shells.

In front of Sarnoski the nose plexiglas dissolved in a jagged shower. Japanese bullets and exploding cannon shells crashed into the airplane in a storm of destruction, smashing equipment, blowing holes in the fuselage and the wings, severing control cables. A 20-mm cannon shell exploded with a terrifying roar and a dazzling flash in the cockpit. Hot steel slammed into Zeamer and Britton. Machine-gun slugs slammed into the body of a waist gunner, hurling him away from his station. Another gunner spun away, helpless from the blows. The men fought to get back to their machine guns. Sarnoski felt his own body jerk as bullets cut into his flesh; he kept firing, kept tracking a Zero. In that first pass five men were hit.

But the Fortress crew drew blood. The lead Zero had taken a long burst from Sarnoski's gun. As it swept up and over the B-17 Able saw a streamer of flame appear. Moments later, its fuel tanks holed, the Zero disappeared in fire that enveloped the entire airplane. It whirled crazily out of control, falling behind the Fortress.

Able in the top turret scored the second kill. His twin fifties hosed bullets into the engine of a Zero. It took only one short, well-aimed burst. Flames erupted from the engine, spread almost at once to the tanks. A blazing fireball hurtled scant feet past the Fortress, its pilot dead.

The Zeros came in again, coordinating their frontal attack by curving in from the left and right, making it a slicing head-on run. Once more the Fortress took a terrible beating, once more the crewmen reeled from the effect of the enemy fire. Ignoring his wounds Sarnoski tracked one fighter, snapping out bursts. His incendiaries cut bright curving paths through the air and found the fuel tanks. A crewman shouted that the fighter had disappeared in a fiery ball. Sarnoski found another Zero slicing into his sights; he pounded out a long burst. He saw the bullets rake the cockpit. The Fortress crew didn't know if the pilot were dead or alive, but the Zero spun out wildly and plunged earthward.

Someone shouted into the intercom that he had flamed a fighter. In the nose Kendrick, still taking his pictures, had miraculously escaped injury. Sarnoski's brilliant work with his single machine gun, Able's accuracy with his top turret, had broken up the attack. The Zeros flashed by, over and under the B-17, every man aboard snapping out bursts as the Japanese tore past the Fortress.

Kendrick called Zeamer. The wounded pilot heard the news gratefully that the photographic assignment was completed. All their pictures had been taken. *Now* they could run for home, now Zeamer and Britton could jockey the Fortress about, swing the tail from side to side as the gunners called in, shouting for better firing position to hit the attacking Zeros.

Two groups of fighters peeled off from far ahead and above the B-17, sweeping down into another coordinated, two-formation frontal pass. Someone sang out, "Here they come—twelve o'clock!"

Again the Fortress took a beating. The bomber was hurt—badly. Control cables snapped as slugs cut through the metal. Hydraulic lines sprayed out their fluid, smoke poured from the radio equipment. Then the oxygen system took a blast of enemy fire. They were at 28,000 feet. Several men would soon be short of oxygen. They were too high; Zeamer started down in a long dive, picking up speed, hoping the speed would help in outrunning the attacking fighters.

As each gunner shouted his calls of incoming fighters, Zeamer and Britton banked and turned the speeding bomber so that several fifties could be combined to bear upon a single Zero. The gunners were taking their toll. In the cockpit the pilots heard a crewman's exultation as he shouted a report of a wing tearing off a fighter.

But in the nose of the Fortress all hell was breaking loose. Inrushing Zeros had again found their mark with their massed firepower. A 20-mm cannon shell exploded with a terrific roar in the bombardier's small compartment. The shattering blast flung Sarnoski's body through the air and back along the narrow catwalk beneath the cockpit. A crewman ran forward to assist the stricken bombardier; he stared at the gaping hole torn in Sarnoski's side. Blood streamed over his flying suit.

"I'm all right," Sarnoski gasped, pushing away help. "Don't worry about me." The Zeros were still coming in, now a long Indian-file, one after the other, each raking the Fortress with bullets and exploding shells. Mortally wounded, Sarnoski crawled back along the catwalk already slippery with his blood. Gasping with pain he pulled himself up to his gun, swung the heavy fifty against the roaring wind, aimed, squeezed the trigger. The heavy gun chattered wildly in his weakening grasp. Sarnoski had just enough time to see a Zero whip into a vertical turn and drop its nose. Then he collapsed over the gun, unconscious.

Someone rushed to his side. As gently as he could in the rocking, shaking bomber he lifted Sarnoski from the gun, away from the pool of blood, and cradled the bombardier in his arms. Moments later Sarnoski died.

There was no respite from the fury of the attack. Zeamer and Britton, soaked in sweat from their exertions, ignoring their own wounds, worked the controls constantly, banking, turning, skidding. Rapidly the Fortress was coming apart at the seams. The B-17 was already a flying sieve, holed and slashed from nose to tail, across the wings. It was a miracle that the engines still functioned.

The Zeros swept in again. Two more men fell from their guns.

Even Jay Zeamer joined the firing. The bastardized Fortress had been fitted out at Zeamer's orders with a single .50 caliber machine gun, fixed to the fuselage to fire dead ahead. One Zero came in from behind and above after the diving Fortress, raking the bomber. The fighter flashed ahead of them as the pilot rolled over and began a long pullout to swing back for another pass.

Zeamer threw his weight against the yoke and the Fortress steepened in its dive. The engines screamed from the increasing speed. The weakened structure of the bomber groaned audibly from the added strain as the speed continued to build. Zeamer worked the controls, banking to stay on the tail of the Zero ahead of him. The Japanese pilot looked back—they could see his head turning in his cockpit—and gaped at the sight of the Fortress hammering after him. He hauled back on the stick and Zeamer squeezed down for a long burst. Fifty-caliber slugs smashed the prop, chewed up the engine cowling, and then churned the Zero cockpit into an exploding froth of blood and glass.

Zeamer and Britton pulled the bomber, carefully, slowly, from its careening dive. The Zero pilots seemed to have gone wild with fury at the lone Fortress that had already shot down at least five of their number. They tore in recklessly, closing to point-blank range, almost brushing wings with the battered, staggering bomber. The cannon shells poured into the Fortress and once again they found the cockpit. A dazzling flash; an ear-smashing roar as a cannon shell exploded at Zeamer's feet, shattering the control cables. Slivers of steel tore into his body. To his right Britton also reeled from the impact of multiple wounds. Another pass . . . bullets thudded and ripped into both arms and legs of Jay Zeamer. Almost every part of his body had taken steel. He sat in a pool of blood, still at the controls, still flying.

A sudden explosion in the air as a Zero tore apart from the fire of several machine guns.

The fighters came in again, reckless, the pilots furious.

They couldn't understand why the Fortress wouldn't go down. The Zero pilots were skilled and they were good marksmen. They proved it—again.

John Britton in the copilot's seat slumped unconscious from shock and loss of blood. Yet another cannon shell exploded in the cockpit, tearing into the body of Jay Zeamer. The blast shattered one leg, breaking the bone, mangling his flesh. Zeamer had already been hit in both arms and legs. He was able to use only one arm to fly the heavy bomber.

Time had run out for them. But—were the Zeros breaking off the attack? They had been fighting the Japanese for forty minutes. How long could it keep up? A single Zero broke away from the loose formation of fighters, whipped in. Trackers converged on the Japanese plane; the Zero fell, seemingly out of control.

Suddenly, with that last pass, it was over. Low or out of ammunition, far from Buka, the remaining Zero fighters peeled off and headed for their home base.

Relief came not a moment too soon. For forty minutes the lone Fortress had fought for its life and now that the pressure of combat was over, the crew found themselves on the brink of disaster.

The bombardier was dead. Radio operator William Vaughan was severely wounded, as was navigator Ruby Johnston. Top turret gunner John Able was wounded, but able to move around. As the men checked with one another they discovered that only the tail gunner, Pudge Pugh, and, miraculously, photographer Kendrick, were free of wounds. The Fortress was a flying wreck, with metal skin punctured and holed everywhere, and with huge gaping tears in the fuselage and wings opened by the Japanese cannon shells. The radios were shot into wreckage, most of the instrument panel—including their compasses—was a shambles. Most of the hydraulics were gone (they would find out as well that they had no brakes and no flap control). The rudder pedal controls from the pilot's seat had been shot away.

Dobodura, their home base at New Guinea, was still some 600 miles away.

And those were only the beginning of their troubles. Co-pilot John Britton was unconscious. Pilot Jay Zeamer, torn and battered and ripped throughout his body, hit in both arms and legs, with one leg shattered, with only one arm responding to his urging, finally collapsed.

The B-17 had no pilots.

Turret gunner John Able had never flown a B-17. But he had been "up front" before with Zeamer and Britton, and he had watched the things they did with the controls. Now, wounded, calling on memory and instinct, he stood between the two unconscious pilots and leaned forward to grasp the yoke—*and he flew the crippled bomber*. He kept the sun to his back and headed in the general direction of Dobodura.

The other crewmen leaned to the sides of Able and did what they could to keep their two pilots alive, trying to stem the flow of blood. It seemed almost impossible that Jay Zeamer could still be alive. Yet every now and then he regained consciousness, returned to blinding pain. During his moments of consciousness he talked to Able, told him what to do with the controls, how to navigate the airplane. Then he would pass out again.

They flew in this manner for nearly three hours. Ruby Johnston, the navigator, and others finally began to spot landmarks they could recognize. Able started the B-17 down. By the time Cape Endiaidere slipped beneath the nose, Zeamer and Britton had regained consciousness. Able had managed to fly, but to land the crippled Fortress, without flaps and brakes, and the controls half shot away, was too much. Zeamer and Britton decided to try the landing themselves.

Britton operated the rudder from his side of the cockpit. To his left, Jay Zeamer used his one good arm—despite his wounds—to wrestle with the control column. There was no time to fly a field pattern, no time to do anything but bring in the Fortress in just one pass—straight in. At any moment either pilot, or both of them, might lapse again into unconsciousness.

They didn't know they landed downwind. Without flaps and without brakes, the battered airplane rolled the length of the 7,000-foot runway and ground slowly to a halt—at the very end of the long airstrip.

Jay Zeamer shouldn't have been alive. The medics gasped when they saw what remained of his body. They rushed him to the hospital and for three days poured blood into the shattered pilot. No one believed he would survive. Jay Zeamer had lost almost fifty percent of all the blood in his body.

The doctors removed more than 120 pieces of metal from Zeamer. Maybe there was more; there wasn't time to find out then. They also amputated what was left of his leg. They put more blood into him. For three days and nights Zeamer hung between life and death—and then began his slow recovery.

Intelligence got their pictures.

And for days afterward small crowds would collect around a lone Flying Fortress, standing off the runway, torn and ripped across almost every square foot of her metal surfaces. Someone started to count the holes and cannon tears. Finally he gave it up.

He said that after the first thousand holes it really didn't matter any more.

# CHAPTER 2

# CONCEPT AND PHILOSOPHY

A WIDE VALLEY IN northwest Arizona, flanked on the west by the Black Mountains and on the east by the peaks of the Hualpai, was the end of the road. In the summer of 1946 the hot desert winds spilled down the Black Mountains to swirl across the dusty valley. The wind rushed into a huge graveyard many miles wide and miles longer. A sound of wind against metal arose. Sometimes the wind gusted until a mournful wail carried to nearby towns. This was the wind giving voice to great metal shapes no longer able to roar with the thunder that had shaken almost the whole of a continent; this was the wind rushing across curved plexiglas, curling around gear legs and open gear wells, the wind banging ailerons and elevators and rudders, the wind dancing in opened bomb bays and cockpit windows and naked turrets.

This was the wind keening its cry through the graveyard of 1,832 great bombers. Every one of those 1,832 airplanes was a Flying Fortress. This was the end of the road for the graceful machines. More than seven thousand engines were silent; more than seven thousand propellers stood unmoving. The wings they had once borne would fly no more. The war had ended the year before and never again would the great and graceful creatures wheel in stately formation miles high above the crumbling remains of the Third Reich.

It was all over. The end of the tremendous, epochal, unprecedented journey.

Only two years before this summer of 1946, just one factory of the Boeing complex in Seattle, Washington, was turning out sixteen of the great bombers every twenty-four hours. One year later the churning battles of the Second World War had become distant sounds whispering down history. In the different cities along the west coast of the United States the many production lines received their final orders to shut down.

The huge factories ground to a halt. Tens of thousands of skilled workers for the last time walked through the doors, leaving behind them stilled machines, ghostly corridors, the memory of a tumultuous uproar that had been the sounding cry of the greatest production effort ever known.

They had built, and rolled out to the flight lines, the grand total of 12,731 Flying Fortresses.

Eleven years before the last Fortress tried her wings, the first airplane, the ancestor of nearly thirteen thousand great bombers to come, was only a series of lines on paper with the designation of Boeing Model 299. Then, on August 16, 1934, craftsmen and engineers of the Boeing Airplane Company, under the helm of Edward C. Wells, began the greatest gamble in the company's history. Boeing believed in what it had on paper; designers and company officials believed they could produce the greatest aerial weapon the world had ever known. The United States government was as interested as Boeing but less confident in the final outcome. That missing expression of confidence could be found in hard terms—Boeing would have to pay every dollar for the project out of company funds.

If they were wrong the entire firm would collapse beneath a financial disaster.

On July 28, 1935, less than a year after the decision to commit to the gamble, Model 299 loomed over the flight line of Boeing Field. In the predawn gloom the great airplane seemed to be waiting as anxiously as were the men assembled beneath its wings for full daylight. The sun would witness yet another crucial step in the gamble—first flight.

Harold Mansfield[4] recalls the moment: "Before sun-up on July 28, a cluster of men stood on the edge of Boeing Field, shivering a little in the morning mist, their hearts and the soles of their feet catching the rumble of four idling engines at the far end of the field. The rumble grew to a burning, firing roar and the big form was moving toward them down the runway, racing past them. Les Tower lifted her slowly, surely, over the end of the field. As though timed by a stage crew the sun popped over the ridge of the Cascades, its brightness glistening on the polished wings that streaked to meet it, and the 299 was a receding speck in the sky.

"Claire Egtvedt shut his eyes and smiled. Design engineer Bob Minshall turned to Ed Wells who had been promoted to project engineer for the 299. 'That's it, Ed. Great work.' "

The airplane proved to be a stupendous success. Her pilots raved about the solid feel of her controls and the sensitivity of her response. Some airplanes just have a great feel for the sky; Model 299 had it from her first moments of flight. While the test pilots waxed enthusiastic, Air Corps strategists turned to the future so that they might best fit the forthcoming production models of the new bomber into the sinews of national airpower.

In this endeavor they proved to be less than successful. That is, perhaps, the strangest paradox of all. Like many great machines, and some weapons, the intrinsic values of what Model 299 would become were recognized by only a limited number of people. The road ahead, with the staggering production effort, with the expression of American air-power that would help to break the back of the Third Reich, was little more than a hazy dream beset with the reality of financial burdens and seemingly endless political hostility.

The Flying Fortress, despite her spectacular performance and brighter promise, was born not in a surging upsweep of shared confidence, but rather against a backdrop of doubts and insecurity. The problems had begun long before Model 299 first flew, long before it became even a sketch on paper. They began—in theory, strategies, concept and doctrine—even before we were committed to World War I.

Military airpower—the capability of a nation to exercise its intentions through the application of military force through aircraft and their supporting systems—is made up of many factors of which aircraft are only one. Airpower in reality is an expression of doctrine; its use arises from the decisions made as to how that strength should be applied. It is, in essence, a reflection of the success or failure of those individuals and/or groups who champion its use.

The United States, today and for many years the most powerful nation in the world, especially in the air, did not always enjoy that distinction. At a time—before, during, and after World War I—when European nations recognized the inevitability of airpower as a major element of their national strength, the United States indulged in acrimonious debate as how best to "keep down" the young upstarts who represented the new air arm of our military forces. That debate, often heated and always military-political in nature, established the environment in which the future air arm would be nourished—or kept poorly fed. The nature of the debate itself is vital, for it reflected the organization that would ensure as a result of examining the potential of airpower. Organization itself may be said to be "everything" where military weapons are concerned, since organization relates to the control and the purposes of any military component. Before 1914 airpower was held by certain military officials in this country to be a definite threat. Not to a potential enemy, but to their own structure of organization—and their own authority.

This apprehension of an outside authority crowding against firmly established tradition, notes an historical study by the Air University,[5] "foreshadowed a widening rift between the aviators and their nonflying military superiors. This personnel friction was at least as important as theoretical differences in bringing about eventual separation of the air arm from the Signal Corps. The basis for the difficulty seemed to lie in the special restrictions placed on flying officers with respect to age and marital status. The aviators resented such treatment and also chafed under what they regarded as the apathetic attitude of the Chief Signal Officer and the General Staff toward military aviation. The 'high brass,' for its part, found the aviators too outspoken and too indifferent toward conventional military customs. As the Chief Signal Officer, Brigadier General George P. Scriven, explained in February 1916, the trouble stemmed from the 'aviation officers . . . unbalanced as to grades, young in years and service, and deficient in discipline and the proper knowledge of the customs of the service and the duties of an officer.' Scriven imputed further that there was deliberate motive behind the friction which had been created. Behind their 'unmilitary, insubordinate, and disloyal acts,' he charged, was a burning ambition to set up a new and independent organization for aviation.' "

Few veterans of the growth of American airpower would dispute that from the beginning of military aviation there existed no shortage of zealots who desired with a "burning ambition" to set up that separate organization. From the early days of combat the eventual establishment of a separate air force appeared—at least to those who were airpower proponents—to be inevitable, and they were not beyond whipping up flames of controversy in order to hasten that day. In 1916 Secretary of War Newton D. Baker acceded to what must come, when he predicted that in the not too distant future the United States would "add armored and armed planes to its air fleet," and that this development would require the creation of a new fighting arm.

Secretary Baker's vision remained an opinion rather than a fact. And for some time to come it appeared that little change ever would take place. The prevailing conviction that air strength was an integral element of ground forces, and subordinate to those forces, laid down the climate in which airpower, for many years to come, would have to grow. It would be—because of reality and a cementing of existing organization—a role of subordination rather than independence. That in itself constituted the handwriting on the wall—new aircraft, techniques, equipment and doctrine must conform to the officially designated role of a subordinate force.

At that time, the period of World War I, it seemed impossible that it might be any other way. Acrimonious debates over organization were only a reflection of the sharp divergence of view as to how military aircraft and their weapons should be employed in the war raging on the European continent. Those who cried for increased airpower did little more than to shout into the howling winds of reality—American airpower simply didn't exist except as a wish or perhaps on the lurid pages of a Sunday supplement.

As one veteran infantry officer put it succinctly some thirty-five years later, "We first discovered that airplanes could go faster and higher than horses. They took over reconnaissance from the cavalry."

The test of battle carried the divergent points of view between the ground and air leaders from the field of theory to the field of action. And this transfer, notes the Air University, "tended to strengthen the influence of the ground officers, because the war had to be fought with available, not potential weapons, and because the battle on the Western Front had already become frozen in a complex pattern of ground operations. . . . It was a struggle of infantry, trenches, and artillery; of attack and counterattack; of attrition and reinforcement. It is no wonder that the high command regarded air operations as an adjunct to the mighty ground forces which had been committed to the mortal and decisive combat."

General H. H. Arnold, who commanded the Army Air Forces in World War II, spoke of the earlier war, and its relationship with airpower, in blunter terms. Going straight to the point he admitted frankly that in 1917 the American air arm "had no theories of aerial combat, or of any air operations except armed reconnaissance. Despite Billy Mitchell's eagerness to blow up Germany, we hadn't a single bomber. Such things as formation flying, a new German development appearing on the Western front that spring, were unknown to us.... Our first projected task was to provide every two ground divisions with one squadron of aerial reconnaissance and one balloon company. For the moment, a complete lack of combat experience had left American aviation behind."

Where it would remain for many years to come.

The long period after World War I was sparked with the fireworks of controversy and little realistic progress. The strategists decried the absence of the weapons with which they hoped to make of the United States a true airpower, but in their seething frustration, turning to developing the theoretical means with which airpower should be used, they laid the foundations for bombardment aviation that would finally see fruition in World War II.

It was General William Mitchell, insubordinate to higher authority and dedicated slavishly to the airpower in which he believed, who started the long trek toward a true national capability in the air. Mitchell advanced his theories and tactics not simply in terms of hardware—i.e., aircraft, weapons and their battlefield application—but also in respect to the organization and control of military aviation. He emphasized, and this was the crux of his argument that was to be sustained, that airpower should be utilized essentially as an offensive combat arm. Mitchell saw as the greatest effect of airpower its great speed which, in turn, promised an extraordinary flexibility in applying pressure to an enemy. Writing of military aviation, he insisted that, "Like any other military operations, concentration of force at the vital point is what counts."

In these words of Mitchell, which became doctrinal principles of the military air leaders in the period after World War I, lay the foundation for developing the doctrine and strategy that governed the use of heavy bombers in World War II. They are of interest for a specific reason in that they established the thinking that led the Air Corps in the 'thirties to fight for what they considered the first true long-range, heavy bomber—the airplane that became the Flying Fortress.

Mitchell often has been regarded as leaning with greater favor to pursuit aviation than to long-range bombardment, but it is in the latter area that he achieved his fame. Looking into the coming years, Mitchell in 1919 predicted that the principal goal of bombardment aviation would lie not in the battlefield in direct contact with combat forces, but in "hitting an enemy's great nerve centers at the very beginning of the war so as to paralyze them to the greatest extent possible."

Those words could be applied without change to the doctrine of modern arms today.

The Air University reviews the position, historically, of Mitchell:

One does not have to look far to find the airman who dared to challenge openly the conservative concept of war held by the General Staff and the War Department. Brigadier General William Mitchell, the leading figure in America's air effort during World War I, came home from France with a burning ambition and a resolute will to raise the air arm to its "rightful" role in national defense. Serving high on the staff of the Chief of Air Service from 1919 to 1925, Mitchell used his position, as well as his talents for writing and speaking, to spread the gospel of airpower far and wide. He used both bludgeon and rapier to drive home his points; he could be shocking, satirical, irreverent, or all of those together. He was, indeed, the gadfly of the General Staff and the hero of the Army's fliers. In the first half of the '20's, it looked like Mitchell "against the field." He was a one-man show for airpower, a formidable protagonist. He burned brilliantly and defiantly—and then, after overstepping the bounds of military propriety once too often, his official light was extinguished. But before he was forced out of the Army in 1926, "Billy" Mitchell made the nation airconscious—and what is more, he planted the seeds of a new doctrine of war and airpower. That doctrine, in general terms, was to become the American air doctrine for World War II. . . . Mitchell declared that modern warfare included all the population of the nations engaged: men, women, and children. In sharp divergence from the view of Secretary of War Baker, who ruled out all attacks upon civilians, Mitchell insisted that, "The entire nation is, or should be, considered a combatant force." Pressing on, he went to the heart of the issue; with unflinching logic he argued that the best strategy often dictated destruction and killing at points distant from the ground or naval theater. The civilians attacked in such operations might include large numbers of women, children, and others not capable of bearing arms, but they were vastly more important as manufacturers of munitions than if they were carrying rifles in trenches. Thus Mitchell succinctly stated the argument that had no answer. The hard facts of technological warfare placed the production line at the front; in the course of World War II the restraining barriers of convention and humanitarian feeling were to collapse completely, and full, though painful, recognition was made of the reality of "total war."

Mitchell and his fiery eloquence notwithstanding, the entrenched military organization fought every move made by airpower proponents to increase the power or the prestige of the existing air arm. This was no isolated group seeking to preserve its privileged status; the spearhead of opposition represented the ranking military personnel of the Army and the Navy, the civilian heads of the War Department and the Navy Department and to a man the entire General Staff. They achieved an extraordinary solidarity in insisting that aviation was, and must remain, auxiliary to surface forces. The old-line officers appeared adamant against the outcries and the hopes of the small group surrounding Mitchell and what he represented. The opposition to airpower seemed to sustain itself from almost every line of reasoning. Many of the old-line officers contested the air arm and their young officers because of jealousy of their traditional prerogatives and position; others didn't care a whit about airplanes and even less for flying officers, whom they found not only loud and insulting but hopelessly overzealous and unrealistic; and, finally, there were those—and their number was many—who sincerely and honestly doubted the effectiveness of any independently operating air arm. For all these reasons, the protagonists of independent and well-financed airpower ran into a solid wall of opposition. And it did not take long, as the Air University notes, for the young flying officers to realize "that those who opposed air independence represented the majority in the military establishments and held the positions of major influence. At this stage in the contest for control of military aviation, the enthusiasm of the air crusaders proved no match for the numbers and power of the opposition."

## FILLING THE VACUUM

It was against this background of conflicting doctrine, and often outright animosity, that the Army's air officers settled down to the long fight for recognition of and independence for the nation's military air organization. That long fight was represented both in doctrinal argument and, especially where the American public was concerned, in deeds that reflected great courage, skill, and an expanding age of air accomplishments. Pilots and crewmen by diligence and daring overcame their enforced poverty of equipment and funds by making flights that caught the public's attention and gained for the country immeasurable international prestige. Army fliers consistently set new world records for distance, speed, altitude and load carrying; they flew in the worst weather and over forbidding terrain. So many records were broken and so many barriers breached by the military aviators that General Henry H. Arnold, who would become the nation's top air commander, has characterized the '20s as the "golden age of aviation."

These were far more than stunts, although no one could deny the excitement of the aerial circus with its daredevils who strutted about on wings, did handstands at ninety miles per hour, and clambered with heart-stopping expertise from one plane to another while thousands of feet above the ground. Those were the crowd pleasers and the show stoppers, but the important flights were those that took men into the lower stratosphere or for the first time hurdled entire continents by wing.

No one feat in aviation ever prompted greater struggle— or failure—than the first flight around the world. It was a singular tribute to the Air Service, and to the determination of Generals William Mitchell and Mason Patrick, that the Army Air Service in 1924 succeeded in such a venture, where the pilots and aircraft of Great Britain, Italy, Portugal, France and Argentina had failed. The first globe-girdling flight was rife with more hazards than any pilot wished to admit. It meant the air pioneering of desolate and forbidding parts of the world: Arctic ice fields, fog-bound ocean areas, steaming jungles, deserts, dangerous mountain ranges; it meant flying through wild storms without radio and with only a minimum of instruments.

Without exhaustive and year-long preparation the epochal air journey would have been doomed from the start. But the Air Service gained the cooperation of twenty-two foreign governments, and secured for the global planes forty landing fields around the world, each stocked with provisions for emergencies.

The four Douglas World Cruisers assigned to the unique mission took off from a lake near Seattle, Washington, on April 6, 1924. For the next 175 days they fought their way around the earth, covering a total distance of 27,553 miles in 15 days, 11 hours, and 7 minutes actual flying time, cruising between 53 and 103 miles per hour. Two planes were lost. One smashed into an Alaskan mountain; the crew walked away from the wreck, and spent ten agonizing days suffering from intense cold and snow blindness before they reached friendly natives. They made the final leg of their return paddling an Eskimo bidarka—receiving somewhat less tumultuous a reception than was encountered by the crews of the two planes that returned on September 28th, 1924, to their starting point in Seattle to mark the close of a brilliant chapter in Army flying history.

The Flying Fortress was created not from a single and clearly defined mission requirement, but rather from a multiplicity of roles to which the Army Air Corps in the mid-thirties had laid claim. It would be difficult to point a finger at any one incident as the primary impetus which brought the B-17 into existence, but among those of importance one must include the period when General William Mitchell "squared off" against the United States Navy.

Until the advent of the airplane capable of carrying

large and heavy bombs, the lines of demarcation and responsibility between the Army and the Navy regarding coastal defense of the United States were relatively simple and clear. The rise of military aviation vastly complicated this defense situation, and touched off a fierce battle between the two services regarding authority and service capabilities.

Both services in the 1920s were already operating their own air arms, each of which had been developed independently of the other. The ranking officers of both the Army and Navy held fast to their basic concept that airplanes could never play anything but a subordinate role in war; to the Army the infantry was the Queen of Battle, and to the Navy the battleship reigned supreme.

When, however, there arose the question of what bombing planes could do the Navy at sea, the Army brass judiciously took a back seat and gave their flying subordinates free rein in setting their sights against naval power and authority. To the General Staff this was splendid opportunity for the Army to gain even more power than it possessed; the air enthusiasts who scored the helplessness of the Navy to protect the continental United States against attacking enemy airpower could only enhance the prestige of massed ground forces and artillery.

Even the waspish tone of General William Mitchell, agreed the Army brass, could be tolerated if he could "throw the Navy for a loss." Mitchell in his writings and speeches had "destroyed" the Navy again and again, and seapower was ever a fair target for his barbed eloquence. Supported by high-ranking Army officials, Mitchell after considerable haggling, name-calling, and weary months of frustration, managed to arrange for bomb-dropping tests against retired naval warships. In these experiments Mitchell's bomber crews speedily disposed of small vessels;

this served only to add fuel to the bitter arguments of air-power *vs* seapower, since the successes were decried by naval authorities who stressed the light armor and structural fragility of the lesser ships.

The bombing tests were conducted over a period of several years, and the results achieved by Mitchell's hand-picked crews shook naval complacency to its foundations. In 1921, off the Virginia capes, a submarine and a light cruiser went down in short order. The most decisive phase of the 1921 tests occurred on July 21, when seven of Mitchell's Martin MB-2 bombers, each carrying a 2,000-pound bomb, smashed the huge German battleship *Ostfriesland* (called unsinkable by naval experts), causing the warship to roll over and sink 21 minutes after the first bomb exploded.

In 1923, off Cape Hatteras, the powerful USS *Virginia* and the USS *New Jersey* were sent to the bottom with shocking ease. Two more battleships received mortal blows which dispatched them beneath the waves.

In the fury of claims and counterclaims that followed the tests there emerged an inescapable conclusion— seapower from those days on had to be reckoned in terms of surface vessels *and* bombing planes. The brass might choose to ignore Mitchell, but they could hardly escape the official conclusions of the Joint Army and Navy Board which, among other points, confirmed that existing aerial bombs could sink or seriously damage any existing type of vessel. Adequate quantities of bombers were seen by the Board *as possibly the decisive factor in coastal defense*. In any future attack upon the American coast, the Board concluded, the Navy must share with the air arm its primary function as the first line of defense.

The Navy agreed reluctantly, having little choice in the matter, that coastal defense should be shared with the

Army's Air Service. But the extent of that sharing, the Navy made clear, was to be kept to an absolute minimum. The Navy, no one doubted, had no intentions of giving up its dominant role.

Riding high for the moment, General Mitchell set forth an entirely new concept of coastal defense which virtually swept the Navy bare of its cherished authority in this area. The Air Service's General Mason Patrick agreed heartily with Mitchell, and declared (as early as 1921) that the Army air arm could take over coastal defense, that it could perform all the functions of shoreline patrol, sea search and attack on hostile vessels.

There was only one flaw in the new concepts championed so ardently by Generals Mitchell and Patrick—the airplanes with which to carry out these grandiose missions didn't exist.

1926 was a year to remember in the development of American airpower—but not for the same reasons. The Air Corps Act of that year firmly established the Air Corps as a major element of the Army; not a separate organization as had been sought by airpower protagonists, but still a major step in the direction desired.

It was also a year of paradox in the development of the bomber as an advanced weapon. In one move, high-ranking officers of the Air Corps and the War Department deplored the ill-performing fabric biplane bombers that were limiting airpower development. At the same time, however, they imposed severe restrictions on the future design of advanced bombing airplanes when the Chief of the Engineer Division of the Air Corps (supported by the War Department) recommended strongly against the development of four-engine bombardment aircraft.

Hopes for a true strategic airpower capability on the

part of the United States waned appreciably. During the 'twenties the pursuit reigned as the primary element of American airpower, overshadowing the motley collection of lumbering bombers which relegated the United States to a third-rate position among the airpower nations of the world. The bomber planes flown in 1926 showed little improvement over the Martin MB-2 of 1920; the aircraft remained sorely underpowered, could carry only small bomb loads, and had operational ceilings below 13,000 feet. They could fly barely 300 miles from their bases to attack enemy targets—and, flying at speeds of about 100 miles per hour, with little defensive armament, they were sitting ducks for enemy interceptors.

The sanguine expectations of General Mitchell and his fellow-enthusiasts failed to materialize. Without airpower that could demonstrate the claims of the air crusaders, not only did the country lack the means to function as a major power in the air, but it lacked the doctrine through which it might hope to utilize its airpower. In essence, airpower in the United States had dropped to its lowest ebb.

Doctrine, of course, was worthless without the means to apply strength through air weapons. And the country seemed to have stumbled against a wall of performance— the bombers that had been forecast with such fervor remained only words. Something, somewhere, was terribly wrong.

"Much of the delay in bomber development was attributable to insufficient equipment for conducting necessary engineering tests and studies," explains the Air University. "The Engineering Division of the Air Service complained of meager appropriations, blaming the situation on the unfavorable attitude of the War Department toward strategic bombing. At any rate, General Patrick expressed his dissatisfaction with the slow rate of progress in 1924 and ordered the Engineering Division to accumulate data on the desired specifications of an improved bomber and to prepare it in the form of a circular proposal for distribution to the aircraft industry. Shortly thereafter, the Materiel Division urged that the out-moded biplane bombers be completely replaced with multiengine monoplane models, and research was started to find a satisfactory design. However, the work was virtually limited to two-engine models, for in 1926 the chief of the Engineering Division ... recommended against the development of four-engine aircraft. His reasons were: high production cost, difficulty of operation, lack of maneuverability, maintenance problems, and higher fuel consumption. It was not until some years later that designers broke through the barriers of economy, doubt, and fear to build a bomber which could serve as a true instrument of airpower."

That airplane, waiting at the other side of the "barriers," would be the B-17. But it remained almost a decade in the future.

General Mason Patrick, his dissatisfaction with American bombers growing almost daily, in March 1927 initiated a new program to accelerate the still-lagging development of bombardment aircraft. One year later the Keystone and Curtiss companies delivered to the Air Corps new bomber models which had been built to the specifications laid down in 1927 by General Patrick. The new planes showed improvement over those bombers already in service, but they proved a sore disappointment to those who had expected a sharp increase in performance and, simultaneously, in true bombardment capability.

In 1929 the Air Corps tried again—and again they failed to produce the airplane which by now leading officers sought almost desperately. The fight to produce for the Air Corps a bomber designed for the sole purpose of carrying out a strategic mission ran headlong into the stolid opposition of the Army's General Staff. The latter decried the need for a single-purpose design and, largely for reasons of economy, ordered the Air Corps to work on a single bomber to fulfill all roles and missions. The single all-purpose model would also enhance economy in production, decided the General Staff.

The result of the single all-purpose model was inevitable. The Air Corps ended up with a "winged clunker" that couldn't handle any of its missions with an acceptable degree of performance or reliability.

Their patience sorely tried, the bomber enthusiasts came almost to the point of open rebellion with the General Staff. Flying officers and high brass locked horns in what became known quickly among high-ranking officers as the "bomber battle." To many military officials the struggle was as much for retention of power by the General Staff as it was a crusade on the part of those fighting to bring to reality the airpower in which they believed so fervently.

Crusade or not there was no mistaking the insistence of the Air Corps. Weary to death of ancient biplanes, angry with the blindness of design that had produced the aerial abortions of the 1929 design studies, they increased their agitation for more powerful and specialized bomber designs. In 1930 they succeeded.

They had reached the turning point in the bomber battle: In 1930 the bomber enthusiasts managed to convince the Air Corps to issue a design proposal for an advanced heavy bomber. Six of the nation's leading aircraft manufacturers responded to the proposal, and to the official comparative tests they brought new experimental models that left no question that the bomber had finally come into its own.

Exuberant pilots and engineers fairly embraced the new experimental airplanes that featured a host of aerodynamic improvements. The test bombers were years ahead of anything flying under foreign colors. Overnight, it seemed, the long-sought dream of realistic airpower was at hand.

The two outstanding models in the 1930 heavy bomber competition were the Boeing B-9 and the Martin B-10. The Boeing entry, an all-metal, low-wing monoplane of clean design, was delivered first for test flight. Pilots were enthusiastic about its excellent handling characteristics, and nothing less than exuberant about its speed of 186 miles per hour at 6,000 feet—some 60 miles per hour faster than any existing service bomber in the world. Engineers noted that the "quantum jump" of one-third more speed came not from increased horse-power, but through structural refinements and aerodynamic efficiency of the monoplane design, as well as a reduction in drag resulting from a retractable landing gear.

But if the Boeing B-9 was outstanding, the Martin B-10 of the same competition was all that, and more. Its performance exceeded even that of the Boeing monoplane bomber, and pilots said of the Martin that "it looked, as well as acted, the part of a modern bomber." Like the Boeing, the mid-wing Martin was a superb aerodynamic design. Unlike the Boeing, it had enclosed crew compartments and an enclosed turret in the nose. When tested in 1932, the Martin showed a speed of 207 miles per hour and a ceiling of 21,000 feet, performance that rated it as the fastest and most powerful bomber in the world. With these two planes the United States had forged a lead in bombardment weapons that was never to be relinquished.

To the proponents of strategic airpower the Boeing and Martin twin-engine bombers not only established new standards of performance and design, but once and for all removed the obstacles to truly long-range, high-speed bomber operations that still waited for fruition. It was not to be long in coming, and, notes the Air University, it was in 1932 that:

the Material Division took steps to improve all heavy bomber equipment. Emphasis was placed on monoplane design, all-metal construction, and streamlining; the transition from wood-and-fabric to metal was virtually complete by 1935. Even more significant, however, was the consequence of the success of these new bombers upon the development of larger aircraft. Supporters of the strategic bombardment idea had always seen the desirability of large planes, since both range and load are primarily a function of size. However, until this time it had been believed that size mitigated against speed. Development of the B-9 and B-10 demonstrated that aerodynamic efficiency could be increased with size, thereby providing an open sesame for development of bigger and faster bombers.

That "open sesame" was soon established to be, not the fanciful remark of the airpower enthusiasts, but a trend that would swiftly bear its fruit. The mass production of the B-10 graduated an engineering breakthrough to the practical and widespread application of the "new airpower." But there was more to come, and Air Corps leaders were quick to exploit the breakthrough.

In March of 1933 Major General Benjamin D. Foulois, then Chief of the Air Corps, distributed a unique questionnaire to pilots on active duty. Foulois wanted their comments and recommendations regarding the future development of bombers. He reasoned correctly that the secret to proper guidance in such development could best come from those who did the actual flying and, in event of war, would risk their lives in those airplanes. As was expected the responses ran a wide spectrum of novel and revolutionary ideas, not all of which, of course, could be applied in a practical sense. But the overwhelming trend of thought was distinctly toward a large, four-engine airplane that could fly hundreds of miles at high altitude and with a heavy bomb load, being able to attack either sea or land targets.

In the Materiel Division of the Air Corps, engineers launched an intensive research program to meet and solve the countless technological problems of such an aircraft—which would demand more efficient streamlining, greater structural strength to meet the loads imposed by higher speeds and weight of armament, adequate defensive firepower and armor, and more powerful engines. The basic challenge exceeded by far the limited capabilities of the Materiel Division, but it established the trend of thought and set the goal toward which the Air Corps would reach. Further, it made clear that this "ideal" bomber called for the best engineering thought and production skill in the nation. In essence, it would be the greatest challenge ever offered up to American industry.

The Air Corps went at the new bomber program in two phases. First there would be strictly an experimental effort, a hardware development study which was intended to ferret out the hidden problems involved in building and flying the true bombardment giants envisioned by Air Corps planners. There would be, as well, a separate program intended to transform the exciting new ideas into the reality of production and service aircraft.

Early in 1934 Claire Egtvedt, president of Boeing, received a personal telephone call from Brigadier General Conger Pratt, chief of the Materiel Division at Wright Field,

Ohio, Could Egtvedt meet personally with Pratt on May 14, at Wright Field? The meeting was vitally important, the general said, and it was also secret. Egtvedt agreed to be there.

Boeing was about to get into the business of big bombers.

# CHAPTER 3

# FLEDGLING

THE MEETING OF CLAIRE Egtvedt with General Pratt at Wright Field, on May 14, 1934, had been set in motion the year before. Many men were contributing to the growing renaissance in the design of the American bomber. At the Air Corps Tactical School instructors threw convention to the winds. The primary target of airpower, they told students in uniform, had changed. Enemy aircraft, ships at sea, ground forces and other familiar objectives no longer headed the target lists. "The enemy's industrial fabric," the students heard, "will be a more vital target than his armed forces."

Along the western coast of the United States Brigadier General Oscar Westover and hand-picked airmen were flying a series of aerial strikes against selected cities. Their bombers again and again slipped through the defenses arrayed against them. Had the maneuvers been real the target cities would have been struck almost with impunity. The word came back from the West Coast that modern bombers could "go it alone" against the best of fighter aviation. With all factors of the modern bomber considered, stated General Westover, "no known agency can frustrate the accomplishment of a bombardment mission."

Therein lay the dominant theme of the revitalized Air Corps. Considering the progress of the modern bomber, especially in speed and range, the Materiel Division of Wright Field undertook an exhaustive study of bomber potential. The result of the study brought raised eyebrows from the engineers involved—if their figures were correct then a range of 5,000 miles at a speed of 200 miles per hour was within reach.

In December of 1933 Air Corps chief General Foulois took the Wright Field proposal for the new bomber—known as Project A—to Washington. There, before the War Department General Staff, he argued his case. "A plane with a range of five thousand miles," he said, "could protect Hawaii and Alaska. I think it is highly important that we undertake this as an experimental project."

To the surprise of many the General Staff acted promptly and favorably. The concept of an experimental bomber to prove out the feasibility of the new design—or to reveal intrinsic weaknesses—was given tentative approval on December 19, 1933. On February 12, 1934, the War Department approved an Air Corps budget of $609,300 for Project A. On May 12 General Foulois received authorization to negotiate contracts with the Boeing and Martin companies for preliminary designs and engineering data.

Claire Egtvedt received his telephone call from Conger Pratt. Two days later he walked into the general's office to face rows of engineers and pilots—and his competition for the experimental program, C. A. Van Dusen of the Martin Company. Both company representatives—for Boeing and Martin—accepted the requirements for competitive bidding.

They were told to have their designs ready within one month.

Egtvedt returned to the Boeing plant in Seattle grimly determined to win the contract. Everyone knew it would be only for the one airplane, that the project was intended to produce data rather than a production line. But the idea of building a four-engine giant that would span a hundred and fifty feet across its wings, that could fly from the east coast of the United States deep into Europe, or any other objective of comparable distance, fired the imagination of the Boeing engineering staff. There would be no reaching back into past experience from which to draw proven ideas. This would have to be a fresh start, the engineers would be forced to plunge into regions wholly unknown to them. The Boeing staff went at the challenge with unbridled enthusiasm.

On June 28 they proved their mettle—Claire Egtvedt brought back to Seattle from another meeting at Wright Field the Air Corps contract for the purchase of one XB-15 bomber, as Project A had come to be called.

Four years would pass before the XB-15 would take to the air. In that time the airplane more than proved its worth as the direct ancestor of the greatest bombers ever built, setting the trend for the features that enabled engineers to take the maximum benefit of XB-15 experience. The XB-15, largest American bomber ever built at the time (it first flew on October 15, 1937), spanned 149 feet across the wings, was nearly ninety feet long, and weighed over thirty-five tons. Unfortunately for the predicted performance the engines planned for the airplane were unavailable at the time it was completed. Instead of the cruising speed of 200 miles per hour the airplane just reached a maximum speed of 190 miles per hour at full power. It managed to achieve its design range of more than 5,000 miles, but only at greatly reduced speed.

The wings were so thick and huge that passageways were built within so that crewmen could manage minor engine repairs during flight. New problems cropped up at almost every turn; the endurance was so great that one crew could not be expected to man the airplane without tiring to the danger point. Following nautical fashion, sleeping bunks were installed so that one "watch" would be on duty, while the other crew rested or slept. For the first time in an American bomber, the crew included a flight engineer with his own station and control panel—an inflight monitor of mechanical performance. Instead of the tight cockpit the crew enjoyed the large space of a long and wide flight deck. Rather than exposed gun positions the aerodynamically clean fuselage of the XB-15 featured enclosed gun turrets. Engineers decided to concentrate on a majority of electrical rather than hydraulic systems for increased systems reliability. To power the accessories Boeing engineers installed two auxiliary generators powered by gasoline engines in the rear of the fuselage.

The flight engineering tests of the XB-15 alone paid back many times the expenditures to produce the "one of a kind" aerial giant. Yet the XB-15, which through the years proved so reliable on long and grueling flights, earned the name of *Old Grandpappy* through missions never planned at its inception. Its use as a test-bed completed, the airplane was redesignated the XC-105, and served with distinction throughout World War II as a cargo carrier. Before Old Grandpappy retired after its last flight, the Boeing engineers could look with pride not only at many years of outstanding performance, but a long list of world record flights for heavy loads carried to altitude.

And into the official archives of the Air Force went the greatest tribute to the "lonely giant." As Project A, notes the Official History of the Army Air Forces in World War II, the XB-15 "became the parent . . . of the B-17, the B-24, and the B-29, to mention only those heavies which carried the weight of the bombing attack on Germany and Japan in World War II."

During the months in 1933 when the Air Corps studied the possibilities of the Project A experimental bomber it would submit to the War Department, a major effort was made to advance the performance of the bombers that would be assigned to mass production. Project A was a "state of the art" experiment intended only for advanced studies, and once committed to a manufacturer, it could carry its own weight with a minimum of direction from the Air Corps. It was a "side project," and there were more pressing matters at hand. Advancing the operational capabilities of the Air Corps headed the list. Officers looked with great hopes to this issue, since the competition that had produced the Boeing B-9 and Martin B-10 twin-engine bombers, with Martin winning the production contract, still whetted the enthusiasm of the bomber proponents. The next round of competition, they reasoned, bid fair to bring about yet another "quantum jump" in bomber performance.

Late in 1933 the Air Corps notified the principal aircraft manufacturers that sometime in the year following there would be a design competition for a new multi-engine bomber that would replace the Martin B-10 then entering wide service.

On August 8, 1934, the Boeing company was among the industrial teams to receive the specifications required for the next bombers for the Air Corps. The bomb load would be at least 2,000 pounds and the airplane must carry this weight over a range of at least 1,020 miles, with a crew of from four to six. It must have a required top speed of at least 200 miles per hour.

There were other specifications that sounded a warning to the Boeing staff as they studied the Army papers. The Air Corps had listed the required maximum speed and range. But it added the cautionary words that it *desired* a maximum speed of 250 miles per hour, as well as a range of 2,200 miles.

The engineers looked long and hard at the new specifications. Whatever airplane could meet those *desired* requirements would have to be head over heels beyond anything flying anywhere in the world. More than a few of the top Boeing group expressed doubts that it could be done.

They didn't express those doubts easily or quickly. The Air Corps design competition in asking for bids from the different industrial companies held a powerful magnet. The bids were to be directed towards a contract of from fifteen to 220 airplanes.

The more the engineers and company officials studied the papers the more excited—or pessimistic—they became. Claire Egtvedt noted that if Boeing were to be eligible for the competition it must have an airplane *in the air* by August of 1935, and that was only one year off. Could a completely new design be made, and the airplane built, and prepared for flight, in that one year? It was a stupendous task to place on the shoulders of any design team.

If Boeing entered the competition it must be all the way. There could be no halfway measures for an airplane of such demanding performance as specified by the Air Corps.

That meant a stupendous outlay on the part of the company. And if they *lost* the contract . . . Egtvedt preferred not to think about that nasty consequence.

Yet there were other elements to consider, and without delay. Boeing and United Air Lines were in design studies for a new airliner that United wanted in order to compete with the DC-2s, modern twin-engine ships, used by other lines. Thorp Hiscock of United, studying a Boeing proposal for the new twin-engine airliner, tossed an idea into the lap of Egtvedt. "Why not go to four engines?" Hiscock queried.

Certainly it was food for thought. Egtvedt told his engineers to come up with design studies of the four-engine airliner. It would be an entirely new design, sleek and fast, with room for twenty-four passengers who could be carried nonstop on long flights. But while they were working at the airliner, Egtvedt told them, he suggested to the engineers that they also consider the design requirements of a bomber of approximately the same size. They even had a starting point—somewhere between the twin-engine B-9 bomber and the huge Project A taking shape on the drawing boards.

Egtvedt ran all these thoughts through his mind. One item in particular didn't fit and he again studied the Air Corps circular for the design competition. There were the key words: *"multi-engine."* To the aircraft companies invariably this meant twin-engine, but every now and then someone came up with a tri-motored design. The words "multi-engine" were included in the circular to allow some freedom of design expression.

But nowhere did the circular say that the Air Corps would *not* consider a four-engine bomber proposal. Egtvedt flew to Wright Field in Ohio to discuss the matter with Major Jan Howard, engineering project officer for the new design competition. The big question Egtvedt brought with him to Wright Field centered about the "accepted explanation" of multi-engine—which meant two engines. Would the Air Corps accept as qualified a design with *four* engines?

Major Howard grinned at Egtvedt. "The word is '*multi-engine*,' isn't it?" he emphasized.

And multi-engine meant two, three, *or* four engines. Claire Egtvedt returned at once to Seattle with his thoughts in a turmoil. There was still the decision to make, and the more he considered Boeing's position, the more apparent it became that an error in judgment could have catastrophic consequences.

The financial risk was appalling. Boeing held the contract for Project A, but at the moment this was still for a paper airplane. The Air Corps contract called only for the completed design of what *would become* the XB-15. It might be months or even years before the Air Corps would make its final decision about going ahead with the giant test airplane, and there was no guarantee that Project A would ever take wing. Boeing could not afford to count on Project A funds (the contract was not awarded until July 1935).

In many other respects, Egtvedt knew, the situation at the Boeing plant was critical. At the beginning of 1934 the Boeing employees numbered 1,700; at the time he pondered entering the competition for the new bomber only 600 workers remained. The plant situation was considered to be "critical," and matters were aggravated by the sudden and unexpected cooling of United Air Lines toward the proposed four-engine transport. Boeing, to stare the matter directly in the eye, was deep in the red, and operating in the red.

"The prospect of building 25 to 220 bombers loomed like a golden harvest," recalls Harold Mansfield,[6] "but the prospect of risking everything on one costly experiment hung like a menacing thunderhead over it.

"Egtvedt asked Bill Allen, the company lawyer, to come down for a talk. He explained that there would be many unknowns in the proposed project. The design studies for Project A made that clear enough. 'You know what little we have left here, Bill,' he said. 'I don't want to jeopardize the future of the company.'

"Bill Allen had a way of heading right for the point. 'Do you think you can build a successful four-engine airplane in a year?'

"Egtvedt looked over the roof of Engineering to the buildings of the plant. 'Yes. I know we can.' "

With those words the Flying Fortress was to be born. On September 26, 1934, the board of directors of the Boeing Airplane Company voted their confidence in the decision of Claire Egtvedt. The sum of $275,000 was allocated for the design and construction of Boeing Model 299. The experimental four-engine bomber must be designed, built, test-flown and delivered for Army flight trials to Wright Field—only eleven months from that moment.

Many top engineers protested. The job was impossible, they claimed. Boeing was being asked not to build just another airplane, but a machine the like of which had never existed. You don't build engineering precedents in the form of superior airplanes on that kind of rush basis, they insisted.

Claire Egtvedt reorganized the Boeing plant on a basis of a maximum effort to produce one airplane.

They called it Model 299.

The design team to create Model 299 wasn't planned with great care and study; there wasn't time for that. The team evolved from top Boeing talent, an engineers' huddle in the office of Claire Egtvedt. The group was small but was considered even by its competition as an "engineering powerhouse." Present in the room was A. N. Monty Monteith, one of the giants in the business. Monteith was the author of the textbook on aerodynamics used at West Point and regarded by many universities as a "bible" in the engineering field. He was Boeing's chief engineer, and he brought with him R. J. Minshall, one of his top men; E. G. Emery of Preliminary Design; and, Emery's 24-year-old assistant, Edward C. Wells. The latter was only three years out of Stanford University, but he would soon become the most significant of all the men who would nourish the early design into what was destined to become the greatest bomber in history.

Three weeks after the first studies were initiated Boeing knew the road it would travel to reach its new bomber. There was no doubt about using every ounce of successful pioneering by the company. That meant a low-wing monoplane design, construction of stressed dural skin, retractable landing gear, enclosed crew and gun positions, the four engines faired into nacelles ahead of the leading edge of the wing. . . . But this was just the beginning.

Roland Bradley of Boeing recalls the events of the moment:

> There was plenty of "know-how" present at the meeting in Egtvedt's office. Between the "know" and the "how" there would be reams of drawing paper. They went to work.
>
> It is easy to design a plane that will go fast. It is no trick to design a plane that will carry a big load. It is (or was, then) something else to design a plane that will carry a big

load and go fast, too. And that was the problem. Strange as it may seem in anything so scientific, engineering design resolves itself into an intricate series of compromises.

The Army wanted the new bomber to possess a high speed of 250 miles per hour. Other factors being equal, the smaller the wing, the faster the plane. In the Fortress-to-be, the designers had to consider a wing small enough to permit that speed. But, the faster a plane in flight, the faster the landing speed, and the Army also wanted this plane to clear a 50-foot obstacle in landing, and stop within 2,000 feet. A wing small enough to permit 250 miles an hour might also cause the plane to land so fast it would require a 4,000-foot runway. So the designers had to compromise on a wing large enough so the plane *could* stop within the specified 2,000 feet.

But—the larger the wing, the more the "drag" or air resistance in flight. This cuts down speed. In this case, with the engines then available, it might be to less than the 250 miles an hour required. So the designers had to work out a wing size that would retain the landing speed and *at the same time* permit the top speed specified.

So it went, with compromises on the compromises. Actually, many of them never got to the drawing board at all. Such things are juggled around in the designer's head and the bad ones mentally thrown out. Usually he's juggling two or three dozen compromises at the same time, working on them all simultaneously. There is no set order in which they are developed. Airplane designing is like the old riddle, "Which came first, the hen or the egg?"

As the team . . . juggled the facts and figures of the "type spec," one of the first thoughts probably concerned available engines. The Boeing group reasoned that even if they had the biggest and best, two engines would never do to power the type of super-ship they visualized. Mentally they chose four, each capable of 750 horsepower, big for that day. Not only would they make possible the desired power, but four engines would provide an extra safety factor for long-range operations.

By experience, they knew approximately how much weight each horsepower could lift off the ground and carry at the required speed. In this case, they figured it would be around ten pounds per horse. So, by multiplying the total horsepower, 3,000, by 10, the number of pounds each horse must carry, they concluded that with the four engines they were thinking about they *could* have a plane weighing around 30,000 pounds.

Now, theoretically, each square foot of wing is assigned the job of carrying so many pounds. By experience, the designers thought in this case a loading of about 22 pounds per square foot would be most desirable. Dividing the gross estimated weight, 30,000 pounds, by 22, the number of pounds each square foot was to carry, they arrived at a preliminary wing area—about 1,400 square feet.

After that the total wing area had to be shaped for best range and efficiency.

So far, the designing was mostly arithmetic. At this point the designers were seized with the doodle urge. There was enough data to make a start, and they just couldn't wait to see how the new plane might look. The pencils flew. Sketch after sketch was roughed in. Wing after wing was drawn, examined, rejected; or, if a detail seemed especially good, it was kept.

Since the area of the tail surfaces bears a fairly well-established ratio to the area of the wing surfaces, the designers sketched them in the rough, as the wings were sketched, experimentally. Because the bomb load and number of crew were specified, they could decide within reasonable limits how they should house them. They decided on a circular cross-section for the fuselage, and gave it a streamlined profile.

As the landing gear was sketched in tentatively, and the four nacelles, gradually the lethal beauty of the plane evolved. By now the rough drawings were departing from the free-hand doodle. What the designers saw on their drawing boards *should*, they thought, meet the performance characteristics the Army wanted.

Then began the tedious task of checking and rechecking what they thought they had, with what they really had. The gross weight, as they originally assumed it, was compared with the gross weight as it appeared now. The new gross was arrived at by analyzing the drag or resistance characteristics of the whole plane, still on the drawing boards. The more drag, the more fuel it would take. If it turned out the plane was going to weigh more than the wing area and the horsepower they had allowed for, then adjustments would have to be made. As these and other details were examined in the cold light of mathematics, there were more and more compromises to be made in the drawings.

Obviously progress was made . . . so the designers turned to other specific considerations.

The bombers of the day provided nothing for the crew but cold and noise. The Boeing engineers thought a comfortable crew would be a more efficient crew, so they provided soundproofing and a heating system. In the planes of 1934, a machine-gunner stood up behind a small windshield and blazed away. In the earliest Boeing Fortress, each gunner was provided with plenty of armament and streamlined "blisters" in the top and sides of the plane.

Then there was the matter of flight controls. The larger planes of the day took plenty of beef to maneuver. Since the better than 30,000 pounds of Fortress was to be a really enormous bulk to handle, the Boeing designers harnessed most of the control job to the airflow. They put the breeze to work by means of small tabs on the controls which helped to move the big control surfaces.*

Flaps, bomb doors and the retractable landing gear of that day were operated largely by hydraulic controls. Boeing's experience with the "247" [a highly advanced, twin-engine airliner of exceptional performance with which Boeing "took the lead" in airliner sales] and other airplanes indicated that electrical controls could be made more positive and reliable. So the designers substituted electrically driven motors as a safer bet ... the electrical system takes combat punishment as no other type of control can.

All in all, the first edition of the Fortress was a whole series of innovations. It was completed within twelve months from the day of that historic huddle in Claire Egtvedt's office. . . . Apparently, somewhere mixed in the graphite of the pencil points that roughed in the original sketches there was a bit of stardust. . . .

That was only part of the story. The three-view drawings that represented the best engineers had in them came in from the engineering shops to Egtvedt's office for final scrutiny. The designs were breathtaking, and concealed within the superb lines of the embryonic bomber were the best innovations that experience had dictated since the earliest days of military aircraft. The engineering drawings showed a clean wing that stretched 103 feet 9 inches from tip to tip, from the rounded edge of the nose to the tail the 299 would extend a distance of 68 feet 9 inches. The wing itself was neither in the low or high category, and yet it

---

*This one particular innovation more than any other has withstood several decades of aeronautical science—the same system is still in use with the largest jet transports built today.

wasn't fully a midwing design; the best description was for a low midwing arrangement that promised the greatest possible structural strength and integrity. Four Pratt & Whitney Hornet engines of 750 horsepower each would provide the new bomber with an estimated maximum speed of 236 miles per hour. The wing area hewed closely to the original calculations—1,420 square feet. The weight was higher than expected—32,432 pounds, but the engineers were convinced this wouldn't put any brakes on performance. The Army required 200 miles per hour and desired 250 mph in the new bomber—Model 299, if the calculations were correct, would deliver a maximum speed of 236 mph. This was less than the coveted figure of 250, but Model 299 promised to more than make up for this slight lessening of "perfect" speed. The airplane would fly—under necessary control response for combat conditions, and still with a rate of climb of 100 feet per minute—to its service ceiling of nearly 25,000 feet. The required figure for range was 2,000 miles—the engineers calculated that at a cruising speed of 140 miles per hour Model 299 could fly a distance without refueling of 3,010 miles. Over lesser ranges its bomb load would be not the 2,000 pounds specified—but 4,800 pounds. And into the long and slender fuselage with its curving gun blisters would go the crew of eight and five machine guns. The gun blisters were made strong enough to take the heavy .50 caliber machine gun, vastly superior to the .30 caliber weapon prevalent on existing bombers.

The many engineering details received a tremendous support from one hundred hours of wind tunnel testing. Those tests were a godsend to the Model 299 team, and seventy-three design engineers went into a grueling schedule of seven days a week, with many of those days running from twelve to sixteen hours.

The board of directors in September had voted the sum

of $275,000 to "design and construct the four-engine bomber Model 299." By December Ed Wells had been promoted to project engineer, his men were shaping metal and riveting the pieces together. But the project was running out of money.

The board of directors met, discussed the new bomber, and watered down their own enthusiasm. More than one man thought again that Model 299 was purely a speculative gamble and if they failed—the dreaded words were *no compensation.* But these thoughts, grim as they were, passed quickly enough. The board of directors dug deep into the dwindling company funds and came up with another $150,000 to continue shaping metal into the final product.

By the first day of July 1935, the shaping was about done. Draped over with tarpaulin because of Air Corps security regulations the airplane was ready to move to Boeing Field. The shrouding canvas would be only for a few weeks; with the date of the first flight approaching, it would be impossible to keep any secrets at an airport in direct viewing of the public.

The first few days of July were especially significant for Boeing for another reason. A double-sealed envelope arrived in Claire Egtvedt's office. It was from Wright Field and it contained the contract for the huge "mystery ship" that would become the XB-15. Boeing was plunging headlong into the business of really big airplanes.

As the weeks of July passed the intensity of effort increased until it seemed that all involved with the project existed in a world no wider than the sphere of influence of Model 299. For several weeks Superintendent Fred Laudan came in to work at the crack of dawn with the day shift; he watched them leave, remained at the plant to work through with the night shift.

Then the final week was at hand and a fever seemed to sweep the plant. The idea of work shifts went flying out the nearest window; everyone came to work and stayed working as long as they could manage to do so. The schedule for the first test flight went up on the employee bulletin boards—*Monday*, July 28, 1935.

From Saturday morning on no one wanted to leave the plant. Men slept in offices on couches, or catnapped in their cars. The future of Boeing could well ride on what this one all-out effort would produce. When the ground crew rolled 299 out to the flight line for taxi tests, hundreds of men stood around, silent, just watching. Gleaming silver under the sun, Model 299 rolled back and forth on the runway, brakes squealing, the roar of her engines rising and falling as pilots and test engineers advanced and retarded power. The great airplane seemed almost eager for flight, but Les Tower was having none of that. Taxi tests, engine tests, control and systems tests—all on the ground.

Newspaper reporters thronged to the field, as did thousands of spectators who lined the fences and created traffic jams.

Before the sun broke the horizon Monday morning, the tense expectancy of the first test flight gripped everyone present. Les Tower had completed his tests, had checked out all there was to study. He was as ready as any man could be for the momentous test when wings for the first time grip the air. Everything that had happened before now had led to this crucial moment—and despite the tremendous design and construction team, every man at Boeing knew there was a world of difference between the drafting table and the open sky.

Yet, the sight of 299 inspired a sense of deep confidence. There is a saying in aviation that if an airplane looks great, then something has been imparted to the machine, that greatness may have been built into the craft. British air historian William Green wrote of 299 as carrying these unmistakable lines; he said that the still untried craft was "as beautifully proportioned a military aircraft as had been conceived anywhere in the world at that time."

Les Tower took her off into a sunrise that was as dazzling as the potential of the great new machine.

For the next several weeks Tower and the Boeing crew, assisted by technicians and engineers from Pratt & Whitney to work on the engines, and from Hamilton Standard to check out the three-bladed propellers that were more than eleven feet in diameter—propellers with variable pitch to the blades and that maintained a constant speed during flight, a feature that enhanced performance measurably and that utilized to maximum efficiency every ounce of power from the engines—tested the airplane under different configurations of flight, from lumbering slow flight to high-speed dashes. They flew with the gear up and the gear down, at different flap settings, with the bomb doors open and closed; they flew at low altitude and took her way up where the temperature dropped to forty and fifty below zero. Tower and his crew put 299 through her paces, from brute handling of the ship to sensitive control adjustments, every move spelling out the details and characteristics and performance of the airplane. She flew with human hands at the controls, and responded beautifully with the automatic pilot turned on—a robot slaved to the control system and sensing every change in performance and flight attitude.

In every respect Model 299 was a sweetheart. There were minor "bugs" to be worked out, the inevitable thousand little things that can't be predicted before the acid tests of flight itself. But that was just the point—the problems remained minor.

Les Tower said that 299 was ready for delivery to the

Army. She was ready for the competitive tests against all comers. Everyone at Boeing was jubilant—there wasn't a thing in the sky that could touch the gleaming new bomber.

In darkness on August 20, 1935, the Boeing line crew wheeled 299 out of the hangar. In the glare of floodlights the Air Corps insignia colors showed clearly. So did the numbers painted on the high, sweeping tail—X-13372. Model 299 carried Air Corps colors, but she wasn't yet a military airplane—her assigned registration number made that clear. No one doubted the lack of military designation was strictly a temporary thing.

Tower and his crew planned a flight—nonstop—from Boeing Field to Wright Field in Dayton, Ohio. If they were going to deliver 299, they were going to do it up in bright colors. Model 299 had the stuff and now was the time clearly to demonstrate what the ship could deliver. Nonstop for 2,100 miles—a delivery flight right down the pike at top performance.

Les Tower climbed into the left seat in the cockpit. His assistant, Louis Wait, strapped himself into the right seat as copilot. Henry Igo of Pratt & Whitney took his position to monitor the engines, and C. W. Benton came aboard as mechanic.

Claire Egtvedt and Ed Wells had gone ahead to Wright Field, there to form part of the welcoming committee.

Tower and Wait fired up the engines one by one until the four Hornets snarled what had become the clearly identifiable sound of Model 299. Everything checked out perfectly. Les Tower released the brakes, wheeled the big silver airplane around, and taxied down the long strip to the end of the runway. Another final check—oil temperature and pressure, magnetos, controls, instruments, propellers, fuel systems, flaps, trim. The works. 299 went through her checklist like a ballet dancer.

She took off into the darkness like a veteran of the air. Everything went like clockwork. Tower and Wait climbed her out to cruise altitude. At 3:45 A.M. they sliced the night sky toward the Cascade Mountains—and Ohio far beyond.

Two hours after takeoff Igo came into the cockpit to stand between the two pilots' seats. He had been studying with utmost care the engine temperatures and manifold pressure readings. He looked at Tower and grinned. "Let's give her the works," Igo said.

Tower nodded. He eased the propeller controls forward until the blades were in high pitch. The throb of the four Hornets changed perceptibly, took on a slightly higher pitch in sound. 299 forged ahead with greater speed.

Precisely nine hours after leaving Seattle, Les Tower brought 299 down on the final approach to Wright Field in Ohio. It was a sensational flight. Sixteen tons of bomber had raced over a distance of 2,100 miles to average the unheard-of speed for the flight of 232 miles per hour. 299 had cut herself a brilliant record for her first long-distance flight. More important to the Air Corps engineers, Tower had flown the 2,100 miles with only 63 percent power from the four engines. To 299 had averaged an altitude of 12,500 feet for the distance. To add icing to the cake, Tower for the greater part of the aerial journey had used the automatic pilot to fly the airplane—he and Wait sat back to monitor the systems. In more respects than one, they had given 299 "her head," and the silver machine had responded in magnificent fashion.

Tower brought her down with his usual silken touch. The brakes squealed slightly as he rolled 299 off the runway onto the taxi strip, taking her to the flight line. They ran through the checklists carefully, shutting down the engines and the different power systems.

Someone looked through the cockpit window, searching for the large crowd they had been told would be waiting to greet them at Wright Field. But the flight line was almost deserted.

The four men climbed down from the B-17, where Egtvedt and Wells were waiting to clasp their hands and pound them on their backs. Benton turned to the man who was now chief designer of 299.

"Where is everybody?" he asked.

Ed Wells grinned hugely. "You're not supposed to be here," he said with a laugh. "The field expects you two or three hours from now."

It was a great wait for the crowd to show up.

# CHAPTER 4

# "A BURST OF FLAME AND . . ."

NOW 299 WENT THROUGH her most grueling tests. The weeks that followed were exhilarating to the Boeing crew and the men who had come along to participate in the severe competition flights. The Army assigned Lieutenant Donald Putt to Model 299 as the bomber's test pilot. There were some murmurs about a lieutenant being given so great a responsibility, but they didn't come from Boeing. Major Ployer P. Hill, chief of Wright Field's Flight Testing Section, knew Putt's capabilities better than any other man. Putt showed great enthusiasm about the four-engine Boeing entry, and Hill knew as well that a pilot who was enthusiastic about a new machine could tax that plane to its limit and bring forth from it performance that another man might never achieve. And Putt was more than enthusiastic; he was wild about 299.

The competitive tests were held with rigid adherence to the rules. The different categories included speed, endurance, time to climb to specified altitudes with different loads aboard, service ceiling, structure and design, engines and power plant systems, armament and equipment installation, maintenance, landing characteristics, and utility as a type.

Model 299 swept the field. The competition included a Martin 146, essentially an improved and modified version of the B-10 bomber then in active service. The third entry came from Douglas; their DB-1, like the Martin, had two engines. Douglas was betting on a favorite in the race; they had produced the DB-1 based on their DC-2 airliner.

Neither competitor could touch 299. Not only did the Boeing entry sweep the competitions, but it exceeded even the expectations of the Boeing crew and personnel from the company. Egtvedt and Wells enjoyed a mounting air of buoyancy. And with ample reason; they had taken a tremendous risk supported by the board of directors of Boeing, and it was paying off in spades. They shared their enthusiasm with General Oliver Echols who had taken over as chief of engineering at Wright Field. Echols, long an advocate of the big bomber and a solid adherent to the Air Corps concepts of strategic airpower, rooted for the 299 like a rabid fan at the World Series.

No one doubted but that Boeing would walk away with honors in the competition, that it would be 299, given a military designation, that would receive the coveted order for mass production.

October was almost past, and every test series but one had been completed. The final phase of the evaluations called for testing under the category of "utility as a type." That would wrap it up. For the last tests, Major Hill took the left seat in the cockpit as command pilot. Don Putt strapped himself in the right seat as copilot. Les Tower stood behind them. Also in the plane were Bud Benton and Henry Igo.

It was a beautiful day for flying, and 299 responded smoothly to the skilled hands of Pete Hill. The bomber cracked thunder across the field, bringing heads to turn and watch. A gleam of silver as the sun reflected off the wings and fuselage. 299 lifted smoothly into the air.

The duty officer was among those watching. The big airplane had impressed him every time he'd seen it move. Now he watched again as 299 rose from the ground, lifted her nose and began the familiar graceful climb to altitude. He grinned as the nose came up, continued in its soaring lift. It was a steep takeoff. The duty officer knew Pete Hill was at the controls, and he knew what Pete could do with an airplane. "He's really going to put her through the mill," he said to someone at his side.

The grin faded as the nose continued its upward sweep. "Hey, what's he doing!" the duty officer shouted, his face suddenly white. The nose never stopped its now alarming rise; it was *too* steep. Then, incredibly, the great airplane staggered into a vertical climb, the engines howling. For an instant it seemed to hang suspended in the sky. Then, as it must happen, 299 began to plunge. Before the nose swept around and started down the duty officer stabbed the emergency button. The crash signal slammed across the field, alerting everyone within hearing.

The onlookers stared in horror, holding their breath. There! She was starting to straighten out, coming out of what had been a helpless plunge. Men strained at imaginary controls, shouted, or stared mutely. She was still straightening out, still coming out of the plunge.

It wasn't enough. They watched her slam into the ground. There was a burst of flame, followed instantly by oily smoke as the wing tanks ignited with the rupturing impact.

Harold Mansfield recalls what happened next:[7]

Jake Harman, bombardment project engineer, in conference with General Echols, heard the sirens, heard someone say "299," raced out and hailed a field car, teeth set. Fire trucks were pouring foam on the burning plane, and a crowd was standing transfixed when Harman arrived. He scrambled with Lieutenant Bob Giovanelli onto a flatbed truck. "Back it in there!" he shouted at the driver.

Pulling coats over their heads, with arms shielding their faces, Harman and Giovanelli dove from the truck-bed into the furnace and dragged out Pete Hill, the pilot, and Les Tower. Don Putt, face gashed and burned, had jumped from the front end shouting something about "the control stand." Two other crew members scrambled out the back end. All were rushed to the hospital. . . .

Major Hill died that afternoon—a bitter blow. Les Tower, who had been on the flight as an observer, was badly burned but expected to live. Putt and the others would be all right. General Robins telephoned Egtvedt in Chicago where he'd been trying to sell the four-engine transport to United.

"Oh, no. No," Egtvedt whispered. It was news the body couldn't bear. He headed desolately back for Dayton.

There was no airplane now for the final judging. The last item on the evaluation sheet—utility as a type—was all that was left, but that called for flights by operating commanders. The Flying Fortress was ineligible under the rules.

"There must be some justice in the world," wrote Treasurer Harold Bowman. "Maybe we can sell the design to England." He added: "Our bank account is overdrawn."

Les Tower rallied but he was taking the failure personally, blaming himself. . . . It took the heart out of his recovery. Egtvedt assured him that it wasn't his fault. Then word came that Tower was worse, Tower was gone. Losing a airplane was nothing like losing a man.

Egtvedt clung to Dayton and Washington to see what could be done. He found the Air Corps was full of friends. Men like Tooey Spaatz and Hap Arnold insisted the Flying Fortress must be carried forward. Arnold was a brigadier general in command of the first wing of the new GHQ Air Force, under the Army General Staff. Knerr and Andrews took up the campaign for the four-engine plane. At Dayton Jake Harman wouldn't let go of the rope he was pulling. The new engineering head, Oliver Echols, who had been down at the Air Corps Tactical School getting a vision of strategic bombing from General Billy Mitchell's writings and from Captain Hal George, was of like mind.

The six hundred people left on the payroll in Seattle were doing their Christmas shopping with a prudent peek at the bottom of the purse when the news came that the Air Corps had chosen the twin-engine Douglas . . . for production.

What had gone wrong? A great new machine was left on Wright Field as a smoking shambles. Two men were dead, the others injured. Boeing had been dealt a mortal blow, to say nothing of the impact upon those officers of the Air Corps who had taken to the Model 299 as the opening of a new age in strategic airpower.

There were rumors that the 299 was too much airplane for any one pilot (or two, for that matter). To fly this machine, aviation writers noted, a man would have to be a superpilot, and even then he would be leaning heavily on his luck. This contention made great reading for the citizen who received his news of aviation from his daily newspaper, but it left a sour taste in the mouths of those who were pilots and who, of course, knew better.

Model 299 was a big airplane—larger than anything in active service at that time with the Air Corps. But it was hardly the biggest airplane built or flown, and, in fact, it failed to approach the size, complexity, or plain cussedness of many other giants that preceded it.

The Zeppelin-Staaken R-6, a German bomber of World War I, with four 260 horsepower Mercedes engines, had a wing span more than thirty feet greater than that of Model 299, was of greater length, and was an "absolute bastard" to fly. Yet this lumbering monster, created in an age when fabric and wood made every flight an adventure, flew more than fifteen years before 299 ever left the ground on its first flight. The Gothas and Giants flown by Germany in World War I, every one of them creaking, wallowing whales with wings, managed to carry out fifty-two bombing attacks against England during which they killed 857 and injured 2,058 people.

By the close of World War I, England had three models flying of its Handley-Page V//1500—and another 250 of these monsters on production order. Each V//1500 spanned 126 feet across its wings (compared to 103 feet 9 inches for Model 299) and stood twenty-three feet off the ground. With four 350 horsepower engines it could carry 6,000 pounds of bombs (against 4,800 for Model 299), had an endurance of twelve hours—every hour spent at the thundering speed of almost 100 miles per hour.

Bigger military airplanes—bigger, that is, than Model 299—existed in the United States long before the Boeing entry crashed at Wright Field. The Witteman XNBL-1 of 1923, built for the United States Army, was a three-winged goliath larger in size than Model 299 and outweighing it by more than five tons. Complexity was hardly the word for this aerial pachyderm. Its six engines, each of 420 horsepower, barely managed to drag it through the air at a maximum speed (under excellent conditions) of 95 miles per hour.

Then there was the Dornier DO.X which had the appearance of being carved somewhat hastily from a massive block of wood. Here was a giant that spanned 150 feet across its wings and also 150 feet in length. Its wing measured ten feet in *thickness*, and supported *twelve* engines; six pulling and six pushing. This was no mammoth built for a stunt—the DO.X carried as many as 169 passengers on a single flight, and could accommodate seventy passengers in sleeping berths. In 1931 the DO.X showed what the future of air travel might be like when it flew from Germany to New York.

In 1934—the same year Boeing started Model 299 on the drawing boards—Andrei N. Tupolev designed his ANT-20, farmed as the *Maxim Gorki*. The ANT-20 spanned 210 feet across its wings—more than a hundred feet greater than the 299. Its weight was staggering against the Boeing. Where the 299 weighed 32,432 pounds, the ANT-20 grossed more than *116,000, pounds*—58 tons!

That attends to the matter of the 299 being too big an airplane to handle safely. The matter of the size of the 299 is often obscured in a proper statement of the airplane. It was the largest *efficient* airplane ever to fly for its day. It combined size with speed, efficiency, excellent flying characteristics, acceptable landing and take-off performance, and other requirements of an airplane designed to function as a military weapon.

So size and weight weren't the culprits. Neither, apparently, was 299 itself.

The Air Corps put together an investigation panel composed of its best pilots, and engineers, and safety specialists. The official report on the accident is one of the most extraordinary in aviation history in its *vindication* of the airplane in question. The investigation panel took especial pains to emphasize that the loss of the Model 299 bomber could in no way be attributed to:

> structural failure; to malfunctioning or failure of any of the four engines or propellers; to the action of the automatic pilot because it was not in operation at the time of the crash; to any faulty structural or aerodynamic design of this airplane nor to any undesirable or adverse flying or handling qualities of the airplane.

What, then, had gone wrong? As in most cases where an airplane is lost when the fault fails to involve the airplane or its characteristics, the answer is simple. The error was not mechanical, but human.

It might best be termed *oversight*.

There are times when a necessary improvement to a new airplane contains within its design the seeds of hidden danger. New equipment demands new procedures, and if a pilot is not thoroughly familiar with those new requirements, he can place himself in a situation where the mistake, made unknowingly, mushrooms with lightning speed into a disaster. This is what happened to destroy Model 299.

Experience with their own airplanes, as well as the lessons obtained from the use of other very large aircraft, had made it clear to the Boeing 299 design team that size becomes a danger to an airplane when it is standing unattended on the parking ramp. Size in this instance refers specifically to the control surfaces—the ailerons, rudder, and the elevators. In the case of the 299 the elevators proved to be the starting point of the chain of events that caused the Boeing to crash.

A parked airplane with large elevator control surfaces is

liable to suffer damage in the event of high or gusty winds. Since the elevators move easily—in fact, 299 and all subsequent Fortresses delighted pilots because of their superb elevator control response—they are also moved easily by these winds. To prevent their being moved violently, with subsequent damage to the airplane, the Boeing design team included in 299 a control device in the cockpit which, when activated by the pilot as he parked the airplane, *locked the elevators and the rudder.* When the pilot placed his lock to *on,* a metal rod slipped into the lock position, making it impossible to move either the elevators or the rudder.

And you can't control an airplane in flight with those surfaces locked.

There was the killer—299 was taken off the ground with the controls locked. The men in the airplane were doomed from the moment the wheels left the runway at Wright Field.

The official finding of the investigation board stated this fact clearly. It seems almost beyond any question but that the error was human—that not one of the experienced test pilots aboard that bomber remembered to follow the basic pre-takeoff check rules that apply to all pilots before takeoff, in *any* airplane.

They didn't physically check the movement of the control surfaces. Had they done so, they would have known immediately that the controls—and the elevators primarily are critical here—were locked. From the evidence submitted, the investigation board reached the conclusion that the elevator was locked in the first hole of the quadrant on the "up elevator" side when the airplane took off; had the elevator been in either of the "down elevator" holes on the quadrant it would have been impossible for the airplane to take off; with the elevator lodged in the extreme "up eleva-tor" hole, pilot Pete Hill could not have climbed into his seat without first releasing the controls.

The first element of the disaster was that the elevators were locked, that the pilot did not physically move the control column through its full path in order to determine if those controls were free and unrestricted of movement. The second "nail in the coffin of 299" was the position of the control lock—precisely in the only position that would allow the pilot to enter his seat and permit the airplane to lift from the ground.

With these conditions established, the airplane was still unable to fly. There is a paradox in this statement com-pared to the previous sentence; nevertheless, both state-ments are true.

With the controls locked in the position they were found during the start of the takeoff, 299 could never have climbed away from the airfield. It would have gotten off the ground, but without the ability to climb.

That was the situation *at takeoff*. But things changed immediately that 299's wheels left the runway, which wit-nesses testified was in a tail-low attitude. At this time the airplane was accelerating, *and the aerodynamic forces act-ing upon the controls were changing their effect.*

The elevators, with increasing power from increasing speed, tended constantly to change the angle of attack of the wing—adding a lifting force to the airplane. The speed of 299 was approximately 74 miles per hour when the wheels lifted from the runway. From that moment on the forces on the elevators increased steadily, forcing down the tail, and increasing the lift angle of the wings. This contin-ued in an unremitting progression until the nose lifted so high, and the angle of attack was so great, that the airplane stalled—and fell.

Even the small servo tabs on the elevators, designed to ease the forces required for control movement, added to the growing fatal situation. With locked elevators, and the pilot pushing forward—frantically, as the nose ascended—on the control column, the servo tabs acted as small elevators on the fixed elevator—and aggravated instead of helping to alleviate the extreme tail-heavy position.

The investigating board noted that, due to the size of the airplane and the inherent design of the control system, it was improbable that a pilot, taking off under these conditions, would discover that controls were locked until it was too late to prevent the stall and subsequent crash.

To support that contention, one source stated that the locked condition of the controls was due "either to the possibility that no effort was made to unlock the controls prior to takeoff, and as a result the controls were fully locked; the possibility that the pilot only partially depressed the locking handle and as a result the locking pin was only partially withdrawn from its locking hole in the face of the locking quadrant or the possibility that the locking handle was fully depressed prior to takeoff and did not fully disengage the locking pin."

Those are possibilities. None of them appears to eliminate the cold fact that had the pilots moved the controls in the cockpit through their full path *to assure* that the control surfaces of the airplane were free and unrestricted in movement—299 would not have been lost.

And that was the sum and substance of it. Several men were dead, others seriously injured. The gleaming shape of 299 was now charred wreckage. Under the strict rules of flight and testing competition of the Air Corps, Boeing was disqualified automatically as a participant in the production contract to be awarded.

The Douglas entry beat out the modified Martin

bomber. The Air Corps designated the twin-engine Douglas bomber as the B-18 and ordered it into mass production.*

A pall descended upon the Boeing engineering team, the company officials, the entire work force. Close friends were dead. Loss of 299 after its brilliant performance in the tests was especially shattering a blow. With the loss of 299 went every dime the company had invested.

Boeing was in trouble. Serious trouble.

---

*For the record, no airplane in service or under development at the time of these tests, other than what would become the B-17 Flying Fortress, ever flew as a combat machine in primary battle zones during WW II. The Martin B-10 was hurriedly phased out of service when the B-18, of which 350 were built, came off the production line. The B-18 itself, winning the flight competitions through "default," proved one of the greatest white elephants ever built, and wholly unsuited to and inadequate for combat during the war. Slow and lumbering, it was so helpless a target for enemy fighters that it was relegated to training duties and searching for submarines off the continental United States.

# CHAPTER 5

# THE SPREADING OF WINGS

THERE WAS LITTLE IN prospect for the coming year to spread Christmas cheer through the Boeing plant. The holidays that normally brought with them the spirit of warm friendship and sharing of good fortune came now as a black pall. Death and destruction cast its grim shadows through the long spaces of the plant as it closed down for the Christmas season. In those shadows hovered the aftermath of the disasters that had struck down Boeing at the very height of its moment of success. It is often difficult to equate financial catastrophe with the loss of close friends, yet reality could hardly be evaded in grief, no matter how deep.

A new year was about to start with an inevitable deluge of creditors. They must be paid or, at least, accounted to—a long list, from small vendors to the banks. The destruction of 299 meant more than losing the competition for the production contract. Boeing had poured its money into 299 and, in so doing, had virtually closed out all other sources of revenue.

The New Year came grim and bleak.

And yet, there still remained hope. Claire Egtvedt had rallied desperately, along with officers of the company, to retrieve the splendid promise that 299 had demonstrated before the accident. They had lost an airplane, and the airplane itself was proven by impartial scrutiny to be wholly blameless. That same machine had out performed everything else in the air. Surely in this promise there was something to be salvaged. As Egtvedt and the others made their rounds, weighed down by the loss of their friends and the unexpected debacle of the crash, they found, as Harold Mansfield had said, that the Air Corps "was full of friends."

It was more than friendship they needed. They found, quickly enough, that cold impartiality had brought the leading officers of the Air Corps to the same conclusions about the 299 that had been held by Boeing. In 299 there existed the greatest bombing weapon ever known—and adherents of strategic airpower wanted that weapon. These protagonists of a powerful strategic air arm knew that with the production of this four-engine bomber the United States could establish a new level of strength in international affairs. It would be not an offensive weapon, but a powerful defense able to strike from both coasts of the continental United States against any approaching enemy. Here was national defense with a meaning never before known—the means to reach out to sea many hundreds of miles and begin the destruction, long before any actual commitment to ground fighting, of a hostile force.

The small spark of hope never lost by Claire Egtvedt and the key design team that had produced 299 waxed a bit more brightly in the sudden intense support for the Boeing bomber. Such leaders in bombardment doctrine and strategy as Hugh Knerr, Frank M. Andrews, Follett Bradley, C. C. Culver, Herbert A. Dargue, Harold L. George, Robert Olds, Kenneth Walker, Donald Wilson and Walter H. Frank presented a formidable phalanx of military, engineering and political support to retain the promise that had been demonstrated during the flight trial competitions at Wright Field.

It soon became clear that while certain rules of the test competition could not be altered, and that 299 had become ineligible under those rules, there were other means of reaching out for the bombardment airpower the Air Corps wanted. Except for the "utility as a type" category the Air Corps considered 299 as having excelled in virtually every aspect of the competitions. It became evident that the utility tests were considered no barrier to official as well as personal enthusiasm for the Boeing airplane.

A formal evaluation board had yet to convene on Model 299, but the Air Corps had already taken steps to eliminate obstacles to their obtaining the new Boeing machine in quantity. The engineering and test personnel of Wright Field had already completed "all detailed engineering inspection and study of performance data, but before a formal evaluation board had met."[8]

Claire Egtvedt and his team were informed that the results of the studies of 299 had led the Air Corps to recommend that contracts be issued immediately for the purchase of sixty-five of the new Boeing bombers. The enthusiasm that met this news was tempered swiftly with the warning that this was only a recommendation, that the formal evaluations had yet to take place and might require many months. There were yet other serious problems.

Douglas was issued a primary production contract for 133 bombers—the new B-18.

There were no funds in the Air Corps coffers to pay for

the sixty-five Fortress. Fiscal 1936 was a year of appropriations with grave deficiencies as far as airpower was concerned.

Boeing held its collective breath when the Air Corps strengthened its recommendations for the Fortress. "Cancel the purchase of another 185 other aircraft already authorized for Fiscal 1936," the Air Corps recommended. "Use the money to buy the new Boeing bomber."

But the ash-filled wreckage at Wright Field was still too stark to ignore. The reports that the airplane was "too much for one man to handle" were like a plague that refused to go away. The Army balked at the recommendations of the Air Corps. They considered the crash, mulled over the rumors, and sat uneasy with the higher cost of the Boeing airplane.

The War Department let it be known they weren't delighted with the new concept of fleets of four-engine bombers.

The Army balked anew. Then there was a compromise.

On January 17, 1936, Claire Egtvedt brought back with him to Boeing a new promise for the future.

The War Department General Staff had authorized the purchase of thirteen four-engine bombers from the Boeing Airplane Company. They had authorized, also, the purchase of one additional airframe that would be used for static tests—subjected to deliberate engineering tortures in laboratories to determine the "breaking point" of the aircraft structure.

Boeing failed to realize through Model 299 what it had hoped. That failure was all the more bitter to swallow because no one questioned the superiority of the Boeing airplane. Some officials and engineers murmured unhappily that the Air Corps had placed a production order for a clumsy twin-engine whale instead of buying the airplane they really needed, and wanted. Egtvedt and his immediate staff knew better. The General Staff had made the final decision. Douglas had the big contract, but the bomber protagonists fighting for the new Fortress were determined to make the most of the airplanes which Boeing was getting ready to build.

As far as Claire Egtvedt was concerned, he had completed his immediate and demanding role with Model 299. The building of thirteen heavy bombers was in itself a tremendous undertaking, and there were pressing problems to overcome—at once. Egtvedt forgot engineering and design and pondered just where Boeing would go in the new year. There were airlines customers to satisfy—and Egtvedt's staff had been hammering out new designs which they wanted to discuss with him, to meet with the airlines, to set up long-range programs for Boeing. To Claire Egtvedt 299 had become a vindication—not for himself, but for Boeing and the people who had created the most outstanding bomber in the world. He would have to turn the production of the new bomber over to those who would attend best to its myriad problems. There was one last major hurdle to overcome with the bomber—Boeing lacked the physical space to establish a proper production line for what would be the Flying Fortress. Egtvedt spent time with company lawyer Bill Allen. When the men were through they had completed their plans for a great new plant to go up on a site at Boeing Field.

Claire Egtvedt would never be too far from what had started as Model 299, but now he could turn to other matters. His immediate role had been completed. The birth of what would become the greatest bomber in history was a matter of accomplished fact.

Long before the first Flying Fortress started to assume shape on the new Boeing production lines, the battle that would dictate the conditions under which the new heavy bombers would operate had been joined among the military hierarchy of the country. As had happened many times before, the conflict centered about the allocation of authority for the coastal defense; the sum and substance of the wearying argument was the division of responsibility between the Army and the Navy for defending the shores of the nation. The Flying Fortress flew straight into the heart of the controversy before the first bomber ever reached its Air Corps pilots. Efforts to secure agreements in this matter, made all the more complicated by bombers of increasing range, "all too frequently ended in the airing of irreconcilable views, and such was the peculiar perplexity of the problems raised that attempts to secure some authoritative and definitive statement had proved futile."[9]

Early in 1931 there seemed to be some satisfaction of dividing the spoils of authority. An agreement was concluded between General Douglas MacArthur, Chief of Staff of the Army, and Admiral W. V. Pratt, Chief of Naval Operations. In that agreement was the statement that:

> The Army air forces will be land based and employed as an element of the Army in carrying out its missions of defending the coasts, both in the homeland and in overseas possessions. Through this arrangement the fleet is assured absolute freedom of action with no responsibility for coast defense. . . .

Overwhelmingly satisfied with this arrangement—no doubt was left that the Army would shoulder the burden of coastal defense—the General Staff took special pains to assure that the Air Corps functioned within the meaning of the mission that called for protecting the coastlines of the country. In essence, the bombers of the Air Corps would serve, first, to extend the range of vision of coastal batteries through aerial reconnaissance, and, second, they would function as artillery of extreme range. Beyond that point where the big guns of coastal fortresses could reach, the bombers would fly to attack an invading fleet.*

On January 18, 1933, the War Department approved an Air Corps plan to carry out special command and staff exercises that would prove out the worth and effectiveness under simulated wartime conditions of a new system of air command, the GHQ Air Force—General Headquarters Air Force. When first organized its mission was to:

> concentrate a substantial part of the Army Air Corps on the West Coast in exercises to be conducted in the late spring for study of the problem of repelling an enemy overseas expedition. . . . General Westover's report concluded that "all Air Force units could be concentrated on either coast within two and one-half days, and possibly within two days should it be desirable to press the movement"; made constructive recommendations for the organization and command of a GHQ air force as a permanent part of the national defense; and stressed the need for "adequate and suitable equipment and material for overwater reconnaissance."[10]

Another step in what would become the Flying Fortress was forged. The official history of the Army Air Force notes, as the next step inevitable in the growth of what was to become a "true airpower capability," that:

---

*While the role of the B-17 in World War II was to be for offensive bombing strikes, Model 299 and the early B-17s were conceived purely for this defensive mission: the protection of American coastlines from foreign surface fleets. It was this function—not the defensive armament of the B-17—that brought about the name *Flying Fortress*.

the Air Corps after 1935 was characterized not so much by its concern to change the basic organization of national defense as by a purpose to find in the mission assigned to the GHQ Air Force the basis for an ambitious program of bomber development. The Army airman thereafter was, above all else, an advocate of the big bomber, and around the potentialities of that type of plane he built his most cherished hopes.[11]

Those hopes came to materialize in the form of the Flying Fortress. But no one, at the time the first B-17s were being assembled at Boeing in Seattle, could possibly have anticipated the fierce opposition to the development of a powerful bomber arm of the Air Corps. There was fierce opposition from the General Staff itself. The Navy at times took violent exception to the big bombers and their headstart pilots and crews. Political Washington balked at the idea of airplanes costing vast sums of money. And nothing good came out of isolationists who believed, first, that nobody was going to attack America across the vast expanse of the Atlantic and, second, that the nation would be far better off minding its own business than building longrange bombers.

Meanwhile, the GHQ Air Force waited with growing impatience for their first Fortresses. The contract called for Boeing to deliver the batch of thirteen flying aircraft and one static test aircraft by the late summer of 1937.

The first Fortress careened smack into a hostile Congressional investigation.

The Air Corps designated the fourteen Boeing aircraft the YB-17, the letter-prefix *Y* denoting that this group of airplanes was strictly for evaluation purposes under operational conditions. It also made it clear that if these tests "in the field" did not prove to the satisfaction of the Army that the new bomber was everything claimed for it, no production order for further aircraft was likely to be made.

On November 20, 1936, the first Fortresses received a new designation—Y1B-17. Fiscal concern rather than technical modification dictated the change; the number 1 after the letter-prefix of Y signified that this evaluation batch of aircraft were procured from "F-1" appropriations.*

On December 2, 1936, a Boeing test pilot took the first of the Y1B-17s into the air on its initial flight. The crew came back to the field enthusiastic with the response of the big silver bird. One engineer commented that "She's everything we had in 299—only more, and better." Little surprise met his words, for there already were contained in AC 36-149 the first modifications to the basic B-17 design that would continue for many years to come. The landing gear was changed from a two-leg to a single-leg system; a small item at first glance, but significant to utility and reliability, since it simplified the gear operation and reduced its weight. Studies of the airplane's long-range potential brought the Air Corps to request a station for an additional crew member. Flight tests of 299 had revealed problems in the gun blisters and armament and minor corrective action remedied the faults. Additional equipment in the form of radio gear, antennas, and similar auxiliary systems went into the Y1B-17.

The big change was in the engines. Boeing dropped the 750 horsepower Pratt & Whitney Hornets and adopted the

---

*On this matter of designation it is interesting to note that, despite official references to the contrary, there never was an XB-17. Model 299, which would have so been identified, crashed before XB-17 could be assigned to the airplane. Since no serial number of the Army was ever assigned to Model 299, there could be no aircraft designation applied to the machine. The Fortress first accepted by the Army Air Corps carried the designation of Y1B-17 and the serial number AC 36-149. This should keep the record straight for the B-17 buffs.

Wright Cyclone GR-1820-39 (G2) engines that produced 930 horsepower each. The performance increases that resulted were especially gratifying to the design team, since the original performance specifications were being exceeded even more than they had been in Model 299.

The gross weight of the Y1B-17 climbed more than a ton to a new gross of 34,880 pounds. The new dividend in power more than overcame the additional weight. While the maximum speed increased by only three miles per hour to a new high of 239 mph, the long-range cruising speed (where it counts) went up from 140 to 175 miles per hour. And the service ceiling—that height where the airplane can still maintain a rate of climb of 100 feet per minute—rose more than a half-mile to the new figure of 27,800 feet.

Those were the statistical improvements. Those that did not show significantly on paper were the better handling qualities of the airplane. With more power available the Y1B-17 had a better rate of acceleration in the air, improved response under a heavy load, and better handling in almost every way.

Five days after the initial flight the first YIB-17 rolled down the runway with Air Corps Captain Stanley Umstead at the controls. Umstead was the first pilot in a new program intended to speed up delivery rates. Instead of waiting for the Boeing company to flight-test each aircraft and then deliver the plane to the Army, military pilots would begin their acceptance flights at the Boeing plant. Umstead's takeoff and flight went without a hitch. So did his landing. But after the Fortress was on the runway and rolling Umstead skidded into the headlines. The captain tramped hard on the brakes. A screech knifed through the air as the steel-and-bronze brake system heated up, fused, and locked.

The tail went up and the nose came down—right onto

the runway. The first YIB-17 skidded nearly 250 feet on its nose. No one was hurt—except the sensitivities of political Washington. The first Fortress had crashed and burned. The second made an ungainly skid along the runway. Both times the airplane was being flown by military pilots, and the uproar that ensued once again raised the matter of the Fortress being too much for any one man to control safely.

Congress waxed indignant and shouted for an investigation. The investigating committee discovered that Umstead had applied the brakes too forcefully, that the airplane (again) was not at fault. The watchdogs from Congress faded away.

But not the vigilance of those who flew the first of the Fortresses. The word went out—screw up and we may all be kissing good-bye to the heavy bomber program of the Army. Everyone walked on eggshells and flew with the touch of angels.

On March 1, 1937, the officers and men of the 2nd Bombardment Group, GHQ Air Force, at Langley Field, Virginia, assembled along the flight line to watch the first YIB-17 being delivered to their outfit. Lt. Colonel Robert I. Olds, one of the most skilled of the bomber veterans in the Air Corps, received his new plane with kid gloves. Eleven more Fortresses dribbled in during the next six months until, on August 5, the 2nd Bombardment Group had received its full complement of twelve YIB-17s.

A thirteenth YIB-17 went to Wright Field in Ohio for engineering test flights, and the fourteenth Fortress, without instruments or internal equipment, was delivered for static tests and eventual destruction to determine the stress limits of the airplane.

But at Langley Field, Bob Olds was meeting with his best men to find the answers to a problem of pressing urgency. His crews would take out the Fortresses until they knew the gleaming new bombers inside and out, until they could fly them with the kind of skill that comes only from putting the best and most experienced men in the drivers' seats. What then? How best could they use the Flying Fortress? Not simply for formation flights and bomb tests and the standard routine for developing new aircraft into operational machines, but for helping the cause to which they were all committed.

The Air Corps was fighting desperately for a new sense of purpose. They wanted bombers. They wanted big bombers in quantity. And the opposition was getting rougher. Enthusiasm for the big bomber was low in Washington where the battle of the budget was an everyday occurrence. The old interservice jealousies had risen from the ashes of former agreements and the military brass were taking dead aim once again at the Air Corps—and the bombers.

If the 2nd Bombardment Group was to be the predecessor of a new organization in the Air Corps, rather than the last of its line, Olds reasoned, then he and his men had to focus the attention of the entire country—*favorably*—on their new Fortresses. They spent long hours into the night working out their plans. No one needed to remind them that the Air Corps' old enemies were ready to cut the nation's military airmen back down to subservient status in the military organization.

In the summer of 1933 the admiral, who had reached accord with General MacArthur on the matter of jurisdiction for defending national coastlines, hung up his uniform and left it in the closet. With the departure of Admiral Pratt from Washington went the brief period of peace between the Army and the Navy. The old controversies bloomed again and the rain of acrimony between the services clobbered the Air Corps with its debris.

New agreements left little doubt that the Air Corps was considered to be a third-rate adjunct to the Army, and the Army itself, in matters of coastal defense, was subordinate to the Navy. The fleet was supreme, came the word from Washington. And what if the fleet were not present? The message could not have been clearer. Even under those circumstances, primary responsibility for locating enemy invasion or warship forces rested wholly with "naval district forces supplemented by Army Air Corps units." In effect the Air Corps would be taking its orders—in coastal and offshore matters—from the Navy.

Matters were hardly improved when the Air Corps' own parent service, the Army, publicly criticized its airmen for their heretical attempts to create a force of heavy bombers. Colonel Olds and his men moved uneasily through the aftermath of a special study prepared at the request of the Secretary of War which brought in June 1936:

> a most discouraging statement of war department policy. Concentration on the big bomber, an offensive weapon, was inconsistent with national policy and threatened unnecessary duplication of function with the Navy, whose eleven carrier-based bombing squadrons equaled the combined total of such forces elsewhere in the world. No country had at the time, or was likely to have in the near future, aircraft capable of mounting an air attack on the United States. And since aircraft of medium range were "capable of attacking" any hostile naval or land-based aviation within effective range of our vital strategic areas, the request for the much more expensive long-range planes lacked logic. The B-18, then the standard two-engine bomber, was equal to any mission assigned the Air Corps and was much less expensive. Not only did the study advise against the purchase of the requested B-17s but, in a reversal of the atti-

tude more recently governing policy, the paper argued against the development of "long-range, high-cost, bombardment airplanes." . . . Until the international situation indicated a "need for long-range bombardment aviation," the Air Corps should be equipped with "airplanes of reasonable performance rather than to have nothing as a result of our efforts to reach for the ideal."[12]

There was more thin ice for Bob Olds and his 2nd Bombardment Group to skirt with the greatest of care. When they took delivery in late summer of 1937 of their twelve Fortresses, the publicity attending the arrival of the new airplanes was overwhelmingly out of proportion with the cold shoulder from the high brass in Washington. The GHQ Air Force went so far as to declare the YIB-17 was "the best bombardment aircraft in existence, particularly for coastal defense."

There was the rub. Few people argued that anything in the skies could match the brilliant performance of the Fortress. But a great many people who were in the position of authority *did* argue that it didn't matter one whit how good the airplane might be—the country simply didn't need big bombers.

The GHQ Air Force rallied desperately to attach its star to the acceptable mission of coastal defense, and there was almost open chicanery in the manner with which overworked public relations officials, in and out of the Air Corps, made every attempt to spread the belief that without the Flying Fortress we simply didn't have any long-range coastal defense on which we could depend. Because, notes the official history of the Air Force:

Under existing circumstances it proved far from easy to win recognition of the need for such a plane in coastal defense, and under existing national policy it was difficult to find any other justification for the long-range bomber than its capacity to contribute to the defense of our own coasts.[13]

The next question came smoothly on acceptance of the problems. If there were scant justification for the long-range bomber in extending the range of coastal artillery, *could some other justification be created?*

Now there was a neat little possibility if ever one existed. Bomber adherents in the Air Corps knew it was only a matter of time before aeronautical science produced truly long-range bombers both in *and out of* the United States. The day would inevitably appear when the great bombers of other nations could reach this country. When that time did come the best defense against such missions would be not simply to try to intercept the attackers, but to go after *their* homeland.

And if the 2nd Bombardment Group could demonstrate beyond question that such long-range attack was possible in the foreseeable future . . . why, people must start to think of the heavy bomber as something other than coastal fortresses with wings.

How could this be done? The officers of the 2nd Bombardment Group looked out at the Langley Field flight line where twelve answers stood shining in the sun. Twelve Flying Fortresses. Twelve silver machines with which to *imply* what the future held.

Colonel Olds' mission was to develop the operational techniques that would apply to long-range bombing missions. He and his men had virtually free-wheeling authority in this program, since, as they were the first long-range bomber force in existence, they would have to start from scratch. No one had laid any groundwork for them. Navigation in formation, through any kind of weather, over any type of terrain, operations far from home bases, a maintenance capability en route, reliability of men and equipment on a scale never before known . . . These were only some of the ingredients with which Bob Olds and his team might be able to establish a solid base for future bomber strength in the Air Corps.

The YIB-17 itself was the key, the plane and the way in which it was used. That meant not bombing strikes on targets in the desert, or precise navigation over lonely islands, but efficiency, speed and performance in a dazzling manner *before the public.*

The 2nd Bombardment Group went to work.

1938 was still spanking new when Bob Olds took off in a YIB-17 from the East Coast of the United States. Olds' crew was honed to a fine pitch, and the Fortress purred with the efficiency of a fine-made Swiss watch. Olds took the bomber to the best altitude for wind conditions, adjusted his power settings until he was stealing every ounce of speed from the four engines and props, and kept up the pressure all the way to the West Coast of the United States. There, his grinning crew knew they'd bagged it.

A new east-to-west speed record—12 hours and 50 minutes on the nose.

There was a lot of back thumping, some fast dashes to the john, some hot food and close attention to the airplane sitting on the ramp. Mechanics refueled the big iron bird, added oil, inspected, adjusted and preened. Bob Olds and his men climbed back into the Fortress and took off. The plexiglas nose pointed back to their point of departure, and again Olds and his men poured the coal to the thundering bomber.

Ten hours and 46 minutes later they got some more back thumping and uproarious shouts for their trouble.

They also had *another* speed record under their belts averaging 245 miles per hour west-to-east, all the way across the United States.

Not bad—for an airplane that had to be carried into existence by a small group of men dedicated fiercely to their belief in the machine. Not bad, and it was only the beginning. The Air Corps brass told Bob Olds to keep it up.

Someone took special note of the fact that Dr. Roberto M. Ortiz, the new president of Argentina, was soon to be inaugurated in a lavish ceremony. "Why not," someone suggested, "add to the festivities?"

"How?"

"Let's fly on down there and extend our best wishes."

No one knows if it started in this light fashion, but little matter. For the idea of flying a mission to Argentina—a mission to express to Argentina the good will of the American people—caught on like wildfire. The actual flight would be a grueling test of six heavy bombers. Navigation, timing, use of strange-airfield facilities, coordination with foreign officials and operation from foreign bases; the list was long and the more the men studied their requirements the more obvious it became they had really bitten off a big hunk to chew. It was the kind of mission where things could be expected to go wrong. If they did, before the eyes not only of the country but of the entire world, the entire heavy bomber program could go right down the drain.

No one wanted to think of a fiery crash or some other major disaster in someone else's front yard. Again, and with more emphasis this time, everyone would have to walk on eggshells and fly with the touch of angels.

The State Department and other government agencies involved in clearing the political and diplomatic pathways did their work. The 2nd Bombardment Group received the green light, and Bob Olds notified his crews to get ready.

On February 15, 1938, they took off in a long file from Langley Field in Virginia. High over the base the six great airplanes wheeled majestically into formation, and set their course for the long aerial trek southward. Piloting the lead Fortress was Colonel Olds. In the left seat of each of the planes following were Major Vincent J. Meloy, Captain Neil B. Harding, Major Caleb V. Haynes, Captain Archibald Y. Smith, and Major Harold George. Bob Olds had picked his men well. Every one of them would be called upon for their skill and experience when the opening weeks of war would inflict shattering defeats upon the United States. They were the frontrunners of what would become the most powerful aerial force ever known in the world.

All that, however, lay in the future when the six Fortresses pushed their way through thin air high over the United States, and toward the foreign lands beyond. They had taken off from Langley Field at nine A.M., and landed at Miami. From that moment on each Fortress would be on its own. Each navigator would plot his own course, each crew would determine from the performance of their own plane the most efficient speed, altitude, engine and propeller settings, and other data vital to flight effectiveness over long ranges. Each plane would, in effect, carry out its own extensive research on its operation and utility. Most of the time the Fortresses drifted out of sight from one another, maintaining contact by radio. A mass formation flight over long distance would have been impressive, the pilots realized, but it also would have placed severe demands on the performance they hoped to achieve. Formation flying is wasteful of fuel, taxing on the engines, and demanding of the crews. Because of turbulence from the propellers of leading airplanes, as well as from weather, the pilots trailing the leader are required to work steadily to maintain formation position, and inevitably there's jockeying of throttles—which gulps fuel and imposes heavy loads on the engines. Going it alone, with radio contact and scheduled times for meeting on the ground, was the best way to hack this mission. They could fly their impressive formations when there were people around to watch. Olds ordered each pilot to assemble in the air over a specific checkpoint on the ground before anyone could land. That way they would come down to earth as a group—and there are few sights more impressive than one bomber after the other gliding down from the sky. Especially when most of the hundreds of thousands of people who would be watching had never seen a four-engine bomber—or *any* airplane before.

The government gave the aerial trek a name that pleased all concerned—the *Good Will Mission.*

It didn't mean anything at the time, and it wouldn't for some years to come, but there was a young navigator aboard one of the Fortresses upon whose shoulder history had placed its hand. His role as navigator was unusual because he was a fighter pilot. He had transferred to bombers and was training on multi-engine aircraft when the Good Will Mission was planned. He wanted anxiously to make the flight as a pilot. Bob Olds turned him down; he didn't have enough time to check out in the Fortress.

"Well, dammit, can I go as a navigator?" he demanded. The boss of the 2nd Bombardment Group said sure, he could go.

His name was Curtis LeMay—the man whose star became almost synonymous with the name of Boeing. This was the same Curt LeMay who would became a crack B-17 pilot and who would lead hundreds of Flying Fortresses into battle over Germany, who would command the great B-29s that burned out the heart of Japan in World War II. He would go on after that to create the Strategic Air Command where, with Boeing B-29 and B-50 Superfortresses, he would "hold the line" until the jet age could be applied meaningfully in strategic air might. This was the same Curt LeMay who would bring the sleek Boeing B-47 Stratojets and B-52 Stratofortresses, and many hundreds of KC-135 jet tankers, into the most powerful force ever known in the world.

On the morning of February 15, 1938, he was tucked away in the navigator's compartment of a YIB-17, headed for South America in an airplane which still had to pass its acceptance tests—and which still might never be ordered into production.

Bob Olds took off first on the 2,695-mile flight from Miami to Lima, Peru. Fifteen hours and 32 minutes later his tires squealed smoothly on the runway of Pan American-Grace Airways' field. One after the other the Fortresses followed him down. The pilots lined up the silver airplanes in a long row that brought people out by the thousands, staring in awe and wonder at the giants that had descended from the skies in such perfect order. The B-17 crews remained on the ground for seven hours of speeches, welcome ceremonies, and the meeting of protocol requirements which pleased mightily the State Department back in Washington.

The first hitch in the flight developed at Lima when the crew of Major Meloy's Fortress discovered mechanical problems with their propeller-control systems. Meloy and his men stayed on the ground while the others pressed on for Buenos Aires—with a sudden decision to land first at Santiago, Chile. Olds had received reports of violent weather at Buenos Aires; following the path of discretion, he scheduled the Santiago layover until it was safer to proceed.

Over Santiago reports came in by radio that the storms

had cleared at their destination. Olds made the decision while still flying to continue according to their original mission plan and the five airplanes, now in a wide and scattered formation that kept them in sight of one another, wheeled to the east to begin the long climb that would take them above the rugged Andes that separate Chile and Argentina. Wearing oxygen masks the crews watched the temperature needles going down to more than forty degrees below zero. At 21,000 feet they looked down to see the peaks startlingly close—and the tumbled flanks beyond that would lead them to Buenos Aires.

They had been in the air just over twelve hours when they cut the switches on the flight line in the Argentinian capital.

Meloy was hard on their heels. He overflew his "emergency stop" at Santiago when he received the word that weather would be no problem. Weather being what it is, he showed up over Buenos Aires just at that moment when a raging *pontero* (tornado) was chewing up the local scenery. Well above the storm, Meloy circled slowly for an hour until the air had quieted down. Despite his delay over the city, Meloy set a new record from Lima to Buenos Aires—11 hours and five minutes.

Right on schedule the men appeared at the ceremonies to inaugurate Dr. Ortiz as the new President of Argentina.

Then it was back to Langley, via the Panama Canal Zone, and hopes that everything would go as smoothly on the way home as they had on the outbound part of the mission. It did—almost. One B-17 suddenly heeled over when a gear leg and tire crunched through the concrete cover of a gas pit to which it was being towed for refueling. It took five hours to heave the Fortress out of its unexpected snare and check it over for damage—but only those five hours. Captain Smith, at the controls, drove his airplane hard, and caught up with the others on the way home during their refueling stop at Lima, Peru. The six Fortresses landed at France Field in the Panama Canal Zone, went through ceremonies and servicing, and then set off for a nonstop flight all the way back to Langley Field.

Five thousand people came out to greet them at Langley when they touched down on Sunday, February 27. If they believed they had had their fill of protocol and ceremonies out of the United States they were in for a shock. Not only was the airfield mobbed but the dignitaries were out in full strength as well. Major General Frank M. Andrews was on hand personally to deliver a *"Well Done!"* message from President Franklin D. Roosevelt.

"Boy, there's nothing like performing before an audience to bring out the brass," one weary crew member remarked as he and his fellow pilots caught sight in the reviewing stands of Secretary of War Woodring and Army Chief of Staff Craig. Those who had been loudest in deprecating the Fortresses were first in line to shake the hands of those who had flown the airplanes.

Bob Olds and his forty-seven crewmen from the six Flying Fortresses had turned in a performance that was regarded not only in the United States but throughout the world as sensational. The new bombers had flown approximately twelve thousand miles with nothing more than minor incidents to interrupt their mission. The crews had proved themselves and in the process had brought laurels to the Flying Fortress. They had done even better than they realized. On November 7, 1939, in honor of and in recognition for their Good Will Mission, the 2nd Bombardment Group received the coveted Mackay Trophy.

The first rule of success is never to release your grip on a proven winning combination. Seventy-two hours after the MacKay Trophy ceremonies ended, Colonel Bob Olds was in the air again and on his way back to South America. This time there were seven YIB-17s instead of six, and they were headed for Brazil. Major General D. C. Emmons, new commander of the GHQ Air Force, went on the second Good Will Mission as Flight Commander. Bob Olds was Squadron Commander for the flight of twelve thousand miles to Rio de Janeiro and back home to Virginia.

Once again their timing proved superb. Weather, reliability, navigation, distance, servicing . . . all the problems that usually plague such a mission were overcome easily with the seven big bombers, and the crews attended the celebration of the fiftieth anniversary of the Republic of Brazil right on the planned schedule. They flew back to Langley Field in a "pilot's dream" of a flight—without a single major incident to mar the journey.

It would seem this second mission *en masse* would have delighted all who were involved. In the sense of accomplishment this was true enough. But the Air Corps, especially the heavy bomber adherents, were flying under an official black cloud. The men who flew the Fortresses into history and the record books weren't blind to reality. They had learned there was more to winning your battle than flying outstanding missions.

Sometimes you could be so good your accomplishments came back like an unexpected boomerang to whang you right in the teeth.

# CHAPTER 6

# POLITICS AND BLITZKRIEG

THREE MONTHS AFTER THE triumphant good will mission of 1938 the 2nd Bombardment Group received a golden opportunity to demonstrate forcefully just what they could do in the way of carrying out the Army's mission of coastal defense. Word had been received that the Italian liner *Rex* was well out to sea and headed for port in New York. One ship, more than seven hundred miles offshore. A dot in the vast expanse of the ocean.

"Can we go out and find it?" Bob Olds asked his men. They were certain they could do so. Olds picked his best men and put them in three Fortresses. He selected Lt. Curtis LeMay to navigate on the most exacting mission they had ever undertaken. If they could fly out to sea in these three airplanes, find the *Rex* and fly over the luxury liner, there would be no question but that the Air Corps could do its job with capabilities far more than anyone had yet conceded.

The passengers on the ship were startled when someone pointed his finger at the sky and shouted. Three great silvery shapes came thundering from the west—dead on their target which was then 725 miles east of New York. Shouting with elation the crews banged each other around the shoulders, laughing and pointing to their target. Several times they swooped low over the liner and waving forms below. Olds peeled off and made a careful "bombing run" on the *Rex*. As the Fortress swept overhead a crewman tossed out a message that landed smack on the deck of the liner. The three Fortresses flew back to Mitchell Field on Long Island, New York, overjoyed with what they had proven.

Just to reach the *Rex* and return to base meant a distance of some 1,500 miles. But their range had to be far in excess of this distance. They needed fuel for starting, running up the engines, taxiing, climb to altitude, and then the flight to the *Rex*—which might mean a search pattern for some time. There was the long flight back to their home airfield, and they must maintain additional fuel for emergencies such as bad weather that might mean diverting to another field rather than Mitchell. All in all, it was a mission to make bomber men click their heels with delight. That the three Fortresses had found the *Rex* through a sky filled with heavy cloud cover only served to increase the feeling of tremendous accomplishment.

No one could have been more stunned than the crews of these three bombers, or their associates, when reaction to the mission came down from Washington. There was no praise to be found—only a severe reprimand and an order that curtailed all future flights of the Fortresses, and all other Army aircraft. In fact, the order, prompted by unbridled Navy wrath at the Fortress flight, restricted all activities of the Army Air Corps to a distance not to exceed one hundred miles from the coastline of the United States!

Disbelief and shock were the response. At first the men

of the 2nd Bombardment Group refused to believe the new orders. Many of them were convinced it had to be a joke. It wasn't. The Navy was putting on all the pressure it could muster and with the President openly favoring the Navy, the pressure was hot and severe.

"Somebody in the Navy apparently got in quick touch with somebody on the General Staff," General H. H. Arnold said sourly of what had happened, "and in less time than it takes to tell about it . . ." Well, the order couldn't have been clearer. One hundred miles out from the shoreline and that was that.

But the action could cripple the Army in its mission of coastal defense. It was being asked to put on blinders and to tie its hands and then carry out the job of defending the coasts against enemy attack.

*Who* had issued the order? The Air Corps inquired. *No one knew.* The rumor spread swiftly that the "order" was nothing more than a verbal agreement between the Chief of Naval Operations and the Army Chief of Staff. "The hell with that," was the comment best expressing the reaction to this news. Verbal orders based upon a verbal agreement? Hell, this was the Army, not a damned prep school, and you didn't do things any way except the Army way—and that meant written, official, for-the-record orders.

But the orders still couldn't be found. The rumors, as such will do, turned into a torrent. Writing candidly of the incident an Air Force historian has noted that the Navy:

> was maneuvering to eliminate the Air Corps from long-range operations over water. . . . Major General Frederic H. Smith, Jr., who has made a special investigation of the matter, states that air leaders were convinced that an Army-Navy understanding on the ban existed, but "I do not believe that we found good sound documentation substan-

tiating the agreement." General Eaker is perhaps the nearest surviving witness to this remarkable episode. He says that he was present in the office of General Andrews, who was commanding the GHQ Air Force, when a telephone call for Andrews was put through by the Chief of Staff, General Malin C. Craig. According to Eaker, Craig issued the order verbally to Andrews at that moment, and Andrews placed a memorandum of the call in his personal file. After the death of General Andrews in May 1943, the memo could not be found in his papers; Eaker infers that someone had removed it. There remains, so far as Eaker knows, no other documentary proof of the order.

While the Navy moved to check long-distance flights by the Air Corps over water, it also made progress in opening the way to long-range, land-based flights by naval craft. In November 1938 a significant change was incorporated in the Joint Action agreement. In connection for provision for naval air action in coast patrol and in protection of sea communications, the change stipulated that naval aircraft "may be required to operate effectively over the sea to the maximum distance within the capacity of aircraft development." Thus was specifically authorized the development which the Navy had sought and the Air Corps had feared. By the early part of 1939 the Navy had six major air bases preparing to handle some 25 heavy bombardment squadrons.[14]

And that was only the beginning. The United States followed a policy of national defense that gave no weight to offensive operations—which could be carried out best and over the greatest distances from home stations by the Flying Fortress. Most military leaders accepted the official national goal of continued isolation, and they were determined not to rock the boat. On that basis many of these men believed, honestly and faithfully, that we simply did not require long-range bombers and that their construction was a matter of wasted funds and effort.

It was against this solidly entrenched doctrine that the Air Corps leaders were forced to set their energies. From 1935, the year the Flying Fortress first took wing, until the Nazi attack on Poland in 1939, the Air Corps suffered its most crucial period for the procurement and development of bombardment aviation. There was little question of what they fought for—the very *existence* of a bomber force. The Air Corps was not lacking in theories and plans, but without the proper equipment it could not possibly mold the force it believed would be needed to oppose the growing might of Germany, Italy and Japan. Looking back upon the 1935–1939 period from the vantage point of hindsight, notes an Air Force historian, "it seems hardly conceivable that the Air Corps leaders should have faced such a desperate struggle in procuring the big bombers. But the fight was real, and it was in earnest. It was, in fact, a three-cornered struggle involving the Air Corps, the General Staff and the Navy. And in this bitter contest the air arm was almost always opposed by the two senior services."

Ever since October 1937 General Andrews had been waging an all-out struggle to obtain the funds with which to increase the procurement of additional Flying Fortresses. "The General Staff," notes an official survey of this period, "continued to ignore Andrews' repeated protests and exhortations."

The general kept trying. In 1938, in his position as commander of the GHQ Air Force, he went on record to block continued appropriation of twin-engine bombers rather than the B-17. The plane the General Staff recommended for construction, Andrews said acidly, was the same B-18 with which Air Corps leaders were already fed up because of its characteristics—which he described as "unsatisfactory and obsolete in combat performance." The B-18 was slower in altitude by nearly 100 miles per hour than the B-17 and since speed and altitude were the essential defenses of a bomber, Andrews argued, it was clear that the development of new fighters by European nations would leave the B-18 wholly at their mercy.

The General Staff noted that it had placed for the Air Corps, on November 9, 1937, an order for thirty-nine additional Fortress aircraft. That, decided the General Staff, was more than enough. "For the best interests of national defense," stated the General Staff, the bombers that would be procured for the Fiscal Year 1939 would be the twin-engine B-18. In the summer of 1938 the Secretary of War made it a matter of official policy: the United States was specifically not to order any further B-17 aircraft.

The high brass, ever resentful of the Air Corps, openly irritated with the success of the GHQ Air Force with its limited number of Fortresses, was convinced it now had the big bomber in a sack and that it had effectively pulled the cord tight to keep it there.

There would be two major forces to snap the cord and bring the big bomber back to life. One would be Germany, already making its preparatory moves before going on a rampage through Europe. The other would be the Flying Fortress itself.

Oliver Echols, the engineering chief for the Air Corps at Wright Field in Ohio, spent a great deal of his time thinking about the Flying Fortress. Like many others in the Air Corps he wanted more B-17s—desperately. And also like many others in the Air Corps, he knew how slim were the chances for getting them. The Air Corps also needed to accelerate its technical development of the B-17 design, and that was practically impossible when there were only thirteen planes of that type flying—of which twelve were being used by the 2nd Bombardment Group in service tests. Getting some of his B-17s away from Bob Olds would be just about impossible, Echols knew, and the one Fortress assigned to Wright Field was constantly required for special engineering tests and experiments.

Echols called Jake Harman and told him to stop in his office. "Look, Jake," Colonel Echols began, "I have an idea. We aren't going to get any more than thirteen B-17s for a while. We could make it fourteen, if we made a flying airplane out of the one that is supposed to be used for structural tests. I doubt if we need those tests. Why don't we use that airplane to put in turbo-superchargers for high altitude?"

Harman thought it over and said that he felt it was a great idea. Dr. Sanford Moss of the General Electric Company, working with the aid of engineers from Wright Field, had already developed the new turbo-supercharger for large engines. His device was a turbine wheel with steel-alloy blades to be turned by the flaming exhaust gases of an engine. As they spun with great speed the turbine rammed high-pressure air into the engines at heights where they would normally be fed only the thin and oxygen-deficient ambient air. In effect the turbo-supercharger enabled an engine at high altitude to produce the same power it would generate much closer to the earth. The result was an airplane that, at high altitude, could fly faster, carry a much greater load, and cruise a much greater distance than an unsupercharged airplane that needed most of its engine power simply to stay aloft in the thin air.

While Harman pondered the mating of the turbos with the Wright Cyclones of the Fortress, Echols threw him another question. "What would turbos do for the speed of the 17?"

Harman studied his slide rule for a while before he responded to the query. Finally he looked at Echols. "At twenty-five thousand feet," he said, "maybe two hundred ninety miles per hour."

That was enough for Oliver Echols. "Get hold of Claire Egtvedt and find out if Boeing will do it. I'll see if I can dig up the money."

He did. Boeing went ahead with the new program. The Army designated the plane Y1B-17A.

While Ed Wells turned to his new engineering task of raising the speed and altitude capabilities of the Flying Fortress, Boeing cut another niche in its program of building giant airplanes. On August 5, 1937, Boeing had delivered the final Y1B-17 to the 2nd Bombardment Group at Langley Field. Now, two months later, on October 15, the huge XB-15 was ready for its maiden flight.

Harold Mansfield turns back the clock:

Eddie Allen wheeled the giant to the far end of the Boeing Field runway. Gentle, thoroughgoing Eddie Allen was now a consulting engineer and test pilot for various companies and was rated the best in the business. Major Johnny Corkille, the Air Corps representative at the plant, was with him at the controls. Satisfied, Eddie cut loose, rolled ponderously down the runway and took off. The big ship came off the ground like an airplane. The two auxiliary gasoline engines that Bill Irvine from Wright Field had proposed were working away in the back end, charging the ship's seven miles of electric wiring. Eddie found the bomber stable and air-worthy, though sluggish in speed. Tests continued through November, until the plane was ready for delivery. Then it slid down to Hamilton Field, California, to widen the eyes of field crews there. Private R. F. Fowler of the 31st Bombardment Squadron sent the *Air Corps Newsletter* his impressions: "Because of the distance between motors, the most practical means of communication is radio. The crew on one engine may be enjoying perfect weather while the crew on the neighboring engine is engulfed in a blizzard. At the last landing one person got aboard unnoticed and wasn't found for days."[15]

On April 29, 1938, the new Y1B-17A took to the air for the first time. The engine nacelles had a slightly different look to observers who had seen the original group of thirteen Fortresses. The change came from the new turbo-superchargers fitted to the Wright Cyclone engines. Even those were changed; the Y1B-17A with GR-1820-51 (G5) engines had a total of 4,000 horsepower, fully one-fourth greater thrust than Model 299. And the new ship, as sprightly as a fighter, had the power when it needed it most of all—at high altitude.

Boeing test pilots and General Electric engineers were still running experimental flights with the Y1B-17A when word came into Boeing of a wild flight with one of the Y1B-17s. The airplane was AC 36-161, the thirteenth Fortress built, and the model that had been assigned for advanced engineering tests to Wright Field.

Heavily loaded with instruments for recording accurate flight data, the plane was on long-range tests with Lt. William Bentley at the controls. High over Langley Field in Virginia, Bentley found himself boxed in from all quadrants by towering summer thunderstorms. Even in those days most pilots knew better than to fool with the violent "thunder-bumpers" and Bentley made his move to get out from under, and fast. He headed for the nearest patch of clear sky but his luck didn't hold. The Fortress staggered as if struck by an avalanche. In an instant shrieking winds tore the airplane from his control. Bentley and the crew, slammed wildly from side to side, blinded by lightning, discovered themselves upside down, stalled out, and helpless—in an airplane at just about its maximum allowable weight.

"That was all she wrote," a crew member commented later. "The bottom fell out on us."

The big, heavy airplane whipped into a spin. Rotating with punishing speed, the instruments tumbled, the Fortress whirled crazily downward. The altimeter needle was spinning as though an inner spring had snapped. The pilots fought to regain control but there was no stopping the berserk machine. Those men who weren't strapped into their seats were plastered against the fuselage sides like flies stuck on flypaper. The Fortress spun all the way down through the clouds and tumbled out, still spinning, into clear air. The pilots stared in wonder from their windows. The wings were still on! They were still in one piece!

They brought her out of it—and increased the forces that had been battering the big airplane. Tramping rudder, ramming forward on the control columns, they stopped the spin and pushed over into a steep dive. Then came the careful easing back on the controls until the nose lifted. Higher, still higher, until the demon wind subsided to the roar with which they were familiar.

Bentley didn't waste any time getting on the ground. Every man aboard the airplane was still shaking his head in wonder that the Fortress had stayed together. On the Langley flight line they crawled all over the ship. They found some rivets popped and there wasn't any question but that the wings were bent out of shape. But she was together and she could fly.

The recording instruments aboard the Y1B-17 had

made a permanent record of the stresses imposed on the airplane. When Bentley and the others examined the papers there were low whistles of amazement. Airplane Number AC 36-161 had gone past just about every maximum load for which it was designed. According to the Air Corps specifications to which the Fortress was built, the airplane should have come apart by the seams. Not once, but several times.

When the news got to Wright Field, Jake Harman thought of what Colonel Echols had said to him during their discussion of turbo-superchargers for the static test model. He had talked about the structural tests and then commented: "I doubt if we need those tests." Harman had a grin on his face when he went to tell his boss just how right he was.

The results of that "hairy flight" carried great meaning to the entire B-17 program. The mandatory limits of flight performance imposed upon the airframe could be raised in full safety, a free dividend from a near-disaster if ever there was one.

On January 31, 1939, the Air Corps took official delivery from Boeing of the Y1B-17A. It got an airplane that was already a startling jump in performance over its immediate Y1B-17 predecessor. With the new Fortress the Air Corps had a bomber that at its best operational altitude streaked through the high, thin air with a maximum speed of 311 miles per hour, as compared to the Y1B-17 at 239 miles per hour. More than 70 miles per hour in a single jump! The cruising speed also went up, but the most startling improvement was the new service ceiling—38,000 feet. That was more than two miles higher than the airplanes being flown under command of Bob Olds at Langley Field.

The test crews of Y1B-17A had some strange experiences to relate to their friends. One of them was flying through thin air with the temperature down to *seventy* degrees below zero.

Despite the hammering blows rained against the Air Corps by political and military foes, 1939 proved a banner year in establishing even more firmly the outstanding performance of the Flying Fortress. There was, first, the very fact that more B-17s were coming out of the new plant at Seattle. The Air Corps had received its thirteen flight and one static test Fortresses by the late summer of 1937. For a long time to come, that was all. The orders had gone through to build thirty-nine of the new B-17B models, but that would take many months.

1938 came and went without another Fortress added to the Air Corps inventory.

Then the Y1B-17A was officially accepted from Boeing. The Air Corps wasted no time in proving what their prize bomber could do. After initial flights to check out the Y1B-17A, the Air Corps turned it loose. The Boeing brought to the country a new load-carrying record by hauling a payload of 11,023 pounds over a distance of 621 miles at an average speed of 259.396 miles per hour. That was an auspicious start and proved what the airplane could do under short-range conditions. Under more realistic combat demands the Y1B-17A could carry a bomb load of 2,400 pounds over a range of 1,500 miles.

The range left some people less than happy. Could it be improved? Boeing took another long look at their favorite thoroughbred and opined that there was room for additional tanks in the airplane. The Air Corps asked that Boeing make design studies toward this purpose.

There were other steps forward. The Air Corps considered that the Flying Fortresses assigned to the 2nd Bombardment Group at Langley Field had more than fulfilled every requirement of their service testing. The Y1B-17 designation was dropped and new "credentials" were stenciled to the fuselage. Henceforth the airplane was to be known as B-17.

The Y1B-17A fell under the authority of the change, and was redesignated as plain B-17A.

Officers and men of the Air Corps waited anxiously to start receiving the first bombers in the production order for the thirty-nine B-17B models. This would be a *combat* bomber, more powerful than the service test group. It would also have the turbo-superchargers that had made of the B-17A a high-stepping aerial thoroughbred, as well as a host of changes within the airplane that would enhance greatly its performance as a machine intended for combat.

The enthusiasm exhibited by the Air Corps for the B-17B, while shared by the technical staff at Boeing, was somewhat lacking in the company's executive offices. The reason was simple economics: Boeing was losing its shirt on the Flying Fortress.

Every dollar invested in Model 299 had gone down the drain; since the airplane crashed before it could be accepted by the Air Corps the loss was Boeing's. The original service test order involved thirteen flying and one nonflying articles. When the order came through for the B-17B models the total number of planes ordered was only thirty-nine, rather than the "up to 220" bombers on which Boeing had risked its investment. The Boeing prices for each bomber to the Air Corps had been based on large production orders. With lesser numbers involved Boeing discovered that it lost several thousand dollars on every Flying Fortress it delivered to the Air Corps.

What of the future? Instead of a promise on which Boeing might be expected to risk further capital, there was the ominous statement from the War Department General Staff: "No military requirement exists for the procurement of experimental . . . bombers in the fiscal year 1939 or the fiscal year 1940, of the size and type described [heavy, four-engine, long-range bombers]."

Jake Harman from Wright Field had visited the Boeing plant to check work being carried out on the turbo-supercharger program. Ed Wells talked with him, excitement clear in his voice, about the possibilities of a B-17 with a pressurized cabin. "We can get you better than three hundred miles per hour at 25,000 feet and a bomb load of 9,900 pounds," he informed the Air Corps engineer.

Jake Harman shook his head. "I'm afraid I've got some bad news for you," he said sadly. "The War Department has turned down General Echols' request for funds for a pressurized bomber program. They've asked us to put no four-engine bombers in our estimates. . . ."

Bad news comes in bunches, apparently. The top offices of The Boeing Company gave their Washington representative, James P. Murray, clear instructions: come up with some income-producing activities for Boeing.

Burdened with this vexing problem, James Murray stumbled straight into a hornet's nest. Just at that time when Boeing was in severe financial straits, and losing money on what Fortresses it was building and had on order, the Air Corps itself reacted to the financial anemia under which *it* had been placed by the War Department. From their viewpoint there was only one answer: get more airplane for the same dollar. And the way to do that was to get tough with the supplier, to bargain hard and from a position of strength.

Circumstances combined to screw up a rapidly deteriorating situation. The original contracts established for Boeing a price of $205,000 per airplane. Despite the fact that the "gambled" high production orders on the B-17 hadn't gone to Boeing, the Air Corps suddenly insisted that the existing price tag was too high and that the figure had to be reduced. Renegotiations for the B-17 contracts became a tangled snarl which became worse steadily with acrimonious relations between Jim Murray of Boeing and General George H. Brett, with whom Murray had to work out final terms.

Murray had planned to handle the negotiations either with Hap Arnold or Oscar Westover. Just at this time a plane crash took the life of Westover. Arnold went into the number one position as Chief of the Air Corps, and Brett slid into Arnold's vacated spot—to the dismay of Boeing and many others. Brett was fully determined to play the role of the no-retreat buyer, and he told Murray that the Air Corps would pay $198,000 per B-17 from then on and "not a dime more." Murray looked with open disbelief at Brett. The figure was ridiculous and both men knew it. Not only would Boeing lose money at the figure of $205,000 per plane, but because of the innovations in the new Fortresses it stood to increase its loss with every day spent on the production line. New engines and modifications to the basic design had improved the fighting capabilities of the Fortress, but also ripped the cost.

Murray told Brett flatly that he was way out of line. If Boeing attempted to mass produce the B-17 on the figures supplied by Brett it could mean a financial debacle for the company. To Murray's surprise—and shocked anger—Brett changed from a man who was negotiating to an incensed military officer who virtually snarled at the visitor in his office. Brett accused Boeing of not cooperating, of blocking negotiations, and of deliberately holding up the program to produce more B-17s for the Air Corps.

Words flew, tempers flared, and Brett told Murray to get out of his office. As a parting gesture he ordered Brett not to negotiate with anyone at the Materiel Division at Wright Field.

Murray was something less than pleasant when he inquired, somewhat caustically, if Brett minded if he, Murray, went over his head to see Hap Arnold.

Brett was fighting for control. "You can see Jesus Christ for all I care!" he shouted at the departing Murray.

Arnold welcomed Murray warmly, but it didn't take long for Murray to understand that Arnold was fighting the same battle which Murray had encountered. Accompanied by Arnold, Murray found himself thrown out of the War Department.

Murray contacted the executive offices at Seattle, where Boeing had a new president. Bill Allen, the company lawyer, had been trying to assess the future of large military aircraft. The war clouds had been gathering everywhere from Japan to Europe and Africa, and there was talk of tremendous armament programs for the United States. That meant production and as far as that was concerned no one could handle mass production better than Phillip G. Johnson.

Johnson had left Boeing in 1934 when there was a legal breakup of the United Aircraft Corporation. Claire Egtvedt bought Bill Allen's proposals and he went to Phil Johnson, asking him to come back as president of the company. Egtvedt would become chairman but Johnson would run the show. Phil Johnson was reluctant to do so. He wanted to retire.

Something changed his mind. It was late August 1939 and Germany was banging on Poland's door. A few days later the Third Reich introduced its *blitzkrieg* to the world by roaring over Polish defenses. The Red Army came in from the east and between them they began the systematic pulverization of Poland.

Phil Johnson returned to the top chair at Boeing. By this time there had already been further orders for the Fortress. The Air Corps had ordered thirty-nine B-17B models. Then the reality of events overpowered the resistance to big bombers by the General Staff and another order came in. Boeing expected this to be the big one that would make their investment on the Fortress pay off. It didn't. The order for the new B-17C model came to only thirty-eight airplanes—and Boeing just couldn't hack the production problems at $205,000 per airplane, and the thought of cutting the price down to $198,000 meant that Boeing would be losing about $10,000 on every B-17 it flew off to the Air Corps.

That was the situation when Jim Murray and General Brett had at one another in Brett's office. It didn't get better when Louis Johnson of the War Department threw Jim Murray out of *his* office.

Few men within the Air Corps doubted that we could stay out of the huge conflict that was building at different points of the world. And few men outside the Air Corps seemed inclined to share their viewpoint. President Roosevelt had not yet judged the international situation sufficiently grave as to declare that the United States had entered a state of emergency; he would do so soon enough, but that time had not yet come.

Boeing was moving the first batch of B-17C bombers along its production line, and the negotiations—which were now foundering so badly on the matter of price—were for an even more advanced model, the B-17D.

The War Department stiffened its position and refused to budge on price. Further meetings were held, but they did little to alleviate the situation. The War Department got tougher and, as Boeing executives could have anticipated, Phil Johnson got his back up at the War Department, General Brett, and a few assorted officials in the capital. He backed Jim Murray to the hilt.

General Arnold and his close team became alarmed. At new negotiations Arnold sent Carl Spaatz as frontrunner for the Air Corps. Spaatz told the assembled group that either they all got together "or it will mean the end of the heavy bomber program."

What Spaatz didn't know, but Arnold feared, was that Boeing had "bought it." The company was fed up and *it was ready to abandon the Flying Fortress*. You can't stay in business by building airplanes on which you take a loss for every article that leaves your plant. Those were the facts, hard and simple.

What happened next was one of those last-ditch desperate measures that belong only in fiction. People sat around a table and they stripped from the design of the Fortress equipment which, before the meeting, the best brains in the business had felt was vital to the combat capabilities of the airplane. They took away the electrically controlled cowl flaps from each engine, a feature that gave lengthened engine life and increased rate of climb and cruising speed. They removed the external bomb racks which Air Corps leaders had felt were vital to maximum bomb loads on short missions. They stripped from the airplane other features that reduced even further its potential as a weapon.

By doing all this, Boeing's Jim Murray and Wellwood Beall told the Air Corps, they could produce the airplane for $202,500 a copy. Government officials balked.

That was it. Boeing said that this was rock-bottom and they wouldn't step back one inch in the package. The air became charged with a take-it-or-leave-it attitude.

The Flying Fortress hung in the balance. Boeing wasn't going to accept what could become certain bankruptcy. They couldn't do anyone, especially the United States, a damned bit of good by going broke and out of business.

They were at the brink. For the first nine months of 1939. The Boeing Company suffered a financial disaster. The ledgers showed a loss for this period of $2,600,000 and there was little specific to look forward to that might get the company out of the red. The problem was that Boeing's decision to go the route of the heavy bomber, which the Air Corps wanted so badly, was crippling the company!

It was an irony of the times that what would prove to be the deadliest aerial weapon of World War II was fought for by the Air Corps, but rejected by those nations then in combat. Curtiss was waxing fat by selling single-engine pursuits all over the world, and they were pushing dive bombers and a slew of other designs as well from France to China. Douglas was reaping in substantial orders for their sleek twin-engine DB-7 attack bomber. Lockheed had huge contracts for its bombers. Vultee was selling dive and attack bombers, Northrop was building torpedo bombers, Seversky was selling fighters and single-engine bombers. The many companies reaping in cash for the foreign orders were enjoying a financial bonanza—and Boeing, with the greatest bomber in the world, was losing its shirt.

If necessary to stay in existence Boeing would abandon the B-17 and give up producing heavy bombers. The meeting hung at his precarious juncture when General Arnold returned to his office. Spaatz was shrewd in his dealings with people and he knew when to make the best of a moment. He left the meeting and took off for a secret heads-together session with Hap Arnold. Spaatz laid the cards out on the table. Either we set this up *now,* he told his chief, or the Air Corps has really gone down the drain with its heavy bomber program.

That wasn't simply the failure of a program—it could prove calamitous not only for the Air Corps, but the country.

Hap Arnold told Spaatz to go ahead. Spaatz returned to the meeting where patience was at its vanishing point and tempers were honed to a fine edge. Spaatz told them that the Air Corps would exercise its option at the new price upon which there had been mutual agreement. The Army would order forty-two B-17D aircraft.

That meeting likely influenced the course of history. It saved, literally, the entire heavy bomber program of the United States. No one present in those negotiations realized how close to disaster they had come.

In June of 1938, more than fourteen months *before* the critical negotiations that saved the B-17, the German Luftwaffe had ready for combat an estimated 1,000 bombers, and it was outproducing the United States by several hundred combat aircraft *per month*.

Poland staggered beneath the heel of the Nazi Wermacht and fell apart beneath the onslaught from the air. In 1939 Hap Arnold sent Colonels George Kenney and Carl Spaatz to Europe. "Get the facts for me," he told them.

They did. And the facts were not pleasant.

"Germany put more planes in the air in one raid over Poland than we have in our whole air force," they told Arnold.

On November 9, 1937, the Air Corps ordered thirty-nine models of its new B-17B bomber. Much of what the four-engine giant could do in the air was shown by the dazzling performance of the Y1B-17A airplane, and when the first

B-17B flew on June 27, 1939, many of the innovations pioneered in the Y1B-17A were incorporated in its design. To the Air Corps the B-17B was especially significant, for this was the first heavy bomber to be assigned to an Air Corps operational unit. It meant that the Army would soon be able to exert its combat strength with these airplanes.

No officer knowledgeable of the fact of aerial warfare demonstrated in China and Spain believed that with the delivery of the first few B-17B airplanes the United States could count itself a strategic airpower. Even when all thirty-nine airplanes were delivered there would still exist an enormous gap between having the airplanes on the flight line and being able to employ them from foreign bases, under the grueling conditions of combat. There was training to be accomplished: Training not only for the flight crew, but for bombardiers, navigators, radiomen, engineers; for the mechanics who would service the engines, electronics, gunnery systems. A vast effort would be needed to provide maintenance facilities in the field, major repair and overhaul, modification centers, fueling and servicing facilities, and many others involving hundreds of organizations and thousands of skilled men.

There must be gunnery training, navigation tests over extreme range, bombing missions against simulated targets, night flying practice, surprise maneuvers with no advance notice to the flight or ground crews. The vast effort to create a strategic air force would take time, men, materiel and no small cost. There were no shortcuts.

Yet much had already been done. Twelve Fortresses of the 2nd Bombardment Group had done their work in superb fashion. The road ahead was complex and demanding but now well-illuminated by the lessons of Bob Olds' hand-picked airmen. The Y1B-17A had already provided a great store-house of information about high-speed, high-altitude super-charged bombers. These lessons must be integrated into the operational program of B-17B aircraft, while the pilots who would be slated to man the Fortresses could obtain much of their training on the older service-test models from the 2nd Bomb Group.

There was much in the new B-17B to delight the men who would fly them—and possibly in combat. At first glance the external appearance of the B-17B showed few of the major changes and modifications incorporated in its design. The original transparent nose with a bubble-mounted machine gun had been eliminated in favor of cleaner aerodynamic lines gained through use of a new plexiglas fairing. The Y1B-17 had a belly cutout in the nose to serve as a bomb-aiming position. In the B-17B this was replaced with a section of flat optical glass as a part of the new plexiglas nose. Over this optical glass was mounted the Norden bombsight. Gyro-stabilized, the Norden bombsight was linked electronically to the AFCE—the Automatic Flight Control Equipment, or autopilot—so that the bombardier on his final bomb run could control the airplane as he established his coordinates through the Norden sight. This equipment, unexcelled by any other bomb-aiming system used during World War II, drew unusual attention to the Flying Fortress. Government regulations required that the Norden bombsight *always* be kept under armed guard. It was carried by an officer to the airplane in a sealed carrying bag and always with an armed guard present to accompany the officer. And it could not be installed in the airplane until immediately before take-off. As quickly as could be done so after landing, it was resealed into its carrying bag and, again under armed guard, removed from the bomber to its storage facility.

Other external changes to the B-17B could be spotted only by a skilled observer familiar with the airplane. To improve stability and control in flight Boeing designed a new rudder that was slightly larger than that for the Y1B-17 models. Larger flaps were installed to improve takeoff and landing characteristics and to compensate for the increased weight of the airplane.

Within the airplane, crew locations were changed to take advantage of the lessons accumulated during the extensive service testing of the Y1B-17 models. The pneumatic brakes of the original design were replaced with hydraulic systems, not only more efficient but more reliable under hard usage.

The same engines that had made the Y1B-17A a record-breaker went into the B-17B. Four thousand horsepower at first blush seemed tremendous energy for the airplane, but in practice there is always a need for greater power. The gross combat weight of the B-17B was well above 40,000 pounds and would go even higher. (Early models of the B-17B carried 1,700 gallons of fuel; by 1941, modifications to the airplane had increased the fuel capacity to 2,500 gallons. Final models of the B-17G had a "standard" capacity of up to 3,600 gallons—more than twice that of the 1939 B-17B.)

If necessary the B-17B could carry up to 8,800 pounds of bombs. It *could*, but it rarely did. With that bomb load the airplane could carry very little fuel, and the range fell drastically. Without bombs the B-17B could easily fly its design range of three thousand miles—a figure that became vital when replacement aircraft were delivered in ferry flights to combat units in foreign bases. With its "standard long-range" bomb load of 2,400 pounds the airplane had an effective range of just under 1,500 miles. This gave an effective *combat radius*—the distance a bomber flies from its base to attack an enemy target and returns, with fuel reserves—of only 600 miles, hardly the intercontinental strike capability awed but ill-informed newsmen attributed to the Flying Fortress.

The one combat deficiency of the B-17B was, surprisingly, its armament. Initially the plane had only five machine guns, all of .30 caliber, which, as events in the European air war quickly demonstrated, was hopelessly inadequate for defense. During its succeeding months of service the Flying Fortress gained not only additional machine guns, but of .50 caliber size—and proved itself the most formidably armed bomber of World War II.

Pilots had nothing but praise for the improved speed, handling and flight characteristics of the B-17B. The new engines and turbo-superchargers, first tested on the Y1B-17A, gave the B-17B a top speed of 233 miles per hour at 10,000 feet and a cruising speed of 176. Far more important was its performance at 25,000 feet where the new bomber's maximum speed, because of turbo-supercharging, rose to 268 miles per hour and the cruising speed to 230 miles per hour. Five miles above the earth the B-17B cruised at almost the maximum speed of the Y1B-17, perhaps its most important and significant performance gain.

One month after the first B-17B flew at Seattle it was delivered (July 29, 1939) to the Air Corps at Burbank, California. It was almost thirty years to the day since the U.S. Army bought its first plane from the Wright Brothers. The Air Corps was ready and determined to "make hay" with its new favorite bombers on its Thirtieth Anniversary. At Burbank the B-17B was readied for its role in a mass assault on world flight records. Other bombers were prepared at Wright and Langley Fields.

During July and August of 1939, the Air Corps "showed its colors" with its Boeing airplanes. Five international records fell to B-17s—and a sixth to the XB-15, which also established a new world mark for others to shoot at.

Colonel Caleb Haynes and Major W. D. Old lifted the XB-15 from the ground with a payload aboard of 31,167.6 pounds. The date was July 30. Haynes and Old pushed the goliath of the Air Corps with its massive cargo to a height of 8,200 feet, to eclipse by more than a ton the load-carrying record then held by Russia.

On August 1 Haynes and Old took off again in the XB-15, not to land until the next day. The lumbering whale of the Air Corps, despite its inadequate power, set a new world record by flying a closed course of 3,107 miles (between Patterson Field, Ohio, and Rockford, Illinois) at 166 miles per hour with a payload of 4,409 pounds.

August 1st was also a red-letter day for the Flying Fortress. Colonel Stanley Umstead (the same Umstead who locked the brakes on landing and put the first Y1B-17 up on its nose) and Lt. Colonel L. F. Harmon left Burbank, California, in the first production B-17B and smashed the coast-to-coast speed record at 265 miles per hour. Their average altitude was 26,000 feet. *Speed at altitude*—the Fortress was living up to its promise.

Also on August 1st, Captain C. S. Irvine in the Y1B-17A set the closed course record of 621 miles at an average speed of 259.396 miles per hour with a payload of 11,023 pounds. That was only the first set in the double-header. Later that same day Irvine pushed the Y1B-17A, still with the payload of 11,023 pounds, to a new world record of 34,025 feet.

But other records also were being set in late 1939—among them a single air assault on one day by Germany against Poland with more airplanes, as Hap Arnold learned to his dismay, than he had in his entire Air Corps.

Boeing received its commitment for more Flying Fortresses.

In January 1939 Major General Frank M. Andrews, commanding the GHQ Air Force, in a rare public expression of candor noted that the Army Air Corps had a first-line combat strength of less than five hundred airplanes. An alarming number of these, the general said caustically, would not be able to stay in the air with foreign fighters. For these reasons Frank Andrews summed up his Air Corps as being nothing better than a "fifth rate air force."

By September 1939, with the flow of B-17B Fortresses still at a trickle, the combat strength of the Army Air Corps in comparison with the German Luftwaffe was even worse. There were 26,526 officers and men in the Air Corps. Of 1,500 tactical aircraft on Army fields, less than 800 could be considered as first-line quality. The numbers of squadrons was a farce; on paper they showed great strength. In reality they were skeletonized and several were *balloon* squadrons!

The official history of the Army Air Force notes:

By contrast the German Air Force in September 1939 had a personnel strength of over 500,000 and a first-line aircraft complement of 3,750 planes, supported by a 10 to 25 percent reserve of first-line planes. The Royal Air Force at the same time had over 100,000 officers and men and at least 1,750 first-line planes.

The disparity between the Air Corps and these European air forces was even greater than statistics on the number of aircraft would indicate. Probably only in the quality of its officers and men could the Air Corps compare with the Luftwaffe and the Royal Air Corps at that time. . . .

The Luftwaffe, moreover, had the air bases and other installations needed to support a modern air force. The number of first-rate military air bases in the United States could almost be counted on the fingers of both hands. The Air Corps lacked not only bases but also the organization and equipment with which to build them. . . .

Even the planes with which the war was to be fought had yet, with few exceptions, to be developed. Of all the models of aircraft on hand in the Air Corps in September, 1939, only one—the B-17—actually flew as a first-line plane during World War II. . . . In 1939 the B-18 was the standard bombardment plane, the A-17 the standard attack plane, and the P-36 the standard fighter; almost 700 of the 800 first-line combat aircraft of the Air Corps consisted of these three models. By the time of America's entry into the war two years later, all of them would be obsolete. . . .

Only in the field of heavy bombers did the Air Corps hold first rank. The B-17 was superior to the Focke-Wulf of the Germans and the Manchester of the British, but in September 1939 the Air Corps had only twenty-three . . . Flying Fortresses.

If the United States was not a "fifth rate" air power in 1939, it certainly ranked no better than third or fourth. Its inferiority was both quantitative and qualitative, and only the prospect that world events might permit the time necessary to overcome these disadvantages offered ground for the hope that the Air Corps could be made ready for any emergency.[16]

It was at this time that first General Brett of the Air Corps, and then Louis Johnson of the War Department, each threw Jim Murray out of their offices—and Boeing stood on the brink of abandoning the B-17.

On April 9, 1940, combined German military forces slashed into Norway and Denmark. The long period of quiet that had followed the systematic dismembering of Poland vanished in the steel of German arms. The Wermacht and the Luftwaffe stunned their opponents—a juggernaut rolled steadily over Germany's enemies.

Exactly one month later, on May 9, 1940, German armored columns, paratroops, and infantry started their move against Belgium and Holland. The next day, the Stukas roared high over the Maginot Line and plunged against their targets in France.

On May 11, officials of Boeing met secretly with Oliver Echols to pore over data on a huge new superbomber that would dwarf the B-17. The United States was still somewhere about fifth as a world air power, but the wheels within Washington were starting to churn. There were no contracts with the Air Corps on the new design; there might never be any. Boeing had been stung, almost whipped financially, in its production negotiations with the Army. Phil Johnson, Claire Egtvedt and their associates threw those memories out the nearest window.

The secret new plane they discussed, no more at this time than studies and drawings on paper, was destined one day to fly. It would be known as the B-29.

But that was still in the future. The day after Boeing and the Air Corps talked about the superbomber, Belgium surrendered. An alarmed United States heard its President ask Congress for an immediate allocation of $1,100,000,000 for new weapons.

Beall and Showalter of Boeing flew to Ohio to meet with Colonel Oliver Echols to discuss drastic changes in the Flying Fortress. The first B-17C had yet to fly, the B-17D model was way behind that airplane. But Echols, grimly aware of what was happening in Europe, and what must inevitably engulf the United States, was looking far ahead. He told Boeing: "Figure out how to get more guns in those

Forts. Tail guns especially. And armor plate to protect the crew."

Boeing's engineers laughed bleakly at the new requirements. They were being asked to carry out massive redesign of the Flying Fortress. Tail guns? It would make mincemeat out of the careful balance of the airplane. It would add weight, complexity, problems. And it would, they warned, make a mockery of the steadily improving performance of the Fortress.

Echols said to "get cracking."

Beall and Showalter showed up in Echols' office with the engineering sketches and armament studies. Showalter went to a blackboard and wrote down the different possibilities of new guns and gunner positions. Echols stared at the black-board, walked briskly to it and started pointing. "Here is what we want," he said. His finger stabbed to power turrets above and beneath the fuselage, twin guns in the tail, every gun save for a nose position to be the heavy .50 caliber weapon. There was more. Echols wanted armor. He wanted self-sealing fuel tanks. He wanted a hell of a lot.

Beall didn't smile. He told Echols he was asking for a whole new airplane.

Echols didn't blink an eye. "All right," he said. "Get it going. We can't wait for a superbomber now."

Dunkirk ran red with British blood. The Luftwaffe raised hell over England and it promised to get worse.

Major K. B. Wolfe called Boeing's Jim Murray.

"Get set to produce the B-17E," Wolfe said. "We're going to order 250 of them."

Murray passed on the news to Boeing in Seattle.

The first B-17C was still in Plant Two, still on the production line, still a long way from flying.

On June 14 the Germans accepted the surrender of Paris. This time it was Oliver Echols who called in Jim

Murray. "I want to talk with you about the Flying Fortress," Echols said. He didn't talk long.

"All previous estimates are obsolete," Echols went on. "We'll contract for 512 B-17Es. But there'll be lots more later."

Boeing had already started a major plant expansion program. The construction engineers groaned—they would already have to double what they hadn't yet built.

Five weeks after the Germans marched into Paris the first B-17C rolled down the Boeing runway for its initial test flight. The new bomber had a sleeker appearance than observers had noted before. The gun blisters that bulged outward from the fuselage sides were replaced with flat-paneled, lemon-shaped gun stations. Another "flat panel" position replaced the top gun blister. Also gone was the blister in the belly, replaced with an extended "bathtub" gun position. In the nose, sockets could hold two .30 caliber machine guns. The top fuselage compartment now mounted twin .50 caliber guns, as did the bathtub in the belly. Improved fuel tanks reduced the risk of fire. The crew positions were fitted out with armor plating.

With new equipment, armor and heavier armament, the gross weight of the B-17C went up to nearly 50,000 pounds. Once again, however, power made up for the heavier airplane. The new Wright Cyclone engines (GR-1820-65 (G-205A)), each of 1,200 horsepower, not only compensated for the greater weight, but raised the service ceiling to 36,000 feet and brought the maximum speed to 300 miles per hour—the fastest Fortress yet to fly.*

Hard on the heels of the B-17C came its D-model suc-

---

*The reader is cautioned that specific performance figures for any airplane model represent nominal or opimum yield. Speed and height depend upon factors of load carried, guns deployed, temperature, single

cessor. Only a skilled observer could notice the change in the two airplanes which, externally, were to be found only in the engine cowl flaps. Provision was made for an additional crew member, the electrical system was improved, and more reliable self-sealing fuel tanks were installed. Despite a slight increase in weight, the cowl flaps proved to have significant effects on performance. The maximum speed rose to 318 miles per hour and the service ceiling climbed to 37,000 feet.

During the year 1940 the Army Air Corps received a total of fifty-three Flying Fortress bombers. The striking capabilities of the nation, despite critical handicaps in almost every aspect of airpower, began to show a gradual but significant increase.

Beyond the B-17D there was being readied the heavily armed B-17E, the first of the offensive Fortresses and also the first to live up to the name it had been given. The E model, still a long way from flight, would usher in a new era of aerial warfare—and when finally it did become available, it would be not a moment too soon.

On June 20, 1941, still before the first flight of the B-17E, the Army reorganized its entire structure for airpower. The old name of Air Corps fell to history and a new organization was born—the Army Air Force. Much of its strength would be reassembled in numbered air forces, each with its specific area of operational responsibility.

There was no question but that the nation would soon be embroiled in war. Great air battles fought across England and the coast of Europe with overwhelming German successes on a wide array of combat fronts, provided a grim forecast of what our own air force would face. The

---

or formation flying, etc. Two airplanes off the same production line invariably will have slightly different performance, even if both aircraft are loaded to exactly the same weight.

linking of Germany, Italy and Japan boded ill for the future. The Army Air Force (AAF) came into being only two days before Germany smashed into the Soviet Union. Clearly, the United States, if it wished to prevail in the inevitable conflict to come, must create the most powerful air combat force in the world.

General H. H. Arnold, who led the Air Corps through its most trying moments and commanded the AAF through World War II, provides a meaningful comment on the role of the B-17 in the trying times when airpower in the United States still struggled for existence:

"This was the first real American airpower," Arnold wrote in his memoirs of the first delivery of Fortresses to the 2nd Bombardment Group at Langley Field in the spring of 1936. The new Fortresses, he wrote, were not just prophecies but "for the first time in history air power that you could put your hand on." Hap Arnold made it clear that in his opinion the four-engine bomber was the main turning point in the development not only of airpower but of world power.

Arnold also contested those air leaders who argued that had the United States set up an independent air organization instead of tying airpower to the Army, the nation would have emerged sooner as a leading world power in the air.

Not so, wrote the man who commanded the greatest aerial force in existence during World War II.

Airpower lay not in organization or unsupported theory. It came into being through the four-engine bomber.

The Flying Fortress.

In the spring of 1941 the Royal Air Force prepared to test the Fortress under the acid conditions of combat.

# CHAPTER 7

# FIRST BLOOD

*T* *HESE FORTRESSES ARE WONDERFUL aircraft—*
*perfectly maneuverable, steady as a battleship and*
*incredibly efficient. We thank you in America for*
*these bombers."*

The Royal Air Force pilot completed reading the neatly
typewritten notes on the table before him. He looked up at
the lights over the studio door in the offices of BBC. The
red light went out. "We off the air?" he asked the studio
technician. His companion nodded.

The pilot gestured with distaste toward the typewritten
sheet from which he had read his broadcast. "Of all the
bloody rot . . ."

"Hey, have you fellows seen this?" The RAF bomber pilot waved a newspaper in his hand. Other pilots crowded
around. There was a look of disbelief on the face of the pilot who held the paper.

"Christ, listen to this," he began, quoting the news story:

*"The Royal Air Force gave these ships their first baptism of fire, and opened a new phase in the European conflict. News stories speak of these new high-flying Fortresses in awesome terms. From altitudes of seven miles, the crews of these big Boeings unload their heavy bombs with uncanny accuracy, unbothered by squadrons of Messerschmitts far below."*

The speaker lowered the newspaper slowly. For a long moment there was silence. Then one of the pilots who had listened to the story, a British officer who flew one of the "big Boeings" in combat, rose to his feet and started for the door.

"Jesus, I think I'm going to throw up," he said.

There was, obviously, a credibility gap between the words spoken publicly of the Fortress I, as the B-17C bombers of the Royal Air Force were known, and what their crews said among themselves—and just as huge a gap between what the public was told of the performance of the Fortresses in combat and what really took place.

The debut of the Flying Fortress, in the colors of the Royal Air Force, was an unmitigated disaster.

Strange to relate, it was *not* unexpected. In fact, it was forecast accurately by members of the Air Corps and by engineers from Boeing, who went to great pains to warn the British *against* sending their Fortress I versions of the B-17C into combat.

"The British never gave the Flying Fortress a chance," Hap Arnold said testily when he was asked about the performance of the first American heavy bombers in combat.

Indeed the British had not.

The story began on March 11, 1941, when the Lend-

Lease Bill (H.R. 1776) became law. Under the provisions of this new bill the President was empowered to deal with any type of war materials with "the government of any country whose defense the President deems vital for the defense of the United States."

Winston Churchill spoke warmly of the Bill's passage as ". . . the most unsordid act in the history of any nation."

Well, *maybe*. In truth American interests were far from unselfish. The longer the British held Germany at arm's length, the more time the United States would have to build up the Air Corps from a "fifth-rate" airpower into something that could stay in the same skies with German fighters. As President F. D. Roosevelt said:

> There is absolutely no doubt in the mind of a very over-whelming number of Americans that the best immediate defense of the United States is the success of Great Britain defending itself; and that, therefore, quite aside from our historic and current interest in the survival of Democracy in the world as a whole, it is equally important from a selfish point of view and of American defense that we should do everything possible to help the British Empire to defend itself.

There *are* times when candor is the best political move. By proclaiming our *interests* rather than our largesse, lend-lease went into effect, accepted by far and away the majority of the American public.

Immediately the Royal Air Force forwarded to the United States Government its request for as many Flying Fortress bombers as might be available. The quantity of "bombers available" didn't require extensive thought; there weren't that many B-17s in existence. The Air Corps agreed, however, that the first twenty airplanes out of the order for thirty-eight B-17C bombers could be released for the Royal Air Force. This didn't present any problems in time since deliveries to the Air Corps of the B-17Cs had started in 1940; the orders went out to separate twenty B-17C aircraft from the Air Corps.

Instead of flying east the airplanes headed in the opposite direction. In May of 1941 the first B-17Cs were flown from Langley Field in Virginia to Wright Field in Ohio, where they were fitted with new self-sealing fuel tanks. Other modifications were carried out to fit the airplanes to British requirements before they would be ferried to England.

When they departed Wright Field they were no longer B-17C models, having been transformed to their new British designation of Fortress I. Little change appeared in their configuration but there was no question to whom these airplanes belonged. Their stark new camouflage designs, the RAF roundels on the wings and fuselage, drew immediate attention. Since they fitted the official category of day bombers they wore the scattered pattern of dark green and dark earth, with the underside of the wings and fuselage a gleaming silver. In the late summer of 1941 new colors came into use; the undersurface areas were painted azure blue and the upper portions became dark green and dark sea-gray. There seemed to be little consistency with the appearance of the Fortress I. Some airplanes were kept a gleaming polished metal without paint, and several showed up at their home base, in October 1941, with dark undersurfaces, a clear indication that someone in the RAF Bomber Command was determined to send out the planes on night missions.

The twenty Fortress I's were ferried to RAF No. 90 Squadron at West Raynham and became "officially" assigned in May 1941. It had been understood by the United

States Government that the Fortress I would never be sent into combat, but was to be employed for training flight and ground crews and gaining experience with the new bombers. Then, when the RAF squadrons were fully familiar with the airplane, Fortress II models (the B-17E) would be provided under the lend-lease agreements. With the new Fortress II, heavily armed and fitted out with equipment designed from the lessons of air combat in Europe, the RAF would have the nucleus of a new and powerful daylight bombing force. It didn't turn out that way—the British committed the Fortress I to combat. No amount of argument from the Americans then in England could dissuade the British from their course. On July 8, 1941, three Fortress I bombers were tested in battle—but the British had already run into snarls with their new aircraft.

"I was in England when the planes arrived," an Air Corps officer later wrote. "We explained to the British our doctrine for the use of the planes. We told them that the crews had to be well trained, that a crew should drop two hundred practice bombs before attacking a real target; that the planes were designed to fly in formation for protective purposes and that by using them as trainers, trained crews could be ready to operate the new, properly equipped Fortresses when we delivered them. For some reason, they decided to use the planes offensively."

The reason was simple. The British were at war and they had an understandable desire to strike at the Germans with every airplane that could fly. They believed the Fortress I was good enough to stay in German skies. The official flight tests to determine performance capabilities of the new airplanes, held mainly with two Fortress I's (Aircraft Numbers AN518 and 531), proved that at maximum altitude the new bombers could outfly anything except the Spitfire fighter of the Royal Air Force. The more one considers what the Fortress I could do, as determined by these official tests, the more easily one understands why the British, despite the warnings of the Americans, rushed these planes into battle.

Several Fortresses were sent to the Aeroplane and Armament Experimental Establishment at Boscombe Down. Fully equipped but without fuel or bomb load the Fortress weighed 34,560 pounds. At maximum all-up (maximum allowable gross) weight the Fortress I tipped the scales at 53,200 pounds.

Despite the increase in maximum weight from the B-17C model of the Air Corps, British test pilots reported that the Fortress I maintained its service ceiling at 33,300 feet. At a height of 29,000 feet and with a "mean weight" of 43,500 pounds the Fortress I became faster than the B-17C—showing a true maximum speed of 325 miles per hour. Trimmed out for its most economical cruising speed under combat load the Fortress I at 30,000 feet cruised at 230 miles per hour.

Taking off with a weight of 53,200 pounds the airplane required just over thirty-seven minutes to reach a height of 30,000 feet. Carrying a load of 4,400 pounds of bombs the Fortress I had a combat range of 1,850 miles, or an effective radius of action of 700 to 750 miles.

The bomb loads varied according to mission requirements. The loads most commonly carried were: two 2,200-lb. bombs or four 1,100-lb. bombs; two 1,000-lb. and two 600-lb. bombs or, eight 600-lb. American bombs. Standard defensive armament was six machine guns, none of which were in power turrets: one .30 caliber machine gun in the nose, which could be fired from one of three ball-socket mountings and five .50 caliber guns, of which one was mounted in the dorsal position firing upward, two in the belly trough (bathtub), and one in each waist position.

The engines were Wright Cyclone R-1820-73 models for a total of 4,800 horsepower. Normally the Fortress I carried a crew of six—two pilots, an observer-navigator, radio operator-gunner and two gunners.

Things got off to an "absolutely rotten start." The very first Fortress I to land at West Raynham went out of control. The officers and men of No. 90 Squadron watched their first airplane skid wildly down the runway, run off the concrete and go skidding out of sight in a great cloud of dust and airplane debris. The landing gear was destroyed and much of the airplane "pretty well mangled." The airplane never again took to the air, the British using the wreck for spare parts for the other Fortresses. It was finally picked as bare as the bones of a Thanksgiving turkey—hardly an auspicious start of the new heavy bomber daylight force planned by the RAF.

On July 8, 1941, three Fortresses took off from Polebrook on a "trial mission," during which they were to attack the German naval barracks at Wilhelmshaven. The first airplane suffered engine trouble while en route to the target and the pilot elected to strike at a secondary target. No one knows whether the bombs dumped from the ailing airplane managed to do any damage on the ground. The remaining two bombers climbed to 30,000 feet, arrived over their targets, and sprayed their bombs everywhere but on their objective. Which was not unexpected on a first mission; the crews had had precious little time in which to become adept with their new aircraft and were, after all, operating at six miles above the earth. The poor bombing was only the beginning of their woes.

Next the two bomber crews found themselves under attack from German fighters, something they had *not* anticipated at their extreme height. That was bad enough. Things came unglued even faster when the gunners found their machine guns had frozen up and wouldn't fire. At 30,000 feet with fighters coming in that's the kind of discovery that can ruin your whole day. The German fighter pilots, skidding in the thin air, pumped the two bombers full of holes but failed to shoot them down. Both planes made it safely back to base.

On July 24th the Fortresses were "officially" committed to battle. Three airplanes, equipped with the Sperry rather than the supersecret Norden bombsight, left England for a strike against the German battle cruiser *Gneisenau*, berthed at French naval installations in Brest harbor. The Fortresses again climbed to 30,000 feet and great hopes were held that the formation run over the *Gneisenau* would cripple or sink the warship. The crews made their bombing runs, dropped on target—but, despite enthusiastic claims of being "right on," actually failed to hit their objective. The battle cruiser came through the raid unscathed.

Not so the Fortresses. German fighters swarmed up to the bombing altitude and in a running battle gave the bombers a particularly bad time. The guns worked and the Fortresses managed their escape, one of them badly torn up in the air fight. It was so badly damaged the crew considered bailing out, but elected to gamble on the strength of the airplane. The extent of the damage became all the more evident when the Fortress landed—and literally fell apart on the runway from the shock of setting down. It was a small miracle that it had held together in the air, so effective had been the punishing German fire.

That made two Fortress I's wiped off.

A third bomber disappeared in flames when, an RAF report showed, it was "burned from pure carelessness."

On August 6, 1941, the British despatched four Fortress bombers (AN525D, 536M, 532J and 533N), on a long-range mission against the pocket battleship *Admiral Scheer* docked in Oslo Harbor, Norway. The bombers took off from Kinloss, which they used as an advanced base for the operation. The mission proved to be another great misadventure. Squadron Leader Mathieson in AN533N managed to reach Oslo but the crew found it impossible to locate the German battleship. Mathieson set up a run against oil tanks and dock installations and four heavy bombs were dropped. The results of the attack went unobserved. Behind Mathieson two more Fortresses encountered the same problem—namely, where was the *Admiral Scheer?* They followed the suit of their leader and dumped their bombs on the docks. The fourth airplane, AN536M, never reached the target. A turbo-supercharger went out and, unable to climb to altitude, the pilot brought the airplane back to Kinloss with the bombs still aboard.

On August 16th the Fortresses struck at Brest, again with results impossible to ascertain. Aircraft Number 523 came back in trouble, made a forced landing at Roborough, after which it erupted in flames. The airplane was gutted.

There were other raids to follow. On the last day of August three Fortresses took off for independent—solo—strikes against their targets. AN-525WP-D set out for Hamburg. After reaching 30,000 feet one engine developed serious oil trouble and lost power. The crew dumped the bomb load near Heligoland and returned to base, the results of five and a half hours flying a complete waste. AN-518WP-B climbed to 31,000 feet and managed to reach its assigned target—Bremen. Heavy clouds obscured the city and the crew dropped their bomb load blindly. Results—"not observed." Fortress AN-532J struck out for Kiel. En route the turbo-superchargers "acted up," the airplane lost power, and limped back home with bombs aboard.

On September 2nd, in a solo attack on Bremen, a Mr.

Vose, representing the manufacturer of the Sperry bomb-sight, went along as bombardier—an unusual role for an American civilian, whose country was not at war with Germany. Thirty thousand feet over Bremen in AN-533N, Mr. Vose was provided with a spectacular close-up view of heavy German antiaircraft fire. Nevertheless the airplane continued on its bombing run and managed to carry out one of the rare successful strikes from high altitude, as the bombs dropped accurately on target.

Two other Fortress I's on that same day experienced less fortune. AN-532 also had departed for a strike against Bremen but was turned back by poor weather. AN-518 took off for an attack against Duisburg, but came home when the intercom system failed.

Two days later, on September 4th, three more Fortresses took off—and all ran into difficulties. Flight Officer Romans in his first mission with the Fortress I took off in AN-533 for Hanover. The lone airplane left contrails so intense that she was an easy mark for German interceptors; Romans turned to his secondary target and managed a successful attack against the docks at Rotterdam. But the Germans had been alerted and at 31,000 feet a Messerschmitt Me-109F attacked. The crew managed to beat off the fighter and escaped.

Meanwhile AN-532, also en route for Hanover, climbed to 30,000 feet, where an engine failed. With a heavy load aboard at high altitude further flight to the target was impossible; the pilot aborted.

The third airplane, AN-518, ran into difficulties with the intercom system. After climbing to 15,000 feet on the way to Hamburg the pilot aborted the sortie and returned to base.

On September 8th four Fortresses staged out of Kinloss for another strike against Oslo, Norway. Three bombers climbed out steadily after takeoff and reached 26,000 feet before crossing into "German air." The fourth airplane, which had been delayed in takeoff, was soon flying through thick clouds with no visibility. The crew aborted and returned to base.

The leading three airplanes ran into a hornets' nest of enemy fighters. Messerschmitts in their opening pass against the bombers shot AN-533N into wreckage; the airplane plummeted out of control into a mountainside, killing the entire crew. A second Fortress, AN525D, was reported as having shot down two fighters at close range. It was a pyrrhic victory—the bomber crashed in flames.

Sergeant Wood, flying the third Fortress (AN535) about one mile astern of the other two bombers, took immediate steps to try to elude the fighters. As the lead Fortresses were cut down Wood ordered his bomb load jettisoned and set out at full power for all the altitude the Fortress could reach. The crew prepared for the worst by setting up for bailing out while Wood headed for home. Lightened of her heavy bomb load, the Fortress climbed to 35,000 feet where the crew watched Messerschmitt Me-109Fs straining in the thin air to reach their height.

Their surcease was short-lived. A gunner aboard the airplane had misunderstood the instructions about *possibly* bailing out and switched from the main oxygen system to his emergency bailout bottle. Rather quickly he consumed the entire oxygen supply and passed out from hypoxia. Alongside the collapsed crewman, the second waist gunner went to his aid, disconnecting from the main oxygen supply. In his haste he forgot to plug into his emergency bottle and he also fell unconscious. Unable to communicate with them on the intercom, Sgt. Wood reasoned, correctly, that his men had difficulties with oxygen. Immediately he pushed the Fortress into a dive to 29,000 feet. Fifteen minutes had passed since the bombers were intercepted and Wood felt reasonably safe at the lower altitude. But almost at once a Messerschmitt swept in to make a long firing pass. A gunner fell, dead, and a second was severely wounded. A bullet clipped the oxygen line of the radio operator, who soon collapsed.

Sgt. Wood found himself on the edge of complete disaster. The German pilot had proven almost fatally accurate in his attacks. One man was dead, two unconscious, and the Messerschmitt had shot one engine into wreckage. The two pilots feathered the propeller and then discovered, almost immediately afterward, that their aileron controls had been shot away—bullets had severed the cables. The bomb bay doors opened suddenly. The power system was shot away and the doors refused to close. They resorted to the mechanical system which, they found, had also been torn into useless wreckage in the attack. The third gunner, encumbered by his heavy flight clothing, stumbled to the open bays, balanced himself precariously and managed to close the doors by hand. Immediately afterward he pitched forward on his face, unconscious; his emergency oxygen system was depleted. The copilot saved his life by plugging in the gunner's system to another oxygen source.

During a firing pass a bullet tore into the glycol tank. Moments later white smoke billowed thickly into the cockpit, blinding the pilots. Watching the smoke pouring through and from the airplane the German pilot concluded he had set the Fortress afire, and turned back for his base. That move saved the bomber.

Sgt. Wood and his copilot fought to keep the battered Fortress under control—a task made all the more difficult by lack of aileron control, the drag of a dead engine, four crewmen dead or incapacitated, and the airplane generally shot to ribbons. Fighting to reach Kinloss, a second engine failed. Battered but still flying on two engines the Fortress managed a crash landing at Kinloss. The airplane never again flew. In fact, the men at Kinloss could hardly understand how Sgt. Wood ever managed to bring it back to base.

That was the last "raid" to be flown by the Fortress I bombers. For their remaining weeks of operations from England they flew solo missions only, and No. 90 Squadron managed but four additional sorties from Polebrook.

En route to Cologne on September 15th, Fortress AN-536 was over the Dutch coast at 32,000 feet and still climbing, when the crew observed enemy contrails at their altitude and heading for them. Immediately the pilot aborted the mission, turning back for home. The next day, when the same bomber tried again to reach Cologne, the pilot almost lost control when two engines failed suddenly at high altitude. The pilot jettisoned the bomb load and set back for England in a long descent.

Fortress AN-518 which had suffered from intercom troubles made the last successful attack by the Boeings on September 20th; Pilot Officer Sturmey took his heavily loaded airplane to 32,000 feet, and released four 1,100-pound bombs against Emden. Five days later Sturmey set out for the same objective, but aborted at 27,000 feet when the Fortress began to leave a heavy contrail behind.

That was the last combat mission for No. 90 Squadron with its England-based Fortress I bombers.

A series of misfortunes had befallen other aircraft, adding to the toll of bombers lost in combat, as well as the two lost in a misjudged landing and from "pure carelessness."

Lt. Bradley of the Army Air Forces was aboard a Fortress I, testing equipment as an advisor to the British, when the airplane encountered severe difficulties in rough weather. Apparently ice formed swiftly across the wings and fuselage. The bomber went out of control and in the turbulence encountered began to break up. The squadron medical officer managed somehow to get out of the airplane and was the sole survivor.

Another Fortress, flying through heavy clouds, suddenly lost contact with the ground. A shrill thunder came from the sky. As witnesses looked up they saw a Fortress streak from the clouds at about a thousand feet in a vertical dive. The airplane continued its plunge straight into the ground where it exploded, killing all on board.

Difficulties in combat, inexperience with the Fortress I, plain bad luck, and worsening weather brought a premature end to bombing missions with the airplanes. Several of the bombers were used for motion picture and other photography while new plans were drawn up for their use as combat weapons. With heavy cloud cover anticipated over Europe the RAF decided to transfer the bombers to the Middle East.

On October 26, 1941, five of the Boeings took off from Polebrook for Portreath, from where they were to stage on to Shallufa, near the Suez Canal. The bad luck that had accompanied the airplanes stuck with them; Fortress AN-527 had an engine overspend and in the wild takeoff blew a main tire. The crew got her back on the ground, leaving the other four planes to continue to Shallufa. No. 90 Squadron in England had only five Fortresses remaining—combat, accidents, transfer to flight test groups, and transfer of the four bombers to the Middle East had reduced the No. 90 Squadron to these five airplanes, ostensibly for training purposes.

On January 9, 1942, the number was again cut down. Fortress AN-536 took off for an extreme altitude test. At

31,000 feet "something happened" and the airplane fell out of control. Soon it whipped into a spin from which the pilots could not recover; the Fortress crashed near the small village of Shepreth.

In a reorganization of RAF units, No. 90 Squadron was disbanded early in February 1942, and the remaining Fortress I's posted to No. 220 Squadron. A detachment of this same squadron had received the four Fortresses that had flown to Shallufa, where the airplanes were modified for operations under desert conditions. Combat missions flown at high altitude in daylight ran into much the same set of problems that had plagued the bombers over Europe. But there were other "minor disasters" to be overcome, not the least of which was lack of proper maintenance, mechanics unskilled with the airplanes, and a shortage of spare parts. A distressingly low number of day missions were flown, whereupon the squadron commander decided to have a whack at night raids. Four Fortresses were despatched to Nos. 37 and 38 Squadrons to attack Benghazi at night. The crews discovered quickly that the bombers lacked the proper range, at the desired altitude for bombing, and were coming home dangerously low on fuel. There was also the unpleasant problem of the bombs which had the nasty habit of icing and "hanging up" in the racks. The worst job in the airplane was given to the crew member who had to stand on the bomb-bay catwalk, the temperature forty or fifty below zero, a shrieking gale pummeling him, where he kicked with all his strength to rid the airplane of the bombs that hung up on the racks.

Other missions continued with no shortage of unusual adventures to occupy the crews. Fortress AN-529 set out for Tobruk, apparently bombed its target (the records are not clear on this point); on the way back to base an engine failed and the pilot, Flight Officer Swanson, could not keep the airplane flying. He found himself with no choice but to come down in enemy-controlled territory and elected to make a gear-up landing, which was successful. The crew scrambled out, ready to destroy the plane to prevent it from falling into enemy hands—and discovered the tanks to be so empty there wasn't enough fuel left to burn the Fortress! They carried the Sperry bombsight from the plane, set it up on the ground, and destroyed it with several long bursts from the nose machine gun. Under the noses of fast-approaching enemy troops, the crew was swept to safety by a section of their own ground forces.

Fortress AN-518, which had endured its own share of problems, was also on a mission that day and nearly was lost when it ran short of fuel after a sortie at "extreme range." The pilot brought the bomber down safely at Mersa Matruh.

Enemy attacks at high altitudes forced a change in mission assignments. Heavy fighter opposition during the second raid, against Derna, brought the Fortress commander to redirect his bombers from desert targets to convoys that traveled between Taranto and Tripoli, and to warships of the Italian fleet. On one of these missions AN-518, which had *not* expected interception, was attacked by two Me-110 twin-engine fighters. To the surprise of the Messerschmitt pilots the Fortress in the high, thin air proved so maneuverable that the bomber pilot was able to turn inside the fighters, and managed his escape with little difficulty.

The problems of sand and maintenance proved rougher opponents than the Germans. Spare parts were so short in supply that mechanics did their best to make up what was needed from bits and pieces of metal stripped from other wrecked airplanes. A fatal accident just about finished combat operations. On a fuel consumption test, the pilot of AN-521 found himself with a critical emergency when the

No. 3 engine overspeeded and burst into flames. Without an airfield within immediate reach the pilot ordered his crew to bail out. One man impacted with the tail and was killed, the others survived. The flaming wreckage struck the ground only six miles from their home airfield.

Back in England, the remaining Fortress I's were used for anti-submarine patrol, after being modified to carry depth charges. Some were used for training for heavy bombers, as the British were now receiving four-engine Consolidated Liberators, and were waiting for the first batch of forty-five Fortress IIA bombers (the British version of the new B-17E). But the last operational mission of the Fortress I was flown on July 27, 1942, after which the bombers found "non-operational" missions to be their stint—training, cargo and personnel transport, experimental test-beds, and so forth.

Two bombers—AN-518 and AN-532—were flown to India; when they arrived in Bengal the Command Engineering Officer looked at them with open disbelief and refused to accept them for flying operations, stating that both airplanes were completely unserviceable. Yet the end was not in sight for these two bombers which had a tendency to rise like the phoenix.

For the rest of the year AN-518 stayed on the ground, rusting and slowly falling apart. Then British crews swarmed over her, restored the battered airplane to flying status, and flew her on December 1, 1942, to the AAF command in Karachi. With old AN-518 was AN-532. Returned to their original service, the bombers were given their original designations, and received their old serial numbers—AN-518 as AC 40-2066 and AN-532 as AC 40-2079.

But AN-532 had run out of luck. During flight through a severe monsoon the airplane was heavily damaged. A local tinsmith was brought out to the airplane at her Indian base and some jury-rigged repairs put her back in flying shape. Soon afterward, on a flight to Karachi, two engines burst into flames. The airplane crashed and was destroyed.

But AN-518 had apparently found a new lease on life. As AC 40-2066 she was assigned to a transport squadron and refitted with four new engines. Specialists stripped her interior and installed new equipment to bring the airplane up to present day standards. Then seats and tables went in for AN-518's new role as a transport for military V.I.P.'s. At this point the airplane vanished in the maw of worldwide operations; no further record on the airplane appears to be available.

A summing up of the role played by the Fortress I is in order. It is obvious from the outset that the airplane encountered more than its share of difficulties. Perhaps less obvious but of greater importance is the fact that recognition of these problems, and the quick finding of solutions, made an overwhelming contribution to the later success of succeeding versions of the Flying Fortress, and to this airplane's role in combat.

Even the matter of dropping bombs posed a serious obstacle on the early raids. With combat experience behind them the British were justifiably suspicious of the bomb-release mechanism in the Fortress I. The "basic load" of ordnance for the B-17C model, from which the Fortress I was created, consisted of four 1,100-pound bombs. Each bomb was secured within the bomb bay by a webbing strap, one end of which was secured to the aircraft structure, and the other to a magnetic release operated by electrical charge. The system worked fine, except at high altitude where subzero temperatures favored a nasty tendency to icing up. That in turn meant the bombs would be frozen in place, whereupon a member of the crew had his opportunity to become a hero literally by kicking the bombs free of the airplane.

Failure of the intercom—especially between the pilot and the rest of the crew—was considered so serious that a mission was to be aborted. Those were strict orders for all pilots. Without an answer from a crewman the pilot had no way of knowing whether or not the intercom itself was out or if a man had collapsed—as many did from the cold, exhaustion, and failure of the oxygen systems. Experience taught the British quickly to institute a standing order that any order from the pilot not only had to be acknowledged, but must be repeated in its entirety.

The matter of ice plagued operations throughout the active life of the Fortress I. It became clear that for extreme altitude operations, where intense cold always was met, the airplanes needed power-operated turrets. The manual guns often froze in place and could not be moved and even the gun mechanisms iced up and were useless.

The cold became an enemy worse than fighters. One Fortress I pilot reported that during one mission "we climbed into the sky into extreme cold which reached 75 degrees minus Fahrenheit. . . . There was white crystalline frost on the windows; about three quarters of an inch. The frost on the front windows was so thick we had to fly with them [side windows] open. I noticed on the front of my flying suit little beads of sweat which had frozen to ice. . . ."

The electrically heated flying suits used in the Fortress I aircraft were awkward, cumbersome and apt to fail when needed most. Stumbling about in temperatures anywhere from fifty to eighty degrees below zero and a wind of 300 miles per hour shrieking in through the open gun positions did not enhance combat efficiency. Flying in thin air with a need for oxygen made it worse, for the critical oxygen systems also were wont to fail at altitude. The cold froze up the oxygen masks so badly that the crews tried every solution which came to mind, including smearing oil on the faces of the men. This failed to alleviate the problem since the oxygen mask valve outlet often iced up and formed ice on the faces of the crew. Emergency fixes were tested at British research centers, but were slow in coming for the men who suffered the savage cold and wind at altitude. To add to the effect of these wearying and painful conditions the gunners also had to lift heavy boxes of ammunition into position during high-altitude combat. It became evident quickly to the squadron medical officers that the missions were taking such a severe toll both physiologically and psychologically that crews were restricted to only two high-altitude missions for any seven day period.

American observers felt the British had tried to do more with the Fortress I than the aircraft was capable of delivering. Technical observers reported that the British, accustomed to their own bombers with higher load-carrying capabilities, "overloaded the Fortresses and then made their bombing runs from excessive altitude." The observers were unanimous on the matter of use of the airplanes. AAF specialists had always insisted that the airplane should be flown on their bombing runs between 22,000 and 28,000 feet and that the formations should be as large as possible. The more bombers in formation the greater the interlacing pattern of the defensive guns, and the greater the probability of an effective bomb drop on target.

Yet even with greater experience and higher efficiency it seemed improbable that the limited number of Fortress I's could have formed an effective combat force. The crews were, in the opinion of American observers, "appallingly in need of training" in aircraft systems and tactics with the Fortress. The Fortress I itself, lacking power turrets and tail guns, was forecast as being undergunned against the German fighters. And there were the problems that simply had to be encountered before they could even begin to be solved. On one mission a German fighter sent a single bullet through the tail wheel of a Fortress I. The tire wasn't just soft or punctured. It was frozen rock solid and it *shattered*, like so much smashed chinaware.

The final assessment of the Fortress I in Europe clearly showed a great deal of "fixing to be done." On twenty-two missions of from one to four planes per mission, eighteen bombers aborted before reaching primary or secondary targets, and two managed to unload their bombs over secondary targets. Not much of a showing for a total of thirty-nine aircraft. Only fifty percent of the Fortresses despatched ever reached their primary targets. The loss ratio to German fighters, when these were encountered, was enough to make a Fortress crewman think enviously of the infantry.

Harsh critics of the Fortress I in its initial combat role didn't mince their words. British "experts" went so far as to recommend that the United States abandon the airplane altogether and start building the Avro Lancaster for night attacks against Europe, a suggestion received with ill-concealed distaste on this side of the Atlantic. (The same suggestion had been made in respect to the Spitfire. Superb airplane that it was, the Spitfire was a short-range defensive machine. Had we built the Spitfire in large number the effect would have been disastrous; while the airplane was unmatched in defense, it was unable because of its severe range restrictions to carry the war to the enemy. By the time we were ranging deep into Germany the Spitfire was no longer in the forefront of battle—it "lacked the legs to get where the action was.")

The Fortress I more than paid its way in experience. By the time the successor to the B-17C and D models took to the air it had already incorporated in its design the lessons learned the hard way with the Fortress I.

# CHAPTER 8

# "BUILT TO FIGHT"

"We built the early models of the Flying Fortress, from old 299 up through the B-17D, as defensive airplanes. They were to protect our shores, to defend the nation. All that changed with the new B-17E. Now, there was a weapon that was offensive all the way. We built that airplane to beat hell out of the enemy. We built that airplane to fight."

FORTRESS PILOT, AAF

AS QUICKLY AS THE reports from Europe filtered back to Wright Field, detailing the teething pains of the Fortress I in its combat debut, the Army Air Force set out to update all its Flying Fortresses. Of the original order of thirty-eight, twenty were sent to the Royal Air Force to become their Fortress I; the eighteen B-17C aircraft remaining were refitted to the standards of the later B-17D, of which forty-two were built. It was a task complicated by the thousand small details, all of which required attention.

In addition to those problems already noted through the experience of the British, test pilot Eddie Allen and his Boeing flight-research crews had been hammering at the difficulties of flying and fighting at extreme altitudes. Allen dragged his problems from seven miles high into the engineering laboratories of Boeing. "There are a hundred things that can go wrong up there," he told the engineers. "It's terribly cold. Greases won't work. Propellers won't work. The fuel mixture system in the airplane doesn't work. We don't have the proper oxygen system."

The modifications to the B-17D went also into the eighteen B-17Cs. New self-sealing fuel tanks were installed in the wings. Heavier armor, and more of it, went into the airplane to protect the crew and vital systems. Except for the single .30 caliber gun in the nose, all weapons were of .50 caliber. Provision was made for an additional crew member, the oxygen system was modified and the intercom freed of its problems. New electrical systems were put into the airplane. When the revision program reached its end the AAF had on hand sixty four-engine bombers of B-17D capabilities.

There had been one problem plaguing the British which, since it never showed up on the American Fortresses sent to very high altitude, mystified the Boeing engineers and AAF specialists assigned to B-17 development. RAF crews had complained, on enough occasions to make the matter one of alarm, that at high altitude the bomb-bay doors would jam. There was never a pattern to the jamming. Before takeoff the doors would cycle properly. Everything checked out. Then at high altitude with its subzero temperatures, the doors refused to open.

"We went out of our minds trying to get a fix on it," a Boeing engineer told the writer. "But we could never get the same kind of problem that seemed to be giving the British fits. Then we had the chance to talk directly to one of our people who was assigned to England as a technical representative on the Fortress I. When he heard how we were trying to solve the problem of the jammed bomb-bay doors, he stared at us in disbelief. Then he doubled up and roared with laughter.

"It turned out that the British had already solved their problem. You know what it was? It didn't have a damned thing to do with the Fortress or its electrical system or its bomb-bay doors. It seemed that while the airplane was climbing out to altitude the crewmen took the last-moment opportunity to relieve themselves. Some of them urinated into the bomb bay because there's a slight opening where the doors meet. And when the airplane climbed to where it was anywhere from thirty to eighty degrees below zero, you'd better believe those doors were frozen solid. . . ."

On September 5, 1941, the first B-17E rolled down the runway of Boeing Field. Hundreds of spectators lined the fences and the roads. The gear came up smoothly, sound changed as the pilots adjusted power and the pitch of the propellers.

There were mixed reactions to the appearance of the new B-17E. Gone was the clean line of its predecessors. The slim and graceful fuselage had vanished. In its place a deepened fuselage carried all the way back from the trailing edge of the wing. A dorsal fin began at the radio operator's gun position and continued rising until it swept upward sharply into a new and towering vertical fin and rudder. The horizontal tail was larger; greater in area and ten feet wider across the elevators.

"That airplane is a mess," a Boeing engineer commented. He shook his head. "They really screwed up a beautiful design."

The young pilot at his side looked at the squared-off dome extending upward from the fuselage, just aft of the cockpit. He let his gaze carry to the underside of the airplane, where another installation of comparable shape was visible. Then he looked at the tail, where windows revealed a position for a new crew member. The tail guns didn't need power since the man behind his heavy weapons didn't have to fight a howling wind. But the other positions held power turrets. The wind wouldn't bother the men at those guns.

"Yeah, I guess you're right," the pilot said finally. Then he grinned. "But she's a fighting son of a bitch, ain't she. . . ."

And that the new B-17E was. The first of the Fortress line built to carry the fight to the enemy. The defensive role was swept into history. The new mission was to attack—not hostile fleets approaching the shores of the United States, but the enemy. Where he fought and where he lived.

When the B-17 was born, in the shape of Model 299, it received its name of Flying Fortress. The title suggested a coastal artillery battery with wings—a flying platform for rifled barrels. With the new B-17E, the name at last was fitting. The Fortress had sprouted machine guns like the quills on a porcupine.

Pilots accustomed to the slender and graceful lines of the early Fortress said that the new airplane, on the ground, looked like a "humpback hawk." They wondered how it would handle in the air. They didn't have long to wonder.

Boeing had pulled off a miracle. They struck turrets into the airstream and stabbed at the airflow with heavy machine gun barrels. They thickened and deepened the latter half of the airplane and rebuilt the tail entirely. They made the airplane longer and they poured added weight into the structure and equipment as if it were lead. They didn't change the wing one inch and the four engines were no more powerful than they had been in the B-17D model.

The B-17E *should* have been slower. Much slower, perhaps by even forty or fifty miles per hour. Outstanding design engineering paid off in spades. In its initial flight tests, despite all that added weight and all that extra airplane hammering against the wind, the B-17E showed a true maximum speed of 318 miles per hour, just as fast as its lighter, sleeker and smaller predecessor.

More important, the new B-17E was a *better* airplane. It had lost its famous slender lines, to be sure. But with the bigger tail, the dorsal fin, an increase in length of six feet, the new E emerged as an airplane of such stability that she was never challenged in her role as *the* outstanding bombing platform in the world.

The B-17E, standing on the ground on the two main wheels and tail gear, nearly seventy-five feet long, presented a gentle incline to the crews boarding her for a mission. Those were the moments, as the men came through the hatches, when the Fortress assumed a new mantle. There is a saying among the men who fly that when an airplane accepts its crew the airplane becomes *alive*. The difference is so great that experienced crews seem almost to sense, to *feel* the change. An airplane, after all, is made for men, and it is never complete until the men are inside.

The Flying Fortress was a big airplane. But it was not one in which its crew could find comfort. It was a machine for making war, and comfort took a last place in the requirements for the combat mission. It was a noisy airplane, insulated only in a limited area in the forward section. Often it was bitterly cold inside, not only from the ambient cold at high altitude but because of knifelike winds that stabbed through every narrow opening. Guns jutted from the airplane, hatches often were kept open, there was almost always a leak through the bomb bay doors. It's bad enough to be exposed to cold; it's worse when the wind shrieks demonlike and turns the cold into cruel pain.

Filled with the implements for waging war the Fortress presented its crew with a maze of sharp projections and nasty objects against which one often stumbled or brushed. Even with the four big propellers synchronized perfectly there was so much equipment, from machine guns to radios to oxygen bottles, that it couldn't help but rattle and vibrate within: After a while the crews never felt it; it was the sound of flight and it became second nature.

At high altitude, even without combat, every man was remote from his airplane despite his being linked through umbilical cords to its very fiber. A man didn't *touch* a part of that airplane with his naked skin. That isn't wise with the temperature down to forty to sixty degrees below zero. In that cold simply exposing the hands to the ambient air can be disastrous. Placing raw skin against metal at that subzero temperature can mean leaving a patch of skin on the metal—and drawing back bloody flesh. The crews were bundled in cumbersome, bulky flight garments, electrically heated. Heavy fleece trousers with leather on the outside. Jackets, boots, gloves, helmets. Goggles to hold off the screaming wind, to keep a man's eyes from tearing when he most needs his vision.

A man in his flight attire was a clumsy bearlike creature. His parachute, strapped over and around his body, heavy, binding and often distressingly uncomfortable, didn't make matters any better. And then there were the leads to connect. Oxygen masks on the face, strapped tightly, cutting against the skin to prevent the precious gas from escaping when a man needed it most. The mask plugged through a hose into the airplane. The electrical leads to the heated flying suit. Leads for radio and intercom to be plugged in. Symbiosis of ten men and one machine.

Those leads were life itself. Strange, then, that these men should be unable to secure themselves tightly to the machine to prevent stumbling, falling or being hurled about. A bomber in combat can be a wild and flailing creature. There are air currents to begin with. Bursts of flak mean concussion, sharp blows of air rammed to the strength of steel. In formation flying, there's the turbulence from all those propellers ahead, flailing the air with thousands of horsepower.

There are ten men in a Flying Fortress. In combat only two of them are seated—the pilot and the copilot to his right. That's all. Just those two. Strapped in by seat belt and shoulder harness they are snugged tightly to the machine. But only they, who must be certain that they are not blown away by explosion or other disaster from the controls.

Ten men crewed the B-17E and its successors. In the nose, during battle, the bombardier and the navigator crouched like animals at bay, each man grasping a heavy machine gun. Directly behind and slightly above them were the pilots, trussed up in their seats. Immediately behind the pilots was the flight engineer-top turret gunner, standing in his complicated nest of steel and plexiglas and machine guns. Behind this man, past the bomb bays, stood the radio operator, leaning back, awkward in his stance, swinging a heavy machine gun through an aperture in the fuselage, trying to sight on fighters high above and slightly aft. And immediately behind and beneath him, the ball turret gunner, bent into a half-ball of human being stuffed into his round world of a power turret, his feet on a level with his ears, his bottom the lowest part of the airplane. Still further back within the fuselage, two men at each waist, exposed to the howling winds, each grasping a single big fifty. And then all the way back, in the tail, seeing what has happened, looking backward, the tail gunner. He doesn't sit or stand or crouch or roll up—he rests on his knees.

Ten men in a machine five miles above the earth—sitting, standing, crouching, curled up, kneeling—that's how they fought their war.

Despite the size of the airplane, in the cockpit, the pilot and to his right, the copilot, are almost cramped within their cage of steel, glass, controls, hookup leads, and instruments. A wedge of compartment glass before each man is the windshield, with side windows for both. On the ground (or in the air, at low altitude with the temperature at a comfortable freezing rather than intense subzero) these windows can be opened by sliding them backward. Sometimes the cockpit arrangements are varied slightly but they hew to a basic pattern. Directly in the center of the windshield and at its lower edge is a metal container with three instruments dials; in the center is the accelerometer (which gauges the heavy forces of flight in multiples of gravity, such as 2g or 3g or 4g), flanked on each side by carburetor air-temperature gauges. If the men behind the control columns lean forward in their seats—they can do this by releasing the "lock" position of their shoulder harnesses— they can just catch a glimpse of the small plexiglas dome through which the navigator peers at the world above. (The early B-17Es didn't have this dome; it was added when the navigators screamed they needed it for shooting navigational fixes.)

In front of the two pilots are three main clusters of instruments; one before the pilot, another before the copilot, and in the center, a third cluster comprised mainly of the flight instruments. Directly behind this panel, and bordered by the control columns with their yokes for the pilots to grip, are the stands with power controls (throttles, propellers, mixture) and accessories. There is also the AFCE—the Automatic Flight Control Equipment, or autopilot, an integral part of the airplane from the time of Model 299.

In front of, to the sides, between, above, below and behind the two pilots are more than one hundred and fifty controls, switches, dials, gauges, handles, knobs, buttons, grips, and toggles. These run the gamut from navigational equipment and controls to the directional gyro (gyroscopic compass), airspeed indicator, artificial horizon, magnetic compass, turn and bank, rate of climb and descent (vertical speed), altimeter, and still others. There are controls and switches for the bomb doors, for electrical power and hydraulic pressure, for lights and oxygen, for the fuel supply and the engines, for pressure and feed, for the flaps and the landing gear and the brakes, gauges to read vacuum pressure, oil and cylinder head temperatures, propeller pitch, turbo-supercharger regulators, mixture—a fantastic array of knobs and dials thoroughly bewildering to anyone not trained and experienced in their use. But every one of them necessary to the pilots to show how their machine is functioning, to warn of incipient danger and allow them, hopefully, to take corrective measures.

Forward of the leading edge of the wings, the B-17E was arranged in split fashion. Below and ahead of the pilots was the nose compartment, where the bombardier and the navigator had their stations for their particular duties—as well as manning the nose armament of the bomber. Getting into the nose compartment wasn't too bad if you

climbed aboard through the belly hatch. The floorboard behind the pilots' seats lifted up out of the way so there was
access in flight between the nose and the rest of the airplane. That looked great on paper, but presented its own
share of creaking bones when a man clothed and geared up
in his cumbersome equipment tried to crawl along the restricted pathway into the nose. It wasn't tried too often in
flight at altitude.

The very tip of the Fortress was conical in shape, a
formed wedge of plexiglas. Metal stripping laced the nose
for added strength and there were ball-socket mounts
through which the barrel of a machine gun could be poked.
Beneath the horizontal center line of the plexiglas wedge
was a flattened optical panel through which the bombardier peered. There was added visibility in the small half
bubble above the navigator's position, and also several
small windows on each side of the nose. Into one window
on each side went another mount for a machine gun. It was
a busy place up front. The bombardier had his Norden
bombsight and controls with which he worked the bomb-
bay doors, switches to release the bombs either in sticks or
in salvos, or individually at specific time intervals of so
many seconds between the release of each bomb.

Behind the bombardier sat the navigator, surrounded by
radio and electronic navigation equipment, and all the
other complex gear required to plot an accurate course on
missions that might range from a few hundred to fifteen
hundred miles. The radio equipment with which to check
known broadcasting positions and on which an airplane
could home was fine—when there were such stations. Often
as not there weren't, especially in the trackless expanse of
the oceans over which many combat missions were certain
to be flown.

Originally the B-17E, following the line of its predeces-

sors, had only a single .30 caliber machine gun in its nose
for forward armament. But it is difficult to give a fixed description for changes came about so swiftly that often the
new aircraft underwent major revision between the time
they left the factory and arrived in a combat zone. The
nose armament of the three last production versions of the
Fortress—the B-17E, F and G—can scarcely be assigned an
official or permanent record. They changed too quickly for
that. A healthy respect for the cannon of Japanese and
German fighter airplanes brought about swift modifications to the weakest area of the Fortress—its armament firing forward. The .30 caliber machine gun was almost
useless. The fifty was many times more effective. It had
greater range and when it was on target it raised considerable hell because of its weight and rapidity of fire. At the
first opportunity the crews rid themselves of the .30 caliber
gun and replaced it with a .50 caliber weapon. Often as
not, since the gun socket mounts were available, they installed two or three heavy machine guns. Sometimes the
crews said to hell with *all* the books and they reinforced
the nose and installed four guns (there were plenty of
Fortresses with *five* fifty calibers in the nose, although with
four or five such weapons there was severe cramping of an
already restricted space). The nipplelike gun mounts in the
forward and side windows allowed the navigator and bombardier to switch from gun to gun as incoming fighter positions were snapped out over the intercom.

Swinging one of these 65-pound guns manually in the
teeth of a wind roaring by at hundreds of miles per hour
was no simple task, especially when a man was encumbered in his heavy and bulky flight gear and
electrical/oxygen hookups. Harder still when the Fortress
was rocking or pitching violently, for there was little

enough free space to begin with. But all things considered, the "big fifty" was to justify the faith its gunners had in the hefty weapon. In the years to follow, the air war would know everything from 15-mm to 40-mm cannon for aerial battles, and a variety of machine guns, but the .50 caliber was the heavyweight, the most flexible and versatile weapon of them all. Hurling its heavy slugs with a muzzle velocity of 2,900 feet per second it could chop into a nasty mess most parts of its target, including the engines.

In the Fortress models preceding the E the navigator had a pleasant astrodome, a clear plastic half-bubble, extending above the fuselage just aft of the cockpit. This served not only for his navigational position checks by stellar fixes or shooting the sun but also made a dandy site from which to survey the world. In the B-17D model, for example, there were times when the navigator might even find himself preempted from his favorite position. Four upholstered chairs in the D cockpit provided room for the pilot, copilot, command pilot (of the mission) and the flight engineer. The command pilot could crank his seat up so that his head reached within the astrodome. Comfortably ensconced he had a magnificent view of the world about him. "On long cross-country flights," reported a B-17D veteran, "it was like flying in an airliner for those of us up front."

The Army Air Forces, when considering the airplane that would become the B-17E, decided there were plenty of other places from which the navigator could pick out his stars, and the command pilot could bloody well find himself another seat, with or without upholstery. They sent the word to Boeing, and Ed Wells and his engineering team moved things around within the forward fuselage. Instead of the stargazing-sightseeing astrodome they installed a massive power turret with two .50 caliber machine guns. It was an immensely popular addition, even if it did shake up the two men driving the airplane.

The turret was so close behind the pilots that when the twin guns fired off a burst the sound was like a cannon shell exploding directly over their heads. "We never minded the noise," a pilot said wryly. "When that turret fired we *knew* what was going on."

The heavy turret was an electrically operated mechanism into which the flight engineer, who was also the gunner, was required to squeeze his head, shoulders, and arms until an outsider saw only a human face surrounded by steel and glass, framed by the wicked-looking barrels of the twin machine guns. The engineer-gunner, except for coordinating his defensive fire with the remainder of the crew, functioned within a combat unit quite independent of the rest of the airplane. Hand controls turned the turret in azimuth and elevation and fired the twin guns, and the man inside was surrounded with an umbilical array of oxygen tubes and intercom wires connecting his heated suit, as well as gunsights, ammunition belts, and containers. Curved plexiglas panels and a plexiglas dome were fitted into the steel mountings to provide an excellent field of view. From the turret the flight engineer-gunner commanded a full forward view as well as an unobstructed view to both sides. He could look back along the glistening curved metal of the Fortress and see the long barrel of a single machine gun sticking upward from the open hatch of the radio compartment and, beyond that, the towering tail of the bomber. In addition to sweeping a 360-degree horizon (an interruptor mechanism made certain he did not tear up the tail of his own airplane) the gunner could also look straight up and deploy his guns along his line of sight— a capability well appreciated by other people in the airplane when the fighters made their attacks in near-vertical power dives.

Aft of the top turret gunner's position was the "other part" of the Flying Fortress, and to reach the tail of the airplane from the "up front" area, a man had to traverse a narrow catwalk spanning the bomb bay, after which he would emerge into the radio compartment. Once again a certain amount of agility was required, since at each end of the bomb bay there was a structural beam, wide enough for a step, but edged with a narrow slice of metal along its length. "Narrow" is a relative term, of course, but for the writer there has been a familiar intimacy with the edge of the beam. On one occasion over the North Atlantic in a storm, trying to return to the cockpit after working the fuel tank controls in the radio compartment (we had bomb bay tanks on this flight), turbulence caused a sudden upset, and I slammed my knee against this edge of the structural beam. A cracked kneecap is one way of being certain to remember a particular part of any airplane. . . .

The radioman had a single heavy machine gun (some crews mounted twin fifties in this position) from which he fired upward against fighters passing overhead or making diving attacks. The firing field of arc was somewhat restricted. Originally the B-17 models up through the D had *only* this station for firing against fighters overhead, and the crews who manned the B-17E and later models with the power turret atop the fuselage shuddered when they thought of the nakedness of the airplane with only the one machine gun in the radio compartment.

Further back within the fuselage were the two waist gunners, two men who lived and fought from within a tubular world, with the walls, floor, and ceiling made of thin metal skin and its supporting heavy ribs that completely encircled them. Wide hatches on each upper side of the fuselage yawned out into space. Normally plexiglas panels covered the hatches to prevent a thundering wind from entering the airplane. When preparing to enter a combat area the gunners removed the hatches (at first they were removed physically; later they could be slid on runners out of the way). It was through these big squarish spaces that their guns pointed, one fifty to each side of the airplane. By the time a B-17 returned from a running flight in the air the floor was almost impossible to walk upon, littered as it was with the dense rain of empty shell casings.

It is at these waist positions that the paradox of the Fortresses' structural strength could best be understood. This was the bomber that gave new meaning to the word *rugged*, that could absorb punishment (and keep flying and fighting) like no other airplane ever sent into battle. The Fortress could be (and often was) holed, torn, cut, slashed and otherwise mangled, but continued to pound through the air, its gunners firing everything they had at the oncoming enemy. One might think, then, of the Fortress as a machine that was nearly impregnable, a bomber with powerful structural ribs and thick metal skin. It wasn't that at all. Weight is the curse of the aerodynamic engineer and every attempt is made to reduce weight while still seeking the grail of great strength. The Fortress was the most rugged bomber ever built, but with an easy push a man could jab a screwdriver right through the thin metal that made up the skin of the airplane. Strength in the B-17 came from outstanding design. It was the brilliant interlocking of its main structural members that gave to the Fortress its tremendous strength; normally the skin was only a surface membrane.

Major General Dale O. Smith, USAF (Ret.), a close friend of the writer, flew many missions as a Fortress pilot in Europe during World War II (as commander of the 2nd Bomb

Group and later the 384th Bomb Group). General Smith felt the airplane through each model "got stronger and more rugged. Forts would take an incredible amount of battle damage and fly home.

"Once, while enroute to Berlin in a B-17G, a flak shell went through my wing inboard of the Number Two engine and burst above us. Except for a slight wing heaviness nothing seemed wrong so I continued with the mission. Upon arriving home we were embarrassed to find England socked in solidly, so I led my group out over the Wash for a letdown over water. There, luckily, I found a small hole in the under-cast through which I led my boys single file in a dive, pulling up just above the waves. Then we hedge-hopped home to Grafton-Underwood.

"Upon examining my ship the Engineering Officer discovered that the main wing spar had been sheared by the flak shell. *Only the thin skin held the wing together during the seven-hour mission to Berlin and back, and in the dive through that hole in the clouds.*

"That Fort never flew again."

In the very stern of the B-17E, in a cramped wedge that formed the blunt final tip of the Fortress, was the compartment for the tail gunner. The lone gunner—who fired his twin machine guns from a kneeling position with his knees on soft pads (never soft enough)—actually flew beneath the trailing edge of the high rudder. His view of the world was not always the best, although he could, if the time was available, observe with satisfaction the results of bomb strikes. He also had a much slower-moving view of enemy fighters boring in with their wings and noses alive with the blinking orange-yellow lights of firing guns and cannon. The tail gunner position, notoriously absent in the earlier models of the Fortress, made up for perhaps the weakest of all defensive areas of the airplane. There was an unusual occupational hazard for tail gunners—eyestrain. At high altitude the Fortress streamed behind it thick, white contrails from the engines that formed into a cottony swath stretching out for miles. Flying straight into two waiting .50 caliber guns wasn't the best way to attack a Fortress—if you were a fighter pilot—and enemy pilots soon adopted the clever trick of starting their attack miles behind the bomber, flying hidden from sight in the midst of the thick vapor trails, breaking out at the last moment at point-blank range to open fire.

The B-17E carried a crew of ten men, and the newest member of the team was often seen carrying a giant-size bottle of aspirin. In addition to its new twin-gun positions in the tail and at the top turret, the B-17E also closed out another blind spot—against attacks from climbing fighters. The bathtub gun position of the C and D models had proven to be ineffective, and this was one of the major sore spots of the Fortress I with the Royal Air Force. The field of fire was poor and, because of the gunner's physical position, his ability to aim little better.

Beneath the B-17 was a squared-off dome with two heavy machine guns. No manned turret this, but one with power, able to swing in any direction and to cover entirely the field of fire beneath the airplane. The gunner sat within the bomber itself, between the top turret and waist gun positions. He kept one eye glued to an optical sight which was linked to a periscope made up of angled mirrors. Unfortunately the sight itself confused the gunners more than it bothered the enemy fighter pilots, and one immediate result of trying to shoot at fighters tearing by was the giant-sized headache for the gunner.

Of all the modifications in the Flying Fortress, none was such a colossal failure as this remote-control turret. The crews disliked—and distrusted—the turret so much, and considered it so useless (no one *ever* confirmed even hitting an enemy fighter with the periscopic turret) that many crews simply removed the turret. They felt the weight was more of a burden than the turret was worth. Some crews jury-rigged .30 caliber machine guns with tracer ammunition for its psychological effect, while still others left the turret in place but removed all the heavy equipment and replaced the machine gun barrels with wooden poles to simulate the guns.

With reports of total dissatisfaction on the remote turret flooding back to the AAF and to Boeing, Ed Wells and his design team worked on a crash basis to come up with the fix that was needed. They did the job in quick time. The answer was the unique Sperry ball turret, literally a self-contained sphere with operating mechanisms, two machine guns, ammunition loads, sights and, last but by no means least, the ball turret gunner, whose position also was unique since he curled up inside the turret proper.

Unquestionably the loneliest position in the Flying Fortress (or its counterpart, the Liberator) was that of the ball-turret gunner. The turret was like some grotesque, swollen eyeball of steel and glass and guns that seemed to hang precariously from the belly of the Fortress. Colonel Budd J. Peaslee, former group commander, 8th Air Force in Europe:

"It is a hellish, stinking position in battle. The gunner must hunch up his body, draw up his knees, and work into a half ball to meet the curving lines of the turret. The guns are to each side of his head, and they stab from the turret eyeball like two long splinters. Jailed in his little spherical power-house the turret gunner literally aims his own body at enemy fighters, working both hands and feet in deft co-ordination, spinning and tilting, and then depressing switches atop the gun grip handles to fire the two weapons. It is the most unenviable position in a bomber, *any* bomber, and the man most unlikely to escape from a blazing Fortress is that lonely soul in the ball."

The Flying Fortress, especially the B-17E, was an airplane laced with control cables, heating lines, communications lines, and its oxygen system. In the air the various parts of the bomber became welded into a single entity, the connecting links acting as blood vessels and arteries and nerves, sinew and bone, eyes and ears, until the bomber was no longer a collection of many parts and her crew, but a single, living, breathing, flying and fighting creature. If contact between crew members was broken, their chance of survival in the most bitter arena of aerial combat was compromised severely, perhaps lost beyond all redemption.

Before a mission was to be flown in the Fortress there was a ceremony that first took place. *Every* mission, and never was any moment of this ceremony less sensitive or less perilous than it had been before. It was a ritual to which every crew must become accustomed, and to which none ever did.

As the rest of the ten-man crew moved to their stations, the bombardier began his critical task. Takeoff was still some time away but the airplane would never move until the bombardier carried out his work; without his ministrations there would be no purpose in sending out ten men and a great machine at the risk of life and aircraft.

The bombardier climbed out onto the narrow catwalk that spanned the bomb bay. In one hand he held a container that he handled with the most exquisite care. Within that container were the fuses, the tiny little items that made bombs come alive. Without those fuses the bombs

were just so much weight—inert chunks of heavy metal and
the chemicals that made up the explosives. Without the
fuses the bombs could be kicked, pounded with hammers,
or even dropped onto hard concrete (as they often were
during bomb-loading and handling) with no greater damage than the crushing of a man's foot if the bomb loader
proved to be careless, slow or just unlucky.

But when the bombardier began his work, the heavy
ordnance was transformed by the magic of the little fuses.
The bomb-bay doors were kept open, with the thick missiles hanging by shackles in their racks. Beneath each airplane, during this ceremony, stood an armament sergeant.
The bombardier handed down to the sergeant the box of
fuses, and the sergeant in turn reached up to hand the
bombardier a wrench. Then, patiently, carefully, as if their
lives depended on their skill (it did) they went to work. A
fuse was inserted in the nose of a bomb, and tightened.
Then another fuse was inserted in the tail, and that one,
too, was tightened, until finally all the bombs were armed.
Now they were horribly sensitive, and steel casings which
once could be hammered with impunity were now the
thinnest and weakest of explosive eggshells.

There was a standing rule never violated. During this
ritual—*never bother these two men*. They were priests beyond the touch of mere mortals.

In the years to come, years in which thousands of Flying Fortresses stood on hardstands at airbases on several
continents, this same scene would be repeated many tens
of thousands of times. And every now and then the odds
would flip and a finger would point. More than once a
Fortress would suddenly—disappear. Where the bomber
had stood, a searing flash of light and then the blasting,
thundering roar. More often than not men, as many as

forty or fifty, would disappear with the airplane. More often than not the shock waves would tear up other bombers and their crews, adding to the holocaust.

All this lay in the future when the first B-17E, AAF Serial Number 41-2393, rolled down the runway for its initial test flight. But it was a future only months, not years, away.

The airplane *felt* right to those who built and tested it. Only six years before Model 299 had flown for the first time. The new Fortress, as the B-17E, was seven tons heavier when empty than the ancestor of the line. Despite the weight, the drag of turrets and guns and the redesigned fuselage and tail, the new giant was forty percent faster.

Combat loaded, the B-17E was flown at an official all-up weight of 54,000 pounds, a figure of which Ed Wells and his team would have scoffed when they designed the precursor of all Fortresses. The writer emphasizes the "official" in listing the all-up weight for, as might be expected, the exigencies of combat often dictated weights exceeding 60,000 pounds, and sometimes even more.

Even as the first B-17E began its series of extensive test flights, the production line (that would produce 512 B-17E models) was already moving more of the bombers toward the flight line.

They would be not a moment too soon.

## CHAPTER 9

# BEFORE THE STORM

EUROPE WAS THE CENTER ring, the main attraction, the headliner. In the late 30's, as far as the leading nations of the world were concerned, Europe was the crucible in which airpower would be formed. Experts and air strategists attended international air races and competitions, fought with one another for the lucrative profits of growing commercial air service, and pulled every dirty trick in the book to outstrip their competitors in the mass sales of military aircraft. In the air war raging over Spain, the Luftwaffe found opportunity to test new equipment and experiment with tactics that would later be employed in widespread combat. And Germany was preparing to back up Hitler's shouted imprecations with massed steel on the ground and glistening wings in the air.

On the other side of the world Japan began to create one of the most effective air forces on the face of the planet. Air war began in 1932 when the Japanese rolled into Manchuria. It escalated in a series of lurching movements, fitfull starts and stops that always saw an expansion in the use of airpower for successive campaigns.

Literally *thousands* of airplanes were thrown into combat over Asia. Planes built in the United States, Germany, Russia, Italy, France and other nations, all eager to sell their military wares to a desperate China. The Soviet Union seized upon the opportunity to settle a score with an old enemy and shipped five hundred fighters and bombers to the Chinese. To assist in the donnybrook building over China, the Russians brought in another 450 fighters and bombers and flew them with Russian crews. That was in south and central China. In the far north another bitter struggle erupted and the Japanese and Russians faced each other in a savage and undeclared war—in which Japanese airpower tore apart its red-starred opposition.

Finally someone gave heed to the alarm bell clamoring from Asia. General Hap Arnold sent observers to the Asian mainland. They traveled as best they could throughout China to take notes and gather as much information as possible. What they reported of Japanese airpower had an immediate and sobering effect upon Arnold. He was surprised, almost astonished, at the grasp of sound tactical doctrine expressed in the actions of the Japanese. Speaking at the Army War College, Arnold emphasized that the Japanese did not think of their bombers only as an extension of artillery. They thought in terms of *airpower*—a freedom of doctrine not yet enjoyed among even the most advanced nations of Europe. Arnold reported to the War College that the Japanese as their most immediate step in combat sought to achieve complete superiority in the air. With their freedom of movement virtually unchallenged they then struck at enemy airfields, rail centers, warships and aircraft factories. Arnold concluded:

> The employment of the Japanese Air Force is directly in line with the most up-to-date teachings of our own Air Corps Tactical School and with the doctrines of our own GHQ Air Force. That is significant. There is abroad in the world a first rate air power which knows how to use its air strength.[17]

From that moment the Air Corps made every effort to establish a buildup of air power forces in the Far East. But the effort was resisted in many quarters of the government and, like so many similar efforts in the final days before World War II—it was a case of "too little, too late."

At the heart of the "new air power" for the Far East was a new airplane—the Flying Fortress.

Referring to the jockeying for position among the potential combatants in the Far East and Asia, historians of the Royal Australian Air Force noted that:

> It was almost certain that the United States would fight beside the British countries should Japan attack, and, if the United States was an ally, an entirely new appearance would be given the balance of sea and air power in the Far East. The United States possessed a Navy more powerful than Japan's, and naval and army air forces far stronger than the air force which Britain and the Dominions could afford to deploy in the Far East while they were at war with Germany and Italy.[18]

The Australians, unfortunately, saw more in the American fleet than did those who directed that fleet. By no means was there acceptance that the United States would hold the line against the Japanese—nor was there even the belief that this *could* be done. In fact, much of the Far East, had the Japanese attacked, was literally "written off" to the invading enemy. Then a new element came into the picture—the B-17 strength even then being built up by the Army Air Corps. This seemed a panacea for an overwhelming problem. Fear of attack and invasion by Japan was so great on the part of each nation concerned that it seemed impossible to achieve a combined strategy against the war believed to be inevitable. In the official history of the United States Army in World War II is contained this significant and revealing note. Writing of this prewar planning, the official historians stated:

> The notion that the Philippines could be defended, in spite of all the considerations *that had led the planners to reject the idea* [italics added: MC], grew out of a new approach to the problem of operations in the western Pacific, involving the use of long-range Army bombers to neutralize Japanese offensive capabilities. . . . a fairly strong bomber force might be built up in the Philippines by early 1942 to take the place of the strong naval forces that neither the U.S. Navy, on the one hand, nor the British, Dutch and Australian navies, on the other, were willing to commit to the support of the Philippines.[19]

But there existed a fatal flaw in the new idea that the Philippines might so be defended. The entire plan for reinforcing the islands rested on the assumption "that hostilities could be postponed *until at least March or April 1942.*"[20]

Unfortunately, the Japanese weren't prepared to wait that long.

And the United States had to overcome an appalling lack of preparedness in the western Pacific.

By the early morning of December 7, 1941, a total of 231 military aircraft had been assigned to the Hawaiian Air Force. Only half of these could be considered up-to-date, based upon the standards of European air war. Among the obsolescent bombers were thirty-three B-18A's, fit only for limited range reconnaissance patrol. The "modern" bombing force included twelve Douglas A-20A Boston light twin-engine raiders and twelve Boeing B-17D Flying Fortresses.

The Hawaiian Air Force was openly unhappy with its limited number of Fortresses, and the clamor for greater numbers of the long-ranging heavy bombers had been heard for many months in Washington. The lack of equipment was somewhat of a paradox; since 1935 the War Department had given the Hawaiian islands peacetime "first priority" in building up its military strength. But events in Europe modified that decision, resulting in the assignment to the Royal Air Force of twenty updated B-17C aircraft.

Yet there could be no denying that the Hawaiian Air Force must be reinforced, and early in 1941 the War Department approved the transfer to the Islands of twenty-one B-17s. The decision entailed far more preparation than might be indicated at first glance. There had never been a mass flight of heavy bombers over such an expanse of open water, and Air Corps officials were warned that a disaster during the ferry mission might have severe adverse reaction among the public. To this warning the Air Corps retorted that the need for the planes was more than sufficient to warrant the risks involved. Early in April 1941, preparations began for the trail-blazing mission.

The Army obtained the assistance and services of a

group of organizations. The Navy Department, Pan American Airways, and commercial radio stations in San Francisco and Honolulu all contributed to the flight. Four Navy "guard vessels" at 500-mile intervals along the route scheduled not only supplied weather information but stood ready to pick up the crew of any plane that went down. All other Naval vessels anywhere along the line of flight broadcast up-to-the-minute weather data. Soon it appeared as if this was more of a Navy than an Army operation. Naval authorities provided communications facilities in San Francisco and Honolulu and linked the entire system with their ships at sea. Commercial airlines in both cities provided weather forecasts. The radio stations in each city agreed to broadcast continuously at maximum power to provide homing signals for the planes staying on the air until they received the "mission accomplished" signal.

The preparations paid off handsomely. On the morning of May 13th Lt. Colonel Eugene L. Eubank of the 19th Bombardment Group led the first of twenty-one B-17 bombers out of Hamilton Field, California, and set course for the Hawaiian Islands. With accurate weather reports, and homing facilities provided by the land stations and the ships at sea, the twenty-one bombers flew the 2,400-mile overwater stretch without a single midship. The Fortresses' average elapsed flight time was thirteen hours and ten minutes, and they landed at Hickman Field in the Hawaiian Islands within five minutes of their estimated time of arrival.

The transfer of twenty-one heavy bombers to the Hawaiian garrison established clearly the importance of the Hawaiian territory, which was held in continental defense plans as a "main outlying naval base." Yet twenty-one B-17D bombers could hardly be regarded as adequate air cover for the huge ocean expanses around Hawaii. For a long time there would not be enough airplanes to carry out a thorough job of reconnaissance. As a minimum the Hawaiian Air Force would need *seventy-two* B-17s in order to search daily the area within the circle of an 833-nautical mile radius from Oahu, if each plane covered only a sector of five degrees. But there were not seventy-two B-17s in the entire AAF.

Attempts to solve the problem continued nevertheless. In the late fall of 1941, military and naval commanders in the Islands received word of deteriorating relationships between the United States and Japan, and all forces in the Islands were placed on alert.

> Of the imminence of hostilities, there was little doubt; but it was generally felt that the most likely area of attack was in the Philippines. The eve of hostilities therefore found the Hawaiian Air Force continuing, as it had through the fall of 1941, to aid in rushing aerial reinforcements to the Philippines.[21]

Of the air defenses in the Philippines early in December of 1941, much was to be desired. Under Major General Lewis H. Brereton the Far East Air Force (FEAF) had more than three hundred military aircraft. Unfortunately at least half of these machines were outmoded and would be almost helpless in the air against modern fighters. Of the remainder, which were considered to be of a quality at least equal to that of the Japanese, many could not be flown because of critical shortages of proper equipment and lack of spares.

By August 4th, 1941, the Far East Air Force was able to put into the air:

> one squadron of P-40Bs, two squadrons of P-35As, and two squadrons of B-18s, but against even a mildly deter-

mined and ill-equipped foe, this show of air strength would have been sadly deficient. Japanese capabilities argued therefore for a radical upward revision in the apportionment of aircraft to the Philippines; moreover, the geographical position of the islands afforded the United States an opportunity, while providing for their greater security, to emphasize its opposition to further Japanese aggression in Asia. AAF Headquarters felt that a striking force of heavy bombers would be a necessary part of any attempt to guarantee the security of the Philippines, and there was a feeling among War Department officials that the presence of such a force would act "as a threat to keep Japan in line."[22]

There was, of course, an overwhelming problem that had to be faced. We didn't have the numbers of bombers necessary to carry out a massive arming of our forces in the Philippines. Yet the AAF felt, despite the strained relations between the United States and Japan, there would be sufficient time within which to build up a powerful heavy bomber force in the Philippines.

*The program of reinforcement,"* noted the official history of the AAF, was *"based on an assumption that hostilities could be postponed until at least March or April 1942."*[23]

Many AAF officers felt this time prediction was outrageously optimistic, that the Japanese already were preparing to attack and that every plane available should be rushed to the Philippines. This became the hard line of the AAF: get the planes out now. Backing up the outward movement would be increasing production. Twelve Fortresses had been produced in October of 1941. Twenty-five were scheduled for November. There would be thirty-five in December, and monthly production (of the new B-17E) would keep rising.

There were also available the new Liberator bombers. The AAF took a long look at its production schedules. *If* the Japanese could be held at bay long enough, there might just be time to build up AAF bomber strength. "Indeed, out of an anticipated production in the United States of 220 heavy bombers by the end of February 1942, no less than 165 of the planes had been scheduled for delivery to the Philippines."[24]

One problem was solved through improvisation. In the late summer of 1941 not a single group in the AAF based in the United States was fully equipped with heavy bombers. AAF Headquarters made the decision to transfer as permanent party to the Philippines the 19th Bombardment Group, which in May had ferried the first twenty-one B-17Ds to Hawaii. The Group was given "critical priority" in receiving new Fortresses as fast as they came off the production lines.

But even that would take too much time. What about a provisional squadron to "fill in" in the Philippines until the 19th B.G. was ready? The group then in the Hawaiian Islands was ordered to proceed as quickly as possible to their new assignment in the Far East. Once again a massive effort was needed to sustain the unprecedented mission. There was no time in which to pioneer the route with one or two planes. It would have to be done with a large force and it must be done quickly. Operating under "utmost secrecy" the mission began. Australian officials offered full cooperation in preparing facilities at Rabaul in New Britain, at Port Moresby in New Guinea, and at Darwin in Australia. The U.S. Navy rushed runway construction on Midway and Wake Islands. The B-17D crews trained day and night, sharpening their navigational skills. It was not going to be a "piece of cake," and for reasons other than long distance over water.

On the early morning of September 5, 1941, the 14th Bombardment Squadron (H) departed Hickam Field and set their course westward. Major Emmett O'Donnell, Jr., led the nine B-17D bombers, with a total of seventy-five men, on the first leg of the mission—1,132 nautical miles. Seven hours and ten minutes later "Rosy" O'Donnell brought the Fortresses in safely to Midway. That night the crews received their first taste of being on the move. They refueled and serviced the bombers, staked them down securely for the night, ate their dinners, and tried to catch a few hours' sleep. Many of the men spent the night hours sleeping beneath the wings of their Fortresses.

Early the next morning (4:45 A.M.) they were rolling down the Midway runway and headed for Wake Island, another 1,035 miles "down the stretch" which was flown in just over six and a half hours.

Air Force historians note that:

Since the next hop to Port Moresby involved flying over some of the Japanese mandated islands, the planes took off at midnight in order to pass over the territory unseen and thereby avoid any possible international incident. Climbing from their usual altitude of 8,000 feet to 26,000 feet, the bombers turned out all lights and maintained complete radio silence over the islands. Although they flew in a heavy rain and without communications, the B-17s kept their assigned positions, and the 2,176-mile hop to Port Moresby was completed at noon on 8 September (local time). Australian officials were most hospitable to the crews, who remained at Port Moresby until the morning of 10 September. The next hop, 934 miles to Darwin, was covered in six and one-half hours, and early on the morning of September 12 the planes took off for Clark Field, near Manila.[25]

For the first time during the long mission the Fortresses ran into trouble. During most of the aerial journey the weather had not been a problem. Rainshowers, some that lasted for hours, did not interfere with their progress. Now, however, the nine bombers were unable to avoid towering storms. The air became violent with increasing turbulence, rain so heavy it blocked out visibility beyond a few hundred feet. No one could tell what the crosswind effect might be. Formation flying became dangerous, and O'-Donnell ordered his bombers into storm echelon. What had been a long and tedious but essentially routine ferrying mission became some of the wildest flying the Fortress crews had ever known. O'Donnell wanted to maintain visual contact with the earth as long as it was possible to do so. Down from 8,000 feet went the nine Flying Fortresses until they were between 100 and 400 feet above the water. They pounded along, rocking and pitching, every crew acute to the dangers of their minimum height. Finally, by midafternoon they had Clark Field in sight. But only barely, since the entire area was being inundated with a "blinding rain." O'Donnell led the bombers down to perfect landings.

"Successful completion of the historic flight, despite primitive servicing facilities and incomplete weather data," noted Air Force historians, "offered reassuring proof that the Philippines could be reinforced by air."[26]

General MacArthur's headquarters received the "particularly welcome" news that before the end of November they would have at their command a light bombardment group equipped with fifty-two Douglas A-24 dive bombers and a heavy bombardment group with twenty-six new B-17s.

AAF Headquarters remained true to their word. On October 16th the 19th Bombardment Group at Hamilton Field, California, received its alert notice for transfer to the Philippines. Six days later all twenty-six Fortresses staged to Hickam Field in Hawaii. Since the staging areas along the ferry route could not accommodate twenty-six bombers at any one time, the Group broke up into several smaller flights. The ease with which the first nine bombers had made the mission in September was not to be repeated. Engine failures and severe weather plagued the new journey. Despite their adversities, by the 6th of November twenty-five Fortresses were at Clark Field in the Philippines. The last plane, delayed by the need to change engines and fight its way through storms, arrived shortly thereafter.

The Philippines now had airpower that could be measured in appreciable numbers—thirty-five heavy bombers were on hand "for any contingency." The Fortresses assumed even greater importance when the fifty-two A-24 dive bombers failed to appear on schedule, and, despite the passing of several weeks, never showed. The A-24s, in fact, never reached their destination, a loss which was to have critical consequences in the battles that lay only weeks in the future.

With thirty-five bombers on hand under MacArthur, AAF Headquarters felt that only the initial phase of the critically needed buildup had been accomplished. No one held any false hopes that peace would be long continued. By mid-November serious decisions had been reached. The AAF planned to fly to the Philippines every "modernized" Flying Fortress it had available. Several days later, with the international situation worsening, AAF Headquarters recommended that the same be accomplished with every B-24 Liberator that could make the journey. Had the plans gone through immediately, the project would "have left only seventeen B-17s within the Zone of the Interior: five B-17Es which were being used for test flights, one B-17C which was in a repair depot, and eleven B-17As and Bs which were obsolete. So serious was the situation in the Far East that even the twelve B-17s of the Hawaiian Air Force were under consideration for transfer to the Philippines."[27]

But having bombers by itself wasn't enough—they had to be implemented into an air force, and that meant extensive facilities on the ground and the men trained and equipped to handle those facilities. During the season of heavy rains in the Philippines there were only two airfields from which the Fortresses could operate—the others became quagmires. Clark Field was sixty-five miles northwest of Manila, and Del Monte, in northern Mindanao, lay 600 air miles to the south.

In more disastrous condition was the state of support. The warning service to alert against enemy air attack was a grim joke. The P-40 fighters, most advanced in the Philippines (or anywhere in U.S. service, for that matter), flew almost daily, and the severity of operational conditions caused critical maintenance problems. Added to this unhappy state of affairs was the fact that some planes crashed in training and replacements were slow in coming. Other fighters that wore out their equipment had to be towed to dispersal areas and left there—often for months—to wait for the arrival of spare parts.

And as for the Fortresses, which had been needed so desperately, General Brereton said acidly that his command did not have "so much as an extra washer or nut...." Of the thirty-five bombers flown from the States, within two weeks four were already out of commission for lack of parts. Basic methods of protection, to say nothing of advanced systems, afforded their own share of headaches:

> Dispersal and camouflage of the bombers proved difficult, for there was no natural cover near the field [Del Monte]. The one available spray gun was put to work day and night to change the shining silver color of the planes to an olive drab. Huge quantities of coconut leaves were hauled to the field by trucks obtained from a local plantation, for camouflage of the dispersed planes on the ground. Ten truckloads of leaves were required to cover effectively one B-17.[28]

On November 29th all Army forces in the Philippines were placed on war alert. All leaves were canceled. Infantry divisions were rushed to areas where we believed the Japanese might attempt invasion. Long-range patrols by Army and Navy bombers brought back reports of large numbers of Japanese transport and cargo ships at sea. More and more Japanese aircraft were seen in flight.

On the nights of December 3rd, 4th, and 5th, fighter pilots in the Philippines attempted—but failed—to intercept Japanese reconnaissance planes. Antiaircraft batteries went on full alert.

On December 1st, General Arnold in Washington warned the commander of the Hawaiian Air Force that "We must get every B-17 available to the Philippines as soon as possible." Five days later Arnold flew to Hamilton Field in California personally to inspect the preparations for the aerial movement of fourteen Fortresses of the 38th and 88th Reconnaissance Squadrons, which were to fly to Hawaii for the first leg of their ferry mission to Mindanao in the Philippines.

On December 6th, General MacArthur ordered a final alert in the Philippines. "All stations were manned and the number of guards increased, special precautions had been taken against subversive activities, and all aircraft were dispersed as best they could be, each under guard."[29]

On the evening of December 6th, the fourteen Flying Fortress bombers of the 38th and 88th squadrons took off from Hamilton Field, and set their course for Oahu. They were scheduled to arrive on the morning of the 7th of December.

By the time they arrived war had already broken out.

# II
# WAR

# CHAPTER 10

# WAR

"December 7, 1941 . . . will live as the date of one of the most brilliant military performances of all time. Superbly planned and superbly executed . . ."

"On December 7, 1941 he [the Japanese] achieved complete surprise. He struck swiftly, boldly, accurately. . . . He made full capital of the paralyzing effect of his initial assault."

"The attack achieved perfect tactical surprise. . . . From the standpoint of air employment alone, his first stroke was masterful."

"Wherever the fault lay, the AAF in Hawaii, and the fleet whose defense was its chief mission, suffered an overwhelming defeat."

AT FIRST GLANCE THE preceding statements might be attributed to an overzealous Japanese historian preparing an "objective record" of the events that transpired at Pearl Harbor on the morning of December 7th, 1941. Certainly the statements are a ringing tribute to the superb execution of air doctrine, and they leave no question as to the helplessness of the attacked to execute what might generously be termed "a feeble defense."

But no Japanese historian prepared those words. They are sobering, objective, and carefully studied evaluations of what happened at Pearl Harbor.

They were all written by official historians of the Air Force.

The Japanese could have been afforded no more careful or guarded praise than by those who were defeated. And these are only excerpts among many statements from official documents. Nearly three full decades is more than time enough to dull the emotional response to a shattering defeat and to permit the dispassionate appraisal of what transpired.

In this story of the *Flying Fortress* it is not the writer's province, nor is it his intention, to review the history of World War II, other than as it involves directly or obliquely the role which was played by the bomber which is the subject of our attention. Yet, Pearl Harbor set the stage for what was to happen later, and some latitude must be taken in relating, even in statistical terms, what transpired that Sunday morning. For the die was cast and the role for the Flying Fortress established. It was not one complicated by problems of strategy. For a long time to come the manner of use of the B-17 was dictated by the reality of events—as fast as the bombers rolled out from their production lines they were rushed into battle.

\*     \*     \*

This is what happened at Pearl Harbor.

In her two-pronged aerial attack with 353 carrier-based fighters, dive and torpedo bombers, Japan's pilots either sank or rendered useless for a long time to come the battleships *Arizona, California, Oklahoma, Nevada* and *West Virginia*; three destroyers; one target ship; one minelayer and a large floating drydock.

The battleships *Maryland, Pennsylvania* and *Tennessee* sustained heavy damage and loss of life, as did the cruisers *Helena, Honolulu* and *Raleigh*; the seaplane tender *Curtiss*; and the repair ship *Vestal*.

Of the 301 American naval aircraft in the Oahu area the Japanese destroyed or severely damaged more than half.

Another eleven Navy aircraft were shot down during the battle in the area of Pearl Harbor. Steaming two hundred miles from Hawaii, the carrier *Enterprise* launched a group of planes, all of which were armed with live ammunition. Guns were "hot." Antiaircraft fire from Pearl shot down several of these planes but most fell to the guns of Japanese fighters. Nine of the eleven crews were lost. Not a single airplane of the eleven Navy aircraft fired so much as a single shot in defense against the attacking Japanese.

The enemy quickly eliminated thirty-seven bombers and 104 fighters of the Army Air Forces in the opening phase of the strike. Japanese planes wrecked and burned hangars, storage shops and warehouses, barracks, maintenance shops, fuel and ammunition storage dumps, and other vital installations. "Almost all of the bombs," states the official report of the attack on Wheeler Field, "released at altitudes of 200 to 250 feet, struck with deadly accuracy along the hangar line. They destroyed forty-three airplanes by fire and twenty-nine by other means."

No less than 2,844 men died. Another 1,178 Americans were wounded and maimed.

The Japanese lost twenty-nine aircraft and fifty-five men. No Japanese warship was attacked or even sighted.

The Flying Fortress blundered—helplessly—into the thick of battle.

The twelve B-17Ds assigned to the Hawaiian Air Force miraculously escaped destruction. As quickly as was possible after the initial fury of the Japanese attacks abated they were dispatched, along with anything else that could get into the air, on search missions for the enemy fleet. Their mission proved to be fruitless. The Japanese were already steaming at high speed to clear the area and had taken up a course to the west.

But other Fortresses were embroiled in the fighting—unarmed and helpless. They were the B-17D bombers of the 38th and 88th Reconnaissance. Squadrons that had left Hamilton Field the night before. At the height of the attack against Oahu the Fortresses showed up*—easy targets for the marauding Zero fighters.

Because of the 2,400-mile flight over open water, fuel was the primary consideration. Flying from one American field to another, there did not appear to be any necessity for carrying machine guns when the weight could be put into fuel. As a consequence of this decision (the correct one at the time) the Fortresses were stripped of their armament prior to departing California. So critical was the fuel load that even the weight-and-balance of the Fortresses had been compromised. To compensate for the shifting weight as fuel was consumed, the crews removed the ar-

---

*Official records have never clarified the exact number of B-17Ds on this flight. At one point the official AAF history states that thirteen Fortresses departed Hamilton Field; in the same volume there is the statement that fourteen Fortresses were involved. Other records claim fourteen as the number. What does seem clear is that two Fortresses turned back shortly after takeoff, and that twelve bombers continued to Hawaii—and arrived early December 7th.

mor plating from the rear of each airplane and shifted it forward.

They flew into a buzzsaw. . . .

Precisely at five minutes before eight o'clock the morning of December 7th, 1941, Lieutenant Akira Sakamoto peered through the optical sight of his Aichi 99 dive bomber, and pulled the cable that released his bombs. Immediately behind Sakamoto came another two dozen Aichi's, plunging from the sky in wedges to strike at pre-assigned targets.

At that moment six Flying Fortress bombers cruised toward Hickam Field. In the lead B-17D was the ranking officer of the 88th Reconnaissance Squadron, Major Richard H. Carmichael. Behind his bomber came five more Fortresses of the first flight. The second flight, also with six bombers, was some distance behind them. Carmichael and his crew were tired. They had been in the air for some fourteen hours and the prospect of getting on solid ground appealed greatly to them.

It was a beautiful Sunday morning. The scattered clouds only occasionally hid from view the green of the islands. Several men pointed ahead and to the sides, reporting an unusual number of small planes in the air. The B-17D crewmen grinned. Obviously this was some sort of private pilots' welcome to the Fortresses. Most of the other planes were headed in the same direction, toward Hickam Field.

In fact, some of them had already reached Hickam. At their lead was Lieutenant Commander Kakuichi Takahashi in an Aichi 99 dive bomber, with twenty-five more planes behind him, screaming earthward in perfectly coordinated strikes against the planes, installations and defenses of Hickam. In the few minutes' time between the arrival first of Takahashi, and then Carmichael, Hickam exploded into a holocaust.

Carmichael looked with concern at the diving, swarming airplanes and the huge clouds of black smoke billowing upward from Hickam. From the Fortresses the men saw brilliant flames leaping along the flight line and erupting from hangars and other buildings.

The Fortress pilots would land singly, one at a time, breaking away by prearranged plan from their formation. Dick Carmichael wanted nothing to do at that moment with Hickam. It didn't take long to recognize that between the time he had left California and arrived in Hawaii, all hell had broken loose. That was a full-scale war ahead of them. Carmichael broke away from the pattern at Hickam Field to seek a landing elsewhere. Flying off his wing was Lt. Harold N. Chaffin who felt his best course was to stick with the "old man."

The crews felt naked in the air. At this moment all they could see of the other planes was a constant diving, circling and wheeling pattern as they struck again and again at their targets. Several crewmen called out: "For Christ's sake, they're Japs!" Without a single machine gun aboard the Fortresses, Carmichael and Chaffin kept their fingers crossed that the enemy planes wouldn't pay much attention to them. All they could do was to duck—and run.

Hickam Field lies along the south-central coast of Oahu, close to the city of Honolulu. Carmichael flew to the northeast, with Honolulu off his right wing, to reach Bellows Field. He found that base also being torn up by the attacking Japanese, as was nearby Kaneohe Field. Luck was staying with them; the Japanese still hadn't attacked their defenseless planes. Carmichael, with Chaffin right with him, swung now to the northwest, flying across the center of Oahu to reach Wheeler Field. Again the Fortress crewmen were confronted with huge clouds of smoke billowing upward from the ground. Even the air was becoming more dangerous as the defenders began to throw up a thickening barrage of antiaircraft fire. The men in the bombers could see the long rows of fighters parked on the Wheeler flight line. Row after row of the new P-40 fighters was blazing.

A short distance beyond Wheeler lay an emergency fighter strip marked on the charts as Haleiwa. Their fuel was running low and Carmichael was anxious to get down while they were still free of attack. But Haleiwa was only 1,200 feet in length, an airstrip short even by fighter standards. Carmichael felt there was no choice. He turned into the wind, dropped his gear and flaps, and "dragged" the four-engine bomber onto the runway in near-stall flight. Behind him came Chaffin, dragging in his Fortress. Both men landed safely on the emergency strip in an outstanding feat of airmanship.

The next three bombers, flown by Lieutenants Harry N. Brandon, David G. Rawls, and Robert E. Thacker, received an immediate baptism of fire when the pilots made their decisions to land at Hickam, a move prompted by critically low fuel. The Fortresses shuddered as the pilots brought them down through furious antiaircraft fire from Hickam. The sound of metal tearing into the B-17s was alarming, but even more frightening was the sight of strange Japanese fighters (Zeros) slashing in for their firing runs. There were so many Japanese planes in the air that the Americans seemed to be flying formation with the Japanese dive bombers, whose gunners took the opportunity to hose lead at the big American planes. Miraculously, none of the men aboard the Fortresses were hit and the three bombers managed to reach Hickam safely. The crewmen scrambled from their planes in haste to rush pell-mell for shelter as Zeros strafed them from both sides of the field.

Lt. Frank P. Bostrom, flying the sixth Fortress in the lead flight, ran into the hornets' nest. Confused by the carnage and billowing flames and smoke from Hickam, Bostrom managed finally to reach Hickam Tower. They were somewhat more confused than the Fortress pilot (understandably) and in the fury of the air strikes they advised Bostrom to land from "east to west," adding the prize understatement that the airbase was under attack from "unidentified aircraft."

Bostrom started into the landing pattern, only to be met by a roaring barrage of antiaircraft fire. The dazed gunners on the ground, not waiting to sort out a possibly friendly airplane in a sky filled with Japanese, saw the B-17D as the biggest target in the sky, and blazed away with everything they had. Explosions hammered shock waves against the Fortress and the men winced as pieces of steel slammed into the wings and fuselage. Bostrom didn't stick around long enough to be shot down by friendly antiaircraft fire. He went to full power and "got the hell out," as fast as the airplane could take him and his men. They found momentary respite from attack in nearby clouds. But they had to land; fuel was running low. Bostrom swung out of the clouds and headed for Hickam. This time the tower ordered him not to land.

Bostrom started to circle the field when six Zero fighters decided the Fortress made a far more lucrative target than strafing fighters on the ground. The Japanese fighters rushed in for the attack, hammering the Fortress with machine guns and cannon. At full throttle Bostrom tried to escape, diving as low as he could fly. The Zeros stayed right with him.

Bostrom pounded through the air, the Zeros chasing him almost all the way around Oahu Island. By now they had riddled the defenseless Fortress. The airplane was holed and slashed from nose to tail. The wings looked like sieves. Cannon shells knocked out two engines and Bostrom's copilot hurriedly feathered the propellers.

Bostrom hedgehopped across the island. Finally the Zeros figured the big enemy bomber as certain to crash and they pulled away from the running fight. With two engines dead, the bombers a flying wreck and fuel gauges reading empty, Bostrom looked for a place to land. He selected the nearest open patch of ground—a golf course—and brought the four-engine bomber down to a perfect landing.

Forty minutes behind Carmichael came the second flight of six Fortresses, led by Major Truman H. Landon of the 38th Reconnaissance Squadron. At the moment the six bombers came toward Hickam there was a lull in the waves of bombing strikes by the Japanese. Lieutenant Bruce Allen lost no time in setting up his approach and getting on the ground as quickly as possible; he landed without incident. Two more B-17Ds made it onto the runway without any more difficulty than flying through thick smoke and dodging holes and wreckage on the runway.

Then the next wave of Japanese bombers and fighters arrived and, explosively, all hell broke loose. The Fortress flown by Lt. Karl T. Barthelmess found itself with an escort of Japanese dive bombers, whose gunners loosed long bursts at the American bomber. A few Zeroes got in their licks, and then turned their attention to the B-17D flown by Captain Raymond Swenson. No one suffered any injuries during the approach and landing. But even as Swenson tramped on the brakes the Zero fighters came in low and fast, tearing hell out of the Fortress. The men dashed away from their airplane as Japanese cannon shells blew the fuselage in half. All but one man made it safely to shelter. The Zeros killed Flight Surgeon William R. Shick as he scrambled away from the wrecked airplane.

Last in line of the six Fortresses was Lt. Robert H. Richards. He never made it to the Hickam runway. Zeros came in fast and hard, hosing lead and cannon shells from nose to tail. In one long pass two fighters shot away the ailerons of the Fortress, damaged the plane heavily, and severely wounded two crew members. At full throttle Richards ran for safety across southern Oahu. He made it to the fighter runway at Bellows Field where he brought the bomber in, downwind, on the short 2,600-foot strip. The Fortress skidded to a stop on its belly just off the strip, its men finally safe.

Twelve new Fortresses reached Oahu. Only one was destroyed, and three were badly damaged (the three planes were repaired and returned to service). Considering the circumstances of their arrival it was a miracle that greater loss of life, and aircraft, had not been the final results.

In the Philippines, time was running out. Thirty-five of the heavy bombers were on alert, guns mounted and loaded. With those Fortresses, AAF officials reasoned, we would be able to strike heavily against the invaders. There was plenty of warning. There were fighters to protect the fields. Even if we had been struck with disaster at Oahu, the Philippines would be a different story.

It was.

It was worse.

# CHAPTER II

# THE WEARY ONES

THE BEGINNING OF WAR in the Philippines, where the United States had assembled its most powerful force of heavy bombers, was a tragedy made up of indecision, superb Japanese tactics, and an extraordinary run of ill luck. The combination of all these factors in just a few hours broke the back of American airpower in the Philippines, handed air superiority to the enemy with only a minimum of cost, and left the area wide open to Japanese invasion. There would be some resistance, at times fierce, but for the most part ineffectual, and the Japanese were going to have things pretty much their own way. Few Americans realized this during the opening hours of what would become 1,351 days of combat with the Japanese, but the lessons applied by the enemy began to sink in quickly. It started on December 8 (December 7, Pearl Harbor time) in a fitful and spasmodic series of operations. When it ended both the day and the future belonged to the Japanese.

What happened elsewhere on this day helps to place in a clearer perspective the events within the Philippines, and also emphasizes why the loss of the striking force of Flying Fortresses in the Philippines, without ready replacement, set the stage for future Japanese victories.

On the first day of war in the Pacific, Japanese military forces—

Smashed at Wake Island with a large formation of heavy bombers . . .

Attacked the island of Guam with eighteen bombers and ordered into action its invasion fleet which, in the next three days, would overrun the American base . . .

Struck with heavy bomber formations against British defenses on the islands of Nauru and Ocean, lying between the Solomon and Gilbert Island chain . . .

Bombed the island of Hong Kong, and dispatched a strong force of troops against Kowloon on the mainland opposite Hong Kong, thereby wrecking carefully prepared defense plans . . .

Swept through the International Settlement at Shanghai and captured the crew of HMS *Petrel* . . .

Rushed aboard the American gunboat *Wake* and, *while the crew slept*, captured the warship intact; with a fine sense of irony the Japanese recommissioned the *Wake* in their own Navy as the *Tataru* . . .

Sortied an invasion fleet along the east coast of Malaya; troops milled ashore from six transports and two destroyers at Singora and Patani. Other troops started a swift dash across the Kra Isthmus . . .

Sent large bodies of troops across the borders of French Indo-China (previously occupied by the Japanese through agreements with the French), into Thailand (Siam), meeting only light and sporadic resistance . . .

Attacked Singapore with powerful formations of dive

and attack bombers and escorting Zero fighters from aircraft carriers cruising offshore . . .

Smashed against British defenses at Kota Bahru, Malaya, in the face of unexpectedly stiff resistance. Preceding the invasion was a powerful barrage from an invasion fleet of heavy warships; forty dive bombers shattered installations at the Kota Bahru airfield to destroy most of the British airpower in the immediate area . . .

Sank a crippling percentage of Allied merchantmen discovered by their aircraft and fleet units, including three American, forty-one British, one Greek, and seven Panamanian cargo vessels. A bare 200,000 tons of shipping slipped away from the Philippines beneath marauding Japanese planes . . .

Eliminated the Hawaiian Islands as a source of danger or interference to Japanese operations elsewhere in the Pacific and in Asia, and in so doing wrecked much of the Pacific battle fleet and inflicted crippling losses on AAF and Naval airpower . . .

Cut communications and supply lines across most of the Pacific . . .

And, in the Philippines, smashed American air strength on the island of Luzon by wiping out a major force of fighters, heavy bombers, and other aircraft and devastating air defense and ground facilities . . .

That was on the *first* day of the war.

On the morning of December 8, 1941, there were thirty-five Flying Fortress bombers in the Philippines. Two squadrons with a total of nineteen B-17Ds were at Clark Field, near Manila, and two squadrons had flown their Fortresses southward to Del Monte, Mindanao. Of the thirty-five airplanes two could not get off the ground because of lack of spare parts and maintenance.

Shortly after three o'clock the morning of December 8 (it was then 8:30 A.M. at Oahu, where the Japanese had been pounding their targets for thirty-five minutes) telephones in the American barracks began ringing. Excited pilots, officers, and ground crewmen—anyone who could get to a phone—shouted the news. Had they heard the radio? Pearl Harbor was under attack! The commercial stations had been breaking into their scheduled broadcasts with news bulletins. War had broken out.

At Far East Air Force Headquarters, officers on duty relayed the flash to their commanders. What about word from military command at Pearl Harbor?

Not a sound. There was no message from any official military or diplomatic source. FEAF tried to contact Hawaii for confirmation; nothing. They couldn't get through. Anything from Australia? Nothing confirmed. Wild rumors— and the alarming sound of the news bulletins. But nothing *official*.

No matter. At least where putting up your guard is concerned you don't *ignore* news bulletins that all hell has broken loose and you're at war. Immediately the Philippines command ordered full military alert.

At three-thirty A.M. the Iba radar station along the coast of northwestern Luzon flashed the warning of unidentified aircraft coming in from the north. Position: seventy-five miles offshore. Course: dead-on for Corregidor.

The 3rd Pursuit Squadron scrambled its P-40s. In the darkness the fighters passed almost directly beneath the Mitsubishi Type 96 reconnaissance bombers, which broke off to the west, without being intercepted.

The rest of the night was spent sorting out rumors and expressing disbelief—by the bomber crews—that they were doing nothing against the enemy and were not allowed to do anything. The powerful force of B-17Ds remained chained to the ground.

*Rainbow 5*, the standing plan for action in the event of war, went unexecuted. Time began to slip away swiftly from the bombers. Time was changing to an ally of the Japanese.

In the event of hostile acts by the Japanese—construed as to mean open attack—*Rainbow 5* was to be put into action. A strong force of Flying Fortresses was to take off at once from the Philippines and strike at Japanese installations on Formosa, where the Japanese Navy had five major airfields from which to launch its air strikes southward. There were also harbors teeming with Japanese cargo ships, transports, and warships.

General Brereton, at Nielson when word of the strike against Pearl Harbor first came in, flashed the word to his men to prepare for *Rainbow 5*. Takao Harbor in Formosa was to be the initial target. Unfortunately, FEAF Headquarters didn't have a single reconnaissance photograph of Formosa. There weren't any maps. It would be striking in the blind. Yet even that was acceptable, because the bombers sent out would attack "targets of opportunity," which might be anything from a sampan to a carrier, and obtain reconnaissance that was needed desperately. Thinking about the myopia under which he would have to function, Brereton also ordered three Fortresses equipped with cameras for reconnaissance missions. Brereton then reported to MacArthur's headquarters at Fort Santiago where he met with Brigadier General R. K. Sutherland, MacArthur's Chief of Staff, to obtain official authorization for the Formosa missions.

By 5:30 A.M. the word was official—war. That ended all questions. The Fortresses were rushed to battle-ready condition. Men checked their guns, engineers swarmed over the planes, the pilots reported they were ready and "loaded for bear."

At eight A.M. Brereton returned to his headquarters. His operations staff waited eagerly for the news of the strikes.

Brereton gave them the stunning orders that the Fortresses would not, repeat *not*, take any offensive action against Formosa. The Philippines were a commonwealth under the protection of the United States. The Philippines had not been attacked. Technically they had no argument with the Japanese; technically, they were still a neutral nation. If the Fortresses used Philippines bases from which to attack the Japanese, then the United States could be involving in a war a nation against which the Japanese might not have planned an invasion.

It *was* incredible, of course. The men who listened to Brereton's report couldn't believe what they were hearing. But the general, openly bitter and dismayed, left no word for argument. "The word," he said, "is that we can't attack until we're fired on."

His staff shared his dismay and their own incredulity deepened. It *couldn't* be true! But it was. The single greatest hope of the Philippines, the offensive power of the B-17D bombers, had been struck down far more effectively than could have been achieved by a Japanese raid.

Approximately at nine A.M., one hour after Brereton returned to his headquarters, the Japanese made their move in heavy strength against the Philippines. Fighters scrambled to meet the oncoming enemy. Still there were no orders for heavy bombers.

At Clark Field, Major Dave Gibbs, operations officer of the 19th Bombardment Group, decided to take matters into his own hands. Colonel Eubank was absent from the field, meeting with Brereton. Gibbs had an instant nightmare of the Fortresses being caught on the ground while the Japanese pounded them to wreckage. He ordered every bomber into the air (bombs were *not* to be loaded) to increase their chances for survival. With loaded guns and full crews, the Fortresses were to stay out of the way of Japanese attacks, and at the same time patrol the waters around Luzon for enemy surface forces.

By 9:10 A.M. fifty-four American planes were in the air. Anti-aircraft units were on full alert. Thirty-six more fighters were held at "instant readiness" to scramble if any intercepts were made.

Twenty minutes later, still entirely free of interception, Japanese bombers ripped up military installations at Baguio to the north of Manila. Airfields south of Baguio, at Cabanatuan, also took a pounding.

Two hours later the radar stations flashed the word of another enemy attack, this time confirmed as coming from over the China Sea. Curtiss P-40E Kittyhawks were circling the field, gear down, setting up their landing pattern, when bombs rained down from the skies. The Japanese chewed up Iba Airfield, shot down five Kittyhawks (three more crashed, out of fuel), and went home without loss.

At twenty minutes past noon, thick dust and haze at Del Carmen was causing long delays in getting fighters into the air. At Clark Field all but two of the nineteen Fortresses were on the ground. Of these seventeen bombers, three were taxiing out to the runway to take off for the long-delayed photographic mission to Formosa. The remaining fourteen were well dispersed, in revetments for bomb protection, while armorers were loading 100- and 300- pound bombs for future attacks the men knew were now inevitable.

But the field, with its bombers and fighters, was naked to any incoming raiders. Dust chained the 34th Squadron to the ground at Del Carmen, and at Clark itself the fighters of the 20th Pursuit Squadron were still refueling. In the emergency, mechanics jerked out the fuel hoses and, with partially filled tanks, the pilots rushed to get into the air to meet a new raid. Four fighters made it into the air before the first wave of fifty-four Japanese bombers arrived overhead to start the destruction of Clark Field. After nearly twenty minutes of bombing a swarm of Zero fighters came in on the deck and shot up anything in sight for more than an hour.

It was a slaughter—in the air and on the ground. What fighters escaped Japanese bombs were torn to ribbons by the Zeros. The air belonged to the Japanese and they made the most of their advantage. Miraculously, every B-17 escaped destruction from the rain of bombs. But what the twin-engine raiders couldn't do the Zero pilots were out to accomplish. They swept up and down the field and its perimeter, unbelievable in their slow, measured firing passes. One by one the Fortresses were holed, shattered and set aflame. It was methodical destruction executed in flawless manner.

"On the ground," notes the official history of the AAF, "personnel of the Far East Air Force fought back as best they could in a hopelessly unequal struggle. Though some units almost completely disintegrated during nearly two hours of attack, there were countless examples of outstanding leadership and heroism."[30]

Flying Fortresses were turned into improvised anti-aircraft stations as crewmen ran to their planes and swung their weapons around to bear on the low-flying Zeros. Lt. Fred Crimmins (subsequently cited for heroism) tried vainly to save one blazing Fortress in the path of the Japanese fighters and was hit, suffering multiple wounds from which he barely recovered. Among the B-17 crewmen was Pfc Greely B. Williams who remained at his gun within a Fortress, despite several wounds, firing steadily until a Zero's strafing pass ended his life.

Of the two Fortresses in the air during the devastating assault against Clark, the first, flown by Lt. John Carpenter, missed attack from the Zeros. Carpenter had been out on a reconnaissance mission and returned to Clark Field after the Japanese fighters finished their grisly job. The second bomber under command of Lt. Earl Tash, stumbled into the thick of the slaughter and received the immediate attention of three Zeros. They swarmed all over the Fortress, inflicting severe damage. Tash ran to the south for safety; the Zeros, under orders to remain at Clark Field, broke off the attack and returned to their strafing.

By the end of the day one third of all the fighters in the Philippines had been destroyed. Dozens of other planes were burned-out wrecks. Airfield installations, supplies, forts, communications centers and other facilities had been smashed.

Of the nineteen Flying Fortresses at Clark Field, only one airplane was still able to fly; two to four bombers might be rebuilt from the wreckage of the others.

In one blow the Japanese had wiped out half the heavy bomber strength in the far Pacific.

One of the grave questions surrounding the events of the opening day of war in the Philippines—involving the destruction of half the B-17s in the islands, as well as the failure to strike at the Japanese when the moment was at its best—may never be answered. But in reviewing the history of the Fortress it is essential that this aspect of what took place on December 8 (Philippines time) be examined.

For the events that transpired, *and those that were pre-vented from taking place*, profoundly altered the course of the entire war.

There is, first, the inescapable fact that despite the opportunity that was provided, the United States lost the precious advantage it had in failing to blunt, and perhaps even wreck, the carefully planned strike of the Japanese against the Philippines from their Formosa bases. We were fully aware of the location of those bases; for approximately two weeks prior to the Japanese attacks, Navy PBY flying boats had flown reconnaissance missions over Formosa, dodging through clouds to escape Japanese fighters.

The Japanese were convinced that the Americans had gained full knowledge of their five major air bases. They expected to be attacked. The Japanese knew of the Fortresses on Luzon, which they considered a critical danger to their plans.

Commander Masatake Okumiya of the Japanese Naval Intelligence:

Early in the morning of December 8, 1941, thick fog rolled in from the sea completely to shroud our air bases on Formosa. On the very first day of the war, when a coordinated effort was of the utmost importance, our planes could not leave their fields. We cursed and fumed, for even as we paced helplessly in the swirling gloom the Nagumo task force planes turned Pearl Harbor into a shambles. If the enemy in the Philippines had the opportunity to counterattack quickly, he could disrupt completely our carefully laid plans. Finally the initial reports of the Pearl Harbor raid reached us through Tokyo; still the fog did not lift.

The commander of the 23rd Air Flotilla, which was attached to the 11th Air Fleet of the Japanese Navy at Takao,

Formosa, provided a second viewpoint in a statement to
the U.S. Strategic Bombing Survey:

> We greatly feared an American raid, and when heavy
> fog kept us on the ground we became very nervous about it.
>
> Our fears increased at eight A.M. when we intercepted
> American radio transmissions indicating that B-17s were
> heading toward Formosa.
>
> At 10:10 A.M., a Japanese pilot erroneously reported the
> approach of B-17s. We expected the worst, and put on gas
> masks in preparation for an immediate attack.
>
> Immediately thereafter, the fog having lifted somewhat,
> all planes took off for the Philippines. *We were amazed to
> find the American planes lined up on Clark Field.*

By what farce of reasoning could MacArthur's headquarters have *ordered* that the Fortresses not strike at Formosa? The heavy concentrations of Japanese bombers and
fighters on the ground, loaded with fuel and ammunition,
provided a prime situation for a devastating holocaust that
could have broken the back of the Japanese air strength
that was assigned to smash our resistance in the Philippines.

But even before this question may be answered there is
another matter to consider. Brereton has stated that he
wanted to send out a reconnaissance mission, that he had
nothing in the way of aerial reconnaissance pictures or
charts of the enemy installations. Yet the Navy had obtained this vital data weeks before! Somewhere along the
line, obviously, there lay a disastrous gap in liaison between our own headquarters.

We have already examined the position of General
MacArthur that he had no right to jeopardize the position
of the "neutral" Philippines by using Luzon bases for a

strike against Japanese targets. The folly of such reasoning is clear, but MacArthur's headquarters ran the show, and Brereton could only follow his orders.

General Brereton in his diary stated explicitly that the need for such an attack was glaringly obvious, and that he had requested of MacArthur's chief of staff, General Sutherland, the permission to carry out the strike.

Not without some acid, General MacArthur responded to Brereton's claims in a statement made in Tokyo that stunned Air Force historians:

"I wish to state that General Brereton never recommended an attack on Formosa to me and I know nothing of such a recommendation having been made . . . ; that he has never spoken of the matter to me either before or after the Clark Field attack; that an attack on Formosa with its heavy air concentrations by his small bomber force without fighter support which, because of the great distances involved, was impossible, would have had no chance of success; that in the short interval of time involved it is doubtful that an attack could have been set up and mounted before the enemy's arrival."

There is little doubt that Brereton and the other air leaders in the Philippines were at severe odds with MacArthur on these points. And it is significant that MacArthur had already conceded, without any attempt to obtain information to support his conclusions, that the Japanese would be in the air and on their way to the Philippines before the Fortresses could strike. But if this were so, why the reluctance to violate a diplomatic nicety by striking first from the Philippines which, as he conceded, was certain to be struck by the Japanese—and within only a few hours!

There exists another serious mistake in General MacArthur's reasoning which has received little attention and deserves more. Because it is obvious that faulty reasoning formed the basis for a series of conclusions, all of which rested on an initial false premise.

MacArthur stated that "the enemy's bombers from Formosa had fighter protection available in their attack on Clark Field from their air carriers. . . ."

Let's stop right there. MacArthur referred to a fighter-escort mission between the Philippines and Formosa, "because of the great distance involved," as "impossible." This was the accepted thinking in MacArthur's headquarters. It was also accepted that the Japanese used aircraft carriers for their fighters in the Philippines.

In other words, if American fighters could not fly nonstop between the Philippines and Formosa, and return, *then it was obvious that the Japanese could not do the same.*

*But the Japanese could—and did.*

Years afterward MacArthur was still insisting that there were Japanese aircraft carriers involved in the Philippines operation. There weren't; the records show that quite clearly.

Firm conclusions based on faulty knowledge, and a total ignorance of operating capabilities of the Zero fighter (which had been flying in combat for more than a year, in China, before the attack on the Philippines), led MacArthur's staff into disastrous miscalculations in their air operations.

At Clark Field men did their best to restore the smoking, gutted shambles to an operational air base. With many of the engineering and maintenance shops destroyed, trying to save the few airplanes left was a task demanding superhuman effort, the ability to work without sleep, and mechanical genius. Most of the hangars were gone, and the men worked out in the open, maddened by swarms of flies that settled thickly on the field. While the mechanics struggled to piece together three or four Fortresses which might be able to fly, others sifted through the debris to restore communications and other vital operational facilities. The main runway was cratered and holed and littered with debris. The men filled in holes until they had a single runway about 2,000 feet in length. That was all. Beyond that one strip the pilots of the B-17s had to weave and dodge to avoid craters and huge chunks of concrete and metal.

The field was short-handed. Many men were still missing; they had bolted for the hills during the Japanese bombing and strafing. There were many dead, more wounded. Others had worked and slaved around the clock and were faltering from exhaustion. They knew they had to prepare the field for operations. Six hundred miles to the south, we still had Fortresses unscarred by the Japanese attacks. Those bombers would be staging into Clark for attacks against the Japanese. A few had already gone out, on December 9th, for reconnaissance missions. They carried a few bombs "just in case." But there were no attacks.

Still shaken by the opening Japanese assault, the men did not doubt that the invasion would soon come. The air was thick with rumors of vast Japanese forces. Naval intelligence later reported that "an extraordinary crop of incorrect enemy information" came into headquarters, including accounts of "enemy sightings when nothing was actually sighted and when a vessel was really seen she was usually reported in one of two categories: irrespective of size, she was either a Transport or a Battleship." (As it turned out, the Japanese did not commit to their Philippines operation any battleships or aircraft carriers.)

The bulk of the reconnaissance missions to obtain accurate information on enemy movements fell to Navy PBY flying boats and to the P-40 fighters of the AAF. Early on December 9th Major Cecil Combs led six Fortresses, each loaded with twenty 100-pound bombs, on a "blind hunt" for the Japanese near Catanduanes. Having failed to sight the enemy Combs went on to Clark Field, where the formation landed. Immediately they were refueled and sent out again, to cruise away from Clark in order that they would not fall prey to Japanese bombs or Zero fighters. They were to return to Clark after nightfall.

Also on December 9th, Major Emmett O'Donnell's 14th Squadron with seven Fortresses flew up from Mindanao. Clark Field tower warned O'Donnell away from the field and they went on to San Marcelino. As Harold Mansfield relates:

> At dusk in a coastal valley off to the southwest, where no B-17 had landed before, they squashed down on tall grass. Filipino guards peppered them with bullets on their way in. The men spent the night in their planes, or in the dew under the wings. "Can we take off from here?" the crew asked.
>
> "We got in. We can get out," said O'Donnell.
>
> "The wind is against us."
>
> "From now on winds don't matter."
>
> At 4 A.M. O'Donnell said he was going into Clark Field to get orders. He took off into jet-black night, made a forty-five degree turn where he knew there was a hill, and climbed on out. When he got into Clark, he radioed his squadron to follow at dawn.[31]

Units of the Japanese Third Fleet were landing troops and equipment at Aparri in the extreme northern section of Luzon, and at Vigan on the northwest coast. The major invasion yet to come, the AAF reasoned (correctly, as it turned out), would be at Lingayen Gulf. The Japanese fleet split into the Aparri and Vigan invasion fleets, while a third force, primarily of warships, stood by to apply its firepower wherever it might be needed.

At six A.M. on December 10th, Major Cecil Combs led five Fortresses from the wreckage of Clark Field. Still carrying their loads of twenty 100-pounders per airline they raced to Vigan. En route they rendezvoused with P-40E Kittyhawk fighters of the 17th Pursuit Squadron.

The Fortresses selected as their targets a group of transports unloading troops and supplies. The pilots elected not to attack in the "mass pattern" for which the Fortress had been intended, but went in either solo or in twos, and at altitudes extending from 7,000 to 12,500 feet, releasing long strings of their small bombs. Below them the Kittyhawks of the 17th Squadron, and ancient P-35s of the 34th Pursuit Squadron, went in at minimum altitude to strafe the Japanese and draw anti-aircraft fire away from the bombers.

When the strike ended three American fighters had been shot down. One Japanese transport exploded and rolled over, sinking almost immediately, with a heavy loss of life to the troops still aboard. It was the only loss to the Japanese from troops still aboard. It was the only loss to the Japanese from an attack by five heavy bombers and a swarm of fighters.

Another bombing mission scheduled for that morning, to coordinate with Combs' strike at Vigan, had been delayed by the necessity of staging O'Donnell's bombers into Clark Field.[32] The big Fortresses slid into the runway at Clark two and three at a time, staging in low and cautiously to avoid the attention of prowling Zero fighters. It took expert piloting by the Fortress pilots to bring their heavy planes down on the short strip cleared by the sur-

vivors at Clark. As quickly as the planes taxied off the runway they were moved to protected dispersal areas for
bombing-up. The pilots assembled for a briefing by Colonel
Gene Eubank, 19th B.G. commander.

A warning of large Japanese bomber formations on the
way to Clark interrupted the bomb-loading; to protect the
Fortresses they were ordered into the air immediately. Five
B-17Ds took off one after the other. The first three air-
planes, piloted by O'Donnell, Captain E. L. Parsel, and Lt.
G. R. Montgomery, headed for the invasion beachhead at
Vigan.

First over the target area, O'Donnell went into a bombing run from 25,000 feet. He spotted a huge ship below.
"My God," O'Donnell exclaimed to his crew, "I think it's a
carrier. Let's take it." They ended their first bomb run with
monumental frustration from a stuck bomb release mechanism—and no bombs dropped. For the next forty-five minutes, flying at successively lower altitudes, O'Donnell and
his crew tried to get their bombs on target. Japanese antiaircraft blazed away at them, upsetting the aim of the
bombardier and forcing repeated runs over the enemy
ships. The Fortress roared in for another run and the faulty
mechanism hung up most of the bombs. Again and again
during those forty-five minutes O'Donnell returned
doggedly to the attack (during which the "enemy aircraft
carrier" mysteriously failed to send up any defending
fighters). The combination of Japanese flak and faulty
equipment defeated him—none of his eight 600-pound
bombs struck a ship.

Parsel made his try from 12,500 feet against a warship
his crew judged to be either a cruiser or a destroyer. Four
300-pound bombs produced spuming columns of water instead of hits. On a second run during which three more
bombs were dropped, they again missed their target ship.

One bomb, however, was reported to have struck a transport. (The Japanese denied that any hit was made; examination of their records confirms that Parsle did not hit any targets.)

Montgomery showed up with only one 600-pound bomb in his airplane. He missed.

The two remaining Fortresses left Clark Field at 9:30 A.M. Lt. G. E. Schaetzel headed for the Aparri invasion force and made an attack from 25,000 feet. The bombs were released against a cluster of transports, the crew claiming the bombs exploded "in the midst" of the enemy vessels. (Again the Japanese, after the war, produced records to show that no ship was struck in this attack.) Schaetzel ran into more bad luck; Zero fighters from Formosa arrived on the scene as he made his bomb run and cut the Fortress to ribbons. By "a miracle, no one was hit," and Schaetzel managed his escape, landing at San Marcelino.

The fifth bomber departing that morning from Clark Field was piloted by Captain Colin Kelly, who had been ordered to seek out and attack a Japanese "aircraft carrier previously reported along the northern Luzon coast." With three 600-pounders aboard Kelly completed his search pattern without sighting the enemy carrier. Finally navigator Joe M. Bean sighted a "concentration of enemy ships"—*officially* reported as consisting of a 29,000-ton battleship of the *Kongo* class, six cruisers, ten destroyers, and from fifteen to twenty transports. (There was no battleship below. Instead of the seventeen warships and twenty transports reported by Kelly's crew, the invasion force, as Japanese records showed, was made up of *one* cruiser, six destroyers, and four transports.)

Kelly set up his bombing run at 22,000 feet over the "giant battleship." Sergeant Meyer S. Levin released in train the three 600-pound bombs; the crew later reported that two bombs straddled the target and one exploded dead-center on the warship. They said the "battleship" had come to a dead stop in the water, was trailing oil and burning. It was somewhat of an exaggeration; the cruiser had not been hit.

Official reports of the attack only compounded the false reports of striking the target—and increased wildly the extent of the "damage." An Army communique of December 10th from Nanila stated that Kelly had attacked a battleship of the 29,000-ton class and "scored three direct hits and two very close alongside. When the bomber left the battleship was blazing fiercely."

It should be noted that Kelly had managed to score three direct hits and two near-hits with only *three* bombs. . . . And for the record, the *Haruna*, which the Army identified as having been sunk, was then steaming unharmed off Malaya, where it remained until December 18. (To add to the hysterical tone of battle reports, the Navy on December 11th claimed one of its lumbering Catalinas had also bombed another 29,000-ton battleship and had left it flaming and stopped dead in the water. That made *two* battleships sunk where there had been none.)

The first indication the Japanese had of Kelly's attack was when three towering columns of water appeared near their invasion force. The pilots of twenty-seven Zero fighters circling at 18,000 feet were startled to notice the water rings on the ocean—*their* first warning that the enemy was nearby. Kelly was still 4,000 feet above the Zeros and fleeing at high speed when the Japanese pilots sighted his Fortress. Three Zeros remained over the invasion force, while the other two dozen fighters raced after the bomber.

Kelly was about sixty miles from Clark Field when several Zeros, one piloted by Saburo Sakai, closed to firing distance. Three fighters swept ahead, peeled off and made head-on firing passes, fortunately with poor aim. Seven fighters then rushed at the Fortress. Each Zero peeled off from a loose formation and made a diving firing pass from above and behind. By the time the ten fighters had completed their attacks Kelly was almost over Clark Field. The Japanese pilots were amazed that the bomber still flew. They had poured bullets and cannon shells directly into the Fortress, apparently with little serious effect. Instead of falling from the sky in flames the big airplane flew on, seemingly unperturbed by the attacks.

Kelly pushed the B-17D into a shallow dive, picking up speed as he raced for safety within a thick overcast. Sakai and two Zeros continued to give chase, going to full power and diving after their quarry. Sakai slipped beneath the Fortress and then came in from beneath and to the rear. Unknown to Sakai, the B-17's radioman had left his belly gun position to contact Clark tower. That proved the undoing of the bomber. Unnoticed by the crew Sakai came up to point-blank range.

The first warning of the renewed attack came with the shuddering impact and explosions of cannon shells within the fuselage. Kelly walked his rudder back and forth to give his waist gunners a crack at the fighter, but it was too late. Sakai watched chunks of metal explode off the right wing, and then a thin white film trailed behind the plane. The Zero bored in, Sakai snapping out short bursts. Then flame appeared within the fuselage.

His ammunition exhausted, Sakai rolled away to permit the fighter behind him to attack. It was a wasted maneuver; the Fortress was doomed. The flames spread rapidly and the second Zero pulled up in a steep climb, the pilot half-rolling to watch what was happening. Three men bailed out from the bomber before it disappeared within the overcast.

Five men bailed out successfully. The left waist gunner had been killed in Sakai's attack. Kelly and his copilot, Lt. Donald D. Robins, were bailing out when a tremendous explosion tore apart the blazing Fortress. Robins was thrown clear and pulled his ripcord; his parachute opened safely. Kelly's body struck the ground near where the Fortress crashed; his parachute was still unopened.

That was the first B-17 lost in attacks against the Japanese. A second was soon to follow. Lt. Montgomery, who had made his attack earlier that day with a single 600-pound bomb, returned to Clark and took on twenty 100-pound bombs. He made a hurried takeoff to follow Schaetzel and Kelly. When he arrived at Aparri he failed to sight the other two Fortresses; he made his bombing run over the beaches for the greatest possible effect. His crew claimed one ship afire, but this could not be confirmed. Montgomery returned to Clark Field, somehow remaining clear of the Zero fighters. Clark Tower ordered him to abort his planned landing and return to Del Monte.

Luck ran out for the Fortress on the southward run. Darkness fell and with it came unexpected storms. The bomber rocked and pitched in severe turbulence. Their anticipated time of arrival at Del Monte came and passed and Montgomery knew they had missed the field. Several times they tried to find their home base but without avail. Then, with minimum fuel left, Montgomery went out to sea. Four miles offshore, in a howling rainstorm, he dropped the Fortress into the water in a perfect ditching. There was enough time for everyone to get into life rafts and paddle safely to shore.

That was the closing episode for B-17 operations from Clark Field. So shattered was the air base it could no longer be used for staging bombers through for flights to the north. The Japanese had devastated the American fighters trying to protect the Fortresses and there was no air cover from the attacks of Japanese bombers and strafing missions by the Zeros. Without fighter cover the remaining handful of Fortresses could never survive.

There was another matter to be considered. The bombers were being wasted in their missions:

> The employment of heavy bombers on December 10 bore little resemblance to prescribed AAF practice, which called for their use against shipping targets in flights of sufficient size to assure a pattern of bombing large enough to cover any possible move of the target in the interval between release and impact of the bombs. Not only was there an inadequate number of planes available, but unsatisfactory communications with outlying fields, insufficient protection of airfields, and the consequent necessity of putting planes into the air for their security added to the difficulty of maintaining anything approaching standard operations. . . . with the rapid depletion of our interceptor forces and with Japanese landings promising the early establishment on Luzon of enemy land-based aviation, it was already apparent that American bomber operations would be still further restricted.[33]

The bomber pilots received their orders. Fall back to Del Monte, six hundred miles to the south.

The Fortresses abandoned Clark Field.

The sighting of Japanese convoys sliding up the coasts of Luzon—at Zambales on the west and at Legaspi on the southeast—brought the Fortress quickly back into battle. On December 12th Major Combs flew a single-plane mission against enemy transports at Vigan; the unhappy crew made no claims for hits. Two days later, on the 14th, six Fortresses were readied for a strike against invasion forces at Legaspi.

Lieutenant James T. Connally was at the controls of the first B-17D taking off. A tire exploded during the takeoff roll. Connally saved the airplane and got it onto the taxiway. Lieutenants Lee B. Coats and Walter Ford made it into the air, but returned when their planes suffered engine trouble. That left three to go, flown by Lieutenants Jack Adams, Elliot Vandevanter and Hewitt T. Wheless. The latter pilot lost an engine and started down; at 10,000 feet Wheless managed to get the engine going again. In murky weather he proceeded to the target area, following the other two planes that had gone ahead.

Vandevanter made three bombing runs over a beach reported to be swarming with Japanese troops, equipment and ships. From 20,000 feet he dropped his bombs and then set course for Del Monte, free from attack by the Zeros.

Adams wasn't so fortunate. Zeros ripped into his Fortress as he released his bombs. Adams went into a steep dive for thick clouds two miles below with the Zeros cutting in close for their attacks. They wounded two men and shot out two engines. Adams ran for the beach at Masbate, couldn't find a level area of sand, and headed for a rice paddy beyond the beach where he bellied in the bomber. The crew pulled the two wounded men from the Fortress as the Zeros swept back and forth in strafing runs. When the Zeros left finally, Adams set the B-17 on fire to keep it from falling into Japanese hands. He and his crew were picked up by Filipino guerrillas, served as impromptu draftees in the artillery and infantry, and made their way eventually back to Del Monte.

"Shortie" Wheless was to be awarded the Distinguished Service Cross for his mission. Harold Mansfield recalls:

... Wheless got separated from his mates in low clouds. He went on alone. He was on his bomb run at 9,500 feet, when eighteen fighters swarmed him. Four of them closed in, one on each side, two on the tail. Gunners in the Fortress poured it to them. One of the fighters went down. Wheless called back to his crew, "You're getting 'em. You're getting 'em."

Then Private Killin, the radio operator, was killed at the belly gun. Navigator Meenaugh came to take his place, shouting, "I'll pay 'em back."

The fighter on the other side dropped away in a smoke-trailing spin. More explosive bursts came through the sides of the ship. Both waist gunners were wounded and had to leave their posts. Sergeant John Gootee, with a bullet in his right wrist, grabbed one of the guns with his left hand, swung it after a fighter. The two fighters on their trail were riddling them mercilessly. With the ship holding straight on the bomb run, the side gunners couldn't reach them.

"Bombs away."

Wheless hit the rudder and swung the ship sideways to give the gunners a chance to pick off one of the pursuits on the tail. Bombardier Schlotte came back to lend Gootee a hand at the side guns. Fifteen fighters remained, attacking in waves, in a bedlam of noise and action. The belly gun had been shot out. Gootee got another fighter, then his gun jammed. Number one engine was dead. Everything was riddled. Finally all the guns were shot out of action or jammed. They sat back and took it.

Twenty-five minutes after the running battle started, the Japanese fighters were silent, out of ammunition. Some of them came up close to look in the windows. The radio was destroyed; one fuel tank ripped wide open but not on fire; oxygen system shot away; front tires shot flat; two thirds of the control cables shattered; side walls a sieve; but they were staying in the air, droning on at low altitude.

At dusk they sighted Mindanao. Drizzling rains obscured the hills ahead. Wheless sighted a small airfield near the beach and headed his crippled ship for it. Too late he saw the field was barricaded. They smashed on through, rolled two hundred yards on flat tires, then the wheels locked. They stubbed up on the nose and settled down again to rest. Seven shaken and injured men climbed out and patted the battered ship. "Good old gal. Wonderful gal."[34]

The end was in sight. The Japanese ruled the air over Luzon and had moved fighters into the airfields captured near Aparri and Vigan. Land-based Zeros, with their extreme range, meant the Japanese would quickly control all the Philippines. Moving the Fortresses 600 miles south to Del Monte no longer guaranteed the protection of distance—they were still an easy mark for the Zeros.

On December 16th FEAF made its decision—fall back another 1,500 miles to Darwin, Australia. The next day the first of the remaining B-17D bombers began the withdrawal. It wasn't a moment too soon. On December 19th a dozen Zeros swept low over Del Monte, caught three Douglas B-18s out in the open, and shot them into blazing wrecks. The B-17Ds still on the field, dispersed and buried beneath coconut leaves, escaped detection by the Japanese. That night most of the Fortresses, loaded with men, took off for Australia. By the 21st of December the survivors of the 19th Bomb Group, fourteen Fortresses in all, were at Batchelor Field near Darwin.

The AAF official history notes that:

In spite of the decision to transfer all heavy bombers to Australia, there was no intention of abandoning the defense of the Philippines. The morale of officers and men on Luzon remained high, in part at least because they constantly expected the arrival of reinforcements. According to one writer, the Army at this time traveled as much on rumors as on its stomach. . . . There was news that the Navy was coming to the rescue, "sweeping everything before it."[35]

But the Navy wasn't coming, and all that was left to strike back at the Japanese were the fourteen surviving B-17D bombers. The day after the Fortresses completed their evacuation to Australia, nine B-17Ds left Batchelor Field to attack Japanese shipping at Davao in the Philippines. Late in the day, with the light failing, and the sky filled with a growing storm, the Fortress pilots were forced to seek out holes in the clouds to drop their bombs. The crews reported hits on the docks and one tanker sunk, although the sinking couldn't be verified. What happened next was all too typical of such missions. The bombers staged back to Del Monte, *hoping* it would still be in American hands. It was, and all that night plane crews and mechanics worked to get the bombers ready for another mission. By morning only six Fortresses were ready. Two suffered engine trouble, and then only four bombers were left to proceed to their targets at Lingayen Gulf. Far below them the crews stared at the major Japanese invasion fleet spread far across the water. The warships seemed ablaze with the steady firing support they were giving to the Japanese troops storming ashore. The four Fortresses dropped their bombs; results were "difficult to observe." Disheartened with the sight of the powerful Japanese fleet—and the inevitable success of the invasion—three Fortress crews flew on to an airfield in the Dutch Moluccas (one returned to Del Monte) where they refueled before returning to Batchelor Field in Australia.

Their return only helped to stress the futility of their operations. They had flown nearly five thousand miles, exacted a heavy toll on engines, beat the crews into weariness, to drop their light bomb loads, ineffectually, on the Japanese who were able easily to brush aside the "annoying slaps" of the Americans.

The crews were beat, the bombers rattling and desperately in need of parts and maintenance. To fly a mission the men and planes had to cover thousands of miles, with staging at airfields en route to pick up fuel and bombs. They were being harassed by fighters at almost every turn and things promised to get a great deal worse before they even started to get better. On Christmas day only eleven Fortresses could be counted in the roster of the 19th Bomb Group, and of these only three were still in commission and able to fly combat. The crews felt that Batchelor Field was the outpost of a lost and condemned world.

The year ended on a note of bleak despair.

## CHAPTER 12

# THE PACIFIC: PHASE II

O N DECEMBER 11, 1941, Japanese invasion forces stormed ashore on the northern coast of Borneo in the Netherlands East Indies. One week later they crashed into Kuching, capital of Sarawak. The Dutch, defending stubbornly, found it necessary to split their forces by committing to the British in Malaya every Dutch bomber available.

Nine days after Kuching fell, on December 27th, General Brereton ordered every available B-17 to depart Batchelor Field in Australia, to fly immediately to Malang, Java, some sixty miles south of Soerabaja. Their new airfield was Singarasi, six miles from Malang, along the southeastern coastline of Java. Ten weary, battered Fortresses of the 19th Bombardment Group made the 1,300-mile flight. As soon as the crews dispersed their planes Dutch officers briefed them on the camouflaged, advance fields they would use at Kendari, Celebes and Samarinda, well inland on Borneo. They would help to defend the vital Balikpapan oilfields.

More Fortresses on the way . . . that was the cheering word the B-17D crews brought with them. General Brereton said they would be the new B-17E. Power turrets, massive firepower, hundreds of improvements—the promise was music. For several days three B-17E bombers would leave the states every day. Three new bombers a day. Then, before New Year's Day, the rate would be doubled. Six new Fortresses every day on their way to the Dutch East Indies, to Australia, to fight back in the Philippines.

The promise was exorbitant. It didn't take long for the new numbers to be reduced. But everyone was working day and night to do their best, to reinforce the battered bomber groups. By January 6th twenty B-17E Fortresses and six LB-30s (export versions of the B-24 Liberator, taken over by the U.S. Government) were actually on their way. In the air and flying westward across the Far Pacific. The promise, if not kept in its full, was certainly being given substance. While the first twenty-six Fortresses and Liberators were staging across the ocean, another forty-five B-17E and nine LB-30 bombers were being prepared to follow immediately. From AAF Headquarters in Washington came the word that still another 160 Fortresses and Liberators would be behind the initial groups. They would be flown to the Pacific just as quickly as they came off the production lines. The first reinforcements would be a trickle, but the flood would be soon behind the first planes.

On January 12th the first three B-17E bombers of the promised flood landed in Australia.

But in the interim of waiting there was a war to be

fought. Singarasi wasn't the best base of operations. The runways, though 5,000 feet in length, were sod—unpaved. Radar defenses were nonexistent. There were no antiaircraft defenses. The Fortresses would be virtually naked to attack from the air. The crews had the unhappy feeling it might be the Philippines all over again.

On January 2nd the Fortresses set out for Samarinda in Borneo. Nine B-17Ds struggled through storms to reach their advanced base of operations. They brought their bombs with them; four 600-pounders to each plane. On the 4th, Major Cecil Combs led eight bombers on a strike against Davao Gulf, 730 miles distant from Samarinda. It turned out to be one of the better missions for the Fortresses. From 25,000 feet they dropped their missiles in the pattern for which the heavy bombers had been intended. A destroyer took several hits that nearly tore it apart, and a cruiser was heavily damaged. The Fortresses returned to Samarinda, and on the next day were back at Singarasi near Malang.

The mission was definitely a success—but at a cost that would soon cripple the weary bombers. The men had flown almost steadily for three days, had consumed many thousands of gallons of fuel, had worn out their airplanes even more—to drop approximately ten tons of bombs. It was the kind of opposition the Japanese could stand.

*We* couldn't. The one mission had drained all the 100-octane fuel at Samarinda. For a second mission to Davao the Fortresses staged through Kendari, leaving Singarasi on January 8th. Engine trouble plagued the mission from the start; four bombers aborted. Five made it to Davao Gulf, but found poor weather and terrible visibility. The results were best described as "uncertain."

On January 11th Japanese troops crushed resistance at

Tarakan, and swept aside failing Dutch defenses to occupy the northern Borneo city. Major Combs took seven Fortresses to Tarakan to hit the Japanese, but found the weather a worse enemy. Severe storms, turbulence, and heavy rains forced four B-17s to call it quits and return to base. The remaining three bombers pressed on, fought off attacking Zeros and shot down two of the enemy fighters and, for all their pains, found the visibility so bad no one could even make a pretense at accurate bombing.

Everyone in the Pacific, it seemed, was learning the hard way about the Zero fighter. The official history of the Royal Australian Air Force[36] tells of the long-awaited arrival of the celebrated Hawker Hurricane fighters that would give the Zeros real opposition; when the Hurricanes first appeared over Singapore:

> At the sight of those planes morale skyrocketed 100 percent, and the sun shone again and the birds sang. . . . That evening at all the night spots the gay topic of conversation was "Hurricanes." The miracle had happened. The Hurricanes were here and the world was saved. "Boy! More stengahs—long, with ice!" . . . The RAF boys flying them began to mix it with the Zeros which we knew was practically impossible. The Zero was just about the nippiest, most highly maneuverable fighter in the world. They buzzed around the Hurricanes like vicious bees.

By January 22 strikes against the enemy were regarded by Australian historians as "pitiful." An attack by five Fortresses was thus described:

> Using Palembang as an advanced base, the Fortresses flew 1,500 miles to make the attack, but in effect it was but

a token raid reflecting the glimmer of a hope on which Far East Command scarcely dared count.

Reinforcements in the form of B-17E and LB-30 bombers continued to come in. The opposition was getting tougher as the Japanese moved their fighters down to advanced land bases.

Top Japanese ace Saburo Sakai relates this story of a battle in late January against a formation of eight Fortresses:

Late in the morning, several specks appeared in the sky, approaching from the general direction of Java. They came in fast, swelling in size until two formations of four planes each became clear. Fortresses, in close flights . . . The rear flight flew slightly above the lead group and, as we approached, the second group of planes moved closer to form a defensive box.

The B-17s passed about a half mile beneath me. I rolled, Uehara glued to my wingtip, and dove against the formations. I was still out of gun range, but flicked a burst as I passed them. I saw the bombs falling as I flashed by the planes. We rolled back and climbed steeply. . . . I moved into position again, a half mile above the rear of the formations. . . . I shoved the stick forward and rolled as I dove. The fighters picked up speed quickly! I kept the stick hard over, in a long rolling dive, firing with both guns and cannon. No results. Everywhere around me the Fortresses seemed to be filling the sky, and tracers arched through the air as we flashed through the formation. We slipped through without damage, and I climbed again for another dive.

Again. Dive, roll, concentrate on one bomber! This time I caught one! I saw the shells exploding, a series of red and black eruptions moving across the fuselage. Surely he would go down now! Chunks of metal—big chunks—exploded outward from the B-17 and flashed away in the slipstream. The waist and top guns went silent as the shells hammered home.

Nothing! No fire, no telltale sign of smoke trailing from behind . . . the B-17 continued on in formation.

We swung around and up, and rolled back in for the third run. The enemy formation continued on, seemingly impregnable, as if nothing had happened. The third time down I went after the bomber I had hit before, and again I caught him flush. Through the sight I watched the shells exploding, ripping metal from the wings and fuselage, ripping the inside of the fuselage apart. Then I was past the plane, pulling out in a wide, sweeping turn, going for height.

The plane was still in formation! No fire, no smoke. Each time we dove against the B-17s their gunners opened up with heavy, defensive fire which, fortunately, seemed to have been impaired by the tightness of the formation. So far I had felt no damage to the Zero. I made two more passes, each time swinging down in a dive, rolling as I dove, Uehara right with me, each of us snapping out bursts with the machine guns and cannon. And every time we saw the bullets and shells slamming into the bombers, seemingly without effect.

We had just completed the sixth firing run when the eight B-17s split into two flights. Four banked to the right and the other four to the left. Uehara pointed excitedly to the flight bearing to the right; a thin, black film trailed the left engine of the third B-17.

We *had* gotten through, after all. I turned to follow the four bombers and pushed the throttle all the way forward, closing in rapidly behind the damaged plane. He was hurt, all right, dropping behind the other three planes. As I moved in I saw tangled wreckage instead of the tail turret; the guns remained silent. At maximum speed I approached to fifty yards' distance, and held the gun triggers down. Every last round poured from my guns and cannon into the cripple. Abruptly a cloud of black smoke burst from the bomber, and he nosed down steadily, to disappear into a solid cloud layer below.[37]

But the Japanese were learning their lessons quickly on how to deal with the new B-17E. The official history of the AAF notes what happened to a mission of nine B-17s on the morning of February 8th when, halfway across the Java Sea, the formation was hit by nine Japanese fighters:

In what the survivors agreed was the best-executed attack yet encountered, the Japanese concentrated first on Dufrane's plane, which almost immediately burst into flame. Only six of the crew succeeded in bailing out. Captain Donald R. Strother having moved into the lead, the enemy's fire in a second attack knocked out one engine, damaged another, and blew out the hydraulic system of his plane. Again the Japanese made a frontal attack, and this time the plane piloted by Lt. William J. Prichard, who had arrived from the United States just two days before, burst into flames and exploded. Three other planes sustained serious damage as the fight continued. Finally, what was left of the flight turned back; *only three of the original nine planes returned to their base.* [Italic added.] Though five of the Japanese had been shot down, the enemy planes had shown superior qualities. Moreover, the top turret of the B-17 had been unable to cope with head-on attacks, the 30 cal. machine gun in the nose had lacked sufficient range, and the bottom turret had failed to prevent attacks from below on vulnerable bomb bay tanks. Such lessons of experience would prove of great value to the AAF in later days of the war, but there was little comfort for those who provided the experience.[38]

Two things were never in short supply during these grueling air battles—the enemy, and operational difficulties. It was almost impossible to fight a war with a minimum number of bombers sadly in need of maintenance and flown by crews on the edge of exhaustion. To fight that war on many fronts where the enemy was always plentiful stretched matters to the breaking point.

No clearly defined boundary of operations existed through Malaya, Sumatra, Borneo, Java, Timor, Celebes, the Philippines, New Guinea, and the intermediate points during this time. We struck at the Japanese whenever the most likely targets seemed to appear, and the campaign carried out from Australian bases (in addition to the short-lived Java campaign) encompassed air strikes extending from New Ireland and the Bismarck Archipelago on the west all the way northwest into the Philippines.

As fast as new planes and crews arrived in the theater they were thrown into the breach. Some were exhausted before they ever got to Australia. Men of the 88th Reconnaissance and 22nd Bombardment Squadrons of the 7th Bombardment Group (who landed at Oahu just as the Pearl Harbor attack was getting under way) were long delayed in reaching Australia. They had spent the two months after their arrival at Pearl Harbor in flying 168 patrol missions out of Hawaii. Not until February would the Hawaiian command release them. They were patched into a new squadron of twelve bombers and started south along the supply line to Australia. It wasn't a fast trip. In the Fijis they were commandeered to fly another twelve missions.

Finally, on February 18 and 19, they made it to Townesville, Australia. They had no ground crews with them. They did their own maintenance. And for the next thirty days they flew reconnaissance and bombing missions on a steady, enervating basis.

It was difficult to grasp the feeling of utter weariness of the Fortress crews. After flying long missions at high altitude during the day, their strength sapped by the roar and vibration of the bombers, and breathing thin air at operational heights, to say nothing of combat, they returned to their bases to face all-night sessions to maintain and repair, refuel, rearm, and bomb up the big Fortresses. There wasn't any fighter protection (it was being decimated by the Zeros) and there weren't more than a handful of anti-aircraft guns. So that the Fortresses could survive on the ground they were dispersed deep within the Australian interior. The crews thus had to make two separate flights for every mission; first they flew from their remote "survival bases" to advanced fields on the Australian coast, and then they started out for combat.

Despite crippling obstacles and personal weariness the crews managed to keep their bombers flying. On February 23rd six Fortresses of the 7th Bomb Group assembled over Magnetic Island, and began the long flight to make the first attack on newly held Rabaul, New Britain. The weather was rotten, but the B-17s managed to sink one cargo vessel and damage another. They fought off Zero attacks during which three gunners were wounded, but no one was killed. It was a rough trip home. One B-17, torn up in the air fight, belly-landed 220 miles from Port Moresby on New Guinea. Not until April 1, malaria-ridden, half-starved, and exhausted, did the crew return to their squadron.

Despite new reinforcements from the States, the situation failed to improve. Operations from Australia were wearing out planes and crews faster than they were hurting the enemy. The planes in Java were there on borrowed time, and only the most hopeless optimist believed otherwise. "The Flying Fortress crews," noted RAAF observers, "claimed successful attacks on enemy shipping and the destruction of aircraft on the ground. But in fact, like the whole Allied effort from Java at this time, these could best be described as 'successful failures'—the enemy could well afford such harm as they inflicted."

The enemy could afford our blows, but we could not afford his for very long, a fact starkly demonstrated in two raids of February 18th and 19th against the port area of Darwin, Australia. One hundred and twenty-five bombers and eighteen fighters wreaked tremendous devastation. The bombing, survivors said, was superb. One American destroyer and two troop transports went to the bottom, as did four Australian vessels, and seven more suffered heavy damage. Japanese fighters and defending bombers shot down nine P-40 fighters, and on the ground seven bombers and two fighters vanished in flames.

The AAF official study of the raid noted that these "gave tangible proof of the enemy capability and intention of bringing the war to the continent of Australia. . . . Immediately following the Darwin attacks, therefore, the Australian Army authorities ordered the demolition of Keats Airdrome, 130 miles southwest of Darwin, and ordered certain other west coast airdromes prepared for demolition. . . . It was becoming increasingly evident that Allied resistance could no longer continue. . . ."

Japanese paratroopers and crack invasion forces swept steadily through the Dutch East Indies; by February 14th they overran the rich Sumatran oil fields. Six days later they stormed Bali, east of Java, and started cutting down resistance on Timor, the island lying between Java and Australia.

Throughout the steady forward push by the Japanese the Australia-based Fortresses went out again and again to hit the enemy, striking mainly at warships and airfields. On rare occasions the Zeros did not intercept. Most of the time, however, the fighters mangled the Fortress formations. Unless the Zero pilots exploited the weakness of the new B-17E the crews found they were immeasurably better equipped with their new bomber to hold off the enemy than they had been with the older models. Fifteen Zeros attacked two B-17Es over Menado Bay, and confidently came in with stern attacks. In the running battle of more than one hour the Fortresses claimed six fighters; Japanese records showed the claims as authentic.

But the Japanese never let up. Both bombers were refueling at Kendari when five Zeros swept low for strafing attacks. One B-17E got away after a running fight, starting on its take off roll. The other was burned on the ground.

Early in February the Japanese began pounding the air bases from which the hard-pressed crews operated. Enemy bombers under heavy Zero escort on February 3rd ripped Malang, Madioen and Soerabaja. Among the thirty-one American and Dutch planes blown up or burned in the attacks were four new Fortresses. Attrition was high and getting worse. Japanese fighter pilots escorting their own bombers were delighted to see a Fortress blunder almost into their midst. The crew had been on an engineering test flight and drifted into the Japanese attack. The Zeros cut down the airplane almost immediately. Then a Fortress on a mission caught fire in the air. Five crew members bailed out of the flaming airplane, but the pilot withstood the flames as long as he could and made a crash-landing on an island. During a Zero sweep of Allied bases, a B-17E and a B-18, the latter used as a transport, were caught in the air and gunned down.

Reinforcements were being used up with a frightening speed, and the enemy could claim only a share of the damage. A spanking-new Fortress completed the long haul across the Pacific and let down for its landing at Singosari airdrome near Malang. The pilot overshot the runway and went crashing at high speed into *another* new B-17E mired in deep mud near the end of the runway. The airstrips of Java often were not paved and pilots fresh from the states, accustomed to concrete beneath them, had wild problems with the rain-slicked and muddy fields.

Things might have been better with good fighter protection, but the pursuits had their share of aggravated woes. Forty P-40s were sent from Australia to a secret airbase southeast of Djombang, near Soerabaja. Before they reached their goal, engine failures, Japanese bombings at intermediary fields, and aggressive sweeps by Zeros reduced their number by fourteen fighters!

Of a total of 120 P-40s sent from Australia to Java, "only thirty-six reached their destination." Most of them were sent to the ocean bottom, still in packing crates on the ships carrying them through waters over which the enemy ruled the air.

Japanese invasion fleets in their successive landings on defended islands came in for maximum attacks not only from the Fortresses, but also from fighters, attack and dive bombers. It was like swatting at charging rhinos with straws. Enemy fighters and bombers were rushed to newly captured airfields throughout Sumatra, Malaya, Borneo, Celebes, Timor and Bali as the Japanese set out on a relentless campaign to wipe out the last vestiges of Allied airpower.

On February 22nd five new Flying Fortress bombers

went up in flames at Malang as Japanese raiders in perfect formation and under escort of weaving Zeros pounded the field in textbook strikes. A Fortress pilot noted that the raid "just about cleans that field out and reduces our air force by one-third. Our bombers have accomplished little since Major Robinson was shot down a month ago. *Too much caution and fear of what a Jap Zero can do to a B-17.*"

At Jogjarkarta four Fortresses were torn apart by enemy bombs. The harassed defenders assembled their fighters at a secret airbase. But Japanese intelligence got wind of the new field, waited until the Allied fighters were on the ground, and came in with a low-level attack that destroyed *every* P-40, Buffalo and Hurricane on the field.

On March 3rd, Broome, Java, was the scene of a mass evacuation by air, just one step ahead of the advancing Japanese. In the harbor, flying boats were taking on women and children, and a few fortunate men—mostly wounded. At the airstrip American, British and Dutch planes also were loading evacuees. Then twelve Zero fighters—only those twelve—tore the place apart.

The Japanese fighters caught the flying boats just as they were starting to take off. Packed from nose to tail with refugees, almost every one of the big flying boats went up in flames or crashed. Some two hundred people died in the disaster. One B-24 Liberator made it into the air with twenty men aboard—it was shot down in flames. And on the airfield, the Zeros, taking their time, shooting carefully, burned and destroyed two B-24s, two B-17s, six Dutch planes, three British, and one Australian aircraft.

There was no opposition in the air. The Zeros ruled the sky.

Much has been written about the two major defeats the Japanese suffered in the spring and summer of 1942.

In May, in the Battle of the Coral Sea, the Japanese ended up the loser in a spirited engagement with the United States Navy. It was the first time two major naval forces slugged it out with punishment to both sides, but without any surface unit ever getting within gun range of the enemy. It was an air battle from beginning to end, during which the Japanese lost the carrier *Shoho*, and took terrific punishment to the *Shokaku*, putting the carrier out of action for a long time. They also lost a heavy cruiser, suffered damage to another cruiser, and lost one hundred aircraft.

The victor was the United States Navy. It wasn't a matter of victory in terms of numbers of ships lost, because the United States saw the carrier *Lexington* (33,000 tons) go down, along with the destroyer *Sims*, the tanker *Neosho*, sixty-six planes, and personnel losses of 543 men.

But the Japanese failed in their bid to invade Port Moresby in New Guinea, and they had to postpone indefinitely invasion of the northern coast of Australia. The Navy bought us freedom from two invasions, and some time in which to build up our forces in Australia.

Many stories exist about the major role played in this first Japanese defeat by the Flying Fortresses then in the southwest Pacific. This brief episode of the Battle of the Coral Sea is to set the record straight. The Fortresses had little to do with it, and that is a matter of fact. Records show that B-17s first discovered the Japanese fleet. They didn't—a B-25 took those honors. The twin-engined bomber was from the 90th Bombardment Squadron operating out of Port Moresby, and its crew spotted a carrier and two heavy cruisers to get the ball rolling for the battle that would follow. The next day another B-25 "contacted a carrier south of Bougainville, shadowing the vessel for an hour and five minutes while sending out homing signals, hoping to guide B-17s to the target." Unfortunately, the Fortresses never got the signal and never went out to bomb the carriers.

After flying many reconnaissance missions, B-17Es on May 7th attacked Japanese transports bound for Port Moresby. The next day they again struck at the troopships.

Unfortunately, they failed to hit any of the Japanese vessels.

Even more unfortunately, due to mixups in signals and lack of recognition of American warships, the Fortresses *did* bomb several vessels of the United States Navy.

It wasn't their best performance.

The next month there came the Battle of Midway in which the U.S. Navy inflicted upon the Japanese their first major defeat in 350 years. In short, the Navy broke the back of Japanese naval surface and air strength, and changed the course of the Pacific war. It was a four-day struggle of vast confusion, swift action, several periods when the Japanese reigned supreme, attacks by Army, Navy and Marine planes against the Japanese and, finally, a savage assault by Navy Dauntless dive bombers that wrote *finis* to uncontested Japanese sweeps anywhere in the far Pacific.

The Fortresses played their part in this battle—a minor role as compared to that of the Navy, but one in which the record, while not nearly as glowing as the reports of past years have indicated, was still vastly better than what had happened at the Coral Sea when we bombed our own ships.

Midway began on June 3rd with reports from Navy patrol planes of a powerful Japanese force approaching the island on a bearing of 265 degrees. Shortly after noon Lt. Colonel Walter C. Sweeney, Jr., led nine B-17Es from Midway on a flight of three and a half hours to reach "cruisers, transport ships, cargo vessels, and other escort ships." At precisely 23 minutes past four P.M. the nine Fortresses caught the transport force by complete surprise. The bombers dropped in pattern from 8,000 feet, releasing thirty-six 600-pound demolition bombs. The bomber crews attacked in two flights, and claimed five direct hits and several near misses. The "hits" included strikes on a battleship or a heavy cruiser. The crews claimed that from thirty miles away they could see both the heavy warship and a transport blazing "with huge clouds of dark smoke mushrooming above them."

But the final tabulation and studies of the Battle of Midway, which continued after the war when Japanese survivors and records could contribute to the "scorecard," placed these claims in serious doubts. The Japanese insisted that the claims were exaggerated to a gross extent. The writer, somewhat in the middle of honest claims by experienced airmen, and the Japanese who certainly were in a position to know, is forced to refer to the comments on this matter made by the official historians of the AAF, who noted that after the days-long battle, careful studies led the AAF to believe that "a fair percentage of the bombs had struck home." But in the studies made *after the war* this note of caution was added:

Assessment was difficult and in part was based upon the statements of the handful of enemy survivors picked up after the action; not until the war ended and the teams of interrogators invaded Japan was it possible to interview a number of the survivors of this initial action. And even their testimony had suffered from the destruction of records, from the lapse of three and one-half years between the action and the interrogation, and from the fact that the

Japanese officers reporting were not always aware of the source of the bombs which were dropped upon them. But their evidence indicates the necessity of a radical scaling down of the original claims as sent in by the Seventh Air Force. At any rate, in some cases these enemy officers stood on the decks of the targets and were in a fair way to determine when and by whom they were bombed, better perhaps than pilots who bombed from 20,000 feet and saw tall geysers spout up around their rapidly maneuvering targets, for it has been demonstrated repeatedly that damage to carriers is particularly difficult to assess from the air. With this in mind, it would seem that the first attack produced a probable hit upon one transport, causing a small fire which was extinguished without delaying the ship, but that the combat craft escaped damage in the attack.[39]

Which was a "radical scaling down" indeed . . .

The early morning of June 4th was the day of the "real" battle when we threw our combined strength against the Japanese carriers. For horrifying minutes that seemed to stretch into an eternity, Japanese fighters and antiaircraft carried on a wholesale slaughter of attacking American planes. Torpedo bombers, dive bombers and fourteen Fortresses hammered at the Japanese early in the day—seemingly without effect. For the grisly log of the morning of the 4th of June showed that out of six Grumman TBF Avenger torpedo bombers, five were shot down. Hits: *none*.

Two of four Martin B-26 Marauder torpedo bombers were lost. Hits: *none*.

A total of twenty-eight Vought SB2U Vindicators and Douglas SBD Dauntlesses of the Marines and Navy made dive-bombing attacks. Twelve went down in flames. Hits: *none*.

Twenty-four Marine fighters intercepted a Japanese formation and were jumped by Zeros. Fourteen Marine fighters were shot down for the loss of two or three Zeros.

In the first wave of fighting we lost thirty-three planes and their crews without hitting a single enemy vessel.

Then fifteen Douglas TBD Devastator torpedo bombers from the Hornet's Squadron 8 went in low and slow. The Japanese blew *every* bomber out of the sky. Hits: *none*.

Twenty-six more torpedo planes went in. Twenty of them burned or crashed into the sea. Hits: *none*.

But the Japanese fleet was maneuvering severely. Fortresses overhead were forcing them to take evasive action. Almost all their guns were depressed to lash out at the low-flying torpedo planes. The Zeros were on the deck after the same targets. Stop the torpedos; they were the most dangerous.

They heard the shrill scream from the sky over the thunder of their own guns when it was too late. Dauntless dive bombers from *Enterprise* and *Yorktown*, coming vertically at their targets from 17,000 feet. They plunged for three miles, the carriers expanding steadily in size to the pilots.

In three minutes—

*Soryu* took three, 1,000-pound bombs in her vitals.

*Akagi* took two big bombs and virtually exploded.

*Kaga* took four big bombs amidships and vomited gigantic sheets of flame.

All three carriers were finished. Flames enveloped them and they went down.

Later that day the *Hiryu* was caught by the dive bombers and torn apart. She was left disabled and sinking.

Two cruisers collided and had to withdraw from the battle. The next day dive bombers sank the *Mikuma* and heavily damaged the *Mogami*.

The Seventh Air Force claimed that the B-17Es in the

battle had made twenty-two direct bomb hits on carriers, battleships, cruisers, destroyers and troop transports, that they had sunk a destroyer, left transports blazing and had shot down eight Zero fighters.

These claims have been vigorously contested. Even the Navy, which at first lent credence to the claims of hits on Japanese cruisers, backed off from such confirmation.

The arguments have not ended. As the official historians of the AAF noted: *"One of Midway's legacies was an enduring debate."*

Meanwhile, far to the north of Midway, another air war on a smaller scale, involving a limited number of B-17s, was under way. The Aleutians also were under Japanese attack.

"No one in his right mind would want anything to do with the Aleutians. It's the goddamned end of the goddamned world."

It was a typical comment of men who served in the Aleutians, a long curving chain of 120 volcanic islands utterly bleak, miserable, cold, windy, packed with mist, snow, ice and pure misery. They ran all the way from the Alaskan Peninsula to within ninety miles of easternmost Soviet territory. Timber was so scarce as to be counted a miracle. The lowlands were miserable swamps blanketed by tundra or muskeg, sometimes three feet thick. The spongy carpet absorbed a man's feet like wet muck. And under the muskeg there was a fine volcanic ash best described as slimy. In addition to the rain and wind and fog the Aleutians were famed for sudden storms that came up with no warning but of predictable extreme violence that blocked the entire world from view. Much of the Aleutians couldn't count two weeks of clear weather every year.

But as a diversion to their attack at Midway, the Japanese put together a small task force of two light carriers with accompanying cruisers and destroyers and sent them out to disrupt our installations in Alaska. They did not intend to invade Alaska or to occupy even exposed Dutch Harbor. They were content to shoot up whatever they could find in the way of American targets, and then occupy the western Aleutians. It seemed as if even the Japanese didn't look forward to the prospect of fighting a war in that miserable part of the world where violent weather was its only export. They were content to hole up as far from Alaska as they could.

We didn't know that at the time, of course. And that meant building airfields under appalling conditions. On Umnak Island, engineers worked in torrential downpours to build airstrips that seemed to be animated. Rains, blizzards, and mud were more common than any other form of weather, and that's just not the stuff out of which airstrips are made, even aided by the use of steel matting.

The Umnak strip *was* animated. It was so unstable that a fighter upon touching down would be tossed thirty feet into the air on impact with the strip. Twin-engine bombers literally formed *waves* in the matting—waves that rippled up and down the length of the strip. Landing a Flying Fortress on that steel matting was an adventure.

The Aleutians combat took a back seat to just staying alive during a mission. Weather dominated everything and killed more crews than the enemy.

Beginning on May 29th the weather turned "absolutely foul." A group of six B-17E and one LB-30 bombers made it into the area just in time. They came to reinforce the reconnaissance duties of the 36th Squadron at Kodiak (before moving on to Umnak) which had been carrying out its job with *one* B-17E.

On May 28th the lone B-17E, flying from Umnak, began its daily reconnaissance of the Aleutian chain. Russel A. Cone, the pilot, said that taking the Fortress off Umnak, or landing on the strip, "had the effect of . . . an innerspring mattress." The lone Fortress flew its recco missions, saw only clouds, snow, and water. The crew returned to Umnak where "conditions were extremely primitive." Combat crews pitched their own tents, cooked their own meals, shared everyone else's mud. During the long alert they went without sleep forty-eight hours at a stretch, much of which was spent in the air searching for the enemy. When they came "home" they pumped gas from barrels and performed their own maintenance.

The Japanese on June 3rd hit Fort Mears and Dutch Harbor with bombers and fighters. The next day they launched another strike, and the American command sent out PBY flying boats, B-26 Marauders (loaded with torpedos), and all available B-17Es. That afternoon (4th June) five B-17E and one LB-30 bombers wasted six hours looking for the Japanese task force. They saw only different phases of terrible weather.

But later that same day two B-17Es managed to ferret out their quarry. One Fortress pilot pulled up *into the overcast* to drop his bombs blindly. Lt. Thomas F. Mansfield went down through the clouds, right above the waves, and went thundering straight at a cruiser. This was the *Takao*. The Japanese, well warned of the attack, were ready and waiting. Mansfield's plane smashed into the frigid waters. One man was picked up by the Japanese from the ocean.

That was the end of the fighting for the Fortresses. There was, in fact, only one more attempt to hit the Japanese during the "Dutch Harbor episode." Five B-26s went out, two came home, three attacked the enemy carriers. Without results.

That ended a brief, miserable combat phase in the most miserable part of the Pacific.

Later, there would be strikes against the Japanese in the western Aleutians. The Fortresses would initially carry out most of the raids, then the Liberators slowly would take over until they replaced entirely the Boeings.

An American who hid out nearly two months on Kiska before surrendering to the Japanese watched several attacks by our heavy bombers. "The bombs did very little damage," he said, "because the ground was so soft. They made craters about five feet wide and thirty inches deep. Finally the raids quieted down to where a B-17 would come over when it was a nice day. They never seemed to hit anything—just splashed water on a ship or two."

The Fortress' combat log didn't set any fires. . . .

On June 12th the crews of five B-17Es struck at Kiska; the crews claimed they had set aflame two cruisers and a destroyer. Confirmation of the full damage was "lacking."

On June 19th a single Fortress *confirmed* the sinking of a cargo ship, the *Nissan Maru*.

During July, weather reconnaissance planes reported fifteen "open days" for bombing. The weather on these "best days" was so bad that half the missions sent out were canceled before the planes reached their target.

July 30th: Fortresses and Liberators arrived over Kiska atop a solid overcast and dropped their bombs blindly. The Navy made some scathing remarks about the value of "hit-or-miss" raids.

July 18th: Zeros shot down a B-17E over Tanaga Island, 350 miles west of Umnak. The next day a B-24 searching for the missing crew also vanished.

August 3rd: P-38 fighters used a B-17E for navigation on a sweep to Adak. They found three huge Kawanishi flying boats, shot down two, chopped up the third which escaped in clouds.

The weather got worse. The Japanese were easier to take. . . .

On December 9, 1942, a Liberator found all airfields closed in by fog, finally crashed on a beach. Everyone survived.

Then things fell apart in the next few days. One Liberator groped down to a belly landing at Adak, smashed two P-38 fighters and was itself destroyed. Another flew 2,500 miles up and down the Aleutians trying to find an open airfield and finally crash-landed along the beach. A third made a crash-landing on an island when it ran out of fuel, trying to find an airfield.

Two other Liberators vanished without trace of any kind.

In rough weather near Adak, two Fortresses collided in mid-air. Miraculously, one made it back to base. The second vanished in the sea.

In two days, six fighters, two twin-engine bombers and one Liberator were lost in crash-landings because of weather.

By the end of 1942, the Liberators had taken over the brunt of heavy bomber operations in the northern Pacific.

No one envied *those* crews. . . .

# CHAPTER 13

# THE PACIFIC: PHASING OUT

THERE WASN'T REALLY ONE air war in the Pacific. There were a dozen fronts on which the Flying Fortress made its appearance, held the line, opened the first major assaults to cut back at the enemy, and then began to be phased out in favor of the longer-ranging B-24 Liberator. Many of these campaigns were wholly separated one from the other, and to the men involved in combat operations it seemed each was a war unto itself. Only through the eyes of Washington, which held the viewpoint of "the big picture," did the many facets mesh into the whole.

One of the least known areas of Flying Fortress operations was the domain of the Tenth Air Force, which came into being on February 12, 1942. For a while the Tenth existed only on papers stamped *Secret.* It didn't have any bases, equipment, or manpower. It had a future mission in Asia, but that was all. It would still have to be created in substance.

During the last days of February 1942 General Brereton

(Commander, FEAF) and a small group of officers began working their way to India. Their identities and destinations were kept secret, and not only from the Japanese. What they had to do would be to manipulate men and the officials of different governments under the noses of Japanese sympathizers. The flight to be made was one of tremendous distance. In a B-17 and an LB-30 the group flew from Java to Ceylon, and then hurried on to Dumdum Airfield near Calcutta, India. In the Fortress was their secret cargo, $250,000 cash wrapped in a blanket, with which Brereton was to bargain for local labor and supplies to get the Tenth into being. For his pains, Brereton was given command of the Tenth, a dubious honor in a country with only ten airfields, not one of which was fit for military operation. His means to get going? Steal, buy, borrow, beg, take at gunpoint; it didn't matter. The British worked closely with Brereton, and agreed he had problems enough to make a strong man weep. We were being beaten back and hammered everywhere we fought the Japanese, and Brereton was supposed to create an air force when the shortest distance to the States, going around Japanese bases, was 13,000 miles. The transit time for supplies could be reckoned safely at two months, with a few weeks thrown in for good measure.

The Mission? Not combat operations immediately as one might suppose. Supply. That was the key for the Tenth. The chief port of American entry for supplies was Karachi, fully a thousand miles from the center of combat operations. Surface transport was a gurgling laugh. Indian railroads were decrepit and guaranteed only to be unreliable. The roads were narrow, rough, and generally impassable. Only one way was left—by air.

Thus the initial task of the heavy bombers in India was to fly supplies. Dropping bombs could wait; it *had* to wait.

The bombers had to supply themselves with ordnance, fuel, parts, food, crews, and the like. From March 8 through 13, the starting force of seven B-17s and one LB-30 hauled 58,000 pounds of supplies, and a battalion of 465 native troops, from Asansol to Magwe, Burma. On the return trip they brought out 423 frightened and grateful civilian evacuees. Three weeks later the Tenth flew its initial combat missions.

That's glossing over lightly what the crews had to face. Within a month of arriving in India and Burma the Fortress crews were sick to death of the place and were more than willing to hand it over to the Japanese, whom they felt should be cursed with all its evils. There was, above all else, heat, insects, humidity, rain, mud, terrible food, primitive facilities and, finally, the enemy, who would have to be fought with a force of bombers and fighters so ragged and short on material that its existence depended on a precarious supply line stretching over 13,000 miles.

The Japanese bases scattered across Burma, Thailand and the Andaman Islands were the primary targets of the Tenth; enemy shipping came second on the priority list. With all their other problems, the Fortresses that first came to the Tenth were so beat-up that they needed major overhauls even for training flights. Nevertheless they had to be committed to battle with crews about as weary as their flagging machines. The 7th Bombardment Group with which the Tenth received its initial strength was made up of those same planes and crews that had been caught at Pearl Harbor. After fulfilling combat and reconnaissance roles from different bases all across the Pacific, they had finally made it to India. The ground crews were scarcely fresher. After a torturous routing through Brisbane, Fremantle, and Ceylon, they finally arrived in India in March 1942. Replacements literally *wanered* in, finding themselves footloose and scattered after their own outfits had been torn up by the Japanese. There were ground crew veterans of the Flying Tigers. Some of the bomber pilots were survivors of the famed Doolittle raid against Japan on April 18th, 1942. After bombing Tokyo they had flown on into China, and were then smuggled through Japanese lines down to India.

No one ever found out what the Tenth might really do in battle. It was the bastard stepchild of the AAF, and any time someone needed men or airplanes for a "critical" theater, the word went out to "get it from Brereton." In June 1942, *every* heavy bomber of the Tenth Air Force was rushed from India to the Mediterranean to join in the air war of North Africa. After flying months of round-the-clock operations they were "released" to return to their original mission of fighting a vastly superior Japanese foe in Asia!

On April 2, 1942, the Tenth flew its first mission—and roared into disaster. It was a dual mission. Two B-17Es made the initial strike against Rangoon—or were *assigned* to the mission. On take off the lead airplane crashed and exploded, obliterating the airplane. *And* its entire crew. White-faced and shaken, the second crew nevertheless took off. But engine failure crippled the heavily loaded bomber, which was forced to limp back to its base at Asansol.

The second part of the mission met with somewhat greater success. Two B-17Es and one LB-30 staged in low—3,500 feet—against enemy shipping, dropping a total of eight tons of bombs. Anti-aircraft fire was intense and accurate, damaging all three planes heavily. They returned safely, however, to base.

The next day six Fortresses struck at Rangoon. One B-17E disappeared. The word is meant in the literal sense. No one ever saw the Fortress leave the formation and it was never determined how the bomber was lost.

The mission of six bombers—a "heavy strike" for the Tenth—was the last of its kind for nearly two weeks. The group settled back to make its airplanes flyable. For thirteen days mechanics and crews worked day and night patching up the Fortresses until, on April 16th, another six-bomber formation went out to blast shipping in Rangoon harbor. They dropped a wide pattern of forty-two bombs of 250-and 300-pound weight against Japanese supply vessels.

Again another thirteen days passed before the next mission. On April 29th the Fortresses returned to Rangoon. They were improving rapidly in their accuracy. Long rows of 500-pound bombs caused "very heavy and widespread damage" to the Rangoon docks.

During May the Fortresses in their limited strength struck shipping, dock facilities and especially Japanese airfields. The Myitkyina airfield in northern Burma was laid waste after one B-17E strike destroyed every building in sight and chewed the runways into cratered mud. On May 25th Rangoon received another call from five Fortresses. Then, for the next eleven days, the B-17Es went out on small-formation strikes, until the monsoon season thundered in to drench the fields and transform runways into quagmires. The mechanics cursed the mud but blessed the black skies. Now they had time to really work on the bombers.

It wasn't to be. In mid-June the call came in to rush every bomber immediately to North Africa.

The summer of 1942 was the period of great decisions to be made and, immediately afterward, to be executed. The war still belonged to the Japanese; it was the enemy and not us who maintained the offensive. It was the Japanese who occupied territory and pushed invasions and ruled the Pacific.

But at the very least the backward momentum had ended. The odds no longer favored the Japanese in every direction. The Battle of the Coral Sea gave the enemy their first taste of slugging it out so that it hurt. The Battle of Midway was something else again; the U.S. Navy had scored the greatest triumph of Allied arms of the war. This was more than something to hurt the Japanese. The losses of Midway broke the back of Japanese plans for further expansion. The lights in Tokyo burned long into the night as the Japanese reshuffled their master plan.

Guarded optimism might represent the highest of AAF hopes at the time. The Japanese had run us out of the Philippines and everywhere else we had made a stand. They had run wild over the British and the Dutch, and the Australians, as well. It was a Japanese Pacific. But at least the Navy had stopped the rampage.

New bombers were flowing to the Pacific. How best to use the new long-range striking aircraft, the fighters, the twin-engine raiders, was the question. How best to establish a uniform command of operations was an even more critical problem that demanded an immediate solution. When the Japanese threw us out of Java there was a great shuffling of feet and rearrangement of paper commands. Brereton, for all his efforts in the Philippines and elsewhere, got the ax instead of kudos and was hustled off with his handful of battle-weary Fortresses to India, carrying a quarter of a million dollars in a blanket.

MacArthur's staff fought with more bitterness among themselves than they did against the Japanese. Not until MacArthur brought in Major General George C. Kenney to run his airpower team—first the Allied Air Forces and then, after reorganization in the southwest Pacific, the Fifth Air Force—did the Japanese encounter well-run, hard-hitting and meaningful opposition across the island bastions of that part of the world. Kenney's attitude was like a cool breeze over the weary men who had fought the long delaying—and losing—battles against the Japanese. First, he said, it was necessary to whip his own house into proper shape. When that was done, his men would "take out the Jap air strength until we owned the air over New Guinea. . . . There was no use talking about playing across the street until we got the Nips off of our front lawn."

In the meantime, the Seventh Air Force had thrown its B-17s into the war in the South Pacific. . . .

Hawaii, Samoa, New Zealand, the Fijis, Polynesia . . . These were the names with which Fortress crews of the Seventh Air Force became familiar in the early months of World War II. Anti-submarine patrols occupied much of their time, using a variety of planes that included a number of old B-18s that "were left standing around" after the war began. But there were long-range reconnaissance flights as well, and to the B-17D fell one of the secret missions. On January 2nd, 1942, Lt. Cecil Faulkner put the "long legs" of the B-17D to good use when he flew from Midway Island to photograph Wake Island from a height of 18,000 feet. It was a flight that stretched the Fortress's range to utmost; Faulkner returned to Midway with only fifteen minutes' fuel in his tanks.

The following August, Major George E. Glober repeated this mission, but in a B-17E. Having the greater firepower of the later-model Fortress meant the difference in life or death; Glober's crew shot down four intercepting Zeros, and struggled home battered from nose to tail.

The Fortresses (later to be replaced by Liberators for

these missions) were pressed into service not only because of their range, but because of their ability to defend themselves. Navy PBY Catalinas had the range but not the means to defend themselves, and the Seventh's Fortresses received the nod for continuing the seven-league boots flights. On July 23rd, 1942, showing a typical mission, three Fortresses left Canton Island to make a photographic sweep over the Gilbert Islands, a mission of more than one thousand miles.

But the Seventh lacked a meaningful number of planes. It was saddled with targets at extreme range, and other groups often called upon the Seventh to supply trained crews and aircraft. The Fifth and Thirteenth Air Forces were the major recipients of this activity.

In the entire first year of war the Seventh counted only one bombing mission that could be called a major strike, and the longer range of the Liberator shunted aside the Fortress for the assignment. Colonel Wm. A. Matheny, staging through Midway, led twenty-six B-24D Liberators against Wake Island two days before Christmas, 1942. Once again it was one of those raids where the big question was: "Is it worth it?" All told, the four-engine heavies had to fly a total of 5,000 miles from their home base to the target and back.

Once George Kenney began whipping his new command into shape in the southwest Pacific, the Japanese found things changing rapidly. Before too many months passed they would feel the weight of not only Kenney's Fifth Air Force, but the Thirteenth, as well, when we began the long road back in the Solomons, starting at a place called Guadalcanal. Many times the planes of the Fifth and the Thirteenth would join in the same strikes.

In the late spring of 1942 what would become the

mightiest tactical air force in the entire Pacific—the Fifth—was still a dream of many months in the future. Months of Japanese successes had battered to dullness the senses of the men flying against the enemy. American historians noted that in the late spring of 1942 the air crews, especially in the New Guinea area, suffered from an "unsatisfactory state of morale." Speaking bluntly, the historians of the Royal Australian Air Force confirmed this critique:

> Whatever it lacked, the R.A.A.F. was virile, well-trained and proud. Confident of their own professional capacity, some members of the force were disdainful of the "Yanks." They were critical of the Americans' failure on occasions to find the bombing target; they suspected the Flying Fortress crews bombed from high altitude because they were afraid to come lower; they were disparaging of the "softness in American morale." ... There was some justification for such criticism, but it was never expressed resentfully, or without consciousness of lapses in R.A.A.F. morale, by any who knew the reasons and the counter-measures that were being taken. Members of the R.A.A.F. readily praised American combat crews and ground staff who provided examples of courage and devotion to the task of fighting the Japanese, and they not only respected but virtually idolised such officers as Wurtsmith and Wagner, the American fighter group leaders, and Carmichael, the commander of No. 19 Bombardment Group.[40]

Early in September 1942 General Kenney created the Fifth Air Force. At every opportunity he struck—with everything from fighters to Fortresses—at enemy shipping whenever it came within range and there were planes available to go out. The enemy pressure was relentless. Raids with fifty fighters and bombers were common; on

August 17, 1942, the Japanese struck with over one hundred fighter-escorted bombers at the Port Moresby airfields. Allied fighters spent most of their time supporting ground troops struggling desperately to hold back the Japanese. It was an unremitting, bitter war that increased in intensity as our own strength slowly accumulated. In the Burma campaign more than 25,000 American and Australian troops fought a no-holds-barred slugfest with the Japanese. At least 20,000 of these men were *flown* into forward combat areas. So critical was the need for their support that even B-17s were thrown into use as transports. In the battle near Dobodura, the Fortresses ferried into the combat area, over high mountains of New Guinea, a four-gun battery of 105-mm howitzers along with their crews and ammunition supplies.

By the fall of 1942 not only the combat action had changed but there was a severe change in attitudes. The historians of the R.A.A.F. were quick to note this shift.

First priority in operations necessarily was given to attacks on enemy ships approaching Buna. The Japanese missed no opportunity to take cover when the weather and darkness offered it. For this reason the more aggressive of the American heavy bomber captains were bombing from low levels. A somewhat extreme example of this was provided on 24th November when Captain Kenneth McCuller, the commander of one of seven Flying Fortresses sent to attack five Japanese destroyers in the Huon Gulf, made his first bombing run at only 200 feet. When antiaircraft shells hit and started a fire in the tail of the aircraft, McCuller pulled out while the tail gunner smothered the flames, and then turned in for another attack. On this run three members of the crew received slight wounds. In a third run an engine was hit. Still McCuller kept on bombing. In the fourth attack a second engine was put out of action. The crew claimed hits on at least two destroyers.[41]

Well before McCuller drew the admiration of Americans and Australians alike, other Fortress pilots and crews were taking advantage of improved maintenance and better airplanes to show their mettle. The end of the line for the Fortress in the Pacific was in sight; AAF Headquarters had made its decision in July of 1942 to commit the Fortresses to Europe and send most of the Liberators to the Pacific. But for some time to come the Boeings would be in the thick of things.

Rabaul, the main Japanese bastion in the southwest Pacific, came into the focus of our attacks with the passing months and, when the Marines went ashore on Guadalcanal in August of 1942, Rabaul received even more attention in attempts to draw off Japanese airpower from the Solomons.

Captain Harl Pease had completed a mission one day with three engines working to bring his Fortress home. The next day a big mission was scheduled against Vunakanau. Not wanting to "miss the big show," Pease and his crew worked all night to get a standby Fortress in condition for the raid. They pushed their way back to Port Moresby with an engine faltering, kept the news quiet, and had their airplane fueled and loaded with bombs. There was enough time for three hours of sleep. The next morning their mission began with a climb from Moresby over the 12,000-foot mountains of New Guinea, which had to be exceeded in a heavily laden bomber on the very start of a mission that would cover more than 1,100 miles round trip. The weary airplane, in company with other Fortresses of the 19th Bomb Group, kept her position. By the time they reached Rabaul several other Fortresses had dropped out to return to base with mechanical problems; eighteen bombers went into the target.

The Zeros—between twenty-eight and thirty-four of them—came in fast. Pease was now flying on three engines and could have—*should* have—turned back for Moresby. But with one propeller feathered he went on in against the target, and took the brunt of the Zero onslaught. Not until the bombs were away (an estimated seventy Japanese fighters and bombers were destroyed on the ground) did Pease stagger from the formation. The bomb-bay tank erupted in flames and was jettisoned by the crew. The Zeros hammered in relentlessly. Then it was over. The flames spread through the Fortress until a huge blazing arrow disappeared into the sea.

Pease, who fought to get on the raid, who should have turned back with a dead engine, was awarded the Medal of Honor.

To support the Marines and the Navy in the fight for Guadalcanal, the Seventh Air Force moved its B-17E Fortresses of the 11th Group from Oahu to the southern New Hebrides Islands. Eight Fortresses of the 431st Squadron went to Fiji, and twenty-seven staged into New Caledonia as the start of a new striking force. When needed, the Fortresses of the 19th Group from Australia could be called into action to coordinate strikes.

The 11th Group went into action immediately to obtain reconnaissance photos of Japanese areas. It was a service-integrated mission with special meaning. The Fortresses were so short of trained personnel and proper equipment they borrowed Navy cameras and then had the Marines come aboard to take the needed pictures.

On July 31, 1942, the Fortresses started their bombing attacks against the enemy in the South Pacific. The range was so extreme that the B-17Es carried auxiliary fuel cells not only in the bomb bay, but in the radio compartment as well. Nine B-17Es flew a mission of nearly 1,800 miles, coming over their Guadalcanal targets at 14,000 feet. The lead flight strung 500-pound bombs along airstrips and the others showered 100-pounders against Lunga supply depots. All the Fortresses came home.

The week that followed was one of maximum effort. Unfortunately it was also a dispersion of Fortress strength. Fifty-six bombing sorties were flown, as well as twenty-two search and reconnaissance sorties. But Fortress effectiveness was best measured in large flights, and only six times during three and a half months were there more than six bombers simultaneously over one target.

Guadalcanal came in for almost daily raids. Intercepting Zeros gave the Fortresses plenty of occasion to test their strength. Crews reported the Japanese pilots were less effective in pressing home their attacks, and all bombers returned home after nearly a week of heavy attacks. Not until August 4th did we lose the first Fortress and that was from a "heartbreak routine." Defensive fire from a Fortress killed the pilot of a Zero. The fighter spun wildly out of control and smashed into a bomber unable to get out of its way. Both planes exploded; two parachutes were seen from the disintegrating B-17E.

The casualties began to mount. The next day Zeros cut down a Fortress over Guadalcanal. Two days later, on August 7th, the day of the invasion by U.S. Marines, a B-17E out on search failed to return. Japanese records indicate it was shot down by Zeros.

The 11th Group asked the 19th in Australia to step up its attacks against the Japanese bastion of Rabaul, on New Britain Island, to draw off pressure from Guadalcanal. Rabaul was a powerhouse of Japanese strength. It was hit several times by twin-engine bombers, but they were flying at extreme range and, without fighter cover, they were being decimated by the Japanese. War correspondent Vern Haugland wrote: "Rabaul was the exclusive, unenvied target of the B-17s for the first year of the war, and the missions were grueling and costly. In addition to concentrated batteries of antiaircraft guns—the crews of which became deadly accurate through their frequent practice—the Japanese at Rabaul for a long period had a formidable strength in fighter aircraft. The Fortresses had to fight their way into the target and half the way home again."

It was on the next mission, with thirteen Fortresses, that Harl Pease went down in his blazing bomber.

On August 19th a single B-17 out on search patrol found a Japanese light cruiser off Guadalcanal and pressed home a determined attack. There was no question but that the crews were getting better. Marines watching from the shoreline cheered as the cruiser exploded in flames, limped away to the north and finally sank near Savo Island. That was well confirmed. . . .

The Japanese and American naval forces went at one another in a tremendous sea-air engagement several weeks after the Guadalcanal invasion. Every Fortress was thrown into the fray. Three B-17Es attacked a carrier and claimed four direct hits. No one could confirm the strikes since the carrier had already been damaged by Navy dive bombers. The mission was costly in a manner unexpected. Coming in to land at night pilots found the airfield was covered by a rainstorm. One Fortress hit a hillside and exploded, killing five of the crew.

Other Fortresses went after another "carrier." Hits were claimed, but the "carrier" was stricken from the final scorecard. There was no doubt that a warship had been struck, but that it wasn't a carrier was made clear when a ball-turret gunner noted that the 500-pound bombs which hit the enemy vessel had "knocked her turrets off." It was a better mission than most for another reason—the crews claimed five Zeros definitely shot down, and all bombers returned.

The scorecard went higher for the Fortresses. There might be some question about the type of ship involved, but not of the steady rise in percentage of hits. On August 25 eight Fortresses put three heavy bombs directly into the light cruiser *Yura*. The crews stayed around to watch the Japanese warship break apart and go down. No questions; sinking confirmed.

And from the Japanese came one of the most unexpected signs of improving accuracy and effectiveness on the part of Fortress crews. On August 25th the destroyer *Mutsuki* was escorting a transport that had been badly damaged in previous air strikes. The lookouts reported the approach of a formation of Flying Fortress bombers. The captain of the *Mutsuki* looked up and decided not to get under way, but to help the transport. The Fortresses were very high, noted the enemy skipper. They were so high, he said later, that "if they should hit us, we would be the first ship struck by horizontal bombers in this war."

A salvo of bombs tore the *Mutsuki* into wreckage that sank quickly. When they fished the hapless skipper from the sea he muttered: "Even the B-17s can make a hit once in a while." His superiors were little pleased with him. . . .

The war became a grind of going out again and again, fighting worsening weather as deadly to long-ranging bombers as was the enemy. On September 14th seven Fortresses struck at a Japanese formation of warships north of Santa Cruz. But the same day wild storms turned back another flight of seven bombers. Later in the week, during a search for a Japanese carrier, towering storms and violent winds forced fifteen Fortresses to call off their mission.

The storm was so severe that three Fortresses went down into the sea, having run short of fuel. Two crews were rescued, but the third drifted on the ocean for a week, watched two men die from the sun, and were picked up finally by the Navy.

The Fortresses moved onto Henderson Field on Guadalcanal. On October 14th Japanese barrages from offshore warships wrecked two B-17Es on the ground, holing the bombers in so many places they had to be abandoned. The Fortresses that survived the attack were so endangered that at daylight they were ordered out of Henderson. The takeoffs were "wild," since the remaining runway was only 2,000 feet long. Every bomber lifted its wheels before it reached the 1,800-foot mark. When things quieted down the Fortresses went back.

The "old days" of staying up high—changed by men such as Ken McCuller—were being abandoned by still other pilots. A Fortress piloted by Lt. Tom Trent, on a long reconnaissance mission without bombs, discovered a Japanese radio schooner standing off the reef of Greenwich Island in the Carolines. Trent said to hell with it, alerted his crew, and went down to the deck to slug it out with the heavily defended schooner. For nearly a half hour the Fortresses shot it out with machine-gun fire. The schooner holed the bomber badly, but the Fortress gunners kept up the pressure as Trent bored in as low as fifty feet. When they turned for home the schooner was on the beach and burning.

Captain Vince Crane followed suit. He came down alone over Rekata Bay and buzzed angrily through the Japanese area at a height of 200 feet, the Fortress gunners pouring it at the enemy from every gun position. They sank two anchored seaplanes, shot up buildings, sent several hundred Japanese scurrying wildly along the beach, and broke off the attack only when an explosive shell severed a control cable. Crane struggled all the way back to Henderson Field, fought the bomber to the ground. His crew used bailing wire to hold together the severed cable. Then they took off for their home field.

The weather nearly ended the career of Lt. Sam White and his crew. The "weather incident" also proved once again why the Fortress crews swore so strongly by their airplane. On a recco mission, White was at 8,000 feet with cumulus cloud buildups all around him. He flew into what he described later as "an awfully pretty white cloud." Inside the cloud, however a tremendous downdraft struck the bomber and wrenched it violently out of control. White and his copilot were helpless as the Fortress whirled crazily and flipped over on its back. Men were being tossed about the airplane. Inverted, the controls loose and ineffective, White hauled back on the throttles. As the Fortress plunged downward he managed to get it righted, but found the bomber dropping with terrific speed. Finally they burst through the bottom of the cloud. The Fortress was in a vertical dive, vibrating from the speed of its descent. The wind howled as the men had never before heard that sound.

The pilots stared in disbelief at their instruments. "She was indicating 340 miles an hour straight down and with the motors idling," White related. "We were at 2,800 feet before I could get the nose up."

The Fortress brought her crew—shaken and bruised, but safe—home again.

Sometimes not even military parlance in official documents can disguise the fury of combat. The recommendation for the Silver Star for Staff Sergeant William H. Schiffer of the 43rd Bombardment Group, refers to action of May 31, 1943:

Sergeant Schiffer was the side gunner on a B-17 type aircraft, which started on an armed reconnaissance of the north and south side of New Britain on the afternoon of May 31, 1943. When about twenty miles southeast of Finschhafen, New Guinea, at 4,000 feet, this aircraft was attacked by sixteen Zeros, which came out of cloud cover directly in front of the plane. This aircraft started evasive action immediately by going into a light low haze and dropping the bombs and the bomb bay tank. Approximately five minutes later as the aircraft came out of the haze, enemy aircraft, which went under the haze, attacked from below rendering the lower turret, the radio equipment, oxygen system, hydraulic system and No. 3 engine inoperative and damaging the control surfaces, and the right landing gear, and putting cannon holes through two cylinders of number two engine causing it to throw oil badly, and severing some gas lines. For the next thirty minutes of this engagement this aircraft was forced to fly at such a low altitude that it was impossible for Zeros to attack the unprotected belly of the plane. While barely clearing the tops of the foothills near Finschhafen seeking cloud cover, the enemy aircraft made individual and simultaneous attacks from all possible angles. That altitude during the attack was extremely difficult to hold because of evasive maneuvering and loss of power because of damaged engines. After approximately thirty-five minutes of combat, this aircraft escaped by following scattered cloud cover out at sea. Although three members of the crew were wounded in the first few minutes, thus decreasing the efficiency of the crew, five Zeros were definitely destroyed and were seen to crash, another was last seen going down as the aircraft entered cloud cover, and in several other instances tracers were seen to enter the attacking planes. After interception had been broken off, the pilots and crew elected to bring the damaged plane, if possible, back to its base, although the oil and gas from broken lines was being blown into the fuselage, and number two engine was smoking badly, threatening to envelop the plane in flames. Although wounded, this sergeant remained at his gun in spite of overwhelming firepower and definitely removed one enemy aircraft from its service against the allied forces of the Southwest Pacific area. And his act of electing to try to bring the aircraft back without regard to personal safety shows gallantry in its highest sense.

But the end was clearly in sight for the Flying Fortress in the Pacific. The war in Europe was mounting to a crescendo. Fleets of a thousand bombers were to be surpassed again and again. For this mission in the roughest air war theater of the world, against the Luftwaffe, the AAF wanted the B-17. The Liberator would take over the task of long-range missions in the Pacific, holding the line until the new Boeing—the B-29—would be ready to strike at Japan itself.

As a final closing to the story of the Flying Fortress in the Pacific, fate stepped in to play its hand. The shoulder it touched was that of Ken McCuller, who had drawn the wild admiration of Australians and Americans alike for his daring low-level attacks against heavily defended Japanese targets.

Ken McCuller was taking off from an airfield in Australia, his Fortress loaded heavily with bombs. He never made it.

A kangaroo hopped from the side of the runway directly before the speeding airplane and struck one of the main tires. The ground crews and other Fortress crews watched in horror as McCuller's bomber flipped wildly over onto its back, slammed onto the runway and exploded.

Ken McCuller, and his crew, would fly no more.

# CHAPTER 14

# EUROPE: THE BEGINNING

ON JULY 1, 1942, Boeing B-17E, Serial Number
19085, banked gracefully in the landing pattern of
Prestwick Airfield, England. Hundreds of men
watched the sweeping lines of the bomber that had just
completed its flight across the Atlantic. They watched it
turn out of base leg onto final approach, saw the flaps
lower to their final position, heard the throbbing change of
power as the pilot went to flat pitch on the propellers.
Number 19085 came across the fence with a sigh of wings
as the pilot flared the heavy bomber gently into a perfect
landing.

Three days later an officer of the 8th Air Force made his
first aircraft notation in the table of equipment for the
fledgling strategic air arm. *"Arrival of Aircraft: B-17E. Total: 1."*

During the next several weeks more of the B-17E
bombers made their seven-league boots crossings of the

North Atlantic. The nucleus of the new force of heavy bombers was taking shape. The airfields were becoming units that knew how to function. Flight crews, mechanics and ground personnel transformed the huge spaces into centers of life, activity, meaning. They all had the same job, of course. Carry the war to the enemy, to where he lived, and, in somewhat ungracious terms, beat the living hell out of him. With bombs. Thousands, and then tens of thousands, and then hundreds of thousands of bombs.

But it all started slowly.

At thirty-nine minutes past three o'clock in the afternoon of August 17th, 1942, the last of twelve B-17E Fortresses of Colonel Frank K. Armstrong's 97th Bomb Group, the first American heavy bomber organization to be formed in England as the spearhead of the 8th Air Force, lifted from the main runway of the American airdrome at Grafton Underwood. The names of the twelve raiders on their first mission indicated the spirit and the mood of their crews—*Baby Doll, Peggy D., Big Stuff, Butcher Shop, Yankee Doodle, Berlin Sleeper, Johnny Reb, Alabama Exterminator, Birmingham Blitzkrieg.*

Another six Fortresses headed for the coast of Europe, but they were out of the limelight. They were decoys to show up on German radar screens, to lure the Luftwaffe on a wild goose chase. The six decoys snuggled comfortably within a thick covering of escorting Spitfires.

The twelve bombers that were to strike for the first time at the German enemy assembled in tight formation, took up a steady climb while on course for the English Channel, and pointed their twelve plexiglas noses toward the city of Rouen, in France. Four squadrons of Spitfire IX fighters weaved in close as escort. As they left their target smoking behind them another five squadrons of the graceful-winged Spits slid into protective position to escort the Fortresses home.

In this initial strike by American heavy bombers in Europe during World War II, the embryonic force dropped on its target from an altitude of 23,000 feet a total of 36,900 pounds of bombs. Of this amount, approximately half fell within the target area.

The enemy seemed more fascinated than upset by the advent of the Fortresses. Antiaircraft fire, desultory at best, inflicted slight damage on two Fortresses. Three Messerschmitt Me-109 fighters swept in against the formation. Well aware of the Spitfires nearby and somewhat in the dark about the defensive firepower of the heavy bombers, the German pilots did not press their attack aggressively. They failed to damage any of the American aircraft.

There were, however, two casualties. During the return flight from the target a pigeon failed to get out of the way in time and skewered itself mightily against the plexiglas nose of a Fortress. The bombardier and navigator within the nose were showered with flying particles.

The target—the locomotive depot and rolling-stock repair shops of the Buddicum concern within the Rouen marshaling yard—escaped serious damage. Nevertheless, air planners were pleased. The crews had been blooded. The first raid was history.

Two days later the Fortresses went out again to begin the long and growing list of mission numbers. No. 2 on August 19th was carried out by twenty-two B-17Es (two Fortresses had turned back after takeoff) against German fighter airfields near Abbeville. It was a good mission in that the Fortresses had excellent formation, flew their bomb run with precision, and sprayed carpets of bombs across the runways and flight lines of the German fields, from which fighters were trying to take off to strike at the Dieppe beachhead, where the Germans were mauling a "reconnaissance in force" made up of British Commandos, American Rangers, Canadians, French, Belgians and Dutch forces.

Six more missions were carried out in August. New targets went up on the briefing maps. Amiens-Longueau, Rotterdam, Le Trait, Rotterdam again, Meaulte, Courtrai-Wevelgem. They were test missions, so to speak. Small forces of bombers protected with heavy escorts of Spitfires. The penetrations of German-ruled air were short in both distance and time. But the crews were learning how to handle their heavy bombers. How best to assemble in formation, coordinate with one another and outside commands, how to rendezvous with the fighters, how to ignore flak and hold a steady bomb run for the critical space of at least fifty seconds, how to cope with the attacks of German fighters.

The 8th Air Force and its Fortress crews were learning the ropes. More and more bombers were coming in from the States, making the long flights from their factories to Canada, Greenland, Iceland and finally to England. Bases were absorbing the influx of machines and men, maintenance shops were learning how to patch torn metal and holed skin.

Steadily the number of bombers available went up, reflected in the Fortresses dispatched to their targets within German Europe. With each succeeding raid the men who ran the 8th Air Force and planned their part in the destruction of the Third Reich found parts of the answers to the questions that lived with them every waking hour of the day or night. Some of those questions, as related to the writer by Colonel Budd J. Peaslee, B-17 and P-51 pilot in Europe during World War II, were:

> Could a bombardment formation fight its way un-escorted over a route of several hundred miles when op-posed by a vigorous defensive fighter force? Could a bombardment formation, in the face of heavy defensive an-tiaircraft and fighter opposition, accurately strike vital strategic targets located in the sprawling and complex sys-tems of an enemy city? Could bombardment formations, rising from many separate airdromes, assemble and organ-ize themselves into complex defensive formations under adverse weather conditions, and could they, upon return from their missions, break up and find their way back to base under these conditions? And, finally, could the nation produce bombers and bomber crews to do the job, and would the cost be too high to bear? The answers to these and still other questions had to be provided before day bombardment could be recognized by all as a strategic force in being. The British had the answers to night bom-bardment; the 8th Air Force had no answers, only questions and faith in an untried concept.

The initial six missions followed a pattern of learning. First the missions were to be flown under the best of all conditions—speed, altitude, formation, timing; the ele-ments which help to build mission success, measured in terms of bombs on target as against losses of the attacking planes. Heavy fighter escort by the British was accepted as a "must." Good weather was essential for green crews, and Europe, noted for its terrible "bombing weather," as-tounded everyone with skies so clear that from bombing altitude the crews could see for hundreds of miles. The

Fortresses went against their targets between 22,000 and 26,000 feet, their best fighting altitude.

On the 21st of August a mission suffered its first lapse in coordination. Twelve Fortresses arrived sixteen minutes late for their rendezvous with their escorting Spitfires. Long before the bombers reached their target, the Wilton shipyard, the Spits turned for home. The Fortresses pressed on and by the time 8th Air Force could get out its recall message to bring the bombers home and prevent their going over target without escort, it was too late. Only nine B-17Es were left in formation; three had turned back because of mechanical problems.

Approximately twenty-five Messerschmitt and Focke-Wulf fighters roared in to attack. This was it; the first real test. Fortresses against the Me-109s and the FW-109s, and no friendly fighters to help.

The running battle went on for twenty minutes. One Fortress lagged behind the formation and the German fighters singled it out for special attention. Five Focke-Wulfs went in close, shooting steadily. A 20-mm cannon shell exploded on the right side of the cockpit windscreen, wounding the pilot and copilot severely; later the copilot died of his injuries. A burst of fire chewed up the top turret. Two engines lost power, but continued to function despite damage. The Fortress gunners claimed two German fighters definitely shot down.

"It was the first time the Fortresses had been exposed to concerted fighter attack without the protection of friendly aircraft," noted an AAF historian, "and the results must have impressed the enemy pilots with the ability of the Fortress to defend itself."

Certainly the impression was deep on our side of the fence. The Americans were reassured of the B17's defensive strength. Even the British were surprised—perhaps at their *own* reactions to an airplane they had written off as help-less against German fighters. An official history of the 8th Air Force noted of this period:

> The kindergarten missions continued with what now seems a pathetically small token force of aircraft. The ship-yards at Le Trait were attacked by twelve Fortresses. Eleven reached the target at Meaulte—the Avions Potez aircraft factory and repair depot where the Luftwaffe was presum-ably licking the wounds it had received during the furious air battle that had accompanied the Allied landing at Dieppe. Thirteen were dispatched to bomb the German fighter airdrome at Courtrai-Wevelgem, in Belgium. From every mission new lessons were learned.
>
> All these missions were carried out in weather which was so good that later it seemed like a happy dream. And as mission after mission ended with no aircraft lost, the British press, cautious at first, became more and more enthusiastic. They speculated with amazement on the stamina of the American crews who failed to be affected by altitude. The *Evening Standard* surmised wisely that it was probably be-cause the American airmen were such husky specimens—baseball players, no less. A British doctor went aloft with a crew to study the effects of high-altitude flying and promptly passed out himself—an incident which merely en-hanced the legend. . . . [42]

On 6th September the Fortresses flew their tenth mis-sion and it became a hard-knuckled graduation day. The Germans had decided they now knew enough about the new American bombers to slug it out more fiercely. Forty-one Fortresses were assigned to hit the aircraft factory at Meaulte, another thirteen flew a diversionary mission by striking at the German airfield at St. Omer. From the moment the bombers reached the French coast the enemy fighters started to press home their attacks. They battered the Fortresses all the way to their target and all the way back to the French coast during withdrawal. Three Focke-Wulfs concentrated their fire on one Fortress which became the first American heavy bomber to be lost. The B-17 went down over Flasselles. It appeared to be under control but helpless to continue level flight. Returning crewmen reported four parachutes, but that was all. Before the mission ended another Fortress was lost. Crews reported the bomber straggling, "chewed up and smoking badly." It was evident the pilot was trying to get as close as possible to the English coast before going down. The British sent out air-sea rescue teams. They never found the airplane or any of its crew.

On October 2nd, Fortresses returned for the third time to the Avions Potez factory at Meaulte. The Germans attacked in strength and they butted heads all through the mission with the American bombers. Air planners noted that the long running battle "was all the more remarkable because the heavy bombers had flown under the cover, direct or indirect, of some four hundred fighter aircraft, in spite of which the Germans had been able to drive home their attacks on the bombers."

The reports spoke also of the "enthusiasm engendered by the remarkable defensive power displayed by the Fortresses."

What it was like on that mission, from which all the bombers returned, is told in this following extract from a pilot who barely made it home:

At 5:00 A.M. on the morning of October 2, 1942, I was waked up in a Nissen hut at one of our bomber stations in

England. It was dark, and for a moment I didn't know quite where I was. I dressed quickly and gulped down the tea that was brought to me. After that I went to the Intelligence office, where they gave me the exact location of the objective. It was the Potez aviation plant at Meaulte, in occupied France.

When the signal for the takeoff came, I was so scared that I could hardly talk. Somehow, though, I managed to make it.

We were in Vee of Vees all the way into the target. Our ship was *Tail-end Charlie*, the rearmost left-hand ship in the formation, and hence the last to bomb. We hit scattered heavy flak on our way in, but it was slight and did no harm. We got well over our targets, in formation and unmolested, and the bombing part was easy.

But that's when the enemy fighters started to pour it on. The Germans' strategy was obviously to pick on the last ship and shoot it down. All the gunners in the crew started calling through the interphones: "Enemy aircraft at three o'clock, Lieutenant!...At five o'clock!...At nine o'clock!..." They were all around us.

The fighters were employing two tactics that were new to me. When they peeled out of their formation to attack, they came in so close together that by the time one ship had shot up and banked away, the next in line had his sights on us.

The other dodge they used was to pretend to come in on one of the other ships, and then do a twenty-degree turn and shoot the hell out of us. Mostly they came from the rear, but at least one of them came up under us from in front, stalled, and as it fell off, raked us the length of the Fortress' belly. I could feel his hits banging into us. As a matter of fact, I could feel the effect of all their fire. It was rather like sitting in the boiler of a hot-water heater and being rolled down a steep hill.

There was an explosion behind me as a 20-mm cannon shell banged into us just behind the upper turret, and exploded; and I kept thinking, "What if it hit the flares?" If it hit the flares and ignited them, I knew we'd go up like a rocket.

Then I looked out at the right wing and saw it was shot to hell. There were holes everywhere. A lot of them were 20-mm cannon holes, and they tear a hole in the skin you could shove a sheep through. The entire wing was just a goddamn bunch of holes.

About that time, several other unpleasant things happened at once. First, one of the waist gunners yelled through the interphone: "Lieutenant, there's a bunch of wires slapping me in the face!" which meant the tail surface controls were being shot up. Second, the right-hand outboard engine "ran away" and the engine controls were messed up so we couldn't shut it off. Third, the left-hand inboard engine quit. And fourth, the ship went into a steep climb, which I couldn't control.

I forgot to say that the whole left-oxygen system had gone out, and that I was trying to get the ship down to 20,000 feet to keep half my crew from passing out. One gunner passed out from lack of oxygen, and the radio operator, seeing him lying by his gun, abandoned his own oxygen supply and put the emergency mask of the walk-around bottle over the gunner's face. The gunner revived just in time to see the radio operator pass out. He, in turn, took the emergency mask off his own face and revived the radio operator with it.

To return to the fourth unpleasant thing that happened—when the ship went into a steep climb, I simply couldn't hold her level. There was something wrong with the controls. I motioned to the copilot to help me, and between the two of us, we managed to get it forward and assume normal level flight.

Then I started to think. The enemy fighters were still shooting us up, we had a long way to go to reach England and safety, we were minus two engines and it took almost full left aileron to hold that damaged right wing up. It was time, I decided, to bail out of the aircraft. So I yelled into the interphone: "Prepare to abandon ship."

But just about that time the top gunner slid out of the top turret and fell between me and the copilot. His face was a mess. He was coughing blood; I thought he'd been wounded in the chest. It later proved that he wasn't, but he was clearly in no condition to bail out of an airplane.

I called for the bombardier and navigator to come up and help us with the top turret gunner, and they did. Back in the waist one of our gunners was manning two guns despite a bad bullet wound in his leg. I don't know how many fighters we damaged or destroyed; there wasn't time to worry about that. We got out over the Channel, finally, and a flight of Spits came racing out to meet us. Brother, they looked mighty good. We nursed the Fort across and made a belly landing on the first airdrome we could find. We nicked a hangar on the way in, but somehow we made it....

"*Lille,*" said a Fortress navigator thoughtfully, "*was our first real brawl.*"

Lille was many things. A target. In the 8th Bomber Command's files it was also Operation 54. Or if you used another system of reckoning it was Mission Number 14. If you looked at it with the view of the AAF historians, Lille was "the formal entry of the American bombers into the big league of strategic bombardment." The men who compiled the operational history of the 8th Bomber Command said, also, of Lille, that it was an "air battle, the first head-on collision between the American spearhead and the massed strength of the Luftwaffe."

At Lille, one of the great French industrial cities, were locomotive factories and great steel plants, targets "made to order" for precision bombing. To do the job the 8th Air Force planned its mission on a scale unprecedented in the brief history of heavy bomber operations in Europe. For the first time the twin-tailed, high-winged, slab-sided Liberators were to go into combat. For the first time there would be more than a hundred heavy bombers on a single mission—twenty-four Liberators and eighty-four Fortresses would strike at Lille and seven more B-17s would take a diversionary whack at Cayeux. Not all of them reached their objectives. Of the 115 heavy bombers sent out, thirty-three aborted and went home. There was still a lot to learn about even getting into the combat zone. . . .

German fighters hammered at the bomber formations "to the practical exclusion of the combined British and U.S. fighter escort, which in this instance numbered 156 aircraft, including thirty-six P-38s from the VIII Fighter Command. Unusually heavy fighter opposition brought reports of numerous combats. Three B-17s and one B-24 failed to return, although the crew of one Fortress was picked up at sea. In all, thirty-one crew members were reported missing and thirteen wounded, four B-17s were seriously damaged, and thirty-two B-17s and ten B-24s were slightly damaged by fighter action."[43]

The Lille raid of 9th October produced some new and cautious methods of examining crew reports of antiaircraft effectiveness, of fighter combat, and of claims of enemy fighters shot down, probably shot down, and damaged. A reporter took down the exciting account of furious action from one gunner who exclaimed that the Lille raid produced "the worst flak I've ever seen!" Not until later did the reporter learn that this was his first mission, and that not only was the flak the worst, but the first, he had ever seen. . . .

Initially the bomber crews claimed they had destroyed forty-eight German fighters and probably destroyed another thirty-eight. Raised British eyebrows brought a drastic reduction of the claims to twenty-five kills and thirty-eight probables. Inspection of German records shows that only two fighters were destroyed that day, according to an official AAF study. The discrepancies seem hard to accept. Either the Fortress gunners exaggerated grossly, or the Germans were lying in their record-keeping. The truth probably lies somewhere in the middle.

After the Lille mission, intelligence officers took a more skeptical attitude in evaluating gunners' claims. In a massed formation of Fortresses, gunners from several different planes might all be blazing away at the same enemy fighter. If it was hit, they all could and probably would claim that fighter as *their* kill. As a result, with nine gunners claiming the same fighter—nine fighters might be reported destroyed when, in fact, only one had been downed. Many fighters were claimed as destroyed when flames erupted from fuel tanks or engines, yet it was always possible, and often it happened, that the flames could be extinguished and the fighter landed safely. One Me-109F that was confirmed—*on film*—to have exploded violently in fire was proven to have survived. The belly tank on the Messerschmitt had been hit and it did explode in flames that virtually enveloped the rear half of the fighter. But the German pilot jettisoned the blazing tank and emerged from the momentary holocaust still full of fight, and came roaring back in for more passes at his four-engined adversaries. A fighter would be accepted as destroyed only if it had lost a wing or tail section, was completely in flames, was abandoned by the pilot, or was seen to crash.

So constricting were the new restraints put on gunners' claims that many crewmen were openly disgusted. Inevitably there appeared the story (probably apocryphal) of a Fortress gunner who watched his mate hammer a long burst at an enemy fighter attacking their bomber—without a single other bomber or fighter nearby. When the attacking fighter exploded not a hundred yards away, the gunner turned to his friend and asked: "You going to claim that one?"

The victorious gunner watched the disintegrating remains of the fighter—in many separate pieces—falling into clouds. "Nah," he replied with disgust, "I didn't see the damned thing crash."

Another major problem revealed during the Lille raid of 9th October was that most of the gunners, lacking experience, were trigger-happy and *very* sensitive to the approach of what might be German fighters. At least they weren't certain whether or not approaching fighters were ours or theirs. There wasn't much problem with the unmistakable twinboomed Lockheed P-38 Lightning, but the Spitfire was another matter. Head-on or even in side view, at high speeds, seen by a gunner squinting into the sun or bright glare from a rocking bomber it could easily be mistaken for a Messerschmitt. If the British pilot was unwary or approached too quickly or from out of the sun he could easily be provided with a hot reception—in the form of tracers suddenly splitting the sky all about him. Spitfire pilots adopted the trick of flipping up one wing so the gunners could see the elliptical shape of the airplane. It didn't take long for the German pilots to follow the maneuver—

while *their* comrades came tearing in for attacks in those few seconds of advantage.

All in all, with the numbers of airplanes and the many hundreds of heavy machine guns blazing away, it was a small miracle that the Fortresses didn't shoot each other up more often. But there were mistakes, of course. At the close of a critique, a Group commander asked if anyone had any matters to be drawn to the attention of the others in the room. A tall pilot who had led a flight in combat that day, rose slowly from his chair and stalked to the front of the room.

"Fixing a piercing gaze upon the pilots of the two wing ships that had flanked his own bomber, he drew from his pocket a battered metal object and held it up for all the room to see. It was an American .50 caliber slug that the pilot had found in his own plane. One of the wing-ship pilots got up, red-faced, and whispered in the ear of the Group CO. Whereupon the CO hastily remarked that it would probably be better if nobody had anything more to say. The meeting was adjourned, with laugher."[44]

On one point there was no argument. The Fortress was the most rugged and powerful aerial machine ever to go to war. No matter how fierce the opposition—and Luftwaffe fighter pilots were men of great courage and skill—no one could fault the Flying Fortress. The official records frequently remark "amazing durability," and even before the first combat mission of the 17th of August, the men who crewed the Fortresses knew what they had. There was an accident in mid-August, only a few days before the first raid was to be flown, and the details of what happened swept through the ranks of the men who were about to be blooded.

The pilot of the episode was in training formation at 32,000 feet when his number four engine—the far right engine—suddenly ran away. Immediately he feathered the propeller. The crew looked out from their windows and ports to see that one of the propeller blades had broken off. Instinctively they hitched tighter their parachute harnesses. They had anticipated correctly the extent of the danger. Moments later they heard the alarm bell as their pilot warned them to prepare for any contingency. He dropped the nose and put the Fortress into a glide, starting to ease his way earthward. But the bomber had descended barely two thousand feet when the Number Three engine—the right inboard—exploded and erupted flames. Again the alarm bell sounded, and this time the pilot, aware that he had a disintegrating airplane on his hands, ordered the crew to bail out immediately. Then, in the pilot's own words:

I started the plane down in a circle to the left, keeping the two good engines down. By the time I reached 14,000 feet, fire had spread all the way back to the ailerons, over the Number Four engine and all along the side of the fuselage.

At 12,000 feet the Number Two engine sputtered, backfired, and then quit. This sort of made me mad.

Up until then I'd been too scared to do anything. I looked over at the Number Three engine. It was hanging over the side of the wing, held by a few cables. The oil tank was visible and on fire. I started to get out of my seat to bail out, but the wings were still on and I thought I'd try to get it down.

Control was nearly impossible, since the bottom of the right wing had been blown off, and a piece of cowling had knocked off the vertical fin. I broke through the cloud layer at 9,000 feet and looked for a field. It was a heavily wooded area, but I spotted a pasture about 800 feet long. I circled the end of it, losing altitude, and as the tires had been destroyed by fire I came in with a wheels-up landing. The entire right side of the airplane was in flames by this time. I started to leave the ship. The place where I had landed was the rifle range of a British Rifle Brigade. About five hundred of them were there, and as I came out they came running up, about a dozen of them with fire extinguishers. Though the gas tanks were leaking we managed to get the fire out.

The crews knew that they had something great in the Fortress—and they knew also that they would need every ounce of strength they could get. Often they saw the results of deadly hits with cannon shells—hits that took the metal off wings and fuselages like the skin peeling away from an onion. The Wright Cyclones in the Fortress were unquestionably the most durable and reliable engines ever put into an airplane. The 8th Bomber Command's official records speak of flak bursts that "knocked whole cylinders out of engines that still kept turning." The crews in Europe were learning what the Pacific crews had already come to know—you could shoot away the hydraulic systems, tear up the oxygen systems, chew up the control cables, blow holes and sieve the Fortress from one end to the other, knock out engines and otherwise commit general mayhem to the airplane, and she would still fly. With one engine dead and the prop feathered pilots could still maintain formation. Many a Fort came home on two engines. Some lost three engines, and if they were at high altitude and the pilot knew, really knew, what he was doing, he could stretch that powered glide enough to bring the cripple all the way back to England. They not only could—more than a few did. Other Fortresses arrived over England with engines that quit or fuel tanks that ran dry and the pilots brought those bombers in as well—dead-stick landings in a four-engine heavy, though, could be quite an adventure.

And there was nothing left wanting in the caliber of the men who crewed the Fortresses. One incident speaks for the men who carried the war into German territory:

I was radio gunner in a Fort called the *Jersey Bounce*. We were getting along all right until the flak caught up with us and a fragment sliced through the fuselage into the ankle of our navigator. The pilot called me on the inter-phone to come and administer first aid to the navigator, but I was too busy fighting off enemy planes that were attack-ing from the rear. As soon as I had a chance, I crawled for-ward to the nose and found the navigator sitting on an ammunition box cheerfully spotting fighters for the bom-bardier, who was leaping from one side of the nose to the other, manning both guns.

I applied a tourniquet to the navigator's leg, gave him some sulfa pills, and sprinkled the wound with sulfa pow-der. Three times I had to stop to take a gun and help the bombardier ward off attacks from dead ahead.

Then the lead ship of our element was hit in the Number One engine and began to fall back. We dropped back, too, holding our position on our leader's wing. Just then an FW flashed in like a barracuda, came right between the two Fortresses, and raked our ship with cannon fire. I could feel the hits slamming into us. Word came through that the tail gunner was hit, and then just afterward the interphone went dead.

The wounded navigator seemed all right, so I crawled

back to the tail gunner. He was intact, but he told me that the ball turret had received a direct hit. I went back to take a look and found it completely wrecked. The gunner was crumpled in the wreckage. I tried to do what I could for him, but it was no use. I don't think he ever knew what hit him. I reached into the turret and fixed the broken connections of the interphone, then I went back to the nose and gave the navigator a shot of morphine to ease his pain. Then I went back to the radio compartment to man my own guns again.

That's all there was to it.

It didn't take the German pilots long to discover the weakest spot in the B-17E's defense. The frontal, or head-on, pass became their favorite attack. Sweeping ahead of the bombers they would turn into position and then, at precisely the moment calculated to bring about the most effective use of their heavy cannons and machine guns, they bored in for the kill.

Sometimes the gunners were able to force the German fighters to break off the attack, or waste their firing pass. Sometimes, even with the lack of forward firepower in the early B-17E models, they could pour enough slugs into the onrushing fighter to explode it in flames or to kill the enemy pilot.

Sometimes they were successful in defending themselves. And sometimes in their success they created disaster. The writer's good friend, Budd Peaslee, recreates such a moment:

The coastline is nearing and the fighter attacks dwindle to a few, and then there are lengthening gaps in their frequency. Finally, they seem to desert the formations. But there is to be one more, a finale.

Far out in front a Focke-Wulf FW-190 completes a turn toward the bomber formations. It bores in straight and level. All possible guns in the bombers swing to bear on the loner; they spit and chatter in an unbroken staccato thunder as hunted and hunted close at the combined speed of the two. No flashes are observed from the guns of the fighter, and there is no indication that he has been hit by the withering fire he faces from the half-hundred bomber guns. The approach of the fighter takes a matter of seconds, yet those seconds are rare in a lifetime and can live as long as the witness. The fighter makes no move to break away as is the practice in head-on attacks. There is time, then, only for a flashing thought that occurs instantly: "My God, he is going to ram!" Then it is over... except that what happened lives in the mind in slow motion, and can only be described in time-consuming words.

The tiny fighter and the massive bomber come together. The impact is only a few yards away from our bomber yet no sound is audible. It is as though the bomber opened its mouth and swallowed the fighter with a single gulp. Where the nose of the bomber had been, including the bombardier-navigator compartment and the pilot-copilot cockpit, there yawns an empty void. Small pieces seem to drip from the chin of the bomber and it appears to stop in midair. The propellers continue to turn as though trying to struggle on toward England.

Out of the very tail of the bomber there appears a single object. It is the great engine of the fighter that has ripped from its frame. It gives the illusion of slow motion as it drops away toward the rear. Then the bomber falls forward into a vertical dive and disappears behind and below the wing of its neighbor. The sky is clean again. Death has come with the suddenness of an electric shock to eleven

brave men—ten in the B-17 and a loner in the Focke-Wulf
their earthly remains commingled inseparably forever.

The war went on. But in the States, across the length of
the continent, a new Flying Fortress was being born.
B-17F, the AAF called it.

# CHAPTER 15

# THE QUEEN

THE MONTH OF APRIL 1942 was a mixture of disaster and promise. Disaster was real in the form of one Japanese success after the other throughout the length of Asia and across the vast reaches of the Pacific. The Battles of the Coral Sea and Midway lay in the future. The start of the bombing campaign in Europe was a dream, vast in its promise but tenuous in its actuality. The invasion of North Africa was yet to be committed.

The history of the Flying Fortress is, of course, a reflection in many ways of the course of the war. The B-17E, committed to production before the catastrophe of Pearl Harbor, was the first Fortress intended to carry the fight to the enemy—the first offensive heavy bomber of the long and famous line. The AAF called for a production run of 512 of the gun-bristling B-17E model. Yet even as the airplane began its flight tests, and before it blooded its first crews in battle, the Boeing engineers at Seattle were completing their design work on the model that would succeed the E. This would be the new B-17F, the Fortress variant that established the Flying Fortress as the Queen of the bombers.

In April of 1942 Boeing Model 299P—AAF designation B-17F—was introduced onto the production lines of the Boeing plant that was working round-the-clock to turn out Fortresses. But Boeing would be only one of three giant aviation firms to manufacture the new B-17F and its successor—the B-17G. The other companies assigned to producing Fortresses were Douglas, which used two factories for Fortress production, and Vega.

Originally the Army Air Forces had established the Boeing-Douglas-Vega manufacturing pool to assist in the rapid production of the B-17E model. But the F version was as great an advance over the E as the E was over former models. The industrial complex stretched across a vast section of the country and involved hundreds of thousands of people, and by the time the three companies were ready to produce as a concerted effort, the decision had been made to change the production lines to the B-17F. This was the first of the Fortress series to be manufactured by all three firms on a joint basis. Boeing expanded its Seattle production lines and put up a huge new plant in Wichita, Kansas. At Long Beach, California, the Douglas Aircraft Company built another great facility solely for the Fortress; the firm also set up production lines at Santa Monica.

In order to identify the actual manufacturer (for purposes of equipment, modifications, servicing and operation) the AAF assigned suffixes to the basic identification. Fortresses turned out by Boeing were identified as B-17F-BO, those by Vega as B-17F-VE, those by Douglas at Santa Monica as B-17F-DO, and those by Douglas at Long Beach as B-17F-DL. Thus, a typical designation for a Fortress might read: B-17F-11-FO. The B-17 represented the seventeenth major bombardment design accepted by the AAF. *F* identified the sixth major design change to the B-17; the *11* identified the eleventh minor equipment change to the B-17F, and BO, of course, identified the manufacturer as Boeing.

The industrial team directed into being by the AAF had no equal anywhere in the world. By March of 1944 the three-company team in the five factories produced, for that one month alone, a total of 578 Flying Fortress bombers! (Production declined later only because of the huge effort already being thrown into mass production of the huge Boeing B-29 Superfortress.) By the time production of the Fortress came to an end in May of 1945 with the defeat of Germany, the Douglas-Vega team had turned out the formidable number of 5,745 of the heavy bombers.

The untrained observer would have been hard put to tell the difference between the B-17E, of which 512 were built, and its B-17F successor, of which 3,500 rolled off the production lines. The only change in the airplane immediately visible was in the nose, an extended plexiglas molding which lacked the supporting rib frames that so readily identified the E model. The only blemish in the smoothly molded plexiglas was the optically flat panel through which the bombardier directed his Norden bombsight.

The experienced pilot, crew member or mechanic who knew his airplane intimately would have noticed also a change in the propellers. The blades were fatter, known to the crews as "paddle blades." Their greater surface area gave them a heftier bite of the air, and they were considered a godsend to the pilots who flew the B-17F under hot tropical conditions. Low-altitude performance improved measurably with the new propellers. There were other small visible changes: engine cowlings were modified to take new dust filters, and to provide sufficient space for feathering the wider blades of the new propellers.

To the eye, the B-17F looked very much like the B-17E. But beneath the shining metal skin of the F there were more than four hundred important modifications—changes that improved greatly its fighting capabilities and gave it that "last extra touch" in superb handling characteristics that so endeared the F version to its pilots. Of all the Fortress models, it was the B-17F that pilots acclaimed as the Queen of all the bombers ever built.

Initial combat experience showed the need for better fire protection and the F model had self-sealing oil tanks. This one change alone promised longer life from engines shot to pieces by enemy fire. An engine that survived major damage from direct gunfire would still fail without its oil supply; the self-sealing oil tanks thus assured a greater chance that the Wright Cyclones would continue to deliver power when most needed—to bring the crews home again.

More and more, combat experience proved the validity of the basic design of the Fortress in which electrical power was preferred to hydraulic systems. Again combat experience dictated the actions of the Boeing engineers, and into the B-17F went additional power sources for the electrical systems—a vital surplus under the hammering strain of battle. Improved design of the power quadrant (control settings) system met with the immediate satisfaction of pilots. The bomb racks and their release systems had long been troublesome; these were redesigned and improved. The brake system, oxygen system, communications equipment, gun mounts, ammunition feeds, were only a few more of the four hundred major changes that went into the airplane.

After production of the B-17F was under way, another major modification was instituted that brought about a remarkable advance in performance. Into these late-model F bombers went the new Wright Cyclone GR-1820-97 engine. Under normal conditions it delivered the same 1,200 horsepower at takeoff as in earlier models. But the engine had a "war emergency rating" for limited periods of operation when power was increased greatly to compensate for overload conditions or combat situations. So effective was the new engine that at 25,000 feet the-97 turned up 1,380 horsepower—15 percent more than at takeoff. With the war emergency power ratings and the new paddle-bladed props the B-17F, despite increased weight and complexity, was the fastest of the Fortress line, with a rated maximum speed at gross weight of 325 miles per hour. The reader is cautioned once again that maximum speed was a condition achieved only rarely in flight, as continued flight under full power would swiftly reduce the engines to clattering junk.

Greater range was another virtue of the B-17F that endeared the airplane to its crews. In order to carry out long-range attacks, the B-17E and previous models flew with reduced bomb loads so that auxiliary fuel tanks could be fitted within the bomb bay. Sometimes tanks were added even in the radio compartment. The F model was built with new wing fuel cells—later known as "Tokyo tanks"—that gave the airplane a maximum range of 4,220 miles.

The maximum gross weight—including the so-called overload weight—was an important factor in determining the range of an airplane. But the weight of normal and auxiliary fuel cells, and the bomb loads could not be increased beyond a point or the landing gear would collapse beneath the load. Compensation for this problem was a major feature of the new B-17F. The normal gross weight had been increased by 2,000 pounds over the E model to a new normal maximum gross of 56,000 pounds. But exigencies of war rarely permit strict adherence to technical manuals, and, since the landing gear of the F was strengthened greatly over its predecessor, the war overload gross went almost at once to 65,000 pounds. But even this limit was surpassed, and often the B-17Fs were sent down the runway with a gross weight of 72,000 pounds—the sort of takeoff where an engine cough could mean a flaming disaster.

The armament of the B-17F went through many minor modifications to improve the ability of the airplane to defend itself against enemy fighter resistance and fly back home again. Take the clear plexiglas molded nose, for example: head-on attacks by Japanese and German fighters dictated improvised changes in the field which were to become standard for most F models. Many of the F variants were built with cheek guns on either side of the nose aft of the plexiglas molding. But these proved ineffectual to meet the shattering firepower of enemy fighters barreling head-on against the bombers. The gunners rigged mounts within the plexiglas molding that, in the most common version, took a brace of .50 caliber machine guns. (The original production versions still retained the single .30 caliber gun of the B-17E. From what the reader has seen so far it should not be difficult to understand why the crews threw away these light weapons and installed single and twin-gun mounts of the heavier, longer-ranging "fifty.") Most B-17F models in battle were seen with as many as four .50 caliber guns in the nose, and the standard armament of the top turret with two guns, the radio compartment with one, the ball and tail turrets each with twin guns, and the two waist positions each with a single .50, for a total of thirteen heavy machine guns.

The maximum bomb load of the B-17F, as with any bombardment aircraft, depended on many factors, the most important being the weight of the fuel carried. The initial production-order F models had an official maximum bomb load of 9,600 pounds, but the airplane rarely flew combat missions with so heavy an ordnance load crammed into the bays. The actual bomb load carried on combat missions in Europe, over a maximum range of 1,400 miles, was usually 4,800 pounds. Depending upon the size of the bomb to be carried the load would vary, but after long experience the records showed the normal load was between 4,000 and 5,000 pounds.

When necessary, the B-17F could drag a staggering load of bombs into the air. It was possible (and some bombers did so) to carry eight 1,600-pound bombs in the internal bomb bay, as well as one 4,000-pounder tucked up beneath each wing, for the overwhelming load of 20,800 pounds of bombs. But with this massive ordnance aboard the pilot had to fly as if he were walking on eggshells loaded with nitro. The stress on the wings was brutal; any severe flight maneuver could exceed the structural limitation even of the rugged Fortress and tear away the wings or the tail surfaces. The effective range of the airplane suffered, as might be expected, and with extremely heavy loads of this nature, the missions were restricted to close targets. Nevertheless there were times when the Fortress would be called upon to serve in this manner.

## CHAPTER 16

## ON THE EDGE

The B-17 took it again at Utah's Salt Flats when we started flying a blind landing system—the original Instrument Landing System, I guess you would call it—except that we observed no minimums; we just flew right into the runway and, as you can imagine, the ship took a tremendous pounding as we hit the ground at 120 miles an hour, often at the wrong angle. But she was a real ship. She took it all, shook it off and flew again. I've seen a lot of airplanes in combat . . . but the B-17 was always the best . . . she was the airplane that took the most punishment and came back for more.

ROBERT K. MORGAN
B-17 PILOT, 8TH AF

BEFORE THE FORTRESS EVER went to combat it had to be molded into a fighting weapon. That requirement had at its base the crew which would transform so many tons of metal into a juggernaut of the air. The crew and the airplane as a single entity had to be created—and that meant a vast logistics, supply, servicing and training organization. It demanded the smoothly functioning apparatus made up of an extraordinarily complex mixture of men, machines and the units into which they were formed.

The men who flew the Flying Fortress in World War II were not professional killers. Not when they came into the AAF, when they completed basic training; not even when they were assigned to operational units after learning how to fly and shoot and fight. Yet their job was intended to culminate in smearing other people until these people came to the decision that further resistance was futile.

That kind of job took killers. To make killers of men who were lawyers, mechanics, farmers, clerks, cab drivers, copy writers, seamen—and every other occupation in the kaleidoscope of American life—took a special kind of training organization. Men were formed into crews, and the crews came to know one another as members of a tightly knit group so that they might fulfill, for a brief period, the purpose for which they were equipped and trained. To do unto other men as they were trying to do unto a great many . . .

When the 384th Bombardment Group (Heavy) of the AAF wrapped up its training in the United States, it was described starkly by one of its leaders, Colonel Budd J. Peaslee.

And now the 384th stood ready as a machine of destruction. It had been brought to a peak of efficiency; its mission to kill, maim, burn, destroy. It had been taught these functions without emotion, simply as a job to be done. Final leaves were granted for the men to visit their homes for the last time, the girls had been kissed, and the wives, who had followed their men from base to base, were dispatched to their places of residence for the duration. The group awaited the order to fly.

And fly they did. Day and night, in clear weather and foul, during weekdays and through long holidays. They wore out more Fortresses and other heavy bombers than were being chopped out of the heavens by the Germans and the Japanese. The training machine of air combat crews was a huge grinding mill. It was implacable, and yet it was intensely personal to every man who was about to lay his life on the line.

It was complicated, time-consuming, wearying of soul and limb, and costly in terms of dollars and materiel. The training of men for combat in the Army and Navy is guided by traditions, systems, experience. Tactics and weapons might vary from one generation to the next, but each service remained closeted in its own philosophy, proven and accepted.

That changed when men flew off to war. The musket may have evolved into the automatic rifle, the Gatling into a deadly .50 caliber that fired at 900 rounds per minute, but the machine with wings was new. With the airplane came revolutionary new methods, equipment, and doctrine. The weapons of advanced technology called for radical revisions in training.

The basic training of a soldier—everything from the infantry drill field to memorizing the Articles of War—simply steeped him quickly in the military system and its methods. Now he was ready to learn the real business of waging a technological war. That meant not a hasty run-through. It meant a year at the least of concentrated education and training. The bomber pilot, supported by his crew, could destroy an entire factory, could sink an aircraft carrier and destroy a hundred planes and thousands of men and wreck the results of several hundred million dollars' worth of effort.

"The airman," Budd Peaslee reflected to the writer, "had to be trained to use the heavy bomber with a cool and a precise calculation. He had to remain cool and be able to exercise that precision under situations of great tension and appalling personal danger. He had to use his weapon—a giant of destruction—without emotion. That was a luxury he had to be denied. He had to consider only the accuracy of his task. He had to do that without thought of compassion for the recipients of his bombs. That they might be women and children and noncombatants could not—must not—be a matter of his concern."

It was a rule harsh and unwavering. It was war.

The writer followed the history through training and information of the 384th Bombardment Group (Heavy), of which Colonel Budd J. Peaslee and Captain "Pop" Dolan, intelligence officer, kept excellent records. This chapter is not intended as a complete discourse on training in B-17s, for such a narrative would fill an entire volume. Rather, through a brief search of the events involving the 384th we may obtain a look into "what it was like," which, along with the historical record of the Fortress itself, provides us with another and important facet of the machine and its men.

Like most other bombardment organizations that flew in combat, the 384th was activated after the war began. On January 1, 1943, Budd Peaslee, commanding officer of the new group, and Pop Dolan, its intelligence officer, surveyed their "home", a desolate, wind-whipped, miserable stretch of real estate about one hundred yards east of the Nevada-Utah border. The remote area lay along the edge of the Bonneville Salt Flats, although the site, known as Wendover Army Air Base, was itself on desert. Nothing in the world could have been more barren. The salt flats themselves are the flattest stretch of land in the world—the only place that is so flat you can see the curvature of the earth. On a clear day one may see telephone poles disappearing over the horizon. More specifically Wendover lay 125 miles to the east of Salt Lake City, Utah, and some 500 miles to the east of San Francisco. Wendover itself was barren—and the countryside for miles around, composed of salt flats, mountains, and sandy hillocks, offered nothing in the way of welcome relief. As a site for training bomber crews it was outstanding—there was nothing to do but fly and pay full attention to what was going on.

While Peaslee and Dolan set themselves to the task of creating the organization-to-be, the combat crews who would make up the 384th began to arrive by rail. They had come from Gowan Field in Idaho where individuals were being molded into ten-man crews, personalities welded into teams. First they had been brought together and then they had initiated their transition training in the Flying Fortress, the airplane that they would take into combat as part of the 8th Air Force. The records forwarded to Colonel Peaslee indicated the arriving crews were at the point where they were ready to begin combat crew training and their final course before being committed to combat in the Big League.

"Other troops also began to arrive from the reception centers and specialized schools throughout the country," relates Colonel Peaslee. "These were the 'filler personnel' trained in the hundred and one specialities needed for a self-sustaining organization—cooks, intelligence specialists, operations personnel, armament, instrument, engine, automotive, ordnance, supply, police, administrative, medical, weather, finance, firemen, and communications personnel, to name just a few. Add to these the less specialized personnel to take care of the housekeeping, who had received only the barest training prior to assignment to the group.

"The task confronting us was to take this great variety of specialists and nonspecialists and make them into a smoothly functioning whole with no weak links."

The first airplanes to arrive for training didn't help matters. The 384th was cursed, as were most units in assembly, with airplanes that had been used by not one but several preceding groups. Thus the newly formed crews of the 384th began flight operations in B-17 bombers that Peaslee described as "in anything but good condition—student flying ages an aircraft far more quickly than is normal with experienced crews and well-qualified maintenance mechanics. In other words," the Colonel said with a sigh, "these were dogs with an extremely high out-of-commission rate. Great pressure was placed on the commanding officer, his maintenance engineer, and maintenance crews to keep the aircraft in the air day and night to build up the flying time and experience of the combat crews. As a result, the workdays were 24 hours long and those aircraft not flying were being worked on around the clock. It was a standing joke that at some bases aircraft occasionally logged over 24 hours of flying in a single day."

As might be expected, the pressure on all personnel was severe, and it got worse as the weeks passed. The natural result of this would be tempers rubbed to the raw and personal dislikes brought to the explosive point. However, as Colonel Peaslee relates, "to the surprise of all concerned this did not often occur. Hot food, plenty of coffee, a sympathetic understanding, and a careful watch maintained by the flight surgeons seemed to maintain a good morale. Those who labored through the long night hours seemed to feel a responsibility to those who were to face the enemy in conflict. Toil and discomfort were their lot; while physical danger was the accepted future of the combat crews, rarely has such a balance of effort and effect been achieved."

It is difficult, except for those who have been there, to picture the Rockies in the height of winter. The cold came spilling down the flanks of the mountains and was snatched up by winds that blew with appalling force and regularity across the vast dry and salt lake beds. Even when the air cleared the wind had a vicious bite from the cold and the great snow-banks heaped upon the mountains that on three sides surrounded the base. Often the sky vanished beneath howling storms of wind-driven snow, and it was cold, it was always cold, in those bitter winter months. Protective gear was plentiful but less than needed to shield a man from the sudden snow squalls which, when the temperature rose during the heat of the midday sun, turned to rain squalls and then, at night, to sleet and ice.

The weather did more than to accent the misery of the isolated B-17 training installation. The winter storms would normally have forced most aircraft out of the cloud-ridden sky and kept them on the ground. The exigencies of preparing for war dictated otherwise and demanded maximum possible flight and training. What was worst of all, Budd Peaslee recalls, were "those long practice navigation missions that had to leave the broad lake basin and cross the towering mountain barriers reaching toward 15,000 feet."

Sometimes the storms inflicted their toll. "The hazards of winter flying," relates Peaslee, "were brought harshly home to the 384th almost at once. The 100th Group, preparing to move on to final phasing, was scheduling the last of its long-range, night navigation flights over the mountains and desert wastes of central Nevada. It was the last night of such flights when one of the bombers failed to return. At once, in the clearing weather of daylight, a search was mounted, using all available aircraft, over the route the flight had been scheduled to take following its final radio position report. At mid-afternoon the wreckage was sighed high in the Humboldt Mountains near Elko, Nevada. There were no survivors. Such tragedies had come to be accepted as the rule rather than the exception. At least one crew of each group to pass through training had come to a similar end or had been lost in some training accident."

Wendover was the end and the beginning of nowhere. After the heated activity of flight training during the days, the base came almost to a standstill. Almost, but not quite. Those who had flown or worked in the cold for long hours were grateful to fall into their beds, for the mornings came early and first calls to renew training came even earlier. There was little to do, anyway. Except for skeleton servicing crews and the maintenance teams who would work the night through to prepare the Fortresses for their aerial stints the next morning, Wendover went to sleep. The lights all across the base went out, one after the other, until only the minimum needed for nocturnal activities remained.

Each group completed their combat training at Wendover in 90 days. This was actually the final tour of training which for some men had already lasted more than a year. For the 384th there came an unexpected break in the monotony of routine when the meteorologists promised two weeks of intensely bad weather—and no flying. Impossible—the training couldn't be held up that long. With so many military bases at its disposal the Army was certain to find one that could harbor an entire group-in-training for two weeks. They did. The 384th roared out of Wendover and transported itself into the deep snows of Great Falls Army Air Base in Montana. They kept up the routine of flying every day and, often through the nights.

Then there was a change. Colonel Peaslee relates—

"On April 1, 1943, the 384th—rough, tough and eager—

moved out of Wendover, Utah, and descended on Sioux City, Iowa, like a funnel-shaped cloud. At Sioux City came the long-awaited new B-17s. They were beautiful to behold. There were new guns, new bombsights, new everything; there was even a smell of newness to the aircraft."

As only he can from his position as commanding officer of the 384th Bombardment Group, Colonel Peaslee provides a summing up of the effort:

As the month of April 1943 ran its inevitable course the training time of the 384th Bombardment Group was running out. Its members had been given the nearest experience possible to actual combat in the peaceful unbombed American countryside. They had fired their machine guns against moving miniature replicas of Focke-Wulf and Messerschmitt fighters on a Utah hillside with combat-experienced instructors looking over their shoulders and talking in their ears. They had dropped their bombs after long, complicated navigation missions on targets outlined to scale on the Utah salt flats. They had sat through endless hours of classroom study and lectures, memorized procedures, practiced techniques, and perfected themselves in every foreseeable area in the performance of their combat function. They had been instructed and drilled in every emergency, lifesaving, and self-defense method known, to the point of being thrown, fully clothed in heavy flying equipment, in a swimming pool with a packed rubber life raft to simulate a ditching in the North Sea. They had sat through mock briefings during which actual enemy targets were described and shown in photo enlargements, and on practice missions they had been intercepted and "attacked" by "hostile" fighters. They had been taught the use of hand weapons and survival kits in case they should be downed in enemy territory.

Returnees from Eighth Air Force combat operations

were back in the United States, after having participated in
several missions and with firsthand knowledge of the enemy. Commanders of groups in training were given the pre-
rogative of requesting that these veterans be brought in to
tell the men and officers of their experience in combat. In
the 384th this optional service was declined. With the
group training complete, there seemed no benefit in use-
lessly adding to the worries and apprehensions of the men.
Some of these men were going to die, still others would disappear, with their fate never to be known with certainty.
This much all of them knew and seldom mentioned or even
allowed the thoughts of it to invade their minds. To have
the morbid gruesome facts stated aloud in open meeting
was not the best method of building the strong morale upon
which they must depend when hope would be dim. . . .

It had not been easy. Every man in the group, now
numbering well over a thousand individuals, had had to
contribute his fair share. All had not been love and kisses.
There had been strict patterns of behavior and rigid rules
and regulations, also there had been infractions and penal-
ties. There had been those, too, who did not fit; those who
had been morally unacceptable as associates to the many.
There had been high-spirited deviltry that had resulted in
disciplinary measures for both men and officers. There had
been misassignment, and shifting to make the machinery of
organization function more smoothly. But there was one
thing there had not been—that was a fatal accident or serious injury of any kind. This was a record in any air force.
Never before had there been a group that completed its
training without a death. The goddess of good fortune had
ridden along on the missions.

And now the 384th stood ready as a machine of destruction . . . its mission to kill, maim, burn, destroy. . . . The
Group awaited the order to fly.

# CHAPTER 17

# ANOTHER WAR

THERE WAS A LEGEND in the 8th Air Force about a Flying Fortress with the call sign George 309.

After a raid deep into Germany, cut off from the rest of its formation, slashed and battered, the lone straggling Fortress crawled through the air back to England. Approaching its home base the pilot radioed the control tower:

"Hello, Lazy Fox, hello Lazy Fox. This is G for George, 309, G for George, 309, calling Lazy Fox. Will you give me landing instructions, please? Pilot and copilot dead, two engines feathered, fire in the radio room, vertical stabilizer gone, no flaps, no hydraulics, no brakes, control cables shot away, crew bailed out, bombardier wounded and flying the ship. Give me landing instructions."

After a brief pause the tower replied:

"I hear you, G for George. Hello, G for George. Here are your landing instructions. Repeat slowly, please, repeat slowly. Our Father who art in heaven . . ."

\*    \*    \*

Sometimes, to the men who planned the bombing of Germany, there appeared to be as much difficulty in deciding on objectives as there was in fighting the German once you arrived.

The obstacles were many and they ran the gamut from technical to global policy.

In the summer of 1942 the strategic plans of the Allies for the proposed aerial devastation of occupied Europe and Germany floundered in a sea of uncertainty. No question but that the hammer must be applied against Germany at the earliest opportunity. But to what extent should the offensive against Japan be sacrificed to accelerate the air war against Germany? To create the sledgehammer and assist in preparations for the invasion of France—Operation BOLERO—the U.S. decided in the spring of 1942 to establish a powerful heavy bomber force in the British Isles. This was the Eighth Air Force which had come into being—on paper—in January 1942; three months later it was committed officially to BOLERO.

As might be anticipated, the early life of the new command was a frenzied nightmare of jumbled logistics and a shortage of men and planes. Major General Carl A. Spaatz took over the 8th and organized it into bomber, fighter, composite and service commands. Spaatz set up his headquarters at Bushy Park, Teddington, in the suburbs of London. In keeping with the use of code names for security purposes, Headquarters Eighth Air Force was henceforth known as WIDEWING. No doubt the Germans knew it too.

Brigadier General Ira C. Eaker received as his special charge the 8th Bomber Command. Into a hurriedly evacuated girls' school at High Wycombe in Buckinghamshire, thirty miles west of London, went Eaker and his staff. Inevitably the code name was applied, and the 8th Bomber Command headquarters became known as PINETREE.

The task of creating a great aerial striking arm defied the imagination. No history of the Flying Fortress—which constituted the essence of power of the 8th Bomber Command—could be complete without acknowledgment of the superb cooperation and selfless labors of the British, without which the 8th would never have come to be. The British offered more than cooperation and direct assistance; they had the priceless ingredient of experience. The Royal Air Force had already proven its mettle in combat. While the growing numbers of Fortresses and Liberators under Eaker were still in the "kindergarten" stage of preparations, the British were hammering Germany with massive aerial blows. Early in 1942 the British had begun to create the airdromes, installations, facilities and communications required to support the huge organization promised in the 8th Air Force. There were, to be sure, differences of opinion, bitter arguments and appalling frustration. But the conflicts arose more from the vexing problems created by the Americans' frequent changes of plans than from vacillation on the part of their hosts.

Setting up a total of 127 airdromes and other facilities necessary to sustain the fighters, the bombers, the service and maintenance units, in the midst of fighting their own harrowing, costly, and bitter war was a herculean task. But the British did the job so well that in June of 1942 General Eaker was prompted to write to Carl Spaatz that the British had "cooperated 100 percent in every regard. They have lent us personnel when we had none, and have furnished us clerical and administrative staffs; they have furnished us liaison officers for Intelligence, Operations, and Supply; they have furnished us transportation; they have housed and fed our people and they have answered promptly and willingly all our requisitions; in addition they have made available to us for study their most secret devices and documents. We are extremely proud of the relations we have been able to establish between out British Allies and ourselves..."

These early months of the air war in Europe—when American participation waxed from paper reports to formations in the air—were a time of extraordinary underestimation and overestimation. The British, helpful to the point of embarrassment, were also brutally frank in their appraisal of the B-17E, stating flatly that the Flying Fortress could never survive in German air. The Americans, on the other hand, were overly optimistic in believing that the Fortress even without fighter escort could batter its way through any aerial defenses and return home with an acceptable minimum of losses. And everybody was hopelessly optimistic in judging the ability of the Allies to move quickly in invasion strength against occupied Europe.

Out of this optimism came one of the most grossly unrealistic war plans of all time—Project SLEDGEHAMMER, which presented seriously the possibilities of a cross-Channel invasion as early as September of 1942. The Germans quickly demolished this disastrous illusion, and the Allies in turn came up with a new overall scheme for smashing the enemy—Operation ROUNDUP, which called for a massive assault against Europe in the spring of 1943. That plan also was destined for the wastebasket.

The original plans for BOLERO, the buildup of heavy bomber strength in Europe, began to suffer a series of drastic blows from within the Allied camp. It became all too clear that if SLEDGEHAMMER had been ridiculously optimistic, Operation ROUNDUP was scarcely less so. And there loomed larger and larger in all considerations a combat theater that had been conveniently relegated to a backstage role—the Mediterranean. Events in a distant theater of conflict had raised the Mediterranean, and Africa, to a new status.

The Russians were being hammered brutally by the German Army. And if the Russians kept falling back, if they continued to yield before the savage German pressure, all hell would break loose. In the summer of 1942 the Wermacht was bludgeoning the Russians and clearing them out of the Don bend. No one doubted that the Germans would next strike toward the Volga and the Caucasus with its wealthy oil fields—*and* its geographic placement as the land bridge to the Asian Continent. And the Japanese. The critical area of the Persian Gulf would be endangered. Egypt might prove to be beyond hope of keeping in Allied hands.

"These possibilities," notes the official history of the AAF, "seemed to put flesh on the nightmare of Allied strategists, the junction of European and Asiatic enemies on the shores of the Indian Ocean. That Germany and Japan had no such plans for a coordinated strategy was not then known to the Allies."

But were it to come to pass, it would be "a defeat of catastrophic proportions." The time was ripe for a massive Allied blow in the Mediterranean.

The AAF history notes that:

By August the American and British governments had decided to mount in 1942 Operation TORCH, landings on the Atlantic and Mediterranean coasts of northwest Africa, as the most practicable means of relieving the pressure on the U.S.S.R. and of removing the menace of Rommel from Egypt. TORCH was to be coordinated with a renewed offensive by the Eighth Army. It replaced ROUNDUP, the landing in France projected for the spring of 1943.[45]

The decisions that led to TORCH were to affect drastically B-17 operations in Europe, and cripple the buildup of strength needed to destroy German industry from the air. The secret orders for TORCH were read in H.Q. 8th Air Force with dismay. The bombers, the fighters, the pilots, the crews, the support teams, all had to come from *somewhere*.

They would be supplied by the 8th. And in making that contribution—to a new airpower organization that would be the 12th Air Force—the 8th was almost to break its own back. The records show that:

> By 1 November . . . in addition to four fighter and two heavy bomber groups, the Eighth Air Force had turned over trained personnel to the extent of 3,198 officers, 24,124 enlisted men, and 34 warrant officers, of whom 1,098 officers, 7,101 enlisted men, and 14 warrant officers came from the VIII Bomber Command alone. The remaining heavy bombardment groups . . . suffered considerably from loss of such essential equipment as bomb-loading appliances and transport vehicles. They suffered even more from the complete lack of replacements, both crews and aircraft, a fact which made it impossible to keep a large force in the air even when weather conditions permitted; and no prospect was in sight of receiving any during November.[46]

From this point on, the 8th Air Force, especially the 8th Bomber Command, would continue to suffer from this unpredictable depletion of its strength, so carefully trained and so exhaustively built up to carry the air war into Germany. After the landings in Morocco and Algeria in November 1942, the fighting in North Africa made it all too clear that there would be another lengthy postponement in any plans for invading the European continent. But at least a new target date for 1944 might be established. The hopes were bolstered when, by the spring of 1943, it appeared that requirements for the North African and Mediterranean campaigns would drop sharply. Without this enervating drain on its resources the 8th Bomber Command could once again build up the massive air strength it coveted. BOLERO, the buildup of heavy bomber forces in England, would be on again. The British in the Western Desert had at least uprooted the Germans from their main positions in that area, and combined American and British land forces were grinding slowly toward a meeting in Tunisia where the surviving German elements could be crushed and all of North Africa secured by the Allies.

Thus it was that by early 1943 hopes brightened for the 8th Air Force. But it was not to be. The increase in strength for BOLERO, had it continued on the original schedule, would have weakened critically the buildup of bomber forces in other parts of the world. The 8th Bomber Command was finding it very necessary to live with the facts of life. Fifteen entire bombardment groups originally committed to BOLERO went, instead, the other way around the world to hammer at the Japanese.

Not until the late summer months of 1943 could the 8th Bomber Command begin to assemble the numbers of bombers and crews its planners had always known were indispensable to their strategic air plans for reducing Germany. By that time a new program, CBO—Combined Bomber Offensive—would be transferred from paper to reality. But in the late summer of 1942 CBO was a long way in the future, and the invasion of North Africa loomed as the highest priority in carrying the war to the Germans.

During battle for priorities at the highest levels of the Allied commands, there was another battle being fought, in which the Flying Fortress played the dominant role.

The lines were defined clearly. The AAF looked upon the B-17 as the great hope for vindicating its concept of strategic air bombardment. But the British sounded the warning that American airmen would be flying their gleaming new bombers straight into a disaster of terrifying proportions.

The Flying Fortress, insisted the most experienced airmen of the Royal Air Force, while heavily armed, was no match for the powerful German fighter airplanes in daylight combat. British experts who had cut their teeth long before in open combat with the enemy said that the Fortress' defensive firepower was overrated and that the number of guns carried had little to do with the ability of a bomber to survive enemy fighter attacks. They arched their brows in quiet horror at the severely cramped position of the tail gunner and dismissed the ball turret in the belly as "so awkward as to be useless." They castigated the small bomb load of the Fortress in comparison to the heavy tonnage carried by night bombers of the RAF. They insisted that the fabled Norden bombsight would be useless over German targets. Not that the sight itself had any basic failings, but the pilot of a bomber would have to be dodging continuously to offset the aim of German fighters and, even if he didn't, flak would throw the bomber about so severely that it would be impossible to hold a steady course long enough for the Norden bombsight to be effective.

In short, the Germans would slaughter any massed bomber formations foolish enough to attempt penetrating German airspace during daylight.

Now, the veterans of the RAF had come to this conclusion by dint of their own bruising experiences at the hands of the Germans. They felt qualified to speak with authority on this subject, and they did not hesitate to do their best to dissuade the Americans from the course upon which they had set with the Flying Fortress.

What seems strange, however, is that the British themselves were not offering their advice from a position of strength. One would believe from the honest vehemence that they had found the winning combination in night instead of day attacks against enemy targets. But the facts are otherwise.

The *official* history of the Royal Air Force[47] notes that up until 1941 Bomber Command "had laboured under a host of difficulties." It also notes:

> ...the truth about our night bombing on 1941, though it was little known, was depressing in the extreme. In September 1941 a full assessment was made from photographs taken in a hundred recent raids. It showed that only one in every three aircraft claiming to have attacked had arrived within five miles of its target. Over the Ruhr alone the number of aircraft arriving within five miles of their target was one in ten. Indeed, no greater contrast can be imagined than that between on the one hand the enthusiastic reports of the bomber crews...and on the other the bleak pictures of scarcely damaged towns now being brought back by the photographic Spitfires. The intelligence concerning the campaign was certainly conflicting. But the Air Staff were realists. They accepted in full the distasteful "evidence in camera" of the photographic reconnaissance machines. And, under the cloak of a complacent publicity which kept everyone happy, they proceeded to build up a force that could do what the optimists imagined was already being done.

This writer has never seen *this* aspect of the early phases of the European bombing war brought to light when there has been mention of the obstinate American planners who flew so quickly into the teeth of British experience that had "proven the validity of the doctrine of night bombing."

More than one history of bombing operations in Europe makes careful mention of General H. H. Arnold's remarks on this matter as indicating his grave concern with the ability of the American bombers to survive daylight raids. One major work states that the British had solved their problems in their doctrine of night bombing, and quotes Hap Arnold after a visit to England as saying that "the British have a lot to learn about bombing. But who am I to question the experiences of the RAF in two years of bombing in a real war?"

It makes great copy, and perhaps Arnold did voice these thoughts—although this now seems somewhat questionable—but if he had any doubts about RAF experience he had only to refer to the British themselves who, with laudable candor, were taking grim looks at their own efforts. We have already heard their own comment on the inability of their night bombers even to find their targets, and we have seen that over the Ruhr less than ten percent of British bombers *even came within five miles* of their targets. But the official history of the RAF of this period has more to say:

> The choice of German transportation as the main objective of our bomber force, and German morale as the secondary, was plainly a confession of failure. We had not succeeded in bombing Germany by day; and we had now found out that attacks by night against small, scattered or well defended targets like oil plants and aircraft factories were inflicting little, if any, vital damage.

Having been severely mauled in bombers that were disastrously ill equipped to survive daylight missions, the British understandably would have no further truck for some time with daylight bombing. They admitted to themselves they could not hit small strategic targets at night. But if during periods of moonlight (weather not interfering, at least for one week out of each four) the crews could identify and attack in mass raids "nine great railway centers of Western Germany," then the RAF could strike a severe blow at Germany's industrial war machine. Very heavy blows against these targets, the British Air Staff felt, "would isolate the industrial Ruhr-Rhineland from the rest of the *Reich* and the occupied territories."

What would happen when the railway centers could not be identified and moonlight was not available? The British reasoned that then their "bombers must have some target other than railway centers ... Only an objective large enough to be found and hit with certainty in the dark would suffice."

That was the beginning of the so-called saturation bombing on the part of the Bomber Command of the Royal Air Force. The British raiders, said the Air Staff, would carry out strikes "by heavy, concentrated and continuous area attacks of large working-class and industrial areas in carefully selected towns."

There is another point to make. Was the daylight bomber—the British daylight raider—wholly out of the picture? Not entirely, it would seem, despite the British opinion that daylight bombers didn't stand a chance. The history of the RAF shows, also, that at some date in the future the Air Staff hoped to combine the effects of massive night attacks "with daylight raids on precision targets by the new heavy bombers." The reference is of course to British heavy bombers ... !

The writer has no intention of launching a discourse on the relative merits of the British and the American methods for carrying out heavy bomber attacks in Europe. Both were devastatingly effective.* But the British technique for the use of long-range bombers was diametrically opposed to the American plan. Their selections of targets, their preference for lightly armed bombers, striking in nocturnal raids; the very bombs and methods of attack they employed, yielded little experience that the 8th Bomber Command could apply usefully to its own future role.

The British clearly preferred attack by the stars. There is another matter to be emphasized. Darkness was to have cloaked the British bomber with a mantle of protection. Losses thus must be far less than those endured by bombers suffering attack in broad daylight.

The single greatest daylight loss in the European air war would come on October 14th, 1943, the infamous *Black Thursday* when sixty Flying Fortresses would go down before German guns.

Yet, there would come a night when a swarm of great Lancasters, huge four-engine raiders, one of the finest bomber designs ever to take wing, would strike into Germany.

On that night, *ninety-six* of the Lancasters would fail to return to England. . . .

Enough said.

Essentially the 8th Bomber Command's program in Europe called for a sustained daylight bombing campaign, carried out with high precision, which, rather than attempting to destroy entire cities in saturation raids, would wreck carefully chosen industrial objectives. The 8th's planners worried their hair gray trying to resolve the com-

---

*In *The Night Hamburg Died*, I have given ample testimony as to the effectiveness of British attacks against the cities of Germany.

plex and interwoven factors of the formidable German antiaircraft defenses, the depth and efficiency of their radar and fighter-control operations, and the known skill and courage of the men who flew the German fighters. Still unanswered when TORCH began to bleed the 8th Bomber Command of its strength was the crucial question whether the American heavy bomber could enter German air territory without escort and defend itself against the superb German pilot and his airplane. All of 8th Air Force's plans could be measured only through the sustained test of battle. And now because of combat in North Africa and the Mediterranean that test must be delayed indefinitely.

# CHAPTER 18

# TORCH

THE FLYING FORTRESS WENT to war in the Middle East months before Operation TORCH, the invasion of North Africa in November of 1942. That the B-17s were committed to aiding the hard-pressed British in June of 1942 is a matter of record. Unfortunately, it is also a matter of record that the Fortresses dispatched to assist our Allies were barely capable of remaining in the air even *without* encountering enemy flak or fighters.

General Brereton had received on 23rd June 1942 emergency orders that directed him to rush to Egypt to throw his weight with the British in the form of "such heavy bombers as he could muster." The bedraggled Tenth Air Force, unfortunately, had little to offer. In fact, Brereton could scrape together from his 9th Bombardment Squadron only nine B-17s, and these so badly in need of repairs that Brereton felt he was being generous in describing them as "near cripples." Two days after a telegram that interrupted a staff meeting at New Delhi, Brereton was on his way from India to Egypt. His entire force added up to the nine sagging Fortresses, all the transports he could steal from under outraged logistics officers, and an entourage of 225 officers and men. On 28th June the planes arrived in Cairo, bolstering a force of B-24 Liberators already carrying out combat operations in the theater.

The heavy bombers were hurled against German supply-lines in day and night attacks. To the Liberators, with experienced crews and established maintenance facilities, went the brunt of the missions. Out of nine missions flown between June 26th and July 5th, the Fortresses flew on only two, one a night raid. The official records attach cautious significance to these operations, pointing out that "no more than ten American bombers" ever set out at one time on a single mission and that "available records do not give any detailed estimate of the damage inflicted." There was a furious air war under way, to be certain, but it was the Royal Air Force with attack bombers and fighters that fought that war. The participation of American heavy bombers on a scale calculated to affect directly and severely the enemy was an event yet to come.

By July 20th Brereton had under his command in Egypt and Palestine a total force of nineteen Liberators and his same nine Fortresses. But by now the drastic demands of desert operations, compounded by supplies and parts that were always too little and too late, had slashed his ability to function in strength. Of the twenty-eight four-engine bombers, only seven Liberators and three Fortresses were able to get off the ground for combat missions. Brereton and his men had to mark time until promised reinforcements arrived. On July 25th new Liberators of the 98th Group roared into Ramat David, Palestine. Wisely, the squadrons brought with them enough spare parts to keep operating until the ground echelons followed them into the Middle East.

For the period of July 5th through August 30th Brereton's weary staff maintained, considering their operational difficulties, a commendable record of activity against the enemy. The bombers averaged five missions a week, flying day sorties and sometimes joining up with British bombers for night strikes. The Fortresses concentrated their raids on Tobruk, the single most important supply depot for the German army in Africa. The Liberators took on an ever greater share of the combat workload, being more ably equipped and maintained, and of greater range than the Fortresses available to Brereton.

During August the Middle East theater saw a steady and formidable buildup of American airpower—preparations for the forthcoming TORCH invasion. Fighters and medium bombers arriving in Africa were "fed into existing RAF formations." The heavy bombers, without fighter escort of sufficient range to accompany them on their raids, operated pretty much as an independent striking arm on what might loosely be termed "Middle East strategic targets," although the missions flown invariably had a direct relationship to the situation on the battlefield.

The weeks that followed repeated the pattern: the Liberators bore the brunt of the missions flown. The Fortresses went out again and again, whenever a plane was fit to fly and fight. On the 14th October the Fortress crews had the rare opportunity to see the direct results of a mission when, in Tobruk harbor, three B-17s sank one ship and "badly mauled" another.

Another indication of the minor role played by the B-17 during this phase of operations is seen in the roster of Allied aircraft. Of a total of 1,098 fighters, bombers and reconnaissance planes, there were no more than ten B-17s by the 16th October 1942, and four of these Fortresses were grounded. Once TORCH became a reality the situation would change drastically as the strength of forces from England were thrown into the battle. But for the moment the B-17s remained strictly a splinter effort.

Splinter though it might be, the handful of Fortresses were proving painful to the enemy. The crews by now were seasoned veterans and they knew how to use their airplanes. On November 2nd, only six days before the great invasion was to take place, five B-17s caught heavy concentrations of enemy shipping in Tobruk harbor. Two merchant vessels were left smashed and burning and the harbor was hit so hard that the fires started during the bombing "were seen blazing two days later."

Then—invasion.

On November 8, the invasion forces of TORCH struck at Algiers and Oran in the Mediterranean and Casablanca on the Atlantic. Most of the air support of the British forces was naturally British; in addition, British fighters and bombers struck well out from their own immediate areas of assigned combat. Where the Americans landed, against unexpectedly stiff resistance from the French, United States Navy carrier fighters bore the brunt of the fighting, while Navy dive and torpedo bombers struck in heavy raids at both the French and isolated German units. The Twelfth Air Force, which would eventually take over the air offensive throughout North Africa and the Mediterranean, working northward into the islands south of Europe, and then Europe itself, was virtually uncommitted in the TORCH landings. While the Twelfth waited for air bases from which to operate (P-40 fighters were flown out from Navy carriers the moment land areas were secured), the furious activity continued. Navy Grumman F4F Wildcat fighters battled with American-built and French-flown Curtiss Mohawks, as well as French Dewoitine 520 fighters. The United States fought a series of pitched battles with the French, inflicting swift damages against the collapsing French forces. The latter found themselves in black disfavor with the Germans, who savagely mauled French defensive positions, drove out the French, and took over these installations themselves.

At El Alamein the British 8th Army had cracked the line of Rommel's defense, and the famed Desert Rats were hellbent to continue their sweep, eventually to meet with the Americans and other combat units in Tunisia, where a linkup would seal the doom of the Germans in North Africa.

At Biskra, near Oran, engineers worked day and night to prepare the airdromes for the heavy bombers of the Twelfth Air Force. The Fortresses of the 97th and 301st Air Groups would shoulder the greater burden of heavy bomber operations, and the B-17 crews would find their role somewhat different from what they had expected. In Africa strategic bombing was seldom possible; the purpose of most missions was to help the ground forces break the back of their opponents' mechanized and infantry strength. The key to success in Africa was logistics; supply was the artery of battle, and supply lines became the prime targets of the Fortresses. Supply, and enemy airpower.

On the 16th November the battle was joined. Six Fortresses of the 340th Squadron, 97th Group, struck at the Sidi Ahmed airdrome at Bizerte. Small though it might be in strength, the attack was eminently satisfying to the men of the 340th. They had staged down from England through Gibraltar; at Maison Blanche the crews fueled their heavy bombers with five-gallon tin cans. The attack proved successful, no bombers were lost, and the gunners claimed one Me-109 shot down.

On 19th November the Fortresses went out again with P-38 escort to hit enemy air on the ground; at the El Aouina airdrome they pounded hangars and installations and destroyed eight fighters and bombers caught by their bombs. All bombers and fighters returned. The Luftwaffe flew from bases in Sardinia to hammer at Algiers and nearby targets. On the night of the 20th the Germans came over in strength with more than thirty Ju-87 Stukas and Ju-88 light bombers. Allied fighters, lacking night inter-ception equipment, were caught on the ground. The Ger-mans exhibited outstanding accuracy and destroyed four Spitfires, three twin-engined Beaufighters, two P-38s, one Flying Fortress, and an entire reconnaissance unit of the Royal Air Force.

Maison Blanche, if this raid was a measure of German ability, was too exposed for the heavy bombers. They were reassigned to Tafaraoui; there maintenance was simplified, and major targets remained within B-17 range. One major exception dampened the enthusiasm of the Fortress crews— Tafaraoui turned out to be an appalling quagmire where the mud, as several famous rhymes had it, was "deep and gooey."

We have come now to the moment when it is no longer possible to continue the combat history of the B-17 by de-scribing sequential missions. Bomber strikes now involved vast numbers of men and machines. Bomber missions were being flown simultaneously to many targets not in one but in several theaters, and mission operations often over-lapped areas of designated authority and responsibility. From a clear-cut sequence of events the war became a huge and complicated panorama. Thus it is necessary, in our review of events in Africa and the Mediterranean, deliberately to ignore, for the moment, the massive operations under way in England, over Europe, and in other combat theaters where the Flying Fortress was not only in action in great number, but where the numbers were increasing with every passing month. Again with increasing frequency the missions were flown by B-17s and B-24 Liberators operating together. Finally, raids were now scheduled every day, and missions conducted on a basis of all-day operations. In sum, the multiplicity of effort could not but shroud, through sheer mass of numbers, the daily events which until now have occupied our interest.

Selectivity now takes precedence over comprehensiveness in reporting operations, and what follows in these pages must be read as representative of the whole. From the massive effort, there emerge certain exploits of individuals or crews or groups of bombers, but inevitably, the lapses in narrative must pass over details which may be of interest to certain readers. In later pages we will return to the air war over continental Europe; for the moment our interest remains concentrated on Africa and the Mediterranean, where the Flying Fortress and its crews were proven to be one of the most outstanding and effective weapons to be employed in any theater of battle, by any of the combatant nations.

The initial strikes of American bombers in Africa were to support the advance of the First Army by grounding or destroying the air strength of the enemy. The major airfields in Tunisia, harboring German bombers and frightening swarms of fighter planes, came in for the concentrated attention of American bombs. On the 28th November a force of thirty-seven B-17s smashed at the Bizerte airfield and the docks adjacent to the air base. Without P-38 es-

cort, the Fortresses were set upon by a large force of Focke-
Wulfs and Messerschmitts, of which the bomber gunners
claimed ten fighters shot down. It was not a one-sided affair; two B-17s were blown out of the sky.

Two days later the Fortresses took another whack at the
north quay of Bizerte harbor, trying to catch German supplies before they could reach the combat units to which
they were destined. Heavy cloud cover frustrated two
thirds of the force from releasing visually. There was no in-
discriminate bombing. With supplies still a critical problem
the crews had been told: "If you can see your target, destroy it. If you can't see your target, bring your bombs back
home." Most of the B-17 force returned with full bomb
bays to their home base.

Two days later the Fortresses were battering the German airfield at El Aouina. Long lines of bombs were
"walked" down the hangar line and into the built-up sections of the base. German operations slackened appreciably
at El Aouina. But the Germans were not to be put down
lightly. Under cover of darkness and then, as ground battles increased in intensity, during daylight hours the Luftwaffe rushed in reinforcements. On 2nd December the
Twelfth went back to El Aouina where intelligence reported
at least fifty new German fighters and bombers on the
ground. In the heavy attack eighteen Fortresses of the
301st Group hit Sidi Ahmed and nearby Bizerte harbor.

The next day, 3rd December, B-17s again struck at Bizerte harbor, smashing two ships in the canal entrance and
scoring effectively against dock installations. The Germans
met the Fortresses with a heated reception; the flak had
been heavy before, now it seemed to have doubled in the
number of guns. Bizerte, obviously a target of great interest both to the Germans and their opponents, had also been
ringed with the latest German radar. Warned well ahead of

time that bombers were approaching, the Luftwaffe had their fighters at altitude and waiting for the Fortresses. On this mission Me-109s at 25,000 feet swarmed into the P-38 escort with an unquestionable urge to mix it up with the twin-engined American fighters; three P-38s and three Me-109s went down in the fray.

On 5th December the P-38s were out in escort of light and medium bombers; the B-17s went unescorted to Tunis. It was "another mission" of heavy flak and light fighter resistance, but there was nothing routine about the still-improving accuracy of the B-17 bombardiers. Reconnaissance photos showed a "very respectable degree of accuracy" in the strike which caused severe damage to the supply facilities of the Germans.

Hard as they were fighting, and effective as they were in disrupting German logistics efforts, there was no stopping the enemy on the ground. The Wermacht again and again pierced Allied lines, drove back our forces, and in isolated but major engagements ripped apart major Allied units. One large command, mired in gripping mud during a withdrawal, was pounced upon by the Germans, who destroyed four fifths of the American tanks and artillery caught under their guns.

The situation had deteriorated and the Allies "had already lost the race. . . . The rains which glued the Eastern Air Command and the Twelfth Air Force to their bases gave a high degree of protection to the enemy build-up. What Eisenhower aptly termed the logistical marathon had begun. TORCH had failed of complete success."

Finding decent airfield sites for the Fortresses was a prime requirement. The two Tafaraoui runways were excellent, but something of a false gift in that the ground immediately off the runways remained muck most of the time. A

Fortress taxiing off the strip needed to be towed free by several bulldozers, and all-prevalent mud crippled bomber operations. Onto the plateau between the Saharan and maritime ranges of the Atlas Mountains went the bombers. Biskra, an oasis and winter resort that lay beyond the Saharan Atlas, became the new home for the Fortresses. Airborne engineers gave the AAF a runway so wide that three B-17s could make a line-a-breast takeoff. Later, as the Allies planned their long-range attack program, the Fortresses would move to the Telergma area, but for the present Biskra was an engineering task fondly remembered by the crews as "successful and spectacular." The heavies were ready to resume the aerial pounding of the enemy.

The B-17s were given an unexpected—and dubious—accolade in planning the daylight strikes against Bizerte and Tunis. Flak defenses and radar-controlled fighters were so fierce by mid-December that the targets were listed as "too hot" for medium and light bombers, and only the Fortresses were considered strong enough to run the gauntlet of enemy defenses. In fact, wherever the twin-engine bombers encountered severe opposition, they were restricted from these targets unless the "B-17s were along to saturate the defenses."

New yellow-nosed Focke-Wulf FW-190 fighters moved into the Bizerte area fields to counter the B-17 raids. The flak became so intense that "Tunis and Bizerte soon compared with the more heavily defended targets in northwestern Europe." Nevertheless the B-17s of the Twelfth Air Force struck again and again at Tunis and Bizerte. Several factors contributed to losses far less than had been anticipated. As the official history of the AAF notes, the B-17s "usually had P-38s escorting, not many P-38s but enough to divide the opposition's attention. Moreover, the German pilots had not evolved any very satisfactory way of attacking the heavily armed B-17, and they were properly respectful...."

The raid of 15th December typifies many of these strikes. Two B-17 formations departed Biskra for simultaneous raids against Tunis and Bizerte. Six P-38 fighters shepherded seven Fortresses to Tunis and another six flew with twelve bombers bound for Bizerte. Despite severe flak and heavy fighter attacks all planes returned. The seven bombers that flew over Tunis left behind them, torn apart and sinking to the bottom, the 10,000-ton Italian freighter *Arlesiana*.

But the Fortresses did not always return unscathed. Three days later, on the 18th December over Bizerte, the Germans shot down four P-38s, destroyed one B-17, and forced another Fortress to crash-land on the way home.

For several days at a time the Fortress crews found themselves grounded by heavy rains. Maintenance was brought up to date and the crews kept in readiness for the first break in the weather. When finally they did get off the ground they met violent weather conditions on the way to their targets. Two missions of the 21st and 22nd December aborted; all B-17s arrived over their targets to find the earth completely shrouded beneath them. On the 23rd seventeen Fortresses made it off the ground. Five bombers iced up so severely they dropped their explosives and returned early to base. The others found their endeavors wasted when the targets remained cloud-covered. The weather forced the formations to break up, B-17s landing at a half-dozen fields across Africa as they fought the worsening elements.

The last week of December—after the "Christmas interlude provided so conveniently by storms"—the Fortresses hit hard in seven missions at the east-coast harbors of Sfax and Sousse, "showing the high degree of accuracy the B-17s were showing." At Sfax on the 26th December, the Fortresses sank two large and one small cargo vessels and damaged several others. The next day at Sousse, four ships took direct hits, one of which was torn apart by a violent explosion. Marshaling yards and dock facilities also took a severe battering from the B-17 bombardiers who were proving the "pickle-barrel accuracy" for the Fortress and the Norden bombsight.

On January 5th eleven Fortresses destroyed completely the Sfax power station, smashed one vessel in the port, and turned the entire dock area into a smoking shambles. Three days later another "small" B-17 formation ripped Ferryville, chewing up the docks, oil storage tanks, and reporting "several direct hits against shipping." Not until after Tunis fell in May was it learned just how far along the B-17s had come, and that the Fortress crews were now *underplaying* their achievements. The "several direct hits against shipping" turned out to be a submarine, a sailing vessel, a tug, an aircraft tender, and a combat patrol vessel all either sunk or damaged beyond repair.

Day after day, weather permitting, the Fortresses attacked enemy shipping, "leaving sunken hulks here and there in the harbors." But during January and February they received increasing numbers of missions that brought them "to intervene even more directly in the land battle." On 11th January five bombers struck the Libyan fort at Gadames. Unfortunately their accuracy was off; huge dust clouds raised by the bombs brought the crews to lay in claims of direct hits. Reconnaissance proved the fort to be undamaged by the cascade of bombs.

But strikes against enemy airfields in the Tripoli area were more successful. On 12th January Castel Benito took brutal punishment from the Fortresses which wrecked the hangars and airfield facilities and destroyed at least twenty planes. The air battle was one of the most spectacular of the Africa war. About thirty Italian Mc-202 fighters dove at high speed past the P-38s and tore furiously into the Fortresses to begin a wild and running twenty-minute fight. The Italian pilots refused to fight the P-38s, breaking away from such combat, returning again and again to the bombers. For their part the Fortress gunners had a field day. Not as well armed or as sturdy as the Messerschmitts and Focke-Wulfs, the Mc-202s took a fearful pounding from the B-17s, whose gunners claimed fourteen Italian fighters shot down and another three probably destroyed. One Fortress, battered and shot to pieces, limped back to Biskra hours later, its two working engines sounding like washing machines.

Six days later Castel Benito was reported by Intelligence to be holding at least two hundred enemy planes which had been flown into the field for concentrated operations. The 97th Group sent out thirteen Fortresses which were escorted, to the delight of the crews, by no less than thirty-three P-38 fighters. This time the Italians were wiser in their actions. Twelve Mc-202s attacked the American planes, and the crews observed the Italian fighters seemed to be flown by "old hands." For a loss of only three fighters, the Italians shot down one B-17 and one P-38.

The attack against Castel Benito was listed as "effective," but it paled before the fury of the blow struck on 22nd January against El Aouina where the damage was listed officially as "devastating." Official studies by First Army Intelligence showed that "the B-17s hit an ammunition dump and inflicted 600 military casualties and, by the most conservative estimate, twelve parked planes had been destroyed and nineteen holed in various degrees."

Bizerte on the 23rd January took an especially severe

battering from the Fortresses of both the 97th and 301st Groups. A large merchant vessel was set afire and sank in the channel adjacent to the naval base, while hangars, oil tanks, workshops and other buildings seemed to erupt in all directions from highly accurate bombing. Every bomber and escorting P-38 fighter returned safely while more than a dozen enemy fighters were shot down.

On February 7th a mixed force of fifty-one B-17s and twin-engined Martin B-26 Marauders made the first attack of the Twelfth Air Force against a European objective. They hammered Elmas airdrome near Cagliari, Sardinia (the island south of Corsica), tearing up hangars and buildings and destroying at least twenty-four enemy planes on the ground. Jubilant gunners shot down five Me-109 fighters and damaged two Italian Re-2001 fighters; all bombers returned safely.

On the 15th February, eight days later, Sicily came in for attention from the Fortresses. At Palermo a large merchant ship was left in flames and sinking, the dry dock was torn up, and loading docks left a shambles. For the next ten days the B-17s continued their attacks against both harbors, shipping, and enemy airfields in the growing offensive of what Eisenhower had called the "logistical marathon."

On the 26th February 1943 the Fortresses encountered stiff opposition from German fighters during a raid against Sicily, hunting out several Italian cruisers. The attrition of combat had already thinned the ranks of the heavy bomber groups. At the end of the long and difficult supply line were many other AAF units clamoring not only for supplies, but also for replacements. Flight crewmen of the 97th Group, for example, were accustomed to having their meals served by high-ranking ground officers, so critical was the shortage of men—and KP duty was being pulled by rank as high as lieutenant colonel. The mission was to bomb the enemy, and keeping the flight crews well fed and equipped took precedence over the normal privileges of rank.

*Hell's Kitchen*, which began its combat career over Abbeville during the debacle of Dieppe, was a member of the Sicily-bound force. An indication of the pressing need for skilled airmen was provided in the actions of one of the crewmen from *Hell's Kitchen*. Sergeant Allie Moszyk was belly gunner for the airplane; it was his twenty-third mission. He should not have been along. Because of the shortage of ground crewmen, the flight crew had helped in fueling and bombing their Fortress. During fueling Moszyk slipped on the wing, lost his balance, and tumbled off to the ground. He hit with a severe jolt and he was told not to fly that day. Moszyk refused to be grounded; he knew he would be needed as a gunner in the critical belly position.

Fifteen thousand feet over Sicily the formation in which *Hell's Kitchen* flew took the brunt of a heavy assault by a mixed force of Me-109s and FW-190s. Immediately the Fortress was in serious trouble. Phil Trapani in the tail cursed and worked at his twin .50 caliber guns which had frozen and were inoperative. Trapani was just at the point of getting the twin fifties in action again when an exploding 20-mm cannon shell wounded him severely in both arms and legs.

Moszyk shouted to the pilot to get the tail up so he could get a clear shot at a single FW-190 glued to their tail when *his* gun position also received a direct hit with a cannon shell. The German fighter flashed down and away, out of gun range, leaving Moszyk's position a shambles. The explosion within the confined space of the ball turret was terrifying. The blast riddled Moszyk with pieces of red-hot metal. Swirling smoke and fumes blinded the gunner. He felt one arm go completely dead on him, and then felt blood streaming down his face. He tried to call the pilot but his radio had been shot away. Unable to fire his guns, helpless and wounded in the turret, Moszyk struggled upward into the fuselage, trying to crawl back to the tail. Despite his wounds, Moszyk managed to drag himself back through the lurching, pitching bomber to the tailgun position. There he found Trapani bleeding profusely, in shock, and without his oxygen mask. Hurriedly, Moszyk applied a tourniquet to the worst of the visible wounds of his friend, took off his own oxygen mask and secured it to Trapani's face. Then he found a walk-around emergency bottle for himself and fought his way forward, through the bomb bays, where he told pilot Norbert Kirk he needed assistance for the tail gunner.

It wasn't the best of news for a pilot bedeviled with his own problems. The number three engine was shot away and Kirk had feathered the prop. Number one engine was burning. Kirk left the airplane to the copilot, called the bombardier and ordered him to go along with him, Kirk, to the tail. On their way back through the plane they found Bob Jones, radio operator, also wounded. Jones refused aid and motioned them back to Trapani, who was in danger of dying. When they reached Trapani, they found him in agony from a shattered arm bone. They did their best to stop further bleeding. Then they turned to Moszyk, still bleeding from the slashes in his face caused by the cannon shell explosion within his turret. As a finale, Moszyk climbed back into his ball turret before landing, at the pilot's request. Kirk was afraid that the belly of the airplane might have received serious damage and he wanted to know just what he faced before landing. He was right. Moszyk climbed back from the ball turret with the news that one tire had been shot away.

Kirk bent several propellers on landing, but that was all. No one minded—he'd brought plane and crew back home.

# CHAPTER 19

# THE DEADLY BOMBERS

DURING THE OPENING MONTHS of war in the Pacific Theater there often existed a huge gap between the claims of B-17 crews and the damage actually inflicted on enemy shipping. Claims of ships set ablaze and sinking were often no more than exaggerated reports of near misses that sent up nothing more than towering geysers of water that did little more damage than wetting down the decks of the unharmed enemy vessels.

What had plagued the Fortresses early in the war was a lack of experience as well as ignorance of the best methods utilizing the particular assets of the four-engined bomber. By the time the Fortresses of the Twelfth Air Force ranged along the African coastline and well into the Mediterranean the situation had altered drastically. Where the early days of the war were a time of unjustified claims and unscathed enemy shipping, the "new war" of the Twelfth Air Force saw the Fortresses operating with uncommon skill and effectiveness.

The majority of B-17 targets were either on land, or involved enemy vessels tied up in port. But there were attempts to get the heavy bombers well out to sea where the enemy had been found by reconnaissance planes and his position could be well fixed. On such occasions the Fortresses in strength went after these ships, and their results cheered air-power proponents and brought open astonishment from those who had derided the ability of heavy bombers to "take out" enemy vessels able to maneuver freely on the high seas.

The first attack of this nature was flown on the 26th February, north of Sicily, off the Lipari Islands. Twenty Fortresses were sent out against a convoy of twenty-one vessels. Holding tight formation, dropping their bombs in pattern from 15,000 feet, the attackers brought confirmed claims of one ship sent to the bottom and three others set ablaze. That was the beginning.

On the 4th March fifteen Fortresses hammered a convoy of six ships cruising northwest of Bizerte, sinking *four* out of the six, with a barrage of direct hits from the well-organized pattern of bombs. On two other occasions during March, B-17s in strikes against shipping well at sea hit and probably sank enemy vessels. One other bombing attempt was shaken up when enemy fighters, obviously under orders to prevent the continuing attacks that were proving so deadly, bored in against the bombers in what is described in group records as a "vicious fighter attack just before the bomb run."

The end result of the first month of repeated attacks at sea by the Fortresses cheered the air strategists from the Mediterranean all the way back to Washington. In combat estimates that were "austerely defined," the Fortress groups put in claims of twenty ships destroyed, fifteen badly damaged, and another eleven damaged in varying degrees.

It galled the bomber crews that they lacked the opportunities to go after additional convoys. But the realities of the combat situation in North Africa limited the opportunity for such missions. First the enemy convoys had to be spotted and their position and *probable* course determined. Then the intelligence reports were flashed to the Fortress bases. Even after mission orders were given to the crews it usually required at least two hours to get the mission under way. Another thirty minutes were required for takeoff and rendezvous, and an hour and a half for the bombers to reach the enemy vessels and to search them out. Often, during this time, the convoys came under the protection of swarms of fighters, or had reached land areas where they were defended both by fighters and heavy antiaircraft fire.

The choice, then, had to be made between attacking ships at sea, or going after the port and unloading areas where the B-17s "always" found worthwhile targets. Until the third week in February of 1943, the Fortresses had kept as their exclusive targets those ports where ships were off-loading supplies. Then their mission operations expanded drastically, and they were assigned new targets along the coasts of Sicily and Sardinia. Thus they struck on 15th February at Palermo, and made strikes on the 26th and 28th of the month against Cagliari, Sardinia. The latter port was hit so badly that a full month went by before Intelligence deemed it necessary for the Fortresses to return. During this "revisit" mission the heavy bombers set ablaze two large merchant vessels, hit another four ships, tore apart the adjoining railroad station, wrecked the seaplane base, and left more than half the unloading berths useless shambles. Another raid on the 31st March, to "round off" the month, sent another three ships totaling ten thousand tons, to the bottom.

(The writer spent a month at Cagliari, Sardinia, immediately after the close of World War II. Nothing in the official records of the B-17 groups could possibly have done justice to the shambles that met the eye. There was only one loading dock in usable condition, and the Liberty ship aboard which the writer was present had to be maneuvered with the greatest of care through a harbor that had been transformed into a littered graveyard of enemy vessels.)

But it was at Palermo, on the 22nd March, that the Fortresses scored an epic success against enemy shipping. General Spaatz made it part of the official record that this strike of the 22nd was far and away the "most devastating single raid thus far in the war." The Fortresses went in at a bombing altitude of 24,000 feet, holding formation with a discipline born of experience. The bombs cascaded earthward in precisely the pattern that had been expounded for years before the war. A long string of high-explosive missiles walked across the water and into ships, one of them a munitions vessel that "let go all at once." The blast was so titanic that it battered the four-engine bombers at their height of 24,000 feet! A brilliant flash illuminated the skies for miles in every direction and a monstrous flaming sphere burst upward from the harbor front, writhing and twisting within itself, an ominous predecessor of the mushroom cloud that would one day tower well above the cities of Hiroshima and Nagasaki. The munitions ship vanished in the terrifying explosion; its demise sent out a shock wave that inflicted damage beyond all hopes. Thirty acres of the heavily loaded docks were torn to shreds, transformed into a shambles of smoking and shattered debris. The disappearance of the munitions ship was followed almost instantly by the sinking of four merchant vessels, while another two cargo ships were hurled bodily out of the water and flung onto a wrecked pier.

The majority of Fortress missions were still being laid on the Tunisian ports. British twin-engined Wellingtons had been attacking on a steady basis, but the astonishing successes of the B-17s brought anxious calls for their appearance over Tunis and Bizerte. On the 25th February and 23rd March the Fortresses bored in against Bizerte, where German and Italian antiaircraft had been so intense that fears had been expressed for the survival of the mission. On the strike of 25th February the lead bomber took a direct hit in the bomb bay. Immediately the oxygen bottles exploded in flames, and the pilot hit the emergency switches to salvo the bombs. Other Fortresses, "flying on the leader," took the emergency jettison of bombs as the signal to release their own loads. Away went a mass of bombs dropped prematurely, far from their intended targets. Where skill had become commonplace, now good fortune attended the B-17s. Several bombs of the premature drop thundered into a submarine in Lake Bizerte, either damaging heavily or sinking the hapless vessel.

The raids went on relentlessly. At Ferryville on March 24th the B-17s tore up the port facilities, sank a tug and a minesweeper, and sent two merchant vessels to the bottom. Once again a direct hit paid unexpected dividends. One of the merchant vessels hit was the *Citta di Savona*, busy at the time unloading ammunition. The entire store of explosives went off, wrecking the area for hundreds of yards ashore. La Goulette, Tunis, Sousse also received attention from the rampaging Fortresses. Sousse especially took a frightening battering. The British Eighth Army occupied the port in April, and its officers reported that the "harbor resembled nothing so much as a nautical junkyard."

Other missions were being laid on with increasing frequency and strength of formations against airfields, marshaling yards, and other ports. Each week saw the target roster growing and the effect on the enemy increasing appreciably. Airfields in Africa, Sardinia and Sicily received one attack after the other, the missions often being timed to allow strikes by the Fortresses and waves of medium bombers as well. The airfield of Capodichino, near Naples, took a pounding in which more than half the fifty aircraft were destroyed on the ground by accurate pattern bombing.

## BACK TO THE HIGH SEAS

During April and the early part of May the Fortress crews struck again at enemy shipping on the high seas. Twenty miles west of Sicily, on the afternoon of the 23rd April, the B-17s caught a single large ship at sea, and bracketed the merchant vessel with a well-laid bomb carpet. The crews reported the ship as hit hard and heavily damaged, but made no claims for a sinking. That night, however, air patrols flying out of British bases on Malta reported the vessel foundering and finally going down. There were two other effective strikes; on 6th April a munitions ship took a string of bombs that walked the length of the vessel. The dazzling blast that followed gave ample proof of the effectiveness of the attack—the ship literally disintegrated, and the awed bomber crews watched huge chunks of ship tumbling in the air, sinking where they struck the water. On May 5th, off the northwestern edge of Sicily, another munitions ship took a beating from the B-17s. This time the vessel did not go under, but was written off as a helpless, smashed wreck.

But it was against the Italian Navy that the Fortresses showed their mettle, and a raid carried out against the La Maddalena naval base of northern Sardinia was described in AAF records as the "most celebrated of the heavies' current exploits. . . ."

On the 10th April, twenty-four B-17s came over La Maddalena at 18,750 feet. Four miles beneath them was the Italian heavy cruiser *Trieste*, anchored well within a protecting cove, and heavily shielded by torpedo nets. The warship was considered invulnerable to conventional air attack by torpedo bombers or low-flying planes; bristling antiaircraft defenses made low-level attack a suicidal venture.

From their bombing run, carried out with precision, the Fortresses laid down an exact carpet of explosives. Almost every bomb dropped within the specified area of release. The *Trieste* vanished beneath the cascade of explosives and booming columns of water. As quickly as the air cleared the results were obvious—the heavy cruiser, torn apart from stem to stern, was already going down. The next day reconnaissance photographs confirmed what was already a foregone conclusion—*Trieste*, holed and shattered, had vanished beneath the sea.

Two other attacks also were under way. Thirty-six Fortresses went in against the heavy cruiser *Gorizia*. Although they did not sink the heavily armored warship, the bombs crippled the cruiser and left it "badly damaged." Capping off the thundering blows from the air, still another twenty-four B-17s struck at the La Maddalena harbor and the submarine base.

From the official history of the AAF in World War II:

> The brilliance of these attacks could not but confirm the American airmen's faith that their long-time emphasis on high-altitude daylight bombing had been correct. Spaatz recorded in May that the day-to-day operational premise at Northwest African Air Forces was that any target could be

neutralized—"even blown to oblivion"—by high-altitude onslaught. Even well-dispersed aircraft—once thought unremunerative bomber targets—were far from immune to B-17s and their cargoes of frag clusters. Losses in TORCH had been slight. As of 22 May, only twenty-four B-17s had been lost in combat; and of these only eight were known victims of enemy fighters (the others were charged off to flak or to causes unknown). The signal failure of the German Air Force to fathom the B-17 defense, of course, could not be counted upon indefinitely. All of which caused Spaatz to regret that the turn of the wheel had not allowed the inception in 1942 of a decisive bomber offensive against Germany.[48]

In the months following, the B-17s continued to hammer at their old targets—among them the "milk runs" against heavy flak and fighter defenses of Bizerte and Tunis. Nowhere was there a letup in the effectiveness of the Fortress' strikes. The official histories of AAF units employ such terms as "Ferryville took a fearful pounding from the B-17s on 7th April . . .", and the "most effective attacks against Tunis and La Goulette occurred on 5th May when extensive damage occurred to port installations and eight small craft were sunk by the bombs."

But the bombers were ranging ever further into enemy territory and on the 4th April a force of ninety-one Fortresses hammered at the marshaling yards, port, and major airfield of Naples. Western Sicily became a "steady target" for the B-17s; southern Sardinia came under intermittent but heavy pounding to support the final destruction of German forces in Tunisia. Accuracy continued, and the weight of the raids went higher and higher as more and more Fortresses arrived in the theater. In mid-April three very heavy attacks against Palermo demolished the port

and rendered it useless for several weeks thereafter; reconnaissance planes came back daily with reports of "no activity."

By late May the B-17 crews considered Sicily, a strong
area of support for the beleaguered German forces in
Tunisia, to be an "old target." Coordinating with other
bombers, especially B-24s of the 9th Air Force, and Vickers
Wellingtons of the RAF, the Fortresses pounded Sicilian
airfields and ports in a mounting crescendo of bombs. "As
part of the plan to isolate the battle area in North Africa,"
notes the AAF history, "southern Italian and Sicilian lines
of communication and Sicilian airfields had been bombed
almost repeatedly . . . in an offensive which grew steadily
in size and fury." Then, on the 13th May, the German
forces in Africa gave up the fight. The aerial armadas of
the Allies turned to a new target—Pantelleria.

From the moment Allied planners turned their thinking
to reducing the Italian island fortress, they recognized that
"its conquest might be a troublesome and expensive operation." Fifty-three miles from Tunisia, Pantelleria was more
than forty-two square miles of rugged volcanic rock with
forbidding approaches studded with steep cliffs and lacking beaches required by any large seaborn invasion force.
An AAF study of the island showed, in part, that Pantelleria was "largely of lava, pumice, and volcanic ash . . . the
surface is cut by numerous ravines and eroded channels.
Hundreds of high, thick stone walls, which divide the
arable land into fields, afford protection for defending
ground troops, while each of the island's square houses of
stone or plaster could be turned into a miniature fortress."

The question was not whether Pantelleria could be invaded, but what the cost would be to the attacking forces?
But what if Pantelleria, isolated and so close to land-based

aircraft, could be beaten into submission through air bombardment?

Out of the questions and the obvious possibilities there grew Operation CORKSCREW—"the first Allied attempt to conquer enemy territory essentially by air action. . . ." Approximately one thousand planes would be committed to the operation, but the majority of these were medium or light bombers, and fighters. Four B-17 groups would carry the brunt of the bombardment responsibility. In short, while the mediums and the fighters would lay into tactical targets—shipping, enemy planes, and antiaircraft defenses—it would be up to the concentrated fury of the B-17 formations to break the back of the Pantellerian will to continue its resistance.

In the period before the Fortresses were committed, the tactical air forces mounted a furious assault consisting of daily strikes by fifty medium bombers and an equal number of fighter-bombers. On the 1st June, the Fortresses joined the attack in strength. Their task was to neutralize coastal batteries and gun emplacements "of special concern to the Allied command." The 1st of June saw the Fortresses, along with P-38 and P-40 fighter-bombers, unleashing 141 tons of bombs on their targets. On the 4th June, swarms of planes, including B-17s, dumped another 200 tons on the beleaguered island. Between the 18th May and 6th June, Pantelleria rocked under 1,700 sorties that smashed at the main port and airfield with more than 900 tons of bombs, while B-17s dumped another 400 tons on the gun positions marked for their special attention.

The "second phase" of the aerial reduction of Pantelleria began on the 6th June, when swarms of bombers and fighters hit the island all day long with heavy attacks. The next day B-17s carried most of the attack, with a total of 600 tons showered onto the island, the majority of bombs hitting shore batteries. On 8th June a new level was reached of 700 tons, "B-17s carrying the bulk of the load." If the island defenders thought they had seen the worst they were sorely in error. On the 9th June another 800 tons battered Pantelleria.

All this was only in a way of building up strength and on the 10th June "the Allied command unleashed the full force of its air power." The attack went on all day long. There were so many planes in the air that new waves of bombers found it necessary to circle slowly at altitude, waiting for bombers that had arrived earlier to unleash their missiles. By day's end nearly 1,100 bombers and fighters had completed their devastating barrage, hitting the island with more than 1,500 tons of bombs.

On the morning of 11th June the invasion forces were off the island and prepared to storm the defending positions. The Italians had failed to respond to several radioed demands to surrender, and the full-scale invasion was launched. Shore targets took a beating from warships cruising near the invasion sites and, as the landing craft with troops aboard neared the end of their runs, waves of B-17s came overhead to smash the devastated island "with tons of bombs in a fine exhibition of flying and bombing."

The Fortresses were still in sight, winging their way homeward, when Allied lookouts "reported a white flag flying . . ." from the main invasion area. In the meantime the landings went in; at one beach only was there resistance, and this was scattered and ineffective. A British military study stated afterward that "in effect active resistance on Pantelleria had ceased when the amphibious forces arrived."

The troops were still moving inland when the official surrender was received. All bombing missions, for which hundreds of planes were standing by, were canceled.

There was only one casualty to the Allied forces in the invasion. The official records show that "a British infantry-man . . . was nipped by a local jackass."

The heavy bombers set their sights again for Sicily and Italy.

With Pantelleria out of the way, the heavy bombers were thrown into the campaign to soften up Sicily for invasion. But to render Sicily ripe for the plucking of attacking forces it was necessary to pursue the Luftwaffe far north of the island where, after the bombings during May of Sardinia and Sicily, the Germans had moved the bulk of their airpower. In the meantime, while trying to eliminate the operational forces now in Italy, the heavy bombers also went after the airfields of Sicily itself. On that island the enemy claimed no less than nineteen major airfields and major airstrips, as well as a dozen fields of lesser value which could serve admirably to meet any major sudden threat on the part of the Allies. Sicily functioned, then, as a giant forward airbase of many separated and valuable airstrips into which the Germans could, within only a few hours, move a powerful force of fighters and bombers. The eastern half of the island became the prime responsibility of the Ninth Air Force (flying Liberators) and the RAF. The B-17s which had operated against African targets as well as ranging into Sicily and Italy took over the western half of Sicily as their major targets. The raids were carried out on almost a daily schedule, bombs slamming into runways, along hangar lines and the built-up areas of the enemy fields. It was a progression of steady bombing, with opposition from the Germans a spotty proposition. For days on end there would be little to contest the bombers in the air and then, unexpectedly, swarms of fighters would tear into the Allied formations.

On the 18th June the Fortresses turned their attention to Messina, the "principal line of supply from the mainland to Sicily." Approximately five thousand tons of war materiel passed every day through Messina and it quite naturally became a focus for the B-17 attacks. On the 18th a force of seventy-six Fortresses hammered the supply center. British Wellingtons followed up for nocturnal raids. On 25th June the B-17s came back in force, no less than 130 of the four-engine bombers ripping up ferry docks, rail yards, and warehouse areas. In the succeeding days the Italian cities and targets took a steady pounding from B-17s, B-24s, B-25s and Wellingtons. And on the 28th June, a formation of nearly a hundred B-17s poured 261 tons of bombs with outstanding accuracy into Leghorn's industrial and railway installations. The damage was reported to be especially severe to the vital city.

For the period of 12th June through 2nd July the bombers rained 2,276 tons of bombs against their targets spread far and wide through Sicily and Italy. The B-17s carried the brunt of the missions and also bore the greatest weight of attacks on Messina, which in eleven raids took a total of 829 tons of explosives.

The softening-up of Sicily was going ahead quite as planned. As the AAF history notes:

> The weight of the attack was delivered by the heavy bombers in missions both near and far. Employing usually formations of twenty-four planes in six-plane flights, the heavies went out from their fields in Africa again and again with each flight carefully briefed on a specific target. Experience showed that an attack about noon took advantage of the position of the sun and was more likely to achieve the desired surprise.... Gerbini and its satellites received a thorough battering, the outstanding blow being delivered

on 5th July with an estimated destruction of 100 enemy planes.... [49]

Gerbini had another meaning to the Fortress crews. For days German fighter opposition had been weak and small in number. But on 5th July the Luftwaffe came out in strength with more than a hundred fighters tearing aggressively into the B-17 formations. One of the Fortress gunners who met that attack, and who went into the record books of the Army Air Force with a distinction unique unto himself, was Staff Sergeant Benjamin F. Warmer.

Ben Warmer is the only gunner of the AAF ever to make the coveted list of aces—men who have shot down five or more planes in aerial combat. The figure after Warmer's name reads nine planes shot down in battle—and seven of them were destroyed on this particular 5th of July. It would be unusual not to experience raised eyebrows over the *confirmed* seven kills of this one air battle, especially since earlier in these pages we have examined the problems of gunner claims during the frenzied action of aerial combat. Yet there is no question but that the seven kills established for Ben Warmer on this date were given the most exhaustive scrutiny possible. Every pilot and crewman of the accompanying planes was questioned. Witnesses were interrogated again and again to sift out possible errors or duplications. When the Intelligence officers completed their work they were delighted and not a little in awe of what their meticulous examination revealed. Ben Warmer had indeed shot down seven enemy fighters during a single aerial battle.

Many factors contributed to the epic contest. There was, first, Ben Warmer himself, a giant of a man who stood six feet six inches and weighed in at more than 275 pounds in his stocking feet. That alone accounted for the ease with which Warmer handled his .50 caliber waist gun. In his huge hands and pushed around by his great bulk, the "big fifty" was handled as easily as another man might heft a .22 rifle. Warmer was more than big; he was a man of unusual strength, a former fullback with the University of California. He also had carried the pigskin as a professional in 1937 with the Golden Bears. There followed a period with Warmer serving as bodyguard to former Secretary of the Treasury, Henry Morgenthau. In April of 1942 Ben Warmer enlisted in the AAF—and earned quickly to his dismay that he just didn't fit into the cockpit of fighter planes. (What Warmer didn't know until later, and even more to his dismay, that another giant of a man—Dale O. Smith, who was six feet seven inches in height—had fought his way through flight school and, in 1943, was even then at the controls of a B-17 over Europe.) Despite his repeated attempts to make it into flight school, Warmer found himself a physical education instructor. An afternoon at the gunnery range extricated him from a disagreeable assignment for the man who wanted to fight.

The axiom at the range with the heavy .50 caliber machine gun had always been that "the gun fires the man rather than the man fires the gun." Not with Ben Warmer. The big machine gun seemed like a broomstick in his hands. And there wasn't any mistaking the effect when the tracers hosed squarely into the center of the target.

Ben Warmer made it into the crew of a Fortress, manning one of the waist guns. By the time the North African battle was over, Warmer, as a member of the 99th Group, Twelfth Air Force, had flown twelve combat missions. Early in June he escaped with his life from his blazing Fortress when his crew bailed out over Africa, after returning from a raid in an airplane shot to ribbons, two engines dead, and another burning. It was "just another mission" for Ben Warmer and his crew; they returned to the fray with a new Fortress to fly.

On the 5th July, approaching Gerbini, Ben Warmer looked like a great grizzly bear as he stalked through the fuselage of his airplane. He bulged from head to toes in fleece-lined leather flight gear, his face was hidden from view behind his oxygen mask, and his huge hands seemed even larger than usual in their thick gloves. Until their last mission, over Naples, Warmer had shot a lot of ammunition at German fighters coming in for the kill at his bomber. He'd hit a few, but not seriously enough to claim more than "damaged." Until the mission over Naples when the other crewmen confirmed that Warmer had shot down two fighters. All of a sudden, he found that everything was falling into place. The gun swung easily from the right waist position and he had the technique of leading his swift targets just the way he wanted it.

The 5th of July was a special occasion for Ben Warmer. *Before* the fight that would take place. It was his seventh wedding anniversary. . . .

There were thirty Fortresses in the formations of the 99th Bomb Group. The thirty B-17s led the attack; more would be coming later. The lead formations got the attention of the one hundred German fighters that rose to do battle that day.

The Germans opened the attack with a broad sweep of twin-engined Messerschmitt Me-110 fighters. A fighter came in along a wide pursuit curve. Warmer held his fire, watching the tracers of the Me-110 falling short of his own airplane. Then the Me-110 was in range and Warmer hosed out lead. He was dead-on. Pieces broke off from the fuselage and wing of the fighter; abruptly it broke sharply to the left. Flame exploded in a huge fireball from the wing tanks and the Me-110 tumbled away. *One.*

He caught a second fighter with a long burst into an engine. The Messerschmitt seemed to stagger, then came boring in on a direct collision course. The men braced themselves. They knew a dead man was at the controls of the onrushing fighter. Almost when it was too late, it seemed, the fighter flipped onto its back and skidded wildly out of control, just beneath the Fortress.

"That's two for Ben!" someone shouted over the intercom.

A single-engine '109 came in along a steep diving turn. Someone shouted "Two o'clock high!" and Warmer was ready with a well-aimed short burst. The tracers melted into the fighter; at once the enemy smoked and then rolled out of sight beneath the right wing. No one thought it a definite kill. Until a moment later when the belly gunner reported the fighter now blazing and, after another moment, the Fortress rocked wildly as the Me-109 exploded.

But the Germans were getting through. Holes appeared magically in the wings and the fuselage. Pieces of torn metal flipped away in the howling slipstream. Up forward in the cockpit a cannon shell started a blaze within the B-17. Someone grabbed an extinguisher, put the flames out, and reassured the crew that everything was "just fine."

It wasn't. In the wild maneuvering a blast of sub-zero air pummeled Warmer's face, creating instantly a blanket of ice along the exhaust valve of his oxygen mask. Before it could block the flow Warmer slapped it away from the mask. He breathed deeply, just in time to notice the other waist gunner clawing wildly at his mask and collapsing to the floorboards. Warmer turned from his gun, adjusted the other man's oxygen valve. Moments later his friend nodded weakly and motioned to Warmer that he was okay. Warmer went back to his fifty just as another man called out: "Watch it, Ben! Three o'clock high!"

The timing couldn't have been better. Warmer caught the '109 with a long burst that was head-on. Three men watched the fighter explode into flames and then come apart in the air like a clock with a busted mainspring. Pieces flew in all directions. *Four.*

Another Me-109 came in from four o'clock, just sliding ahead of tracers from the tail guns. As it broke into clear view, Warmer fired a long burst that stayed with the speeding fighter. The heavy slugs hammered into the fuselage along the wing root. At once the German pilot rolled in an attempt to break away from the American fire. Too late; the weakened wing failed to take the punishment of the maneuver. The wing snapped away at the root, sending the fighter tumbling wildly out of control. *Five.*

Another fighter, and again Warmer tracked the incoming Messerschmitt. The heavy gun banged out six rounds and went silent, the ammunition box empty. Warmer cursed as he slipped on the empty shell casings beneath his feet. Once he fell clumsily to his knees. He fought his way upright, grabbed an ammo belt, slung it over his shoulder. He loaded one end of the belt into his gun, slammed a round into the chamber. The Fortress rocked wildly from antiaircraft shells bursting all around them. Gerbini lay far below. The Fortress rocked, bounced upward as the bombs dropped free. Moments later they were out of the flak and the fighters were boring in again.

A single Messerschmitt came in from twelve o'clock high. No defensive fire met the approach of the onrushing fighter; the forward guns had been knocked out. Bullets and cannon shells slammed into the B-17 as the German pilot held down his gun tit for a long firing run. Someone called out to Warmer that the fighter was breaking off to his side. The waist gunner was ready and waiting and as quickly as the Me-109 appeared Warmer poured a long burst into the nose, let the tracers walk back into the cockpit. Where the pilot had been there appeared a bloody froth and pieces of wreckage tearing away. The '109 snapped over with a dead pilot at the controls. *Six.*

There came one final attack. Two fighters in tight formation for concentrated firepower arced up from below in a steep climb. The tail gunner drove one off, smoking, but the other came on, slowing in the upward rush. Warmer jammed his heavy weapon back and down and squeezed off a series of short bursts at the fighter. Tracers slammed into the engine and smoke poured back. The Me-109 seemed to hang in the air for a long moment, floundering helplessly as the propeller jerked to a stop. Warmer hosed a long burst into the fighter as it fell off and dropped away in a wild spin. The crew watched the airplane spin all the way down to earth where it disappeared in an explosion.

That made seven.

And the Distinguished Flying Cross, and a commission, for Staff Sergeant Benjamin F. Warmer, the gunner who looked like a grizzly bear . . .

Allied troops invaded Sicily on the 10th July. The air war had settled down—if this word may be used—to a continuing murderous assault against the disheartened Italians and the grimly defending Germans. During the assault phase alone the Tactical Air Force flew over five thousand sorties to support the ground troops and invading ships. Strategic airpower threw their weight into the fray to smash supply lines and demolish the ability of the enemy to fight in the air. Four groups of B-17s, five groups of B-24s, and five groups of medium bombers flew almost continuously against their assigned targets. Marshaling yards, repair shops, ferry slips, port facilities, bridges, rail lines, and airfields took a steady and savage pounding from the air.

As the aerial bombardment continued, island defenses fell one after the other to the Allied troops. The heavy bombers turned to new targets. Evidence of the mounting weight and fury of these attacks is provided in the missions flown on the 17th July against Naples and Rome. Early in the morning seventy-seven Liberators plastered rail yards in Naples. In the afternoon, with fires still blazing from the B-24 attack, the heaviest part of the raids were carried out by 97 B-17s and 179 B-26 Marauders, escorted by no less than 164 P-38 fighters. Naples took a battering from the 353 bombers which dropped a total of 650 tons of bombs to wreak widespread havoc throughout the target area. The number of planes involved provides the best measurement of the effort under way.

It was but the harbinger of more to come. Two days later, on the 19th July, more than five hundred bombers took on Rome. The Lorenzo and Littorio rail yards, and the Ciampino airfields, took a savage mauling from more than a thousand tons of bombs. Both the B-17 and B-24 formations achieved spectacular results. Four groups of Fortresses tore up the Lorenzo yards to leave them a smoking, ruined shambles. At Littorio the B-24s carried out a repeat performance. For a while, at least, all trains in the Rome area came to a standstill. Both yards were out of action.

"The effect of the damage should be viewed in conjunction with the raid of 17th July on the Naples yards," notes the official AAF history. "The two attacks produced a gap of some two hundred miles in the Italian railroad system between points north of Rome and south of Naples and prevented for at least several days the movement of Axis troops and supplies by rail from central to southern Italy."

The raids grew in size. On 13th August 106 B-17s were out to pound rail yards again, with forty-five P-38s providing escort. Four days later, the B-17 formations had again increased in size as 180 Flying Fortresses ranged northward from Africa to pound airfields northwest of Marseille. In addition to extensive damage to hangars and airdrome installations, reconnaissance photographs showed a confirmed total of ninety-four planes destroyed and another twenty-eight damaged on the ground.

The raids went on, heavier and heavier. The bombers were sent out to soften up Italy for its invasion early in September. The persistent, systematic, and highly accurate bombing of airfields prior to and during the invasion of Sicily had given the Allies complete air superiority, and the drive was on to repeat the past. More than 1,100 enemy fighters and bombers had been wrecked or abandoned on the ground during the campaign in Sicily. Now, mixed in with targets of industrial and communications importance, the airfields came in for renewed attention. The raids were carried out day after day with the pressure applied relentlessly. The single heaviest strike of the period came on the 19th August when 162 B-17s and 71 Liberators went after Foggia. Nearly 650 tons of bombs ripped up rail lines, set factories aflame, and tore apart marshaling yards and rolling stock. It took a long time to get the type of confirmation the bomber commanders wanted most, but on 28th September British troops entered Foggia and sent back reports that the heavy attacks against the city had been "most effective" and that damage inflicted on the rail and industrial targets "surpassed all earlier estimates."

Pisa on 31st August took a battering from 152 Fortresses in an attack that "cut rail lines . . . and caused widespread destruction." Every major rail terminus received the attention of the B-17s, as well as the rail lines through the famed Brenner Pass. On the 2nd September the B-17s scored a tremendous victory "out of all proportion to the number of planes involved." A small formation of two-dozen Fortresses "destroyed the bridge across the River Is-cara and cut the only other line running south (from the pass to Merano), thereby blocking all traffic from Germany to Trento; the same day nineteen other Fortresses cut the Trento highway bridge and the adjoining bridge over the Adige River. The Brenner route was the shortest, most direct line between Germany and Italy, and its interdiction, although temporary, was valuable to the Allies."[50]

In other raids carried out simultaneously against airfields, 136 B-17s escorted by large formations of P-38s made a devastating attack on 25th August against the Foggia airfield complex. It was a fearsome one-two punch, opened by 140 P-38s that came in on the deck in a wild and free-swinging strafing attack. Immediately after the 140 fighters completed their runs the 136 Fortresses appeared overhead to hit four airfields where they destroyed or wrecked some sixty planes and tore up vital ground installations. The AAF history notes that this attack was likely the "major event in the air war in the Mediterranean, for thereafter there was a sharp decline in the number of Allied bombers lost to enemy fighters."

On the 3rd September Allied forces stormed Italy. The B-17s kept up their merciless pounding. Mission after mission went out and the majority of these were marked with the outstanding success that had come to be expected of the formations of Flying Fortresses. The official records use such terms as "heavy attacks," and describe the airfield targets as "smashed" and "battered" or having suffered a "severe beating." One hundred and thirty-three Fortresses ground up Viterbo airfield near Rome. One hundred and twenty-four B-17s pulverized airfield targets near Foggia.

One hundred and thirty B-17s "struck a smashing blow against the town of Frascati, fifteen miles southeast of Rome, where the headquarters of the German high command was located."

Salerno was invaded. Fortresses in formations of a dozen planes to 130 bombers smashed bridges, rail lines and yards, power stations, highways. Again and again reports came in from the field that accurate bombing by the Fortresses had isolated German reinforcements from the scene of combat where they were so desperately needed by the enemy.

The Fortresses also went out in small numbers for night raids. On the 16th September five B-17s joined an armada of 340 British heavy bombers against southeastern France to close up railroad tunnels.

The Fortresses began to extend their range for the heavy air assaults. On the 24th September the B-17s carried out a "solid smash" against Pisa rail yards. Then they "put in three long-distance blows on the 25th with strikes against yards at Bologna, Bolzano, and Verona."

B-17 formations reached out to additional targets in France, northern Italy, and Germany. As the war situation on the ground changed, the emphasis went from communications lines and airfields to industrial centers. Much of the effort was coordinated with the growing fury of bomber operations from Europe, where the Eighth Air Force had run into devastating losses at the hands of German fighter pilots. The nature of the air war was changing, and the industrial cities of Germany itself came more and more to the forefront as the prime target of the Fortresses.

Before we return to the European Theater of Operations and the "island carrier" that was England, there is a finale to our study of the Flying Fortress in Africa and throughout the Mediterranean. It is one of the least-known and most incredible facets of the entire war, and somehow it seems fitting that it involves not only the B-17, but one of its offspring, the YB-40 gunship, a B-17F converted into an airplane bristling with sixteen machine guns and bomb bays crammed with enough ammunition to fill the needs of several bombers.

It is also the story of a bizarre hunt for an American fighter plane—a P-38—and its pilot.

Whose success in *shooting down* B-17s unnerved bomber crews up and down the Mediterranean . . .

It began on the 4th of June 1943 when a formation of B-17s was returning from one of the "hammer" missions against Pantelleria. Well behind the bunched four-engine bombers, visible only as a small dot in the sky, a last Fortress dragged its way home to Africa. The B-17 was crippled, with both engines on the left wing dead and feathered. The pilot, 1st Lieutenant Harold Fisher, fought the controls of his shot-up airplane. This was his twentieth mission, he had plenty of experience and skill to handle the machine. But he didn't know how much longer he could retain full control. Fisher thought seriously of ditching while he could still control the plane for if the crippled bomber ever "got away" from him, his crew would have to bail out, and *fast*. Fisher didn't like the idea of ordering his men to bail out into the sea. He was a veteran; they weren't. For the other nine men aboard the B-17 this was their first mission.

Fisher committed himself to staying with the airplane as long as she would fly. He ordered the crew to dump all excess weight—machine guns, ammunition belts, flak suits; everything that would come loose. He didn't want to think about German fighters. His airplane, *Bonnie Sue*, was already staggering. A single pass by a Messerschmitt or a Focke-Wulf could send them spinning into the water.

Then the dreaded call. "Fighter one o'clock high," shouted the right waist gunner. "Closing fast."

There wasn't much time for panic to well up in the crew who were already checking their chutes. No one could mistake the twin-boomed signature of the P-38. One of the Little Friends, welcome as hell right now. The P-38 came in so close that Fisher grinned at the sight of the pilot waving to him. Fisher went to VHF, asked the P-38 pilot for escort back to his base. The pilot agreed and fell back to take up a weaving escort position above and behind the Fortress. Harold Fisher looked down at the Mediterranean four thousand feet below. That P-38 was good news.

Until a moment later when a locomotive seemed to thunder directly against the Flying Fortress. The bomber heeled over violently from the sudden blow, a roaring, continuous crash as heavy machine gun slugs and exploding cannon shells tore apart the airplane. Fisher had just enough time to see the P-38 closing in fast, the long nose ablaze with the four fifties and the single 20-mm cannon. Just enough time to see the P-38 chopping the Fortress into ribbons; just enough time to hear cold laughter in his earphones. Then the bomber dropped toward the sea in a screaming spiral, Fisher fighting the controls. Just before they hit the water he righted the airplane and brought up the nose. They hit with all the force of smashing into a stone wall. The nose gave way and at more than a hundred miles per hour the ocean burst through the airplane, killing men, trapping the others. Fisher remembers crawling through a shattered windshield. He struggled to the surface, grabbed at a raft floating alongside him.

He was the only survivor. That night a British rescue team fished him out of the water.

The next day Fisher found himself the target of unbridled fury on the part of P-38 group commanders. They'd listened to his story and they reacted to his details of being shot down by a P-38. They didn't like it and they read off the equally angry bomber pilot. The Intelligence officer, Major Walter B. Higgins, soothed the ruffled feathers of those at the interrogation. What he had to say put a new light on the matter. It wasn't much, but it was everything.

Several weeks previously a P-38 pilot, low on fuel, confused and unsure of his actual position, made an emergency landing at Elmas Airdrome, just outside Cagliari, Sardinia. Before the pilot could set his fighter aflame, Italian troops dragged him off the big twin-engined airplane. That was the start of it. The Italians tested the P-38 until they'd gleaned all the technical data they desired. Lieutenant Guido Rossi, a colorful and skilled fighter pilot, looked long and hard at the Lightning, and came up with an idea. He presented it to his superior, who in turn bucked it on up to Rome, where Mussolini personally approved what Rossi had in mind.

The lieutenant's plan was simple. He would leave the markings on the American fighter and, after the Americans made their bombing raids, he would follow the formations, looking for stragglers. No one would suspect a lone P-38; indeed, they would be delighted to see the fighter and gain protection of its speed and guns.

Guido Rossi shot down several B-17s. There were no survivors to report his ruse back to the Allied camp. Until the British picked up Harold Fisher from the sea and he went home with his startling tale of the renegade P-38.

Despite warnings sent to all bomber units, Rossi kept up his unnerving manhunt for crippled or straggling bombers.

Then he swept in against a formation over Naples, and shot another Fortress out of the sky.

Fisher went to Colonel Bill Hall, his group commander, with a suggestion: since Rossi was so fond of stragglers, why not set up a decoy? Not a B-17, but the YB-40, one of the experimental gunships then being tested in Europe. Engineers took a standard B-17F model and carried out a drastic modification of the airplane. They put a power turret with twin fifties beneath the nose to make up for weak defensive firepower against head-on attacks. Where the radio operator had fired a single fifty, they installed a second power turret atop the fuselage. Instead of the single fifties in each waist position, they doubled the waist firepower. Into the bomb bays went ammunition boxes, enough to keep the YB-40 firing long after a B-17 ammo supply would be exhausted. The idea of the YB-40 was to provide a form of self-escort to bombers that ranged beyond the reach of friendly fighters. Each YB-40 had sixteen heavy machine guns. Chances were it could take care of a single P-38, which was the way Rossi always operated. Especially if they were able to sucker in the Italian in precisely the same fashion he had trapped the crippled Fortresses into setting themselves up as dead ducks ... Bill Hall gave approval, and the request for a single YB-40 went up to Eighth Bomber Command in England. The gunship arrived early in August and, as he had hoped, Harold Fisher received orders to fly the gun-bristling decoy.

For the next two weeks Fisher and a picked crew did their best to flush out the renegade P-38. Returning from missions against Salerno, Foggia, Naples and Rome he dragged away from the bomber formations, an "obvious cripple" trailing aft of the other bombers and a sitting duck for fighters. Lt. Rossi came nowhere near the YB-40 and went after the real thing. On the 19th August the Italian flamed a straggler south of Benevento. A week later Rossi chopped down another Fortress and, to cap off the day, flew formation with a strafing P-38 and then shot down the unsuspecting American pilot.

Desperate, Fisher badgered Intelligence for details on his elusive quarry. The break came when he learned that Rossi's wife lived in Constantine—*occupied by Allied troops*. That night Fisher stepped through the apartment door where Gina Rossi and her child—never seen by its father—lived. As soon as he returned to his base, Fisher dragged a squadron artist from his office and put him to work. When the artist completed his task the fuselage of the gunship carried on its side a painting of a beautiful dark-haired woman. Beneath the painting, in large letters, was the name Gina.

On the 31st August the Fortresses went out against Pisa with Fisher holding trail position. They didn't see Rossi during the bomb strike but took a beating from German fighters hitting the Fortress in beautiful formation attacks. They stayed with the Fortresses through the bomb drops and then planned to fall back. But the copilot, Lieutenant John Yates, blanched at what he saw in the air. German fighters were all over the place. Not even the extra turrets and heavy armor of the YB-40 would do them much good against a concerted fighter attack.

The Germans solved the problem for them; two Me-109's poured cannon shells into the number four engine and exploded it in flames. Overloaded from the weight of guns and armor, the heavy airplane swung into a wide, helpless roll and before the pilots could stave off the maneuver the YB-40 was on its back, falling crazily. Fisher had no help from Yates; the copilot had been battered unconscious.

Fisher struggled to bring the gunship out of a screaming dive. For ten thousand feet the airplane plunged toward the sea. Fisher jerked back the throttles, rolled in nose-up position on the trim, and hauled back on the yoke with all his strength. The Fortress should have snapped off its wings from the brutal pullout at five thousand feet. Fisher didn't know when he came out of the dive—the pullout had blacked him out. When he regained his senses—Yates was still unconscious—he feathered engines three and four and pondered their fate. Heavily loaded, the YB-40 would never make it back on two engines. Fisher barked out orders for the gunners to dump everything except the ammunition still in their guns. Yates came to while the emergency jettison order was being met by the gunners. He shook his head and stared out his side window. Suddenly his fist was banging Fisher on the arm.

"Hey! There's a P-38 out there.... He's got one feathered."

One engine stopped and the propeller blades knife-edge into the wind, the P-38 slid beneath the YB-40 and came up on Fisher's cockpit side. The P-38 pilot waved at him. Could it be Rossi? There was no way of telling. Yates went on the intercom and warned the gunners to stay alert for anything from the fighter. Fisher switched to the assigned fighter radio frequency. The pilot told Fisher he'd like to ride home with the bomber; Fisher agreed. Then he turned his attention back to the YB-40. Their altitude was down to two thousand feet and still dropping.

With the P-38 along Fisher thought it safer to dump more weight. He ordered the gunners to dump the remaining ammunition and every machine gun that could be released.

Then he heard a voice that brought him straight up in his seat. It was the P-38 pilot.

"... pretty name, Gina. She's from Constantine?"

Fisher snapped back to reality with warnings pounding in his ears. He shouted for the men to keep the guns. The left waist gunner and radioman had already heaved theirs over the side. Fisher switched back to fighter frequency. During the next several minutes he baited Rossi as best he could—including in his conversation details of what it was like to sleep with Gina Rossi.

That broke the farce. Rossi already had his engine restarted and with a string of oaths pulled ahead of the YB-40. His maneuver was clear to Fisher. Rossi would bring the P-38 back in a long, steady head-on run to pour his bullets and cannon shells straight into the cockpit. Rossi took his time. As far as he knew the YB-40 was now help-less, its ammunition thrown into the sea. He set up his fir-ing run and bored in.

At the last possible moment Fisher roared: "*Now!*" Every gun on the YB-40 that could fire forward opened up. Two turrets blazed away, dead-on their target. The P-38 seemed to stagger in mid-air, then it slid away to the side, trailing smoke. Crewmen called out that the left aileron was shot away. Rossi was the one now in real trouble. As the men watched, flames erupted from the smoking engine, streaming back almost to the tail.

But Rossi wasn't quitting. Cursing Fisher for having slept with his wife he brought the Lightning in without wa-vering. He was going to ram if necessary. The four guns and cannon of the P-38 chopped into the crippled YB-40, slamming the big airplane to the side. The Fortress gunners kept up return fire, pouring it into the fighter. Closer and closer came Rossi, finger jammed on the firing tit, grimly determined to take the Fortress and all its crew with him.

He almost made it. The P-38 was coming apart in the air under the furious battering from the multiple guns of the YB-40. The cockpit canopy twisted wildly through the air, the flames lengthened, and pieces of Lightning kept snapping away in the wind. Almost to the B-17, Rossi could no longer control the fighter. It dropped its nose and headed for the water below.

Rossi regained control, dropping down in a long, flat glide. Aboard the YB-40 the men watched the Lightning hit the water, throw up a high plume of spray. When the water settled they saw Rossi standing on the wing, shaking his fist at them. The crew wanted to go down and shoot "the son of a bitch while we got him." Fisher ordered his men not to fire. Instead, he notified Air-Sea Rescue of the position of the Italian pilot.

The Twelfth Air Force awarded Lt. Harold Fisher the Distinguished Flying Cross, and each crewman the Air Medal, for their roles in the amazing aerial duel.

Harold Fisher and Guido Rossi both survived the war. Several years later, Fisher's luck ran out. During a mission on the Berlin Airlift the plane he flew crashed.

A great many men who knew Harold Fisher mourned his passing. One of them was Guido Rossi. . . .

Of all the Flying Fortresses that became famous during World War II, none was so well known by sight—but not by name—as the B-17 of the 414th Squadron, 97th Bomb Group, known to its squadron members as *All American*. Millions of people recognized the familiar picture of the Fortress with the white circle around its fuselage star, and the number 124408 stenciled on the high vertical fin. They knew the picture showed a scene that was flatly, aerodynamically, technically impossible.

The picture of a Flying Fortress seemingly cut in half and still flying.

The Fortress, flown out of Biskra by Kenneth R. Bragg,

was returning from a mission over Tunisia. During attacks by German fighters, an Me-109 drove from high above against the tail, from the six o'clock position. The tail gunner poured a long burst into the cockpit, killing the pilot.

With a dead man at the controls the German fighter continued its dive and smashed into the tail section of the Fortress. The impact tore apart the Messerschmitt, and in the collison the left horizontal stabilizer and elevator of the Fortress were torn away. What was worse, the fuselage was sliced in half along a diagonal line running from the dorsal fin back and downward to the tail.

It was impossible for the airplane to fly. But it flew. It shook and rattled and the tail swayed wildly. The tail gunner scampered with monkey swiftness out of his small position and into the dubious safety of the fuselage. Every man aboard tightened his parachute, ready to go out the moment the tail separated—as every man expected it would at any moment. Accompanying bomber crews stared in awe. It's not often you see a miracle happen before your eyes.

For an hour and a half Ken Bragg flew that impossible airplane home. They gave him a long straight-in approach to Biskra. And Bragg landed that impossible airplane in an impossible landing.

"You know what happened when that damned airplane came to a stop?" a crewman ventured in awe. "They got a small hatch back there in the fuselage. When someone pulled open the hatch that airplane broke in half...."

But it flew home—first.

# III

# TARGET: GERMANY

# CHAPTER 20

# BOOM TOWN

A WAR CORRESPONDENT DOING human-interest stories about the men who flew the great B-17s cornered a tail gunner as the man descended, cold and weary, from his bomber after a mission of nearly 1,600 miles. In his best newsman's manner, the correspondent asked: "Son, what made you decide to become a tail gunner?"

The exhausted gunner stared at the correspondent. "It's the only outfit I know," he said slowly, "where you can retreat at three hundred miles an hour. . . ."

Turn back the clock.

The time?

The exact date doesn't matter. Time is how you measure it. In England, in the dark winter of 1942–1943, time was measured in numbers of missions flown, numbers of missions left to be flown. Out of the many there emerged distinct crews, distinct aircraft. One such of these was a Flying

Fortress with the name of *Boom Town*. It was an act of derision, a sarcastic title bestowed upon the big airplane by her copilot, Lt. Bill Reed. When the crew took delivery of their new bomber the engines had a tendency to blow oil all over the nacelles and the wings. A disgruntled crewman complained that if they could only sell the oil the ship threw away they could be rich. One quip led to another and the name *Boom Town* was painted on the side of the nose.

She was an ordinary B-17, even if her crew *was* young. The oldest man aboard was the pilot, Captain Clyde Walker. He was twenty-three—the "old man" of them all.

The eighth mission of *Boom Town* was to be part of a small formation of B-17s against the submarine pens of Lorient. That was how Walker and his men reckoned time— the number eight was everything. Number nine would be after that, and then ten, and so on up to the magic figure of twenty-five, when headquarters would punch your ticket for a ride back home. To the States.

But before you could fly Mission Number Nine you had to first survive Number Eight. To Lorient and back. Copilot Bill Reed fidgeted uncomfortably in the cockpit as they started out on Number Eight. He had a premonition. "We're going to get clobbered today," he said unhappily. "I know it; I just *know* it." Someone told him to shut up. There was plenty to do without listening to morose copilots and their triple-damned premonitions.

Turn back the clock. To the moment of takeoff for Mission Number Eight . . .

Clyde Walker stared grimly through the windshield. Heavy fog shrouded the field, swallowed up the dim runway lights that stretched away before the nose of *Boom Town*. Walker didn't like to fly in fog. He hated taking off in the stuff, but there wasn't any way out of that. He pushed the throttles forward, brought up the tail, rushing into the swirling gloom. Fog swallowed them up and Clyde Walker went on instruments. Moments later someone back in the fuselage cheered. They broke quickly through the ground fog and spilled upward among big, fluffy, soaked-in-sunshine clouds. Everyone looked around for the other planes. Walker slid *Boom Town* into place. In the formation of Six Flying Fortresses, they held lead position of the second element of three planes. Wedged together in the sky they climbed out over the English Channel. At eight thousand feet everyone went on oxygen, checked in with the pilot. A little while later, the cold seeping through every part of the Fortress, they tested their guns. The recoil vibrated sharply through the metal structure.

In the nose a small riot was under way. The navigator, Lt. Bill Smith, and the bombardier, Lt. Grover Bentinck, horsed it up with each other. Bentinck was bellowing "You Are My Sunshine" into the intercom. Clyde Walker and Bill Reed in the cockpit grinned at one another. It was lousy crew discipline, but this early in the mission it didn't matter. They were a close-knit group, and everyone was sharing the joy of the bombardier. Back home in Galveston, Texas, Bentinck's wife was going to have a baby. He couldn't keep from bubbling over.

He shouldn't have been in the airplane. He had been ill for weeks, often doubled over with blinding pains from stomach cramps. He couldn't keep down much food. He had flown seven missions and he had severe ulcers. They were bad enough for the doctors to tell him he was ready to return to the States. He was a veteran now and he could go home, and his wife was going to have a baby. But Grover Bentinck had been with this crew since the day they received their Fortress in training. The bombardier shook his head to the doctors. "I'm staying," he said, and went back to his airplane.

They crossed the coast of France at 23,000 feet. The temperature had dropped to forty below zero. Then the sub pens at Lorient were coming in sight, and Bentinck forgot his ulcers and his pain and the baby that wasn't born yet. He glued his eye to the Norden bombsight. Walker called him on the intercom. "It's all yours," the pilot said calmly. "Here we go."

The bombing run would endure for precisely one hundred and eighty seconds during which there could be no evasive action to elude flak or fighters, no matter how intense. Three minutes of flying on the thin edge of the guillotine. Everyone sucked in air, braced themselves. It's not a good feeling to be helpless, to know that the gunners far below are aware of precisely what you're doing, that they can track and lead your big airplane. For the first sixty seconds it was amazing. Nothing happened.

Then it began. *"Flak!"* The belly gunner called it out at the first appearance of the angry black puffs. The bursts came in closer as the gunners five miles below closed the range. *Karrumph!* Each shell went off with a heavy, thudding explosion. Shock waves lashed out at *Boom Town.* Walker wrestled with the controls; some of the hammer blows were too much for the autopilot to take. Now the smoke puffs appeared magically off the wings, sliding by in the air, unreal, floating black cotton.

Oscar Green in the belly, curled up, cramped, spinning around, commanded the attention of the crew. His voice had been high, excited when he called out the flak. With the appearance of new danger he was calm.

"Wolves coming up," he said. "A dozen. Climbing fast."

Twelve Focke-Wulfs.

Krucher in the tail complained that flak was chewing hell out of *Boom Town*'s rear.

Walker kept the B-17 flying straight and level, an old man of twenty-three years. Bentinck, who might cripple a factory, kill a few hundred people, destroy a great submarine, was only twenty-one. He had been a soda jerk, a merchant seaman. Now he was lord and master of this bomber, the keeper of six thousand pounds of steel and high explosives in the bays. He glued his eye to the sight, his hand on the release. The target centered on the crosshairs, and Bentinck's finger twitched. One rack deep in the belly snapped free its catch and six heavy bombs fell away. The bomber lurched upward. The fingers twitched again and another six heavy bombs spilled out into space.

No sooner did Bentinck cry "Bombs away!" than Walker yanked the yoke over hard, tramped on rudder. The flak was bad and it was getting worse with every second. Walker wanted away from that lethal straight run and he wanted it fast. He knew the gunners were zeroing in on him.

Below in the nose Bentinck, staring earthward, gave a joyous shout over the intercom. "Bull's-eye!" He repeated the call, still shouting, and then started to say something else. He didn't make it. The words began in his throat, but a torrent of blood bubbled up inside him, drowned out the message, gagged him. He died in midsentence. A shell had gone off directly beneath *Boom Town*. Steel ripped upward, tore through metal, slashed through Bentinck's body and killed him instantly.

The same burst sent a jagged hunk of hot metal into the navigator's arm. The blow was tremendous. It hurled Smith like a rag doll against the side of the airplane. He hung there a moment with his eyes sill open, pink-glazed, and then slumped down in a heap, unconscious. The Germans had them. Shell bursts went off with a terrifying cannonade, before, above, beneath, all around them. Another burst went off immediately beneath the belly, hurling the Fortress wildly over on her side, standing the big airplane on its wing. The blast and exploding steel tore the heavy bomb doors to shreds. A howling gale thundered through the ship to add to the din.

The flak was bad, the fighters were worse. The Focke-Wulfs were ahead and above the formation and they were wheeling around in beautifully held formation, coming back swiftly, almost invisible in the glare of the sun. All twelve FW-190s opened fire on the call of their leader. Forty-eight cannon and twenty-four machine guns poured blazing lead at the bombers.

*Boom Town* took a beating from the onset of the fighter sweep. The Fortress shuddered and vibrated helplessly before the fierce onslaught. Cannon shells exploded against the wings and fuselage; others crashed within the airplane to explode with ear-blasting roars. Streams of bullets, buzzing like angry hornets, ripped through the fuselage, punching holes everywhere, ricocheting off equipment.

A sudden cry of pain burst through the intercom. Then, calmly, the tail gunner said, "I'm hit. Bad." He was. Blood poured from his wounds. A moment later Green called in from the belly turret. They could hear him fighting to keep his voice calm. It was bad down there.

A Focke-Wulf had come up from below in a screaming climb, raked *Boom Town* the length of her belly. Cannon shells walked along the rounded metal skin, with each orange flash tearing chunks out of the bomber. Then the shells walked into the ball turret. Green was dazed and shocked. One shell carved a gaping hole in the turret and tore up the inside. Hydraulic fluid was burning, de-icing fluid sprayed Green with needle fingers. Smoke blinded him. A 300-mile-an-hour wind at minus forty degrees slashed in through the shattered glass.

Walker couldn't discuss the situation. Lt. John Frisholz, the radio operator, had come on the intercom immediately after the tail and belly gunners reported their troubles. Frisholz was amazingly calm. "Skipper, the radio room's on fire," he said. That was only part of it. "I'm hit. I've got a hole in the back of my head from a piece of flak." He didn't add that blood was pouring from the wound.

Walker and Reed in the cockpit had *their* hands full. The first hammer blows of flak had sent a chunk of flak through the number one engine, smashing the drive shaft. The engine shook madly, threatening to tear off the wing. Hastily Reed chopped power and feathered the prop. Moments later flak banged into number two engine, releasing a spray of oil. At any moment it might catch fire. They feathered that engine, leaving them without power on the left wing.

The Germans dealt them trouble in spades. Number three engine suddenly vibrated, building up as the tremors shook the airplane. Flak chopped a propeller blade. As they watched with eyes wide, the distorted propeller blade began slamming against the engine cowling. Pieces of metal turned red hot and began to fly away in the slipstream.

And then a big hole appeared in the base of the number four engine. The pilots stared at the one good engine left to them. The hole wasn't going to cause them any difficulty, they realized. They crossed their fingers and went to maximum power on the one good engine left to them. Number four was keeping them in the air; the moment it coughed they'd be on the way down.

For a few minutes they seemed to hold altitude. That was all. With one good engine and the bomb bay doors setting up a tremendous drag the Fortress simply couldn't hack it. Abruptly the bomber seemed to lurch, then stagger in the air. The other Fortresses pulled on ahead to disappear in the distance.

They'd bought it and they knew it. A cripple. Just what the fighters loved best of all. The Focke-Wulfs came in eagerly to finish off what they'd started. Walker thought about giving the order to bail out. He knew he couldn't do it. Not with men so badly wounded they would never survive a jump. Walker pushed forward on the yoke and let the Fortress take her head in a steep dive. It was their only chance. Far below waited clouds that promised concealment from the fighters.

The Focke-Wulfs got to them before they made it. Bill Stroud in the waist finally managed to cut some meat out for their side. A fighter came rolling in, so close that Stroud, a kid just out of high school, could see the back of his head and the earphones clamped over the German's helmet. It was a hell of a sight. It became even better when Stroud, yelling like a maniac, poured a long burst into the cockpit. Stroud saw red appear behind the shattered glass just before the Focke-Wulf tumbled wildly out of control. He snapped out a few more bursts for good measure.

A second fighter came boring in on a long curving pass. It was perfect. Stroud just swung the big fifty a few inches, felt it roar and buck in his hands, and hammered out a series of short, steady bursts that were right on target. Pieces of metal flashed away in the air and as Stroud watched the fighter became a disintegrating mass of junk. Scratch two. . . .

Lou Berring, back-to-back with Stroud in the waist, cursed steadily, in a monotone, without let-up. Until his voice rose to an exultant yell as a crimson-nosed Focke-Wulf aileron rolled directly into his tracers. The fighter tumbled away, Berring screaming he'd killed the son of a bitch.

Through all this, Krucher lay in the tail, sprawled awkwardly, bleeding away his life. Pain washed through him. Several times he blacked out. Krucher was known as the best gunner in his outfit, but a couple of slugs in his body had slowed him down badly. He lifted himself on an elbow, stared through the small tail gunner's window. His eyes widened. A German pilot had noticed the damaged tail position, noticed that the guns remained silent. The Focke-Wulf came in from dead astern, taking his time. He was setting up his pigeon for point-blank firing.

Gritting his teeth against the pain, Krucher dragged himself back to his guns. He grasped the handles and took slow, careful aim. Through the sights he watched the FW-190 boring in, rocking in the bomber's slipstream. Then the wings and nose sparkled and Krucher knew the German was firing. Krucher squeezed the triggers, keeping the guns hammering in a long burst. He didn't dare release the pressure; he was afraid he might not have the strength left to squeeze the grips again.

The tracers poured into the wing root of the Focke-Wulf. The left wing snapped away, tearing open a fuel tank. Krucher was still firing when a great sheet of flame leaped into being. What was left of the fighter cartwheeled away.

The clouds were closer. Walker yelled through the intercom for his men to hang on, to keep firing.

Behind the cockpit Phil Judkins in the power turret followed a fighter closing in along a wide curve. The tracers pounded into the fuel tanks of the red-nosed fighter and then there was only a huge dazzling ball of flame in the air.

Green was still in his belly turret, still in a mess. He couldn't see. Pawing at his eyes didn't help; he was blinded. As fast as the wind whipped away the smoke and the de-icing fluid the ruptured lines poured it right back into his face. He was drenched through his flight clothing and shaking from the bitter cold. The cannon shell exploding in the ball turret had knocked out one gun. Green couldn't see, but he could think. He stayed there in the turret, in pain, blind, freezing, and he kept snapping out bursts wildly as he turned the ball around and around, firing in every direction. It was bluff but it worked.

The sky vanished. "We made it!" someone shouted in desperate relief. They plunged through the clouds. The gunners fell back from their weapons in exhaustion.

In the radio compartment Frisholz was in a bad way and worsening. Blood poured in a steady stream from the deep head wound, soaking into his flight suit. But the radio operator ignored the hole, ignored the bleeding. With single-minded purpose he grabbed an extinguisher and put out the fire that had raged in his compartment all through the murderous fighter attacks. Only then did he permit the others to attend to his wounds.

In the nose, Smith regained consciousness amidst an ocean of roaring pain. He felt as if his arm had been sliced down its length with a blazing poker. The copilot climbed down from the cockpit to check on Smith. That done, he placed a blanket over Bentinck's body.

Stroud crawled back through the fuselage to drag Krucher away from his guns. The tail gunner gasped with pain, his face white. He could barely move his arm to gesture to Stroud. The waist gunner stared with mingled sympathy and awe at Krucher. How the man had ever dragged himself to his guns and then aimed and fired those roaring fifties was something beyond the ken of Stroud. Others came to help him with Krucher. They cut away the tail gunner's clothes. One man uttered a low exclamation.

Three bullets had lodged deep in Krucher's back. Two pieces of steel from an AA shell ripped and tore the flesh. Krucher hadn't been joking when he told Clyde Walker that flak was chewing up the rear end of *Boom Town.*

The pilot couldn't keep the battered Fortress in the clouds. Numbers three and four, the only two engines he had working, were rapidly coming unglued. The battered propeller was still grinding at its engine cowling, sending back showers of sparks. Struggling against a stiff headwind that made England seem ever more distant the crippled bomber kept losing altitude.

Light flooded the airplane as they dropped away from their misty concealment. Walker turned to Reed. "Where the hell are we?" he barked. Reed didn't know, either. The navigator had been unconscious for a long time. No one had paid attention to anything except beating off the German fighters and staying alive. Walker groaned with frustration. On top of everything else they were lost.

The altimeter read only eight hundred feet. Still they dropped lower. No one really believed any more they would make it back home. And that meant a crash-landing. Walker couldn't get out of his airplane with men unable to jump. They were committed.

They were six hundred feet up when Reed shouted and pointed straight ahead. Water! The Channel! Still their altitude fell. Clyde Walker recognized Brest ahead of them. "*Jesus Christ . . .*" Brest was a murderous bastion of flak, one of the most heavily defended cities along the French coast. But there was no way to avoid what lay ahead. Walker didn't dare bank or turn the staggering Fortress. Any degree of bank would suck out altitude from beneath them.

They couldn't believe their amazing fortune. They flew right through Flak Row without a single shot being fired at them. And there were *thousands* of German guns down there.

It didn't seem to matter. They had survived flak and fighters both, they had made the Channel, but they were on the deck in a crippled, wheezing airplane and they had another one hundred impossible miles to go. Two engines were dead, they were flying into the teeth of a stiff headwind, *Boom Town* was riddled everywhere with gashes and holes that added to air drag. The wide-open, mangled bomb bay acted as a tremendous anchor on the ship. And one engine—number three—threatened to tear the prop clear off the shaft.

Brest fell behind, out of sight. Walker cursed and fought the lumbering machine. They were down to barely thirty feet above the waves. It looked like the end. If they ditched in the Channel, if they survived the ditching, *if* they made it into the rafts, the wind would blow them right back into the hands of the Germans.

Walker shouted on the intercom. "Lighten the ship!" he ordered. "Jettison everything that isn't nailed down." The waist guns went out first. Ammunition belts. All loose equipment. Everything but their parachutes.

*Boom Town* lost a few more feet.

Walker hit the ditching alarm. At the sound of the bell the crew piled into the radio compartment, dragging the wounded with them. They placed blankets and cushions against the bulkhead. The men braced themselves for the vicious shocks they knew would be coming. More than one ditching bomber had split wide open on impact with the water. The Fortress was almost in the Channel. The two spinning props hurled back spray. Lower. A sudden vibration. She was touching, feeling at the water gingerly, as if she didn't want to go down.

Then—something on the order of a full-blown miracle.

Aerodynamically it might have been impossible. But it happened anyway. Nose just so high, Walker brought his plane down, trying to set her gently into the water. At better than 120 miles per hour the ball turret smacked the waves. The Fortress shuddered from nose to tail. *Now!* Walker hauled back on the yoke.

*The B-17 bounced back into the air!*

In the cockpit Walker and Reed stared at one another, incredulous. It couldn't be! But they were at least 125 feet above the water. . . .

They stretched out every precious foot of their unexpected altitude. Every mile further across the Channel meant that much greater chance for rescue.

Then she was almost in the water again. Miracles don't happen twice. . . . Walker played the controls like a virtuoso, lifted up the nose; there, ever so slightly. Again the hammering vibration as the ball turret scraped along the water. Back came the yoke—and again the Fortress bounced another hundred feet above the waves.

With the two good engines at maximum power they were burning out their fuel swiftly. That meant the ship was lighter now. They stayed up a great deal longer after that second bounce. *Boom Town* flew just a shade easier. They held on, flying, squeezing her along. Reed pointed, his face showing fear of being wrong. Maybe it was just clouds. They stared ahead, straining their eyes. No question now. That was England in the distance. But the Fortress was sinking lower. They wouldn't make it.

Reed didn't need to voice the question. Could they do it once more? Walker said a little prayer. Arms aching from the strain, he eased up the nose, held it, allowed the Fortress to settle until he felt the impact through the vibration. Back on the yoke; quick! Three times now, and *Boom Town* wallowed another hundred feet back into the air.

Now there was hope. They were still burning off fuel, they were lighter. Walker and Reed hammered at the throttles, trying to pull more power from them. At the last possible second Walker came back on the yoke, flying with exquisite precision. The bomber lifted sluggishly. But she lifted, speed dropping. She lifted just enough to mush scant feet above the cliffs. English soil flashed beneath them.

Several minutes later Reed pointed out a British field straight ahead.

Ground crews at the British emergency field heard the clattering sound. They stared in wonder as a flying wreck came over just above the treetops. The men on the ground could see great holes torn in the wings, fuselage and tail. Two engines were dead, the propellers stopped. Sparks trailed a third engine. A big sheet of the rudder was naked, its metal ribs showing where the skin had been shot away. A huge hole showed in the belly. The ball turret was mangled wreckage. Where there had been a smooth plexiglas nose there was now shattered plastic and torn metal. As they watched the fourth engine began to trail a finger of dirty grey smoke.

Breathlessly they watched the cripple lurch its way out of the air. The landing gear slid down, stiff and straight. The pilot of that machine was good. The big bomber bounced lightly, the tires kicking up dust. Halfway down the runway there was the sharp squeal of brakes.

Fire!

An engine exploded in flames. Before the Fortress came to a stop, two men leaped from a hatch, ran forward under the wing and turned fire extinguishers on the blaze. It sputtered, threw out choking clouds of smoke, and died.

The mission was over.

The Fortress was so battered it would never fly again.

Not many people have heard of a Fortress known as

*Boom Town.* An ordinary bomber on an unspectacular raid. An airplane shot to ribbons that came home on guts, skill and a chance that was no better than one in a million. But it came home. With three badly wounded crew members and a dead bombardier, just a kid himself, who would never see his unborn child.

It hardly made the papers.

It was just another mission.

# CHAPTER 21

# THE LONG, DARK WINTER

THE LETTER CAME IN TO the Boeing Company. No one in the front office had ever heard of Lt. Clark M. Garber, Jr. Garber was one of many thousands of pilots trained to fly the B-17; he was also among the men who spearheaded the aerial bombardment of German-occupied Europe. The letter was unsolicited. Garber just wanted to tell Boeing they had built one hell of a fine machine. Garber wrote:

> We had left our base that day with a maximum load of bombs, gasoline, and ammunition, bound for the continent. A big cloud loomed ahead of us and we flew into it, and all the rest of the world vanished. Our squadron was flying instrument formation from then on.... After about fifteen minutes of this, a shadow suddenly loomed big ahead of us. It was another B-17, the leader of our formation, and he was turning into us from ahead and to the side. It was just

one of those things that is apt to happen when the soup is thick as it was that day.

At the speed we were traveling, we were due for a smashup. I yanked the nose of our ship up and to the right, trying to climb and turn at the same time. We were loaded too heavily for that, and we went into a stall. We hung there for an instant, our nose pointing into the sky with the ship's tremendous load pulling at it. Then the Fortress went over on one wing—and fell onto its back. From there it screamed into a vertical dive.

What we had done was a maneuver not unusual for small planes, but one that four-engined bombers were never designed to stand. Something else a heavy bomber was never built to do is vertical dive. And now we were doing that.

It was a pretty sickening sensation, heading down there. All this time I didn't know where we were or where the ground was, because we were in the clouds. Our indicated air speed was better than 350 miles per hour, which means at that altitude we were actually traveling somewhere between 400 and 450 mph. I could hear those heavy bombs rattling around in the bomb compartment like ten pins.

According to the slide rules, there was no chance of our pulling out of the dive. The strain would tear the wings off a loaded ship the size of ours. But there wasn't any choice— we were goners if we didn't try it. So I held my breath and started to pull out.

There were tearing noises. The bombs had ripped loose and they were crashing out through the bottom of the ship. Then—the bomber came up level—and the wings were still with us.

During the ship's tumbling, both the bombardier and navigator had their heads driven through the glass windows. Two of the gunners were thrown half out of the ship, where somehow they managed to hang on by their fingers. Other crew members pulled the gunners back inside.

We brought the ship down to a safe landing, then, and we were a pretty happy bunch of boys. . . . Our ship is back in shape and in service again now, just as good as ever. Meanwhile, we've changed her name . . . to the very appropriate one of *Borrowed Time.* . . . She's a great ship. . . .

*January 3rd, 1943.* En route to the target, the Flying Fortress took a concentrated attack by German fighters. During one pass, a 20-mm cannon shell tore through the fuselage to reach the cockpit before it exploded. The terrific blast at close range killed the pilot instantly, severely wounded and rendered unconscious the copilot. With no one fighting the controls, with the dead pilot slumped forward, the B-17 pushed over into a power dive and plunged away from the formation.

In the brief time it took for the heavy bomber to plummet two thousand feet, the stunned copilot regained consciousness. In an instant he took in the situation. Despite his serious wounds he dragged the body of his dead pilot off the controls, grasped the yoke and hauled back with all this strength. The loaded bomber came out of the dive and started a long zoom, still at high speed. Quickly the copilot made his decision and went to full power on all four engines to continue the climb with all the speed he could sustain. The Fortress astounded the crewmen of the other bombers by climbing back to their altitude and slipping into its former position in formation.

The officer commanding the mission, who watched the incredible episode from start to finish, said the incident "was the most remarkable feat of piloting I have ever seen."

*January 3rd, 1943.* Down on the deck, struggling like a crippled gull over the Bay of Biscay, another Fortress participated in a wild dogfight with at least four FW-190s. Turning always into the attack to give the FWs less time to aim and fire, maintaining violent evasive action with one engine dead and another damaged, the Fortress shot down at least two of its attackers. The pilot, a bullet through his legs, brought his riddled ship back to base.[51]

*January 3rd, 1943.* His name was Sergeant Arizona Harris and he was the top turret gunner in a B-17. January 3rd was the day the AAF awarded Harris the Distinguished Service Cross, the nation's second highest medal for valor in combat. But Harris wasn't there for the ceremony. An officer in his squadron, who saw what happened, told the others about it:

> His name was really Arizona—they christened him that way—and he came from Tempe, which is a little desert town not far from Phoenix. He had a big leonine head and tawny hair and steady eyes and thick strong wrists, and he was one of the best top turret gunners you ever did see. He usually fired in short, quick bursts, to keep his guns from overheating, and he didn't miss—not often. He already had two FW-190s to his credit, and he had an Air Medal, too, that he was going to show to his father and his two brothers and his married sister when he got home.
>
> He went out that day with Charlie Cramner, one of the most popular pilots in the whole group, and I think Arizona was proud to ride with him because he knew that if anybody could bring the ship back, Charlie would. Even when

two engines were knocked out and the whole bottom was blown clean out of the nose, so that the bombardier and navigator simply disappeared and nobody knew what became of them—even then it looked as if Charlie would bring her back, because when the formation finally pulled away from the enemy fighters, there was his ship staggering along with us.

Not quite with us, though. The formation came down to zero feet for protection against possible attacks from below. But Crammer didn't dare lose altitude he couldn't regain, so he kept his ship as high as he could—fifteen hundred feet, maybe—and the rest of us thought he was safe up there. As safe as you can be in a riddled ship with two engines out and most of the nose shot away. So we didn't join him.

But all of a sudden, about forty miles northwest of Brest, six Focke-Wulf FW-190s and a Messerschmitt Me-109 came hurtling out of nowhere. They spotted the limping Fortress, and one after another they made a pass at it from behind.

The other bombers were too far away to help. We saw two parachutes from the Fort flare open after the second attack—although there was barely time for the chutes to open before they hit the water.

We saw the Germans circle the drifting chutes, and whether or not they machine-gunned the fliers is something that can't be proved, so why think too much about it? But when the Fortress settled into the sea—and Charlie Cramner, who had stayed with his ship as a captain should, set her down as gracefully and gently as if he had four engines and a six-thousand-foot concrete runway under him—then the Germans did strafe her, and you could see the steel-gray sea boiling under the rain of bullets.

But there was something else you could see, and that was the guns in the upper turret still blazing, even as she settled. She settled fast; she lasted only about half a minute. But the top turret was still spitting as the waves closed over it. And that was the end of Arizona T. Harris, American fighting man.

To the VIII Bomber Command, suffering drastically the depletion of skilled crews and bombers for operations in Africa, bedeviled even more by heavy fog that kept its planes grounded, it became clear that not until the summer of 1943 would a full-scale bomber offensive begin. During the months of waiting every attempt would be made to utilize the limited forces available to test the fundamental theses of strategic bombing. But the "experimental phase" was already too prolonged, while the lessons needed to launch massive raids remained maddeningly obscure. Many involved in planning felt that the program to smash German industry and communications from the air would fail. Although the War Department had granted highest priority to the heavy bombing campaign against Germany, the necessary depletions for TORCH and the recent rescheduling of fifteen groups of Fortresses for the Pacific had weakened the VIII Bomber Command far more than the public was aware.

Meanwhile, as the AAF official history notes: the questions that so urgently needed solution remained unanswered.

The problems could be more simply stated than answered. Could Anglo-American bomber forces strike German production forces often enough and effectively enough to make eventual invasion appreciably less costly? Could the forces required be provided without unduly hampering air activities elsewhere and the operation of the other arms in any theater? Could the bomber campaign be conducted effectively within acceptable ratios of losses?

For those questions the RAF had answers which, if not conclusive, were founded upon experience. The bombing of industrial cities had in recent attacks wrought great destruction; they had secured a favorable position for the heavy bomber in the allocation of production potential; and in their night area bombing they had learned to operate without prohibitive losses.

The Eighth Air Force ... had no answers. ... But the problem was crucial; upon its successful solution hung the fate of the Eighth's participation in the combined offensive and of the Eighth's claim to a heavy share of the forces later available. ... Eighth Air Force officers continued to experiment, weighing as carefully as they might the evidence provided by combat missions and trying desperately to overcome difficulties which stemmed in no inconsiderable part from the attenuated size of their force.[52]

Many of the early missions had gone off well, with losses almost always less than ten percent of the attacking force. But it was becoming more evident that the Germans had not thrown the full fury of their fighters against the Fortresses; only one fourth of all German fighters planes were, in fact, deployed within reach of the bomber raids. That situation could change drastically, and it could change swiftly. It worried the planners of bomber operations. The long delays were permitting the Germans to assess the strength of the Americans and to develop methods for countering the bombers. The mission of the 20th December 1942, against Romilly-sur-Seine provided much sober thought. Over one hundred Fortresses went after the target sixty-five miles southeast of Paris; seventy-two struck the target with 125 tons of bombs. The bombing results were good to excellent, but of "considerably greater historical significance ... was the fact that, in the course of this deepest penetration yet made by USAAF planes into German-occupied territory, the bombers made contact with almost the entire force of enemy fighters located in northeast France. The ensuing air battle developed epic proportions and provided an important test of the American heavy bombers' ability to carry out unescorted missions deep into enemy territory."[53]

Six Fortresses went down, two were so badly damaged they crash-landed on return to England, and another twenty-nine sustained damage of varying degrees. It was a portent of what was yet to come. And what was to come became evident in the sudden changes of tactics by German fighter pilots in the abruptly increased effectiveness of flak, in Intelligence reports of vast changes and reinforcements that strengthened the entire German system of daylight bomber defense. At first the Germans had not taken the American campaign of daylight bombing as a serious threat. Now they were doing so, the German back was stiffening swiftly.

Then the hopes of daylight strategic bombing were dealt an unexpected blow that nearly wrecked the entire program. Harold Mansfield provides us with a behind-the-scenes look at what went on:

Ira Eaker's 8th Bomber Command, by winter of 1942, was a hardened, scrappy core of combat crews. In the fall the two groups of B-17Es had been joined by a third equipped with Consolidated B-24 Liberators. These three groups and their fighter escort, on twenty-three short-range missions, claimed 104 enemy planes shot down, 108 more probably destroyed and 117 damaged. But they had learned grief, too. They had lost eighteen bombers, thirteen of them shot down by enemy fighters, five by antiaircraft. The losses of equipment and men were not being replaced, because new forces were going to help Major General Jimmy Doolittle in the big North African campaign. In England, in the cold, wet winter with its mud at the airdromes, its fog, its nightly blackout bore and the silent, empty seats at the breakfast table after yesterday's raid weighed heavily.

Ira Eaker was wearying of small hits at nearby targets along the Channel. "If we can get the equipment, we can knock Germany out of the war from the air," he said. "By destroying Hitler's factories we can put an end to his air force. By destroying his munitions plants and communications we can stop his armies." But every week Hitler was building stronger defenses. Now was the time to mount a gigantic air offensive, Eaker felt.

"You haven't tested the defenses over Germany itself," British officers cautioned. "Those targets are impregnable by daylight." The old issue. The crisis came at Casablanca where the Allied High Command was gathered in January 1943. Hap Arnold summoned Eaker there. "I'm sorry to have to tell you this," Arnold said, "but the President has agreed to give Churchill our bombers for night bombing."

It hit Eaker like a Messerschmitt head-on. For a fraction of a second he reeled, then caught fire. It was wrong, dead wrong. The Forts weren't designed for night bombing. They *could* do the job by day. Eaker knew military discipline, but he'd have to fight this decision, even if it cost him his job. "Our planes aren't night bombers," he said. "Our crews aren't trained for night bombing. The losses will be much higher. It's a tragic decision and I won't be a party to it. And I reserve the right to tell the American people at the appropriate time why I quit."

"If you feel that strongly about it," said Arnold, "I'll arrange for you to talk to the Prime Minister."

Eaker had the feeling that Hap Arnold was glad he'd spoken out as he did. He received a message: "The Prime

Minister will be waiting for you at his villa." Eaker had come to know Churchill in England. He went promptly.

"General Arnold tells me it has been decided to turn our bombers over to night bombing," Eaker told the Prime Minister. "I think this is a great mistake. I've been in England long enough to know that you want to hear both sides."

Churchill smiled. "Sit down." Eaker handed the Prime Minister a single sheet of paper on which he had written the case for daylight bombing. Churchill read it. Near the bottom Eaker heard him mumble audibly, "Around the clock." It was the place where he'd said that with the British bombing by night, and the Americans by day, they'd give the Germans no rest, bomb them around the clock. Churchill looked up. "I took this action because I have a strong feeling against your losing your young men," he said. "Your losses are greater than ours. You haven't convinced me, but you have convinced me that you should have an opportunity to prove that you can do this. When I see the President at lunch, I'll recommend that we do this."

In the House of Parliament, Winston Churchill stood up to deliver his report on Casablanca. Eaker had been sent a ticket to the balcony. There was an ovation for the great British leader. He began stating the decisions that had been reached [at the Casablanca Conference between the leaders of the Allies]. Then he announced that the Americans would continue their daylight bombing. "The British will bomb at night and the Americans by day," said the Prime Minister, glancing up at the balcony. "We shall bomb these devils around the clock."[54]

It would be known as CBO—the Combined Bomber Offensive. It would, however, not become an operational reality until the summer of 1943. But already in January

1943, the Eighth Air Force was girding itself for the first daylight bombing attack by Flying Fortresses against the heartland of Germany proper.

The crews got the word quietly, early in the morning, with the sky still dark outside. The briefing officer waited for their attention, for the murmuring to cease, the feet to end their shuffling.

The date was the 27th January 1943. "Gentlemen," the briefing officer said, and with the subtle change in tone in his voice everyone paid the closest attention. "Gentlemen," he repeated, "the target for today is Germany."

A voice in the crowd said quietly, "Goddamn."

Long before the 27th January 1943 it was clear to the leaders of the VIII Bomber Command that the morale of the flight crews had suffered because of inadequate replacements, lack of proper training, "rotten weather," and, by no means least, the fact that after five and a half months of bombing operations not a single American bomber had flown a mission over Germany. The AAF history notes that the "Commanders were impatient and often discouraged at the slow rate of Eighth Air Force operations and at the delay in buildup. Combat crews saw in the statistics of attrition and replacement the likely prospect of a short career. To make matters worse, commanders and crews alike were eager to strike at the German homeland, but hitherto they had been prevented from doing so by tactical and strategic considerations the validity of which they did not always appreciate. In this restlessness they were joined by a considerable segment of British opinion. . . ."

Wilhelmshaven was ripe for the opening blow against the heartland of the Reich. The plans for the attack had been under way since November, but repeated difficulties spared the German port city the attention of the VIII Bomber Command. The strike was laid on for the 27th January. Despite previous British attacks totaling more than a thousand tons which had inflicted serious damage on the town and obliterated a naval munitions depot, production in the U-boat yards was proceeding normally. The U-boat yards and pens were prime targets and what put frosting on the cake was the report that the pocket battleship *Admiral Scheer* was then in drydock on the north side of the Bauhafen. The naval dockyards hummed with round-the-clock production. In every respect Wilhelmshaven was perfect for the initial penetration into the Reich.

It was quite a morni ng for the crew briefings. The Casablanca Conference decisions were being broadcast in the early hours of the day. "Unconditional surrender" of the enemy had become the official hardline policy of the Allies. The British Eighth Army had broken free of German restraints and was starting to pound toward the Tunisian border, while on the Eastern front the Soviet Army, in a huge pincers movement, had annihilated the Wermacht of Stalingrad. At the briefings, notes a history of the VIII Bomber Command, there was a feeling in the air of "let's get on with the war."

The weather that day was far from ideal for high-level bombing. At altitude, the cold was intense. On this trip the crews for the first time tried rubbing the oxygen masks with salt to keep them from freezing. The trick worked. Despite all precautions, however, the knifelike temperatures took a heavy toll of men and machines—freezing gun and turret mechanisms, clogging camera shutters, fogging windshields and bomb sights, and stabbing through the heaviest clothing the combat crews could wear.[55]

A crewman put down some notes of that day:

> At about 1030 [10:30 A.M.] the altimeter indicated 25,000 feet. The cloud cover had ended, far below us, and we could see the surface of the sea—like a sheet of glass. At 1045 the Captain warned the crew to be extra-alert. I looked out to the right and could see the outline of the coast of Germany and the row of islands that lay just off it. It was our first glimpse of Das Vaterland. At 1057 we were just over the islands and at 1100 the tail gunner reported flak at six o'clock, below. It was from the coastal islands and was the first time we were fired upon from German soil. At this time we were beginning to turn and we crossed the island of Baltrum and went into German territory. As we turned, the bombardier elevated the muzzle of his gun and fired a burst so that the tracers arched over Germany. The first shots from our ship, *Hell's Angels*, but not the last!

Ninety-one heavy bombers, Fortresses from the 1st and Liberators from the 2nd Bombardment Wings, departed England for Wilhelmshaven. Of this number, only fifty-three arrived over the target. In fact, the initial attack against a German city came off as something of an anticli-max. The opposition was far less severe than had been ex-pected. Over the Frisian Islands and almost continuously over Germany proper, flak gunners kept up a steady bar-rage at the Fortresses and Liberators, damaging several of the bombers, "but at no time was it intense enough or ac-curate enough to have deterred the attacking force in any way. At Wilhelmshaven, especially, the flak defenses ap-pear to have been thoroughly confused, their effort at a predicted barrage being what a British observer who flew in one of the B-17s called 'pathetic.' "

The ineffective flak defenses came "as a complete surprise" to the bomber force, the crews of which expected the worst. But though the flak failed, the appearance of the heavy bombers brought up more than a hundred German fighters. Before the running battle was over a single Fortress and a Liberator were shot down. Then, the pilot apparently killed, an FW-190 tore directly into another Liberator to take the bomber and its crew down with him. AAF gunners claimed seven German fighters shot down.

It would be stretching a point to consider the Wilhelmshaven attack satisfactory to all concerned, for the number of bombers attacking was far less than the force dispatched, and the bombing results were only fair. Yet the raid was gravely important and, as the AAF notes, "a very interesting one. A relatively small force of heavy bombers, their crews no more experienced than they should have been, had penetrated by daylight, and necessarily without benefit of escort, well into the enemy homeland and had, moreover, done so without appreciable loss."

But if the crews expected the opening blow against the Reich to be the start of a vigorous and massive program, they were foiled in their hopes by one of the worst winters in British history. "The gray core of winter now settled upon the area of operations," notes the VIII Bomber Command. "Rain, sleet, biting winds, and freezing banks of dun cloud spun out from the North Sea to cover both the bases and the targets. The weathermen and Operations Staff at Command spent their days and nights watching the birth and life and death of a succession of storms which ranged from the Arctic to the Equator. In seventeen days but one operation was carried out. Emden was attacked despite icing conditions and temperatures that went below the recording capacities of the thermometers, 45 degrees below zero. Vapor trails formed by the bombers helped guide the enemy fighters in their attack."[56]

The one attack was on the 4th February against Emden where the Fortresses "stirred up a hornet's nest of fighters." The B-17 crews were being given their preview of new German defenses: in addition to the single-engine Me-109 and FW-190 fighters they encountered Me-110 and Junkers Ju-88 twin-engine fighters with heavy machine gun and cannon armament.

VIII Bomber Command tacticians reviewed the results with uncompromising candor.

> The Command's bombing experts, with few results by which to judge the progress of their campaign for accuracy, shook their heads and ordered more practice missions, more runs over the target ranges. On occasion excellent results had been achieved during the earlier missions—on one Lorient attack six of thirty-six bombs dropped from 22,000 feet had hit a block of sub pens measuring 200 by 400 feet. Those exceptions had now to be made the standard of accurary.[57]

Not until the 26th February did the bombers return to their first German target. Sixty-five bombers set out for Bremen but finding the target obscured by clouds turned instead for Wilhelmshaven where they hit with "some effect" the harbor area. But Luftwaffe fighters hit the bombers even harder, harrying the four-engined raiders all the way in to their target and all the way back. Ten days previously the Germans shot down eight bombers in a raid against St. Nazaire. Now, on the 26th February, their prolonged attack coupled with courageous, persistent firing runs took another seven bombers out of the strike force. The toll would have been higher except that the bomber crews had already carried out jury-rigged modifications, installing .50 caliber guns in the nose. Rearranging the bomber formations to increase frontal fire-power also contributed to the suddenly stiffened defense of the Fortresses and Liberator against head-on sweeps by German fighter pilots. The Germans, too, were experimenting. Me-109 fighters flew above the bomber formations to release small bombs intended to explode amidst the tight Fortress ranks; no bombers were hit. New antiaircraft devices also went into action. The crews referred to these as air mines; they were "slightly larger than shoeboxes" and fired into the air above and ahead of the formations. Out of the puff of smoke of the shell burst there appeared the mine, suspended from a small parachute. Used in large number, they were intended to drift into the path of the bombers. But no bombers were damaged by these "intensely interesting, but fortunately ineffective" devices.

The raid becomes intensely personal when viewed through the intelligence debriefing of the crew of the Flying Fortress known as *Southern Comfort*:

We had disposed of six of our bombs when the ship shivered and we knew we had been heavily hit. The bombardier sent away his four remaining bombs on the docks of Wilhelmshaven before turning to see if the navigator had been killed by the explosion of a 20-mm shell in the nose.

The navigator was alive and uninjured, although the shell had exploded only three inches from his head and dented the steel helmet he was wearing. The explosion drove his head down on the navigator's table, which broke under the impact of the helmet. The only ill effect he suffered was that he could not calculate the course of the plane for about twenty minutes. During this time the bombardier handled the navigator's gun as well as his own.

A moment later the right waist gunner phoned: "Sir, Number Three engine has been hit and is throwing quite a bit of oil." The oil had spread over the wing. A tongue of flame appeared. The copilot closed the cowl flaps and pulled the fire extinguishers. The fire went out. The propeller of the crippled engine was now windmilling and chewing away at bits of cowling. Sparks were bouncing off the oil-covered wing.

At this point the pilot noticed that the rudder did not respond. Presently we found that four square feet of it had been shot away. When the tail gunner reported the condition of the tail, or rather the lack of it, he also reported that still another shell had burst just in back of him inside the fuselage.

There was no time to appraise the damage. *Southern Comfort* had lost air speed caused by the drag of the windmilling propeller, and an attempt to rejoin several of the formations proved futile.

It was then that the pilot realized that if we were to return to England we were going to have to do it alone, crippled and out of formation. The loss of the supporting guns of other aircraft in the formation was serious, but more serious was the choice of course. We flew due north, to put as much sea between us and the enemy fighters as possible. Meanwhile the Number Three engine was vibrating and the wild prop kept taking bites out of the cowling.

We were out over the North Sea when the pilot announced over the intercom: "Those who want to, please pray!" Not long after that we sighted land. We weren't sure, but we thought it was England.

As we neared our home base an inquisitive Mosquito spotted us and finally came so close that we could see the pilot shake his head at our battle-scarred condition. He waved his hand and left. Shortly afterward, we picked up our field.

The report of the VIII Bomber Command states that the bomber landed "with a gaping hole where the rudder should have been, a shattered nose section, a wing spotted with ragged shrapnel wounds, and its fuselage riddled from nose to tail with flak and cannon-shell holes. One shell had crashed through the fuselage directly behind the tail gunner's position, leaving a gash the size of a grapefruit.

"One by one, the crew climbed out—*uninjured*."

March 1943 was *the* month for shaking off the doldrums of winter and the frustrations of the preceding months. No one found any miraculous panaceas in the sky, but before April appeared on the calendar it was clear to all concerned that tremendous strides had taken place, that the Fortress and the Liberator crews were being transformed into skilled veterans with the know-how to take on the best the enemy could throw at them—and the German pilots were outstanding.

March was also "a climatic month in the history of high-level precision bombing." Looking back with the advantage of 20-20 hindsight the AAF historians describe an incident "which demonstrated, if demonstration were needed, that small formations could not hope to penetrate the fighter defenses in the Reich without crippling losses."

At Hamm, Germany, are the marshaling yards through which funnels major production output of the Ruhr industries. The yards lie just beyond the Ruhr Valley; more significantly they lie 160 miles "inside the outer ring of Nazi defenses." Compounding such difficulties was the fact that the concentration of railway lines, marshaling yards and workshops, as well as the storage sheds where industrial goods were held prior to shipment, were difficult to find with accuracy on a "one-pass basis." Hitting the small target, in the face of intense antiaircraft and furious fighter attacks, would make Hamm an historical effort. By now the crews were aware that the German pilots considered shooting down a bomber less important than the more immediate goal of breaking up the formations during the approach to the target. If the fighter pilots could keep bombs from hitting the target, they were accomplishing their primary purpose.

Exhaustive planning went into the mission. The main force of seventy-one B-17s took up a course to the northeast, over the North Sea, following the normal route to Bremen or Wilhelmshaven. Halfway between England and the coast of Holland the Fortresses swung to the southeast and struck out for Hamm. During this flight a decoy force of fourteen Liberators tried to lure German fighters away from the Fortresses.

No one knows if the diversion would have worked, for the weather nearly wrecked the mission. Of the four B-17 groups in the air, one encountered such violent weather and thick clouds that all the airplanes returned to their home fields with the bombs still aboard. Two other groups, discouraged by towering walls of clouds, abandoned their initial plans and hammered the "last resort" target of shipyards at Rotterdam. The final group of sixteen Fortresses was another matter.

The bombers flew into clouds too high to escape and continued on instrument flight. When the leader of the formation—a pilot twenty-two years old—came out of the clouds with his small force of bombers he found himself quite alone. Just sixteen planes—the others were nowhere in sight. The young Squadron Commander wrestled with a decision that had to be made immediately and was, quite literally, a matter of life or death. Straight ahead lay Germany. . . .

The soup was getting thinner. We strained our eyes for a glimpse of the other Groups. Not a sign of them. We were approaching the coast now. We could barely see it through the haze. We crossed the coast. The Navigator checked our position.

Where in hell were the other Groups? Should we go on? The weather was getting better now. I asked the tail gunner how many ships we had. "Sixteen, sir." Sixteen Forts—against the best defenses Germany had to offer. Should I risk those 160 boys' lives to bomb Hamm? It was an important target, but the other Groups had apparently gone to attack an alternate. Nothing would be said if I turned back. We went on.

The fighters provided only light opposition on the way into Hamm. Not a Fortress dropped out of formation. More important in the strategic sense, reconnaissance later showed an "excellent concentration among the railway shops and marshaling trackage."

But if the fighters failed on the way into the target, they made up for it in numbers and severity of attack as they hammered the bombers on their way home. During a long and violent air battle, fifty enemy fighters shot down four of the big bombers—a staggering loss ratio of twenty-five percent of the attacking force. Although at least thirteen fighters were confirmed as destroyed, "it was a costly operation," notes a historical study, "but considering the weight and determination of the attack, it is remarkable that more of the B-17s were not lost."

The missions went on, against targets in the occupied countries and within Germany itself. The losses suffered by the Fortresses would have been higher except that "the bomber crews were also increasing in experience. By preserving as good a defensive formation as possible, by turning into the attacks, and by varying altitude as much as was consistent with tight formation flying, they managed often to evade otherwise lethal passes. In addition, the twin nose guns now installed in many of the bombers were credited with breaking up many attacks. . . ."

Six missions were flown during March against targets within occupied Europe; all but one enjoyed fighter escort. On March 12th sixty-three bombers went out. On the thirteenth, another seventy-four bombers made attacks. All planes returned from these missions, showing once again the effectiveness of fighter escort.

Two weeks went by after the Hamm raid before the Fortresses went back into Germany to strike at the submarine construction yards at Vegesack on the 18th March. Seventy-three Fortresses and twenty-four Liberators took on the Luftwaffe in a savage running battle that started long before the target was approached and continued all the way back from the objective, some of the fighters pursuing Fortresses as much as eighty miles out over the water beyond the German coast. The mission paid off handsomely. Vegesack represented the largest force of bombers the VIII Bomber Command had ever placed over a single target. Bombing was excellent to outstanding, with official photographic interpretation showing "extremely heavy damage." Gunner claims went as high as fifty-two German fighters shot down, but Intelligence debriefings lowered this figure drastically, and an official estimate was placed at approximately twenty fighters destroyed, with "many more" damaged.

More cheering to the crews—only two bombers went down out of the entire force dispatched.

But it was the last mission to be flown by Jack Mathis. His torn-up Fortress brought home his mortal remains. The navigator who flew beside him recounts what happened—

We ran into very little trouble on our raid into Vegesack until we started on the bomb run. A very heavy barrage of flak was thrown up at us just as we reached the target. Flak hit our ship and sounded like hail on the roof. I glanced at Lieutenant Mathis, who was crouched over his bomb sight, lining up the target. Jack was an easygoing guy and the flak didn't bother him. He wasn't saying a word—just sticking there over his bomb sight, doing his job.

"Bomb-bay doors are open," I heard Jack call up to the pilot, and then he gave instructions to climb a little more to reach bombing altitude.

On the bomb run, that flak hit us. We were seconds short of the bomb-release point when a whole barrage of flak hit our squadron, which we were leading.

One of the shells burst out to the right and a little below the nose. It couldn't have been over thirty feet away when it burst. If it had been much closer it would have knocked the whole plane over.

A hunk of flak came tearing through the side of the nose. It shattered glass on the right side and broke through with a loud crash.

I saw Jack falling back toward me and threw up my arm to ward off the fall. By that time both of us were way back in the rear of the nose—blown back there, I guess, by the flak blast.

I was sort of half standing, half lying against the back wall and Jack was leaning up against me. I didn't know he was injured at the time.

Without any assistance from me he pulled himself back to his bomb sight. His little seat had been knocked out from under him by the flak, and he sort of knelt over the bomb sight. He knew that as bombardier of the lead ship the results of the whole squadron might depend on his accuracy. And he didn't let anything stop him. Part of my job as navigator is to keep the log of the flight, so I looked at my watch to start timing the fall of the bombs.

I heard Jack call out on the intercom, "Bombs—" He usually called it out in a sort of singsong. But he never finished the phrase this time. The words just sort of trickled off, and I thought his throat mike had slipped out of place, so I finished the phrase, "Bombs away!" for him. We don't start our evasive action to avoid the flak until those words go up to the pilot—and we all love that evasive action.

I looked up and saw Jack reaching over to grab the bomb-bay door handle to close the doors. Just as he pushed the handle he slumped over backwards. I caught him. That was the first indication that anything was wrong. I saw then that his arm was pretty badly shot.

"I guess they got you that time, old boy," I remembered saying, but then his head slumped over and I saw that the injuries were more serious than just some flak in the arm. I knew then that he was dead. I closed the bomb bay and returned to my post.

The AAF awarded Jack Mathis the Medal of Honor. Mark Mathis, who flew in medium bombers, wanted only to kill Germans. He wanted to do it in the same manner as his dead brother. The AAF ceded to Mark's request for transfer, and Mark Mathis soon flew in *The Duchess*, the Fortress which bore Jack Mathis' body home from Vegesack.

The crews said that Mark was going to finish his brother's tour of duty, would fly Jack's twenty-five missions. Jack Mathis had been killed on his fourteenth mission.

Over Kiel, on his fourth mission in *The Duchess*, Mark Mathis went down in a torn and shattered Fortress.

It was soon after the Vegesack mission of the 18th

March, where a group succeeded in outstanding accuracy by "placing an estimated seventy-six percent of its bombs within a radius of one thousand feet of the aiming point," that the Commanding General of the Eighth Air Force felt that the turning point had been reached. "The men and the machines," he said, "have proven themselves." The attack of the 18th March, he went on, was "a successful conclusion to long months of experimentation in daytime, high-level precision bombing. After Vegesack comes a new chapter."

You might have heard the comment through the dark and winter-blanketed fields all across England.

It was soft as a sigh, and it sounded like *Amen*.

# CHAPTER 22

# THE BIG LEAGUE

ONE THING WAS CERTAIN. The Eighth was learning how to fight. The crews of the Fortresses had become hardened veterans. They were learning how to defend themselves, and while they were brushing up on the fine points of survival they were improving their ability to hurt the enemy where he lived. The ultimate goal, of course, was to keep bomber losses to a minimum while inflicting the greatest possible damage on the German.

Those who evaluated what had happened knew that the Fortresses had yet to encounter the brunt of German defensive fury. And the Germans also were learning. From the initial penetrations into the Reich it had become clear that while flak damaged many of the bombers, the enemy fighters were cutting the big airplanes out of the sky with their courageous and skillful attacks. The men who had flown both bombers and fighters in the Eighth Air Force were aware, from their own experience, that the Luftwaffe still had not brought in the bulk of its strength. But they knew what the Germans could do in defense of their homeland.

The need was for long-range fighters that could escort the bombers all the way in to the target, remain there long enough to slug it out with the Germans, and escort the Fortresses all the way home. This was a tremendous requirement that many engineers felt could never be achieved. In fact, the Germans themselves believed the Americans could never develop fighters with sufficient range to escort the bombers on their deep penetrations of the homeland. Fuel capacity alone wasn't enough. A fighter had to carry an enormous load in fuel, guns and ammunition, and still retain the speed and maneuverability to match the Focke-Wulfs and Messerschmitts, fighters which up to this point had been proven to be among the world's best.

In view of these problems, the development of long-range escort fighters by the United States must rank as one of the greatest technological achievements of World War II. But that lay months in the future, and for the present the Fortress crews knew they must run the gauntlet without the protecting guns of American fighters. Once again Operation TORCH had played its decisive role. The P-38 fighters that would have escorted the bombers were almost all in North Africa. Many hundreds of the twin-engined Lightnings, destined originally for Europe, were engaged in Africa and the Mediterranean, where they were performing magnificently. There were other fighters in England—the heavy, rugged P-47 Thunderbolts—but these could not be sent on long-range escort missions. Radio equipment in these fighters, which would one day prove to be the scourge of the Luftwaffe, was so badly put together that most fighters were unable to communicate either with one

another or with ground command. It would take months to
solve that problem. Neither were there long-range drop
tanks for the Thunderbolts, and until these could be produced, and the airplanes modified to receive them, the
Thunderbolts could not carry the fight to the homeland of
the enemy.

In fulfilling its mission of striking at the heart of German industry, the Eighth Air Force not only "had to grap-
ple with the problem of penetrating enemy defenses as a
matter of most immediate urgency," but also strike the enemy with "the utmost accuracy."

"For reasons of defense," states an Air Force study, "it
had become standard operating procedure for the bombing
force to bomb in some sort of formation, and by February
[1943] a considerable weight of opinion favored bombing
by combat box or group, each aircraft dropping its bombs
on a signal from the lead bombardier." Despite experiments
with other systems, the Eighth adopted "dropping on the
leader" as the most effective method of obtaining maximum effect for the bomb tonnage dropped. Experiments
were carried out to improve the bomb pattern through
modified formations or by having an "immediate drop on
signal" by bombardiers watching the lead plane. For small
targets or special missions the technique varied; but for the
average mission of large bomber forces against major targets "bombing on the leader became the normal technique. . . ." It was at this time that the Eighth "began
successfully to employ the automatic flight-control equipment (AFCE) as an aid to accurate bombing. The purpose of
this automatic pilot, which could be controlled by the
bombardier on the bomb run, was to synchronize sighting
and pilotage with mechanical precision and thus provide a
steadier bombing run than could be achieved even by veteran pilots. The few seconds immediately before the bom-

bardier released his bombs obviously constituted the critical moment in the entire mission, for it was then that the bombardier performed his final sighting operation. So it was essential that the aircraft should be held as nearly as possible to a steady course without slips, skids, or changes in altitude, and that the pilotage be as free as possible from the influence of flak and of attacking fighters. Perfection of this sort was impossible even with the best of pilots. With those produced by the hasty training program into which the AAF had been forced it could not even be approximated."[58]

With increasing reliability of the AFCE, and the accumulation of experience by the crews, bombing accuracy continued to improve. The AAF history notes that "whereas in January and February a group could consider its bombing above average if 20 percent of the bombs identifiable by photo reconnaissance fell within 1,000 feet of the pre-assigned aiming point, in March and April it was not uncommon for groups to record 30 to 40 percent in that category, and several instances were reported above the 50 percent mark. Some of the better results were obtained under trying conditions, even in the face of stiff enemy resistance, as for instance at Bremen on 17 April when, in spite of very heavy flak over the target, fierce enemy fighter attacks, hazy weather, and clever camouflage, very satisfactory bombing was accomplished—one group placed 60 percent of its bombs within the 1,000-foot radius. Overall results of outstanding accuracy were obtained at Rennes and Vegesack in March, at Paris in April, and at Meaulte in May. . . ."[59]

*17th April 1943.* One hundred and fifteen Fortresses left England of which 107 bombers struck their primary target, the Focke-Wulf plant in Bremen. They bombed "exceedingly well," tearing up large sections of the huge aircraft factory. But in this largest mission of the Eighth Air Force to date the Germans struck with unprecedented fury.

The enemy had everything going for him. The weather was excellent—which placed the Germans on alert and enabled them to track incoming formations easily and assemble their own fighters without difficulty. The body blow, however, was delivered by an enemy patrol bomber which, while over the North Sea, sighted the B-17 force en route to its target. Staying well out of defensive range the German crew "radioed the location, direction of flight, speed, and altitude of the bombers" and allowed the "enemy to organize and concentrate his forces. This he did with skill and dispatch."

The first fighter attacks came near the Frisian Islands. A small number of fighters harried the formation all the way in to Bremen where, before they could set up their bombing runs, the Fortress crews encountered a mass of perhaps 150 enemy fighter planes ready and waiting for them. "It seems to have been their main purpose," noted an Intelligence evaluation of the mission, "to vitiate the effectiveness of the bombing by knocking down the leading planes and breaking up the bomber formations, because all attacks were withheld until that moment."

The Germans came in with a battering assault the crews described as "the most vicious and concentrated fighter attacks yet encountered." Just as the leading bombers crashed into the flak barrage immediately over the target a wave of more than fifty fighters swarmed against the formations. They flew a variety of coordinated attacks, barely missing Fortresses and ignoring their own flak. One after the other the B-17s took a merciless beating. One bomber fell away from the tight formations. Others began to straggle as the severity of the German firepower crippled the planes. With full bomb loads and open bomb doors a lost engine meant falling out of formation. Men were wounded in large number as the fighters closed to point-blank range. But despite the tremendous onslaught, the B-17 crews proved their mettle. The cold evaluation of the strike against Bremen notes—not without an indication of pride—that "despite the severity of both fighter and flak attack, however, the first groups managed to maintain formation and to bomb with remarkable accuracy."

The fighters kept up the pressure all the way back from the target, maintaining the same fury with which they had met the opening of the bomb run. It was a cruel day for the men who manned the Fortresses. In all sixteen Fortresses were shot down and another forty-six were damaged.

Not until the 1st May did the Fortresses go out again, with seventy-eight bombers assigned to attack the submarine pens at St. Nazaire. Seven Fortresses went down on that mission. One B-17—Number 649—came home with its interior burned out by a flaming holocaust. Awed crews who came to look at the blackened hulk could hardly believe what they saw. Equally awesome was the performance of Staff Sergeant Maynard H. Smith, ball-turret gunner for No. 649. Smith didn't *look* like a hero. He was described by his friends as "short and scrawny." He didn't have much of a combat record. In fact, he didn't have *any* combat record—St. Nazaire on the 1st May was his first combat mission.

But for what he did that day they awarded Sergeant Smith the Medal of Honor. The trouble began with a bad mistake on the part of the squadron leader. He mistook the coast of France for the coastline of England and started what he believed to be a descent for his home field. They found out just how wrong they were when, in the thick haze of the day, setting up their targets precisely, the Germans opened up with a blistering flak barrage. Almost at once the two Fortresses flying just off the wing of 649 were torn apart and went down. Before the impact of their loss could sink in, German fighters struck. . . .

The intercom was alive with the shouted words of the crew.

"*. . . fighter at four o'clock . . . hey, look out for those three coming up from under . . . Jesus, there's a Fort going down . . . bail out, you guys, bail out! . . . watch it, up there on top . . . seven o'clock low, four of the mothers . . . there goes another Fort; I think I saw two chutes open . . . hey, anybody see that fighter I got? I really creamed that son of a bitch! . . . two fighters, nine o'clock . . .*"

The words stop suddenly. Gunners try to bring life back to their communications lines but without use; German shells have torn up their intercom equipment and the men must rely on shouted words to those nearby or hand signals to the others too far to hear their words. In the ball turret Maynard Smith spins around in his attempts to track the enemy fighters, to pour his tracers into the Focke-Wulfs and Messerschmitts. It is a matter of snapping out bursts, shifting quickly from one incoming fighter to another to break up the attacks. Smith hasn't a moment in which to think and it is several minutes before he realizes that no longer can he hear the other crewmen on his headset. He doesn't think too much about that, either. He can feel the Fortress vibrate from the other guns throughout the airplane and he can see tracers whipping away from his ship. But it is discomforting; again and again the Fortress shudders convulsively from direct hits.

Then there are new sensations. It is becoming uncomfortably warm in the ball turret and then Smith's heart feels as if it has come to a sudden stop. He sees smoke swirling down from the fuselage above him. *What the hell is going on?* Smith wonders if they are actually on fire. He bangs his hand against the intercom switch but it doesn't do any good. Nothing. The smoke gets thicker and now Smith is afraid that the Fortress is burning. He's got to find out. He waits for a lull in the attacks from below and works the control to retract the ball turret into the fuselage so he can climb out.

Nothing happens. The controls for turret retraction have been shot away. Suddenly the turret is confining, closing in on him. The smoke is thicker. Sweating from the exertion, Smith winds the emergency hand crank. The urge is overpowering to get up into the fuselage. As he winds the crank the fighters are back; Smith keeps cranking.

Above and forward in the airplane, the top turret gunner has climbed down from his weapons to move into the cockpit. The gunner looks behind him and sees flames. Without the intercom the pilot might not know. The copilot listens to the gunner, leans to his left and looks back, through the bomb-bay compartment. Copilot Robert Mc-Callum later noted that he had "looked back through the bomb bay and all I could see was bright red flames, like looking into a furnace."

The flames were so severe that after futile attempts to extinguish the blaze with fire extinguishers, the radio operator and both waist gunners, blistered and nearly overcome, panicked. Convinced their ship was doomed, unable to communicate with the pilots, the three men lost no time in bailing out. The chances for survival seemed better in the English Channel than in a crippled, blazing airplane.

When Smith finally drags himself out of his turret he faces an appalling sight. Forward is a sea of flames. The radio operator and waist gunners have vanished. What Smith cannot see is that in the nose of the airplane the navigator and bombardier are both badly wounded. Smith turns from the flames again and looks to the rear of airplane where he sees the tail gunner sprawled on the floor of the Fortress, critically wounded by an exploding cannon shell. The flames reach out toward Smith as he tries to get his bearings. Not until that moment does he realize that the airplane is in a dive. The pilot is diving for lower altitude; the German fighters have shot away the oxygen system and getting down low is an immediate necessity.

The wind screams in through the open hatch of the radio compartment, fanning the fire. The Fortress lurches through the air as if the pilots were fighting for control. And this they are; the flames have burned through several of the control cables. As Number 649 plunges from the sky, trailing her death mark of flames and smoke, the crewmen of other bombers write off Smith's Fortress as a goner. They have already seen several chutes and now the blazing airplane is plummeting toward the water below. The men watch and they wait for the blinding flash that will mark the fuel tanks exploding.

It seems impossible that the Fortress can survive. The wings have been so holed with cannon shells and bullets that it will take only a spark to set off the fuel. Only a spark—and fire is chewing out the center of the airplane . . .

And the fighters are back. No question they will come as wolves after the cripple. Smith is torn by the urgent desire to bail out. Three other crew members have already done so and there is every reason for Smith to follow them. He glances again at the tail gunner and he knows he will stay.

Maynard Smith becomes like a man possessed. For minutes he battles the flames in the radio compartment, dragging away flaming objects to the waist windows where he hurls them from the Fortress. He is desperate to keep the fire from the ammunition in the compartment. He battles the blaze with anything within reach—clothing, boots, even his gloved hands. But he cannot stay at the task too long. Convinced the ammunition is for the moment safe from the fire, he rushes back to the tail where the gunner lies collapsed. Smith pulls the man over, rips open a first-aid kit and dresses the man's wounds. He is still stemming the flow of blood when the German fighters attack. Smith shouts reassuring words to the wounded gunner and stumbles back to the waist.

With the tail turret unmanned, his own ball turret empty, the radio compartment gun unmanned and unusable because of the flames, and the waist guns unattended, the Fortress is helpless to attack from the rear. Smith grasps one of the big waist fifties and snaps out bursts of tracers at the incoming fighters. Accuracy is unimportant and bluff is everything, and Smith is playing colossal bluff. The tracers spray out, are seen by the German pilots. Scarcely do the fighters on one side break away when Smith wheels about and grasps the other gun in the opposite waist position.

Long minutes in the lurching, flaming bomber go by while Smith moves from one waist gun to the other, throwing out enough tracers to convince the enemy pilots that the Fortress is still lethal in its defense. Smith is trying to buy time and he gives his airplane a continued shaky lease on life.

All this time, however, the fighters have been scoring. Hammering explosions rip the fuselage and the tail; through the hatches Smith sees gaping holes blown in the wings. There is no time to stare. Unfinished business awaits Smith in the tail and at the first opportunity he returns to the prostrate gunner. He completes stemming the flow of blood, binds the wounds, does what he can to make the man comfortable. It is crude medical care but the man will live.

The fighters are back, tearing apart the staggering, still-blazing Fortress. The Focke-Wulfs take their time; the pilots know they can cut the big airplane to pieces in leisurely fashion. Smith stumbles back to the waist and again opens fire. Once more the arcing tracers do the job; the startled German pilots break off a firing pass. They cannot understand how the shattered airplane remains airborne.

By now the fire in the radio compartment is raging fiercely. The wind-whipped blaze is spreading rapidly and the German pilots see the brilliant flames streaming out the radio hatch and through the waist gun positions. The Focke-Wulf pilots know it is only a matter of seconds, a few minutes at the most, before the Fortress explodes or plunges down, wrapped from nose to tail in flames.

The German fliers may not be wrong. Shattered oxygen bottles are feeding the flames to a white-hot fury. It is suicide even to approach the intense heat. Smith grabs another extinguisher, pauses for a moment, and rushes into the holocaust.

The entire mid-section of the Fortress is filled with the roaring fire. The heat has become so furious that the ammunition in the feed belt to the radio compartment machine gun has started to explode. Armor-plated and incendiary shells scream through the bomber. The radio, the gun mount itself, cameras, and the metal sections of the radio compartment have softened and are starting to run molten. Into the exploding ammunition and liquid-running metal goes Maynard Smith.

With only his flying gloves for protection Smith snatches at the flaming ammunition belt. Fifty caliber ammunition explodes in his face. Despite the heat broiling the exposed skin on his face the little sergeant wrenches the belt free and lurches away from the inferno, clutching the burning ammunition belt in his hands. He stumbles to a waist hatch and hurls the lethal belt away from the Fortress. That danger, at least, is now gone. A moment later Smith is back into the flames. His pain-wracked hands grab at flaming oxygen bottles and these also he flings away through the hatches.

Again he returns to the inferno. One after the other he exhausts the chemical fire extinguishers. Still the flames crackle and roar. Smith is beating at the blaze with his hands when cannon shells explode nearby. Smith rushes for the waist guns. What it is like there in the waist, the flames roaring nearby, the fighters coming in again and again, no one can ever imagine. The wounded tail gunner stares in open astonishment as Smith performs like a man berserk. The instant the fighters bank away he is back in the midst of the fire. There are no more extinguishers. Smith snatches up a large sheet of canvas which has been used to package equipment. He wastes no time in wrapping the heavy fabric about his body and shuffles back into the flames to beat at the fire with his hands.

Long minutes later a smoke-gagged and fire-blackened Smith struggles out of the radio compartment. He slumps exhausted to the floor of the airplane and closes his eyes.

The fire is out. He has saved the Fortress.

Somehow the pilots bring the airplane back to England, get it on the ground. Most of the controls are shot away. The tail wheel has been blown off by a cannon shell. But they land without further incident.

For some time the crew members who escaped death in 649 move slowly through the gutted radio compartment. Outside, hundreds of men wait to crowd aboard the Fortress, to stare at the rivulets formed by metal that had run molten. They blink in disbelief at the empty and blackened brackets from which Smith tore loose the flaming oxygen bottles. They think about the burning and exploding ammunition the little sergeant carried away in his hands.

Some time later Maynard Smith indicated that little had changed, that perhaps the four stripes on his sleeve were held there somewhat precariously. When the moment arrived for the official presentation to Smith for the Medal of Honor, it wasn't difficult to find him.

Staff Sergeant Maynard H. Smith was on KP.

Entry of 8th May 1943 in the diary of Joseph Goebbels, Propaganda Minister, Third Reich: "*Wegener told me about the day raids on Bremen by American bombers. These were very hard indeed. The Americans drop their bombs with extraordinary precision from an altitude of eight to nine thousand meters. The population has the paralyzing feeling that there really is no protection against such daylight attacks . . .*"

One hundred and sixty-nine bombers left England to attack France on the 13th May; 119 bombers struck their targets. To the officers and men of the VIII Bomber Command, the raids of the thirteenth, from which four bombers were shot down, was but a preliminary for the next day.

The 14th may was a day of records, the day when the Eighth Air Force "was ordered to put its maximum force in the air . . . as part of a great combined attack against the German war machine." The British in night raids hammered Berlin and struck at targets within the Ruhr and in Czechoslovakia; the Eighth was to follow up with blows at Kiel, Antwerp, Courtrai, and Ijmuiden. For the "all-out" effort the Eighth sent out 224 heavy bombers and twelve mediums, of which 209 airplanes reached their targets for bomb drops. The size of the effort rose with the inclusion of fighter sweeps—118 P-47s flew with British Spitfires on short-range escort missions. In all, the 14th May, what the British press referred to as the opening of a "great blitz," went very well, indeed.

Kiel held special significance. Struck by 109 B-17s and seventeen B-24s Kiel represented the deepest penetration yet into Germany, with the bombers flying 460 miles from their fields to the target. Eight bombers went down, almost all of them to German fighters. The small force of Liberators carrying incendiaries, required to fly the lowest position in the second combat wing formation, was exposed to German attack. The Germans made the most of this advantage and cut down five of the seventeen Liberators. The severe losses to the B-24s made it evident that these bombers should not be sent out to accompany the Fortresses unless the B-24s were in such large number that they could protect themselves if separated from the main bomber force.

The next day, the 15th, the Eighth proved its stamina. A total of 193 heavy bombers was dispatched against targets. On the 17th a force of 198 raiders struck out from England against their objectives. On this day the Eighth learned the folly of sending medium bombers, unescorted, against their targets in low-level raids. Ten Martin B-26 Marauders in two flights attacked Ijmuiden and Haarlem. The twin-engined bombers ran into a swarm of fighters and encountered severe flak barrages. The Germans were totally effective in their defense—every bomber went down. Four days later two crewmen from one bomber were picked up floating on their raft at sea—the only survivors of the massacre.

Three more missions were flown in May. On the 19th, 211 bombers struck again at Kiel, Flensburg and other targets. On the 21st, 161 bombers set out for Wilhelmshaven and Emden. On the 29th the number of bombers reached a record 279, with strikes against St. Nazaire, La Pallice and Rennes.

As far as the Eighth Air Force was concerned, the heavy bombers had completed their phase of "test and buildup." The 29th May represented the 61st mission. It was now time to study and evaluate. A look at the loss column showed surprising effectiveness on the part of the Fortresses and the lesser number of Liberators that sometimes accompanied them on strikes. During the five-month period of January through May 1943 "the bomber loss rate, expressed as percentage of credit sorties (i.e., sorties in the course of which the aircraft has entered areas normally defended by the enemy or has in any way been subject to attack) was 5.6 percent. This figure includes both those bombers lost in action and those listed as falling in Category E, that is, damaged beyond economical repair while engaged on an operational mission. Expressed as a percentage of aircraft actually attacking the target, the figure rises to approximately 6.4 percent."[60]

By the end of the test and buildup phase—through the 29th May 1943—the Eighth could also count its losses in heavy bombers. A total of 188 great raiders had gone down before German steel. Approximately 1,900 men had died or been taken prisoner; there were other dead and wounded with the planes that returned to England. Operational and training accidents also had exacted their toll. But one thing was certain—there was no longer any question that the Fortresses could do the job.

The time was ripe to begin CBO—the Combined Bomber Offense of Americans and British forces in the sustained and systematic attack on the German war machine. On the 10th June 1943 the CBO went into effect and the Eighth Air

Force entered its "second phase" of operations. From that day forward Eighth would concentrate upon demolishing the German Air Force. It would hammer at factories and Luftwaffe installations and, inevitably, would take its toll in the air of defending German fighters. As long-range escorts in the form of P-38s, P-47s and P-51s became available, the effort to engage and destroy the Luftwaffe in the air would be intensified. High on the target list of Eighth would be industrial centers, petroleum refineries and storage tanks, marshaling yards—those facilities that related directly to the fighting capacity of the Reich.

May 1943 was momentous for yet another reason. Five new B-17 groups were assigned to operational status for combat missions. One group burdened with training duties was returned to combat status. Another group would be ready in June. And in the Mediterranean theater another heavy bomber striking arm came into being with the activation of the Fifteenth Air Force, which absorbed the heavies of the Twelfth.

The target was Germany.

# CHAPTER 23

# MISSION 65/MISSION 69

THERE SEEMED NO END to the fury and growing strength of German fighter defenses. On the 13th June the enemy demonstrated again that deep penetrations into the Reich during daylight could incur devastating losses. A total force of 228 bombers went out from England, splitting into smaller formations to attack several targets. Sixty Fortresses went after the U-boat yards and harbor of Kiel—where they stumbled into the heaviest fighter defenses ever put up against an attacking bomber force. The interception became another of the long, running battles, starting when the Fortresses reached the German coast. There the enemy launched his attacks in force, employing the usual Me-109 and FW-190 fighters as well as twin-engine Me-110s and JU-88s. The Germans were drawing on all their fighter strength to resist the mission, as the crews learned when they encountered black-painted night fighters thrown into the fray. As the AAF official history records the event:

The attacks were pressed with vigor and tenacity, but the small force of Fortresses fought its way steadily through the swarming enemy until it sighted Kiel. There it delivered its bombs with the battle at its hottest and the lead plane already mortally damaged. In the circumstances it would be churlish to blame them for bombing with less than "precision" accuracy. On the return trip the attacks continued. It was a broken and scattered remnant that landed in England. Claims registered by the returning crews totaled thirty-nine enemy aircraft destroyed, five probably destroyed, and fourteen damaged. It is impossible to estimate the planes destroyed by those bomber crews who were themselves shot down (twenty-two of the sixty Fortresses were lost), but considering the intensity of the fighting they must have been numerous. ... Though hailed by both British and American air commands as a great victory, the "battle of Kiel" can be considered so only in terms of the bravery and determination with which the shattered force of bombers did in fact reach the target and drop its bombs. In terms of the cold statistics which ultimately measure air victories, it was a sobering defeat.[61]

Nine days later, on the 22nd June, the crews of the VIII Bomber Command avenged the debacle of Kiel in one of their most successful performances. A force of 181 Fortresses struck at the synthetic rubber plant at Huls with 422 tons of bombs, "of which 88.6 tons exploded inside the plant area. So effective was this bombardment that the entire plant was shut down for one month for repairs and full ... production was not achieved again until six months later."

The Huls Strike—Mission Number 65 for the Eighth Air Force, was also the initial combat mission for the 384th Group, commanded by Colonel Budd J. Peaslee, and, the

381st Group. The success of that mission is evident in the results achieved, but there is another side to mission 65. On this strike, as on many others, a separate force of bombers went out to act as decoys to divert German fighters from the main force. Often such diversionary sweeps were flown, and there is the natural tendency to pass off such an effort as unimportant. This is not so, and to place the diversionary sweep in its proper context, to give us a look behind the scenes, the writer is indebted to Colonel Peaslee, who prepared the following account of Mission 65:[62]

Mission Number 65 for the Eighth and Number 1 for the 384th was conceived with cunning and imagination. There were two bomber groups with identical status available, both having completed the mandatory two-week training period satisfactorily and both ready and waiting to perform their first assignment in the air war. In this way they could acclimate to enemy action with at least one intermediate step. . . . As a part of the mission the two freshman groups, the 384th and 381st, would constitute a special task force to confuse the German fighter controller. These two groups would assemble over their bases and climb to bombing altitude over England. They would fly a dogleg course and their presence would be readily discovered by the German Radio Direction Finding facilities, following which they would depart from North Foreland north of the Strait of Dover and attack the Ford and General Motors plants at Antwerp, Belgium. While this was a relatively short mission with a penetration of the Continent to a depth of only about 30 miles the target was nevertheless important, as these plants manufactured spare parts for the great stocks of Allied vehicles captured at Dunkirk and during the desert campaign.

With the receipt of the field order containing all the details necessary to plan, organize, and launch the attack, the vast blackness that had been the sleeping base came to life. The darkness was spotted with myriads of moving lights which marked the progress of individuals moving toward their places of duty to prepare the 384th for its first mission....

For Mission Number 65, takeoff, or H-hour, was set for 0700 hours, briefing at 0500, and breakfast at 0400 hours. When the crews were called at 0330 there were few who had to be called a second time. For most, it had been a long night of wakefulness and tension, with a few catnaps interspersed as the long night hours passed. In their bunks they could hear the distant and never-ceasing rumble of engines as the ground crews went about their tasks of checking and rechecking. The restless thoughts of the crewmen spanned the ocean and continent and came to rest in their homeland, centered around a wife, or parents, or other loved ones, in a distant land. And then at last the "caller" came and called their number and it was like the voice of doom. But the spirit of youth and confidence surged to the top and with their mutual apprehensions pushed into the background they were gay and boisterous. As they dressed for the bitter cold of high altitude they kept up a chatter of wisecracks and talk of love and conquest....

Just minutes before...takeoff time the sun struck through the white blanket [of fog] and almost with the wave of a magician's wand the runways became visible. A green flare soared up through the last wisps of fog hanging motionless over the base. This was the signal to start engines. Around the perimeter of the base the silent propellers came to life as puffs of smoke whipped back from the exhausts and a great volume of sound grew and grew until the very earth seemed to shake. Majestically the big birds rolled from the hardstands and along the taxiway toward the takeoff point, where they hesitated for a final burst of full power, then lumbered down the runway and into the crisp morning air.

Where the bombers had appeared awkward and un-gainly on the ground, in the air, with wheels retracted, they became things of beauty and grace. The leader began a large gentle orbit of the base at 1,000 feet with the twenty-odd B-17s of the 384th cutting across the wide circle to come into their assigned positions with precision and skill. In the single orbit the formation assembly was complete and the climb began. . . .

It was at North Foreland that the fighter escort of *Ty-phoons* should have made rendezvous with the bombers, but none appeared. It was then assumed by the commander that they had been there on time, twenty minutes previ-ously, and had proceeded on toward the east to Antwerp. Fifty miles east of the English headland the bombers crossed the Belgian coastline and entered hostile skies. There was still no evidence of friendly fighter escort and it became all too apparent that rendezvous had been missed and the bombers were on their own. At this point a decision was necessary in the lead bomber. To penetrate the Conti-nent in the face of overwhelming enemy fighters could be a frightful error costing many B-17s and men. In the com-mander's mind there was the fervent hope that the *Ty-phoons* and *Thunderbolts* were ahead of the formations clearing the way. It was a futile hope, doomed to be shat-tered on the rock of reality. About thirty miles west of Antwerp, hope would come to grief in a flash of gunfire.

In the thin, cold air about 24,000 feet above the Belgian mainland, the formations were rapidly closing the distance between them and their objective. With anxious eyes the invaders searched the great expanse of sky in all directions, eyes that asked the burning question of the moment:

"Where is that fighter escort? Where are the *Typhoons* and the *Thunderbolts*?" Well they knew that in the next few minutes the peaceful expanse of atmosphere around them could erupt with the noise and confusion of cannon and machine-gun fire aimed by man and machine against man and machine with lethal motive. It was then that the dreaded moment came, that the interception the crewmen had anticipated came to pass.

First evidence that they were not alone in the sky came with the suddenness of a thunderclap. Out of the slight haze that seemed to extend inland over the Continent, at a closing speed of 500 miles per hour, came the first wave of the attackers. Actually the first visible evidence was super-bright flashes from the muzzles of cannon mounted in the wings of Focke-Wulf 190s flying abreast and meeting the bombers head-on. In a matter of seconds, actually less than ten, the attackers flashed through the lead bomber formation and into the trailing group. Although expected, the attack came so suddenly that not a round of defensive fire exploded from the bomber guns. There had been no time to swing the heavy .50s to aim at the Germans. No sooner had the first wave of six attackers disappeared to the rear than a second wave came, and a third and a fourth, until the bombers could only guess at how many had come in head-on interception.

After the first attack the nose gunners of the B-17s were ready, and heavy vibrations of the defending .50s shook the bombers steadily. They were joined by the rear guns sporadically, as other gun positions took fleeting shots at the fading targets. As the fighters passed through the formations they broke to the left and in climbing turns; with their great speed they came up on the formations from the rear and on the flanks to make repeated attacks, using the sun at their backs to blind the defending gunners.

Fortunately for the task force the distance that separated them from the target was short when the first interception was made. At nearly four miles per minute they made the intervening thirty miles before the Germans could do extensive damage. There were many bombers that had suffered damage as the fight progressed across the sky, but a B-17 takes a lot of killing and, except for a lucky hit on a vital and explosive part, no single fighter attack ever took out a Fortress in one pass—unless a burst happened to kill both the pilot and copilot.

The bombers never wavered from their briefed course and there came a time, almost suddenly, when the bombardier in the nose must ignore his defensive guns and the fighter attacks, and devote himself to the task for which he had been trained. At the Initial Point (IP), the geographic identification point on the ground, the lead bombardier took over control of the formation path to the target. At this point, ten miles short of the Ford and General Motors factories, Captain Charles Bonnett, of Texas, spoke to his companion, the navigator, and requested that he fire a signal flare. As the brilliant white flare arose from the lead bomber, the formation turned slightly to the left and took a straight course directly toward 111 North High Street, Antwerp, Belgium. Captain Bonnett now flicked the switch that opened the great doors in the belly of the B-17, exposing the two columns of 1,000-lb. bombs suspended from the racks. All following bombers followed suit and the eyes of the bombardiers in each froze on the belly of the leader.

Captain Bonnett now aligned his bombsight with an object on the ground and clutched-in the PDI (Pilot Direction Indicator) which actuated a needle in an instrument on the pilot's instrument panel. By a series of adjustments, telegraphed to the PDI, Captain Bonnett killed the drift of the formation from a direct line to the target. His next adjustment was to set up his drop angle by "stopping" the cross hairs of his sight on a particular point on the earth's surface. During these operations the pilot was meticulously following the indications of the PDI, holding his aircraft at an exact altitude of 24,000 feet, and holding the formation at an exact air speed. While these operations were going on, the formation had flown into the field of antiaircraft fire. There were a few initial black bursts that dirtied the sky well ahead of them as though the German gunners were taking warmup shots. Suddenly there were hundreds of bursts in and around the bombers. These had to be ignored, for the formation was now on the bomb run where for at least five miles the bombardier and lead pilot must devote themselves entirely to the sighting operation, ignoring all else. This one minute was the reason they existed.

The fighters had abandoned their repeated attacks for the moment because the danger from flak was as great for them as for the bombers. The target on North High Street was in view and Captain Bonnett set the cross-hairs of the bombsight on the main structure of the building complex and clutched-in, connecting the bombsight mechanism through the electrical release system to the bomb racks. The black bursts of bursting 88-mm projectiles became notice-ably thicker as the formations approached the bomb release point. The concussion from the bursts made air bumps that rocked the bombers as in a choppy sea, but the formations bored on until at last the moving indices of the bombsight came into alignment and completed the bomb release cir-cuit.

The thousand pounders fell away in regular intervals about fifteen feet apart which would equal 100 feet on the ground nearly four miles below. As the bombs of the lead aircraft began their fall toward the target, all bombardiers in the following aircraft began the release of their bombs until there was a mass of some fifty tons of explosives en route to a violent destiny, and now the bombers were beginning a turn to a heading that would take them back to England.

The first bomb from the 384th formation struck in an open field nearly 500 yards short of the target and was followed instantly by all of the bombs of the formation. They fell through the intervening distance to the target and finally the last of them walked through the factory area. Captain Bonnett in his first drop against the enemy had been fearful that he might overshoot and had deliberately aimed short to assure his last bombs getting into the factory. Otherwise it was a beautiful drop and the bomb concentration would have been devastating had the aim been on target.

As the formations came off the target in a gentle left turn, the antiaircraft fire slackened and suddenly stopped as the guns shifted to the formation following. On looking back, its bomb bursts could be seen making an almost identical pattern with the 384th's. Their lead bombardier too, in his inexperience, had aimed short. The formation now braced themselves for the return fighter attacks, but to their great surprise and joy, none came. Gunners began yelling gleefully over the interphones, telling of a great air battle that raged through the sky about. The *Typhoons* and *Thunderbolts* were there, and the Germans were now on the defensive. Individual dogfights raged through the Belgian skies in a give-and-take among the fighters. Fortress gunners screamed in glee as they watched their rescuers chase the Germans east into Germany. The sight was a joy to behold, but there had been a cost.

Far below the bomber formations two pairs of bombers were going down. They were seen to be under control, but a few enemy fighters that had escaped detection were keeping up a running attack as the lonesome four tried to make the coast. They could not be helped, the main formations had to face the facts of life and leave them to their own devices. In cold harsh terms they had to be written off and abandoned, for the rest must live to fight another day.

The return flight was peaceful and there was a great sense of relief in the crews upon arrival over England. That island country had never looked so good. Back at base the bombers with wounded aboard fired red flares and were allowed to land first in order that medical aid be made available at the earliest possible minute. Ambulances with flight surgeons aboard raced up to the end of the runway to assist in evacuation of those who had felt the enemy's wrath. When all the bombers were down, there were four missing. Two of these were soon accounted for, as messages came in that they had made emergency landings at British bases on the coast with wounded and heavy battle damage. These were the two that, upon seeing their comrades shot out of formation and jumped by enemy fighters, had voluntarily abandoned the flight to accompany the wounded bombers and help them fight off the aerial jackals that sought to destroy them. These two had paid heavily for this folly and would be severely criticized by their commander when the group again came to briefing. The action had been courageous but foolhardy. Nothing had been gained; they had not saved their buddies, they had caused great damage to their aircraft and physical damage to themselves and, above all, they had disobeyed orders by breaking formation. This was a court-martial offense and the group was warned by the commander that any similar offense would be brought to trial. This was not a war in which knightly behavior could be tolerated or rewarded. To break formation voluntarily and without just cause in the face of the enemy was equal to desertion, for in fact they would be deserting their own forces who were depending on them for a share in the mutual defense.

Note by Colonel Peaslee:

*The 384th joined the Eighth in the first week of June with thirty-five combat crews. In the first three months of operations forty-two bombers failed to return from missions over Europe. This represented a loss of 120 percent in less than four months. The tour of each bomber crew had been arbitrarily established at twenty-five missions and, as losses during the first months of the bomber offensive were running at about 10 percent per mission, it was simple arithmetic that the last fifteen missions would be on borrowed time. For every mission a crew survived beyond ten, some new, or replacement, crew would be missing in action in their place. It was truly remarkable that these men remained steadfast with such odds against them.*

Mission Number 69 stood on the edge of disaster. Not the disaster already so well known in the form of bombers shot down and crews lost. The disaster that skirted the edge of Mission 69, flown on the 28th June 1943, has found scant place in the air histories of World War II. Of 241 heavy bombers dispatched, 201 struck their targets. Within these numbers were 158 Fortresses that bombed St. Nazaire. Another forty-three B-17s struck at Beaumont-le-Roger. Of the attacking force sent out, eight bombers failed to return. Those are the statistics—but the almost-tragedy of Mission 69 is not found in statistical files. It is a story this writer has never before seen in print. Before, that is, Budd J. Peaslee was dragged from retirement (a feat of which this writer is undeniably proud) to commit to paper, as only he could, this side of the air war never be-

fore told. The colonel turns back the years to the 28th
June 1943:

The details of this Eighth Air Force day bomber operation may still exist somewhere deep in the historical depos-
itories of this nation. On the other hand, this . . . may well
be the only written record that recalls the drama of Mission
Number 69. Or perhaps somewhere there may be an aging
veteran bombardier, a returnee from the air wars over Europe, who may vividly recall the shocking moments over
Brussels and shudder as recollections flood back into his
mind from days long past. On the other hand, the principal
of this incident may be one of those who failed to return
from the wars and his earthly remains may be moulding in
one of the forgotten junk piles of a thousand bombers that
fell like rain over the aerial battle routes of World War II.

The incident occurred in that task force Mission 69 sent
against the enemy fighter base at Brussels. . . . Three groups
were designated as a diversionary task force to bomb the
German Air Force installations, including shops, fuel storage facilities, ammunition dumps, and living areas of Beaumont-le-Roger airdrome in the outskirts of Brussels. . . . The
airfield was strongly defended by concentric rings of heavy
AA guns. In placing the guns the Germans had located only
a few on the side, thus leaving a definite weakness in the
gun defenses. To take advantage of the thinly placed AA
protection, the route of approach would be from the unexpected direction and the route to the target would be directly across the city. At the Initial Point of Halle, a few
miles southwest of the city, the combat wing leader would
fire a green flare and would turn northeast directly across
the heart of the city. At this signal the groups would break
into bombing interval of one mile, with the 384th following

the leader in the second position. After the bombing the leader would turn left and the following groups would re-form into defensive formation. As in all operations over occupied countries, participants were cautioned against any bombing of other than specifically designated targets. Stress was placed on the unfortunate predicament of the Belgian people under the domination of the German hordes—that these people were our friends and could be counted on for assistance in case bombers should have to be abandoned in the air or crash landings should become necessary. . . . Halle, the Initial Point, appeared, and to the northeast could be seen the beautiful capital of Belgium with its population of nearly a million. At the IP, the formation turned and split according to plan, and the bombers headed directly across the heart of the city. The electrically actuated bomb bay doors opened slowly as each bombardier prepared to drop his bombs when he saw the lethal load fall away from the leading bomber of his formation. The lead bombardier of each element of the strike force became engrossed in his duties of the sighting operation.

As the formations now aligned in a column of groups moved ponderously across the city they encountered no fighters and no flak. The lead bombardier in the 384th, in the second position, had completed his sighting adjustment and was prepared for the bomb run on the airdrome targets. As he watched the city pass slowly beneath his bombsight window he noted, far below, a large rectangular area in the center of the city, indicating a park or athletic field or perhaps a complex of sports areas. For some reason the sight intrigued him and he continued to focus on the installation after it had passed to the rear. As he watched, suddenly his unbelieving eyes saw the area explode in a mighty series of bomb bursts. To his horror he saw the strings of American bombs begin along one edge of the rectangle and walk down the entire length, with about half the bombs bursting in the open and about half in the residences that lined the parklike grounds. In his anxiety he screamed over the interphone to his pilot, "My God, someone has bombed the city!" The impact of his message was shattering. Vivid imaginations could picture the holocaust that was being visited on the helpless and friendly Belgians. The awful impact of what had happened for the moment unnerved those who were aware of it, but not for long. The bombers now entered the field of antiaircraft fire. A few bursts at first and then a massive barrage as the formations entered the heavy defenses. The sky in front and to the sides was filled with bursts. Those behind could easily be ignored. This fire could be classed as "accurate and intense." But the bombers marched on as inevitable as the march of doom, and suddenly the bombs were away and the boys could go home.... The return flight was tranquil and in peace. Only the conversation was sharp and intense as discussions were exchanged among crew members of the 384th leader about the tragic accident they were leaving behind them. It was obvious that a horrible error had occurred in the trailing formation that had been repeatedly and vigorously forbidden by high command. Someone would receive a court-martial for this beyond all doubt.

... On the second day following the fateful mission to Brussels, the Eighth Air Force remained grounded by bad weather. On this day all commanders and the key men of all lead crews were summoned to division headquarters.... Approximately one hundred officers of the division made up the assemblage, and all were in place well before the designated hour.... There was a heavy air of tension hanging over the meeting, reminiscent of a courtroom audience awaiting the dramapacked life or death verdict in a murder trial.... The diversionary strike on the airdrome at Brussels came under scrutiny. The grapevine had spread the knowledge that someone had pulled an error of the greatest magnitude. Outside of the guilty group no one knew who was responsible, and no one knew what his fate would be. This kind of thing had never happened before, although bombs had, in a few instances, gone astray from targets in occupied countries and innocent people had been killed and maimed. These were regrettable mischances of war, but never had an entire group, in seeming deliberation and unharassed by enemy action, dumped its bombs on such an obviously illogical target. There had been severe criticism of the unfortunate incidents of the past by neutral observers. The repercussions of this massive mistake could only be expected to be violent.

The leader of the 384th followed the combat-wing and lead-group discussion and at long last it came time for the guilty man to face the general, to describe his error, and to learn, from the general, his fate. It seemed inevitable that he would have to pay dearly for his tragic mistake even though it was unintentional and explainable. There had to be an international goat. As the "moment of truth" arrived, a young major arose and stepped to the rostrum with face pale and hands tightly clenched. Unsmilingly he faced the general and his aides and in a tense voice said, "Gentlemen, our part of this mission was flown as planned until on the bomb run our bombs were released prematurely and we bombed the city. My bombardier will tell you how it happened."

A slight young man wearing the silver bars of a first lieutenant, hardly out of his teens but with the face and expression of a man twice his age, arose and stepped slowly forward. A sense of impending drama gripped the listeners as if it were a great play portrayed by a fine cast under a masterly director. The young officer spoke in great deliberation as though he had said this piece a thousand times to himself before; his audience hung on every word in a tense silence in which even the breathing of a neighbor in the next chair became audible between the words.

"We turned on the target at Halle as briefed and as we came out of the turn we were in proper position. It was a long bomb run clear across the city, there was plenty of time and there was no enemy action by either fighters or flak. I picked a point on course to kill drift and set up the drop angle. It was a sort of rectangular park and I selected the near corner as a simulated aiming point. I talked to the major and we made a run on the dummy target as it lay directly on our course. All switches were in the ON position except the arming switch, and I had a good run on the aiming point, at which time I unclutched the bombsight to await our approach to the airdrome. I was looking ahead trying to pick up the target when I felt our bombs go away and looked down. I saw our bombs falling away with the arming wires still in place. I looked around and saw the bombs of the formation also falling and saw the arming vanes spinning away. I was panic-stricken, it was like a bad dream but I could not wake up. I wanted to die. It's still a bad dream and I still can't wake up. I don't know how it happened unless I failed to disengage the bombsight, and the sight indices continued to move and the sight to function until the bombs were released. Whatever the cause I alone am to blame—the bombs of the entire formation are on my head, they were dropped, as ordered, on the bombs of the leader. I can only say I have regretted the day I was born."

The lieutenant, with all eyes following him, returned to his chair. The eyes were compassionate with pity and full comprehension.

It was the general's turn to take the rostrum. He was a

stern-visaged thick-set and taciturn man with graying hair. His face was like old leather, seamed and wrinkled by a thousand suns. One eye was sharp and penetrating; the other bland and expressionless, for it was glass. The general was a product of the open cockpit, helmet and goggles era. He had lost his eye in a bombing raid while he watched the Battle of Britain as an American observer. He arose and standing by his chair he faced the assemblage and spoke:

"Gentlemen," he said, speaking without humor and giving these boys who fought the war equal stature and dignity as though speaking to equals in rank or high command. "Gentlemen, you are all well aware of the seriousness of what has happened. Again and again you have been cautioned about irresponsible bombing over occupied countries. No effort has been spared to impress upon you the great responsibility that rests upon your shoulders when you open your bomb doors over the Continent. You have been told of the friendly peoples temporarily under the iron heel of our enemies. Your missions to these countries have been carefully planned to avoid the possibility of accidents as much as possible. On this mission, to avoid the heavy flak defenses and to offer you the maximum possible chance of survival, you were routed across the city. This was a grave error that we cannot afford to repeat. The principals in this case are liable and courts-martial appear warranted. However, high command must assume a considerable share of the blame due to ill-considered planning and being guilty of overzealousness in the protection of crews at the risk of such an accident. Following the mission to Brussels, high command initiated an extensive investigation into the results of the bombing through agents in Belgium and other intelligence sources. We find these results are not so bad as had at first been feared." Here the general paused and a close observer might have been able to discern a certain relaxation of the sternness in his one good eye. "As a matter of fact we are informed that the German occupation command considered the park area and the better-class adjoining residences an excellent locale for the billeting of troops. The entire circumference of the park was used for this purpose; we are informed there were 1,200 casualties among these forces and only a few Belgians were injured or killed. Across the Channel this accident is being called a remarkable exhibition of American precision bombing. Such are the fortunes of war, gentlemen. This meeting and the incident are now closed."

So saying, the general and his party departed as the combat personnel stood at rigid and silent attention.

# CHAPTER 24

# THE BLOODY ROAD

WITH REPLACEMENT CREWS AND new bombers pouring in from across the Atlantic the Eighth Air Force began to put the pressure on the enemy. On the 29th June 232 heavy bombers struck targets in France. On the 4th July a force of 275 bombers went after targets in that occupied land. Six days later, on the 10th, another 286 bombers were on their way from England. Four days after that, 264 more Fortresses hit their targets. On the 17th July the Eighth for the first time went over the three hundred mark in a single strike of heavy bombers when it deployed 332 of the big raiders from their East Anglian bases.

But it was the last week of July, when the weather broke for the better, that the Eighth showed that truly it had come of age as the greatest aerial striking force in existence. On the 24th July, 309 bombers departed England. The next day, the 25th, 323 raiders went after targets in Germany. On the day succeeding, making it three in a row, 303 heavies struck their objectives in northwest Germany. There was a one-day lull, and then three more days in succession of all-out raids. Three hundred and two bombers went after German targets on the 28th July. Another 249 planes hit across Germany on the 29th and, on the 30th, 186 bombers ended the week of intense attacks against the German war machine.

It amounted to much more than a show of strength. Seventeen major industrial targets took beatings. The Fortresses showed what they could really do when they astounded their admirers and confounded their critics by flying from England to Norway and back—a round-trip nonstop mission of two thousand miles—and carried out a devastatingly accurate strike against their targets. The Fortresses also brought the meaning of air war home to the German populace when they ripped up an aircraft factory at Oschersleben. Berlin was only eighty miles distant and the promise of raids on the Nazi capital was clear.

When the month began with a series of especially effective strikes against industrial and airfield targets in France, feeling swept through the Eighth that this was to be a period of maximum effort. It was all that and more. It was a month of wild and savage air battles. The cruel loss of eighty-eight Fortresses in the final week of July, along with some nine hundred men, affected everyone in the bomber command. That the returning gunners claimed nearly three hundred fighters shot down—plus those downed by the bomber crews who never returned—did little to offset the sense of tragedy stalking the Eighth.

The crews had become professionals in a sense that imbued men with deep pride. The waist gunners of one Fortress forgot incoming German fighters when they saw their tail gunner *crawling* along the floor of the airplane to their position, leaving a trail of smeared blood. That didn't stop them dead—the tail gunner was cursing and demanding more ammunition.

Another Fortress, cut to pieces by German fighters, went down into the North Sea. All the crew but one appeared in the water or clinging to rafts. The wounded navigator slipped into the water from his raft, swam back to the Fortress already going under the waves, struggled through the sinking plane, and in the radio room dragged an unconscious gunner out from beneath heavy equipment. He hauled the gunner back to his raft where he then collapsed from exertions and his wounds and had to be hauled unconscious into the raft.

"Coming back from bombing an airdrome on July 14th,[63] a Fortress met a nose attack by three FW-190s with a blast of fire that destroyed two of the fighters and evidently killed the pilot of the third. It crashed head-on into the Number Three engine of the Fortress with an impact that tore off the propeller and knocked the bomber completely out of formation. The German fighter did a cartwheel over the Fortress, cutting halfway through the wing and a third of the way through the horizontal stabilizer. Top and ball turrets on the bomber jammed; radio equipment was smashed; all the instruments, according to the copilot, 'went crazy.' Pieces of metal from the disintegrating Focke-Wulf hurtled through the fuselage. A gun barrel buried itself in the wall between the radio room and the bomb bay. Other crews in the formation later reported that the Fortress had blown up as a result of the collision. It had not. On the contrary, it pulled itself together, shot down one more fighter, limped back under a canopy of sympathetic P-47s, and made a belly landing at an English base. None of the crew was scratched."

*Blitz Week* began on the 24th July with the mission of almost two thousand miles in strikes on Heroya, Bergen and Trondheim in Norway. The crews heard with delight the briefing reports that resistance to the attack was expected to be meager, and the bombardiers perked up when they saw details of their target at Heroya–a "bomber's dream." A gleaming new magnesium, aluminum and nitrate works had been constructed as an island connected to the mainland and city by a causeway. The plant was so new that most of the installed machinery had not yet been placed in operation. "The area was literally crammed with facilities," notes a history of the 384th Group, "and any bomb on the island would be a good bomb." On this mission there was an "interested observer"–a black cocker spaniel with something over three hundred hours of combat flying time to his credit. Since much of the mission was flown at low altitude, *Skipper* didn't need to wear the oxygen mask fashioned for him, and carried out a series of visits from the radio room to up front to see the navigator, bombardier and the pilots.

Of more than three hundred Fortresses sent out, only one was lost; flak-damaged, the bomber made a safe landing in Sweden and the crew was interned. The strike of 24th July against Heroya has been called "the most successful and shrewdly planned and executed mission of the entire war. It caught the defenders unaware, it devastated a great industrial complex, it cost only the bombs and fuel and not a single American life."

A total of 580 bombs burst within the target area and of these no less than 151 were shown by photo reconnaissance to be direct hits. Nothing tells better than Swedish eyewitness reports what happened at Heroya:

> Everything is absolutely ploughed up; not one foot of the huge factory site was spared. One can see complete rows of office buildings totally destroyed, work houses

have apparently been saved, but through charred window openings, twisted machines, bulging concrete walls can be seen. Other buildings have had worse treatment, for example, the first-aid stations, stores, technical offices, laboratory, one of the acid towers, one of the tower-centrifuges, the largest factory chimney cut off by 40 meters; the wharf received several direct hits and is perforated nearly from end to end. A German streamer with general cargo for the *Aerudinium* factory received a direct hit and sank like a stone. The factory buildings around *Metallurge Gunnekleiv* partly undamaged but the front of the buildings forced in. All the factory's machines out of production. Nearly everything was ready for a ceremonious inauguration of the aluminum factory; production would certainly have been in activity by the New Year. The people have been expecting this attack for the Germans were putting the factory to use. The Director of the Factory considers the destruction total and impossible to rebuild during the war.

On Mission Number 77, the 26th July, American airmen had nothing but praise for the British air-sea rescue teams prowling the Channel. Sixty-five men were saved from the frigid water. The pilot of one Fortress, whose crew spent the night drifting off the German coast, related what happened at his Intelligence debriefing:

When the fighters hit us, the wing swelled up like a balloon and then burst into flames, and we went into a dive. I didn't give the order to bail out because I thought I might pull out of it. I got it under control only 150 feet above the water, just in time to ditch. [After ditching we] tied our dinghies together and then started worrying. We were a long way from home and closer to Germany than any other land. We were afraid the Germans might pick us up. We not only watched Kiel burn that night, but we actually sat out there in the water and had a grandstand view of the RAF bombing the German coast. We could see the flak bursting and the fires started by the RAF blockbusters.

About noon the next day a British plane spotted us. He dropped three big dinghies and then hung around to protect us from possible attack by a Ju-88 that hovered in the distance. Soon another RAF plane joined him, and then three more, then three Forts joined up. It looked like the combined Allied air force above us.

One of the RAF planes dropped a launch by parachute. It was a sight to see that boat come parachuting down, settling right beside us. It was all closed, with the hatches sealed. We opened it up and there were sleeping bags, food, water, gasoline and directions for running the thing. I had an idea I might get the boys to head for New York . . .

Before he became a copilot in B-17s, John C. Morgan flew with the Royal Canadian Air Force. He then shifted to the AAF, where he was a rarity—a Fortress pilot with the rank of Flight Officer (and later, Lieutenant). Over the German coast the B-17 in which Morgan flew as copilot took a sudden withering attack from FW-190 fighters. The navigator related what happened, telling why John C. Morgan was later to receive the Medal of Honor:

On their first pass I felt sure they had got us, for there was a terrific explosion overhead and the ship rocked badly. A second later the top turret gunner fell through the hatch and slumped to the floor of my nose compartment. When I got to him, I saw that his left arm had been blown off at the shoulder and he was a mass of blood. I first tried to inject some morphine, but the needle was bent and I couldn't get it in. Then I tried to apply a tourniquet, but it was impossible as the arm was off too close to the shoulder. I knew he had to have the right kind of medical treatment as soon as possible and we had almost four hours of flying time ahead of us, so there was no alternative.

I opened the escape hatch and adjusted the chute for him and placed the ripcord ring firmly in his right hand. But he must have become excited because he pulled the cord, opening the pilot chute in the updraft. I managed to gather it together and tuck it under his right arm and toppled him into space. I learned somewhat later from our ball-turret gunner that the chute opened O.K. We were at 24,500 feet about twenty-five miles west of Hanover. Our only hope was that he was found and given medical attention immediately.

[The Fortress made its bomb run. After "bombs away" the navigator found the intercom system knocked out—]

The last I remembered hearing over it was shortly after the first attack when someone was complaining about not getting any oxygen. All this time, except for what I thought to be some violent evasive action, we seemed to be flying O.K. It was two hours later, when we were fifteen minutes out from the enemy coast, that I decided to go up, check with the pilot, and have a look around. I found the pilot slumped in his seat, the back of his head blown off. *The copilot was flying the plane with one hand and holding the half-dead pilot off the controls with the other....*

[The pilot was a rugged, six-foot man with a will to fight that not even his grievous wound could extinguish. Only partially conscious he fought wildly to retain his grip on the controls and the copilot, John C. Morgan, was forced to struggle almost continuously with his wounded pilot, dragging him away from the control yoke as the crippled airplane went through the violent maneuvers that

other crew members believed to be evasive action. What
the navigator did not realize was that the firing pass by the
Focke-Wulfs that tore away the arm of the top turret gunner and nearly killed the pilot had severed the oxygen
lines; four men in the rear of the Fortress collapsed, leaving the bomber without protection except from the nose
guns and the turret in the belly. The gunners were revived
in terrible condition with severe frostbite. The radio equipment was shattered. The intercom was knocked out. The
decision normally would have been to turn back, to run for
safety. John Morgan continued on to the target. The navigator takes up the story:]

The copilot told me we had to get the pilot out of his
seat as the plane couldn't be landed from the copilot's seat.
The glass on that side was shattered so badly you could
barely see out. The copilot was operating the controls with
one hand and helping me to handle the pilot with the other.
We struggled for thirty minutes getting the fatally injured
pilot out of his seat and down into the rear of the navigator's compartment, where the bombardier held him from
slipping out the open hatch. The pilot died a few hours later.

In 1944 John C. Morgan, Medal of Honor, ended his career as a B-17 pilot. Over Berlin his Fortress was torn apart
in the air. Morgan was blown out of the airplane *clutching
his parachute in his arms*. Falling over the German capital
he hooked up the chute, pulled the D-ring, and floated
safely to earth. He was in a prison camp when the war
ended.

The air war became hotter. After a one-day reprieve on
the 27th July the crews were out again on the 28th, 29th
and 30th. On the 28th, when twenty-two Fortresses went

down, one group suffered a disastrous beating by losing fifteen out of the thirty-nine bombers in the formation. The German defenses included fighters of every size and description. They hammered at the B-17s with machine guns, small- and large-bore cannon, floating mines, and the deadliest of the latest defenses—aerial rockets. One fighter pilot scored a rare triple victory with a single rocket firing. The missile ripped directly into a Fortress. The explosion hurled the bomber out of control, sending it reeling into two others. All three B-17s went down.

The Fortress crews for the first time saw *German* B-17s. These "Intruder" Fortresses had been captured intact by the enemy. They were refurbished for flight. Several of the captured B-17s were used to demonstrate their characteristics to German fighter pilots. Others flew along with the American formations, radioing to ground stations details of the flight—the pattern, speed, altitude, heading and other information on the American armadas. Every now and then a German B-17 would come in close to an American bomber and the gunners would blaze away at their unsuspecting prey.

Early August proved a holiday for the crews. No missions were flown until the 12th, when all hell broke loose again. Of 330 Fortresses sent out, 243 pounded targets throughout the Ruhr. The Germans cut down twenty-five of the heavy bombers. On the 15th and 16th the Fortresses ripped into German airfields throughout France and Holland. A total of 573 heavy bombers flew missions on the two days, of which 527 attacked their targets. Losses were cut drastically to six Fortresses, for which credit went to heavy Allied fighter sweeps and escorts.

Then came the 17th August with a double-pronged blow at ball-bearing works in Schweinfurt and a strike at the Messerschmitt factories in Regensburg.

By the night of the 16th August the Eighth Air Force counted up a total of eighty-three missions into Germany and over the occupied countries. This was the anniversary eve of a year of heavy bomber operations and the penalty for these first twelve months was brutal. A total of 411 heavy bombers had gone down, taking with them more than four thousand crewmen. Dozens of other planes that staggered back to England never again flew. The dead and wounded in the returning bombers were counted in the hundreds.

For many reasons Mission Number 84 on the 17th August is especially significant. It initiated the first of forty air attacks to come on the bearings industry (Schweinfurt alone in the summer of 1943 produced forty-five percent of all Germany's anti-friction bearings). Mission 84 was the single greatest assault yet made on Germany; 376 planes left their bases of which 315 raiders struck targets in the deepest penetration yet, dropping a new record total of 724 tons of bombs. The 1st and 2nd Bombardment Divisions were assigned Schweinfurt in central Germany; they would hit their target and return to England. But the 3rd Division would strike Regensburg and continue on its way, crossing the Alps and the Mediterranean Sea to land at advanced bases in North Africa.

It was a day of perfect flying weather and a day of savage air battles. The Germans struck at the bombers with fanatical persistence and what the crews termed "incredible courage." They came up with every plane they had in their arsenal. The attacks were constant. No sooner did one wave of fighters rip through the bomber formations when a fresh wave screamed in, firing. The fighter pilots "went wild." They attacked in head-on blows, in vertical climbs and dives, rolled through the formations, closed to point-blank range. Entire fighter squadrons struck in "javelinup" formations which made it difficult and often impossible for the Fortresses to take evasive action. The Germans came in with their fighters wing to wing, setting up a huge launching platform from which they lobbed heavy rockets at the bombers. It was the most intensive, violent defense yet encountered and without question the worst day in the memory of the bomber crews.

*Sixty heavy bombers went down.* The Germans shot down thirty-six heavy bombers from the Regensburg task force, and twenty-four more raiders from the group attacking Schweinfurt.

The crews of the returning bombers said they had shot down German fighters in droves. Gunner claims were 288 enemy fighters destroyed. Even if this figure were cut by half it tells the ferocity of the air fighting. One navigator related: "I can't remember looking out without seeing a bunch of them falling out of the sky like big dirty drops of rain." Six hundred men went down in the lost bombers; no one knows how many fighters they may have destroyed.

The bombing at Regensburg was described as "magnificent ... the entire weight of bombs landed inside the Messerschmitt factory area or on the adjacent airfield. All work at the plant was stopped. Six main workshops were hit, five being severely damaged. Storerooms and administrative buildings were wrecked; a hangar presumably used for engine installation was more than half destroyed. . . ."

As the air battle raged, the men in the Fortresses heard the increasingly excited German claims of strikes and kills mingled steadily with shouted cries of "Parachute!" and "Ho, down you go, you dog!" and then, a final gasp, *"Herr Gott Sakramant."*

In the B-17 named *X Virgin* a waist gunner was killed by German fighters. Internal systems were slashed and cut by the enemy fire. In an unprecedented move, four men chose to bail out deliberately so that the remaining crew would have enough oxygen to take the ship over the target and return. Over the target the bomb-release mechanism failed to work. . . .

But a wounded gunner felt he hadn't come all this way for nothing. He left his guns and worked his way to the bomb bay. With a screwdriver he loosened the shackles and then jumped up and down on the bombs until they broke loose and fell free.

Fire exploded loose in the Fortress called *My Prayer*. The B-17 plummeted in a wild dive, helpless, out of control. Seven men bailed out to save their lives. The top turret gunner couldn't jump; his chute had been set aflame. The pilot and copilot stayed with the gunner in the blazing airplane. By superhuman strength the pilot fought the careening airplane out of its dive. Behind him the gunner, wounded severely in the leg, succeeded with the copilot in putting out the flames. *Now* they still had to fight their way home through a horde of fighters waiting to finish off the cripple. The pilot flew the Fortress, the wounded gunner handled the nose guns and the copilot swung back and forth between the waist guns to stave off the enemy fighters. Without protection from below or to their rear the pilot brought *My Prayer* all the way down to the deck. They roared through Germany with their propellers nicking trees.

"We came home at two hundred and ten miles an hour," said the pilot, "buzzing cities, factories, and airfields in Germany. It was the first legal buzzing I've ever done. We drew some fire, but I did evasive action and we escaped further damage. The people in Germany scattered and fell to the ground when they saw us coming, but in Belgium the people waved and saluted us. . . ."

The copilot of a Fortress in the final group of the for-

mation—which that day took a terrible pounding—held debriefing officers fascinated with his account of the mission:

> ... Two FW-190s appeared at one o'clock level and
> whizzed through the formation ahead of us in a frontal at-
> tack, nicking two B-17s in the wings and breaking away
> beneath us in half rolls. Smoke immediately trailed from
> both B-17s, but they held their stations. As the fighters
> passed us at a high rate of closure, the guns of our group
> went into action. The pungent smell of burnt powder filled
> our cockpit, and the B-17 trembled to the recoil of nose and
> ball-turret guns. I saw pieces fly off the wing of one of the
> fighters before they passed from view.
>
> Here was early action. The members of the crew sensed
> trouble. There was something desperate about the way
> those two fighters came in fast right out of their climb
> without any preliminaries. For a few seconds the inter-
> phone was busy with admonitions: *"Lead 'em more ...
> short bursts ... don't throw rounds away ... there'll be
> more along in a minute."*
>
> Three minutes later, the gunners reported fighters
> climbing up from all around the clock, singly and in pairs,
> both FW-190s and Me-109s. Every gun from every B-17 in
> our Group was firing, crisscrossing our patch of sky with
> tracers. Both sides got hurt in this clash, with two Fortresses
> from our low squadron and one from the Group ahead
> falling out of formation on fire with crews bailing out, and
> several fighters heading for the deck in flames or with their
> pilots lingering behind under dirty yellow parachutes. I no-
> ticed an Me-110 sitting out of range on our right. He was to
> stay with us all the way to the target, apparently reporting
> our position to fresh squadrons waiting for us down the
> road. At the sight of all these fighters, I had the distinct
> feeling of being trapped. The life expectancy of our Group

seemed suddenly very short, since it appeared that the fighters were passing up the preceding Groups in order to take a cut at us.

Swinging their yellow noses around in a wide U-turn, a twelve-ship squadron of Me-109s came in from twelve to two o'clock in pairs and in fours, and the main event was on.

A shining silver object sailed over our right wing. I recognized it as a main exit door. Seconds later, a dark object came hurtling through the formation, barely missing several props. It was a man, clasping his knees to his head, revolving like a diver in a triple somersault. I didn't see his chute open.

A B-17 turned gradually out of the formation to the right, maintaining altitude. In a split second, the B-17 completely disappeared in a brilliant explosion, from which the only remains were four small balls of fire, the fuel tanks, which were quickly consumed as they fell earthward.

Our airplane was endangered by falling debris. Emergency hatches, exit doors, prematurely opened parachutes, bodies, and assorted fragments of B-17s and Hun fighters breezed past us in the slipstream.

I watched two fighters explode not far beneath, disappearing in sheets of orange flame, B-17s dropping out in every state of distress, from engines on fire to control surfaces shot away, friendly and enemy parachutes floating down, and, on the green carpet far behind us, numerous funeral pyres of smoke from fallen fighters, marking our trail. The sight was fantastic; it surpassed fiction.

On we flew through the strewn wake of a desperate air battle, where disintegrating aircraft were commonplace and sixty chutes in the air at one time were hardly worth a second look.

I watched a B-17 turn slowly out to the right with its cockpit a mass of flames. The copilot crawled out of his window, held on with one hand, reached back for his chute, buckled it on, let go, and was whisked back into the horizontal stabilizer. I believe the impact killed him. His chute didn't open.

Ten minutes, twenty minutes, thirty minutes, and still no letup in the attacks. The fighters queued up like a bread line and let us have it. Each second of time had a cannon shell in it.

Our B-17 shook steadily with the fire of its .50s, and the air inside was heavy with smoke. It was cold in the cockpit, but when I looked across at the pilot I saw that sweat was pouring off his forehead and over his oxygen mask. He turned the controls over to me for a while. It was a blessed relief to concentrate on holding station in formation instead of watching those everlasting fighters boring in. It was possible to forget the fighters. Then the top turret gunner's twin muzzles would pound away a foot above my head, giving a realistic imitation of cannon shells exploding in the cockpit, while I gave an even better imitation of a man jumping six inches out of his seat.

A B-17 of the Group ahead, with its right Tokyo tanks on fire, dropped back to about 2,000 feet above our right wing and stayed there while seven of the crew successively bailed out. Four men went out the bomb bay and executed delayed jumps, one bailed from the nose, opened his chute prematurely, and nearly fouled the tail. Another went out the left waist-gun opening, delaying his chute opening for a safe interval. The tail gunner dropped out of his hatch, apparently pulling the ripcord before he was clear of the ship. His chute opened instantaneously, barely missing the tail, and jerked him so hard that both his shoes came off. He hung limp in the harness, whereas the others had shown immediate signs of life after their chutes opened, shifting around in the harness. The B-17 then dropped back in a medium spiral and I did not see the pilots leave. I saw it just before it passed from view, several thousand feet below us, with its right wing a sheet of yellow flame.

After we had been under constant attack for a solid hour, it appeared certain that our Group was faced with annihilation. Seven of us had been shot down, the sky was still mottled with rising fighters, and it was only 1120 hours, with target-time still thirty-five minutes away. I doubt if a man in the Group visualized the possibility of our getting much further without one hundred percent loss. I know that I had long since mentally accepted the face of death, and that it was simply a question of the next second or the next minute. I learned firsthand that a man can resign himself to the certainty of death without becoming panicky. Our Group firepower was reduced thirty-three percent; ammunition was running low. Our tail guns had to be replenished from another station. Gunners were becoming exhausted.

One B-17 dropped out of formation and put its wheels down while the crew bailed out. Three Me-109s circled it closely, but held their fire, apparently ensuring that no one stayed in the ship to try for home.

Near the IP, at 1150 hours, one hour and a half after the first of at least 200 individual fighter attacks, the pressure eased off, although hostiles were still in the vicinity. We turned at the IP at 1154 hours with fourteen B-17s left in the Group, two of which were badly crippled. They dropped out soon after bombing the target and headed for Switzerland.

Weather over the target, as on the entire trip, was ideal. Flak was negligible. The group got its bombs away promptly on the leader. As we turned and headed for the

Alps, I got a grim satisfaction out of seeing a rectangular column of smoke rising straight up from the Me-109 shops.

... We were on our way toward the Mediterranean in a gradual descent. The prospect of ditching as we approached North Africa, short of fuel, and the sight of other B-17s falling into the drink, seemed trivial matters after the vicious nightmare of the long trip across southern Germany. We felt the reaction of men who had not expected to see another sunset.

When the Fortresses of the Regensburg mission braked to a halt at their North African airfields the Eighth had completed the cycle of its first year. It was just one year to the day since the first twelve B-17s flew fifty miles to France, bombed Rouen, and returned home.

In the course of that year the fledgling Eighth had dropped a total of 16,977 tons of bombs on enemy targets.

What was to come would overshadow almost completely the effect thus far achieved on the German war machine.

The bloodiest part of the war lay ahead.

Germany heard a clashing of arms all over the sky; the Alps trembled with uncommon earthquakes ... Never did lightnings fall in greater quantities from a serene sky, or dire thunders blaze so often.

VIRGIL—*GEORGICS*, BOOK ONE

# CHAPTER 25

# GRAVEYARD SKY

NOT UNTIL 6 SEPTEMBER," NOTES the official AAF history,[64] "did the Eighth again attempt a mission on the scale of the Regensburg-Schweinfurt operation. Meanwhile, it resumed the simpler task of bombing airdromes and airplane factories in France, Belgium and Holland. With friendly fighter escort for most of the time, the heavy bombers flew during this three-week period some 632 credit sorties at a loss rate of barely four percent. And frequently they were very effective, especially on 24 August when the bombing force followed up its successful attack of 14 July against the Focke-Wulf workshop at Villacoublay, and on 31 August and 3 September, when it severely damaged airdromes at Amiens and Romilly-sur-Seine."

On the 6th September the Eighth again gave it the big try. B-17 strength was up to almost seventeen groups. Three groups of Liberators that had served in Africa returned to the roster of the VIII Bomber Command. The crews had had opportunity to rest from the savage melees and critical losses attending their deep penetration into Germany. Now their commanders believed them ready once again to make the deep plunge into German territory. The target: Stuttgart.

The sky still belonged to the Luftwaffe—as was made clear before the day passed. Fighting through severe weather, a force of 262 bombers out of the 407 heavies dispatched managed to rip up targets in the area of Stuttgart. Out of the 262 planes that attacked, forty-five fell to the German defenses, for the most part fighters. Again nearly five hundred men were missing, wounded, or dead.

"As if to emphasize the importance of long-range escort," notes the AAF history, "the Eighth sent out, on the day following, a force to attack aircraft facilities in Belgium and Holland and the rocket site at Watten in France. Thanks to excellent fighter support, 185 planes bombed without a single loss—indeed, without experiencing a single encounter with enemy aircraft."

For the rest of September the heavy bombers were restricted to sweeps within the Low Countries and France. And, again, the effectiveness of fighter escort was apparent. On the 9th, 330 out of 377 bombers tore up more than ten airfields packed with German fighters. Two bombers were lost near Paris.

On the 15th, out of 398 planes airborne and 273 attacking, six were lost. The next day, 224 out of 295 heavies struck airfields and other targets. Fighters rose in large numbers to intercept the Fortresses, but the escorting Thunderbolts and Spitfires broke up the enemy attacks. Eleven bombers were lost to fighters and flak.

On the 2nd October 370 bombers went out, striking at targets in Germany and Holland. The escort fighters kept back most of the attacking German interceptors. Of the 339 bombers that struck their targets only two failed to return. On the 4th October the strike force was made up of 361 raiders, of which 282 penetrated well into Germany. Losses went up to sixteen planes.

That was the end of the reprieve. The Eighth had once more girded its strength and prepared to make the plunges deep into the enemy's homeland, against his most heavily defended targets.

On the 23rd, 364 bombers went after their targets. Three failed to return. Most of the bombers sent out on the 26th failed to reach their targets; of forty Fortresses striking at German airfields, all returned safely. On the 27th, 332 heavies left their English fields—seven were lost.

It was the end of the reprieve and the beginning of what became known as *the* critical week of the strategic air campaign against the Third Reich. In cold terms it was the roughest week of the entire war for the men of the VIII Bomber Command. It culminated on *Black Thursday*, the 14th of October 1943, with the most savage air battle of history. There were other battles that involved more men, strikes of greater range, missions of greater importance.

But this was the greatest air battle ever fought and it has gone down in history, as it should, for the unprecedented fury and the courage of the combatants, of both sides.

The "critical week" began on 8th October with 399 heavy bombers sent out against Bremen and Vagesack to strike at submarine building and airframe construction. A heavy force got through to their targets—357 raiders actually bombing. The Germans put up a "violent defense of fighters and flak," destroying thirty bombers, and severely damaging another twenty-six. Three out of every four planes in the 1st Bombardment Division took flak damage;

sixty percent of all bombers in the 3rd Division suffered flak damage.

The Eighth kept up the pressure. On the following day, 9th October, another 378 heavies went out, of which 352 got through to their objectives. The mission of the 9th was in many ways significant. It was the longest-ranging mission of the war to date; three task forces totaling 150 bombers flew to Gdynia-Danzig of the Polish corridor where they struck port facilities, naval units and submarine facilities. Another force of almost one hundred bombers sliced into East Prussia, more than two hundred miles *east* of Berlin, to slam the Focke-Wulf assembly plant at Marienburg. Another 106 bombers tore up the Arado aircraft factory at Anklam.

The bombing in the Polish corridor was considered a failure. Not so the other strikes where "bombing at all targets was of a high order." Official records show that at Anklam "the Arado factory, engaged in manufacturing components for the FW-190s, suffered damage to virtually all its buildings. . . . But it was at Marienburg that the most brilliant bombing was done. There the Focke-Wulf plant was almost completely destroyed by high-explosive and incendiary bombs dropped with unprecedented accuracy." General Ira C. Eaker hailed the Marienburg strike as "the classic example of precision bombing."

Losses for the day came to eight percent of the attacking force—twenty-eight heavies and their crews went down.

On the 10th October the Eighty made it three days in a row. A force of 274 bombers hit the main target, the key transportation junction of Munster, north of the Ruhr. A diversionary sweep of thirty-nine bombers was to draw off the attacking fighters. They didn't—and the Munster bombers took a severe beating from the enemy planes. Here the 100th Group gained its new title as the "Bloody

100th" when the group fell victim to a German fighter tac-
tic that "had been the secret dread of most bomber commanders, who had seen the German fighter command miss
the opportunity time after time."

They didn't miss their chance at Munster. Starting at
the IP, continuing to the target and on the way home until
fighter escort came to the rescue, German pilots assembled
in a mass of single-engine Me-109s and FW-190s, and
twin-engine Me-110, Me-210 and Ju-88 fighters. They flew
parallel to the bombers in groups of twenty to forty, beyond the defensive fire of the Fortresses. When they were
ready they peeled off, one at a time or in pairs, in swift
succession to carry out what amounted to a constant running attack, against the lowest elements of the formation.

"Their first victim," notes the AAF history, "was the
100th Bombardment Group which flew in the lead position.
Two minutes after the concentrated attack on this unit began, its formation was broken up, and in seven minutes the
entire group had been destroyed or dispersed. All twelve of
the 100th Group planes that saw action in the Munster battle were lost."

Losses for the day: thirty heavy bombers.

Colonel Budd J. Peaslee recounts:

From October 10th to 14th the Eighty licked its wounds
and rested the tired combat crews and groundmen. Nearly a
hundred four-engine bombers lost in three days of operations was more than the hardiest staff officer or theorist
general could stand. The men who flew the missions were
numb with fatigue and the mental strain of facing death in
one form or another—from hundreds of thousands of shrapnel fragments, cannon projectiles, bursting bombs, bullets,
fire, oxygen starvation, or a fall from five miles up to a
sudden and total destruction on the ground. This kind of

war had no foxholes or dugouts, no hedgerows or earth-
works, no place to hide, no place to run; it was a far different kind of conflict than man had before faced. It was so
new and unknown that the Eighth Air Force was forced to
operate on unproven theories and to set a limit on the capacity of the combat crews that, from the start, was almost
purely arbitrary. Twenty-five heavy bombardment missions
over Europe was one such limit set on the probable ability
of the average young crewman to last before mental
crackup. Some men could go less, some could go more, depending on their mental state and resistance to shock. In
the first three missions of the critical week nearly 9.5 percent of the attacking bombers were lost; thus giving a
crewman an even chance of survival for almost eleven missions. These odds were the cold uncompromising figures
confronting the crews. But youth rebounds and revitalizes
quickly. The rest between October 10th and 14th did wonders for the energy, morale, and will to fight of these young
American airmen. They were ready to go again.

The warning order on the eve of October 13th for Mission Number 115 . . . called for a "maximum effort" on October 14th, 1943.[65]


Mission 115 began in subdued fashion, invisible to the
outside world. At PINETREE, headquarters for the VIII
Bomber Command at High Wycombe, deep beneath thirty
feet of reinforced concrete, five officers sat around a large
table, meeting for the Daily Operations Conference. It was
here, after an exhaustive study of every aspect of recommended missions, that the decision was made for Mission
115.

On the wall before the five officers was a giant map of
Europe. The heartland of the enemy. Red lines laced the
map—the "blood highways of the air," as they were aptly

named—indicating the aerial pathways to and from targets in the Reich and the occupied nations. The "Old Man" completed his conference with his aides. The decision to attack or to keep the bombers on the ground was his and his alone.

General Anderson stared for a long moment into space. He thought at the moment not simply of statistics and tonnage and target evaluations. Human beings, flesh and blood and emotions, made those statistics move, changed the lines on the graphs. For the moment the silence held. How many men would be killed or lost *today?* How many were killed last week, and before that? The general's hand slapped lightly on the thick wooden table.

He looked up. "All right. Schweinfurt it is, then."

*"Schweinfurt it is, then. . . ."*

Those four words signaled a torrent of orders and movements. It began as a trickle, a Warning Order that flashed from VIII Bomber Command headquarters to the air divisions scattered throughout England. The Warning Order was the command to set into motion the vast and intricate machine of destruction that was the heavy bombardment force.

At one base a pilot bent over the teletype machines and read the printed sheet.

"Schweinfurt," he mumbled. He looked up at his fellows. "That's that goddamned killer town."

Shortly after midnight, the B-17 stations in England brooded in the dark. The weather was rotten, the scud sweeping by only three hundred feet overhead.

At Thurleigh, Colonel Peaslee, who was to lead the 1st Air Division into that battle, entered Wing Headquarters' operations office. Here the duty officer kept his ear glued to the red scrambler, the special telephone rigged for secret conversation. Peaslee watched the duty officer, who seemed to be engaged in a one-sided conversation; his only contributions were curt, a "Yes," or "No," or "Twenty-seven" or "Fifty-two."

Peaslee walked to the wall operations map, pulled back the curtain, and stared at the black yarn stretched from England to the target. "One look was enough," he recalls today with distaste.

The duty officer said "Over and out," dropped the red scrambler back on its hook, and looked up.

"Rough show," he commented flatly, "but with this soup outside they'll probably scrub it before takeoff."

"Maybe," the colonel replied, "but we've gone before when it was like this. Remember the morning we lost ten at the end of the runway?"

The duty officer didn't want to remember it, and neither did Peaslee, but it wasn't easy to forget. That particular morning ten bombers had piled up during takeoff. "They all had armed bombs in their bays," Peaslee recalled, "and there were a hundred men aboard. It was the same kind of morning, wet and lousy, and suddenly it was lit by a series of brilliant flashes. And then there was nothing."

One hundred men, and . . . *nothing.*


By the time Mission 115 had been committed in the darkness of night of mid-October, the Eighth Air Force had acquired the legends and the characteristics which would be remembered for decades to come. No force of men could face their trials without the cementing of bonds that transcended everyday relationships, for they knew with mathematical certainty they stood only a slim chance of surviving their assigned twenty-five missions.

In their barracks, this night, as on many others, the men

were restless. The writer has scoured the official records—many of them handwritten—to unearth the notes written by unsigned authors. One such man wrote: "The men lived the battles in their sleep, with considerable mental disturbances. The other night the men went into the barracks and found Captain Fenton flying an apparently tough mission. Apparently his ship was hit and he exclaimed: 'Copilot—feather number four!' *The lieutenant, sound asleep, answered him. Both of them, sound asleep, piloted the severely damaged Fort back home . . .*"

Notation from an official document: "At one time the lack of equipment for cleaning machine guns became so acute that the gunners, having cleaned parts of their weapons with soap and water, *took them tenderly into bed the night before a mission to prevent them from rusting.*"

The men knew that this was war, that some would be shot down and some would be killed. But the empty bed in barracks, the empty seat in the mess, the empty benches at the briefings—these were a constant reminder that cut deeply into the souls of men.

At one station a gunner missed a mission when the surgeon ordered him to stay on the ground for the day. *Every man in his barracks was lost that day on a mission over Germany.* For several days the bewildered and hapless man would run suddenly to the other barracks in the hope that he might recognize one of his friends. Finally he could not face the silence, the empty beds any longer. He was a seasoned and a brave man, but he broke. He fled the station and went AWOL. . . . [66]

What did the men who fought the Germans think of their adversaries? One gunner summed it up for the rest:

*"You gotta hand it to Jerry; he's a beautiful flier, and boy, has he got guts! . . ."*

During the height of the disastrous missions deep into the Reich, an American aircraft firm, following the policy that Americans are better than anybody else, sponsored what was probably the most ill-received advertisement of the war. The advertisement ran full page, and it showed a grinning gunner peering through the sights of a .50-caliber machine gun as he poured tracers into a swarm of Focke-Wulf fighters. Beneath the heroic painting was the caption: "Who's Afraid of the Big Bad Wulf?"

One pilot who saw the page immediately tore it from the magazine and pinned it to his group's bulletin board. Beneath the page was a long scroll with a big red-ink headline: "WE ARE!"

Every combat officer in the group signed below, and the group commander's name headed the list. They mailed it to the manufacturer with their blessings.

Sometimes it is possible to catch an intimate glimpse of the men who manned the Fortresses through the diaries of their medical officers. From a thick stack of files in the Air Force archives I extracted the diary of a medical officer of the 381st Group, a unit that had suffered severely during the "critical week" and was posted for Mission 115 to Schweinfurt. The diary opens slightly the door to the lives of these men. At times the vignettes are pointed—

"Sometimes you don't need combat," wrote the air surgeon. "On the ninth raid of the group, on 14 July 1943, a B-17 simply exploded en route to the target. The ship was over England when it tore to pieces in a blinding flash. Six men were killed instantly; the other four were blown into space, and were able to pull their ripcords."

On the 17th August, in the initial attack on Schweinfurt, the 381st Group sent out twenty-six of their big bombers. One aborted—and of the remaining twenty-five bombers, eleven were shot down.

"Morale was pretty low this evening on the return of the crews," recorded the flight surgeon, "particularly as soon as stories were compared, and total losses realized."

Two days afterward, on a raid to Holland—a "milk run"—one Fortress went down. "The loss of this latest ship seems to have a depressing effect on the combat crewmen, presumably because it was supposed to be an easy one. The line of reasoning, I presume, is to the effect that if losses can be sustained on the simple ones, what chance does anyone have?"

On the 8th October, on the mission to Bremen, seven out of twenty-one bombers were blown out of the sky. Of the fourteen that returned several were slashed to ribbons. There was this addition to the diary:

"B-17 *Tinkertoy* ground-looped just off the runway. *Tinkertoy* had her nose shot out and the pilot had his head blown off by a 20-mm cannon shell. There was hardly a square inch of the entire cockpit that was not covered with blood and brain tissue. One half of his face and a portion of his cervical vertebra were found just in front of the bomb bay. The decapitation was complete."

After the mission of the 8th October, only six days before Schweinfurt—

"After this mission, in visiting the many crews right after they hit the ground, the tense excitement of many crews was apparent and in many cases was border-line hysteria. This was the roughest mission experienced in some time and most of the personnel seemed to feel the losses keenly."

The diary refers to a bizarre incident: "Just as the formation was reaching the Danish coast, a 20-mm shell exploded in the cockpit of Lt. Winters' ship, and Lt. Winters was temporarily stunned or blinded by the flash. When he came to, the bombardier and navigator had already left the ship, the copilot was jumping, and one of the crew members gave him a farewell salute—and jumped. The ship was in a steep gliding turn and there was a fire in the rear of the cockpit. Lt. Winters righted the ship, put on the autopilot, went back and put out the fire, and brought the ship safely back to England. . . ."

*10 October 1943:* "The mental attitude and morale of the crews is the lowest that has yet been observed."

*Three days later:* "Captain———, a squadron leader and a brave man, informed the commanding officer that he had no desire to continue flying."

The next day was the 14th October: "Crews were briefed at 0700 hours and the target was the ball-bearing works at Schweinfurt, Germany. The mention of the word 'Schweinfurt, *shocked the crews completely* . . . [as] on 17 August this group lost so heavily on this same target. Also conspicuous by its omission was the estimated number of enemy fighters based along the route. Upon checking with the S-2 later, it was found that this omission was intentional and that the entire German fighter force of 1,100 fighter aircraft was based within eighty-five miles of the course. The implications are obvious.

"As I went around to the crews to check out equipment, sandwiches, coffee, etc., the crews were scared, and it was obvious that many doubted that they would return."

The bombers for Mission 115 took off into a world of cloying wetness. At most fields the visibility was barely two thousand feet. But that was enough. A mile or more above each field there was bright sunlight. At bomber airbases in England bright green flares hissed into the damp air. At the same instant, from the control towers far from the edge of the runways, answering green flares sputtered through the mist.

That was the signal. Mission 115 was ON.

On the morning of 14th October, Colonel Peaslee flew in the lead bomber of the 92nd Group. Peaslee would lead the raid this day. As commander he flew in the right seat—the copilot seat—of the lead bomber. For the purposes of flight the colonel was subordinate to the captain at the controls; indeed, when necessary, he took orders from the man of lesser military rank.

Let us turn back the years to that moment when the green flares hiss in the grayness of early morning in England.[67]

The throttles move forward, the engine roar becomes a bass scream that claws through the air. Peaslee glances at the pilot and nods. The brakes are released and the lead bomber begins to roll.

The Flying Fortress gathers speed like an enormous boulder accelerating down a steep mountainside. With each passing second of takeoff the propellers bite through an increasing volume of air, imparting lift to the wings. Faster and faster, recoiling with the shocks of the uneven runway surface.

The runway border lights stretch as far as the eye can see, but in the distance they fade into a fog-created limbo. As swiftly as the bomber gains speed new lights glow into being to replace those racing past the wings. The airspeed indicator needle creeps around the dial, pauses momentarily at fifty miles per hour. Far behind, the second bomber is already wheeling into position.

Peaslee stares out into the murk when McLaughlin's

voice comes crisp and clear over the intercom. "I'm going on instruments. Keep her on the runway and pick up the wheels when we're clear."

It's the captain talking to the colonel, but the voice is sharp and meaningful, and it is a direct order. McLaughlin is the aircraft commander, and the colonel is the copilot, and there is absolutely no doubt as to who issues orders, who commands the machine.

The B-17 creeps toward the left of the runway and with the barest touch on the right rudder Peaslee overpowers McLaughlin's foot on the pedal, and the bomber swings back where they belong. McLaughlin is taking no chances, he's making a move that reflects excellent judgment. Right from the runway he begins his instrument takeoff, adjusting his senses to instrument flight while he is still on the ground. From this moment on, while everything is under full control, he will fly the artificial horizon, the airspeed indicator, and the other flight instruments. He will have no reference whatsoever to the real earth. It is an excellent move because it *always* takes several seconds for any pilot to adjust to the transition from visual to instrument flight, and there are more dead pilots than the living want to remember who failed to snap quickly enough from visual conditions to the world of instruments at the end of the takeoff run. If the wing dips the bomber slides off on that wing, and the runway is all too close.

On this day 383 four-engine bombers are taking off in the haze and wetness of an English morning, and of the nearly four thousand men who are in those bombers, not one receives even a scratch because his pilot has failed so near the earth.

Not far ahead of the first of those 383 bombers the runway lights turn red, and Peaslee cannot help but feel a sudden stab of apprehension. Red means the end of the runway and a blinding explosion in seconds if the bomber does not raise itself, but even as the thought half-forms within his mind he sees the needle reach the figure of 88. This is what he calls his moment of eternity, and at that same instant eternity stays its comfortable distance away. The rough feeling of the runway vanishes. That is the only change that Peaslee feels, but after the thousands of hours a pilot accumulates it is the same as a warning bell clanging in his ears. The B-17 is off the ground. In one swift motion the colonel grasps the gear to bring up the wheels and tuck them away.

When he looks up again he sees nothing outside the airplane. The sky is heavy gray and except for the pounding of the engines, lessened because the ground no longer reflects the sound back into their ears, the heavy bomber is in limbo. Peaslee glances at the instruments, everything registers normal, the air speed is an even 100 and is still increasing. McLaughlin has made this takeoff, from this runway, many times before, and he is not greedy for altitude—not yet. He is just high enough to clear all the obstacles he cannot see but knows are there, and he holds the heavy bomber flat as he waits for speed.

At 120 miles per hour he has what he wants. The airspeed needle glues into place at 120, and two other instruments now become active. The altimeter still reads scant 300 feet but the rate of climb rises slightly above the zero point. Then there is 500 feet of air beneath the Fortress and without looking at the artificial horizon Peaslee senses the start of a turn. McLaughlin barely touches the yoke and his foot nudges the rudder pedal with infinite sensitivity, but the bomber responds.

The pointer of the radio compass starts a crawl around the face of the dial, edging toward zero. The airplane is turning under McLaughlin's sure hands for the splasher, the pulsating radio signal on which the bomber centers its initial flight.

As the lead Fortress cleared the edge of the airfield, the sound boomed out from the accelerating machine, rushed through the trees and thickets; the airplane climbed slowly, and the sound spread out, an invisible wash of shock waves heralding the birth of new flight. Even as the echo reverberates into the homes of the countryside, the second ship is on its way. The lead aircraft emits its trail of thin blue smoke, sign of engines under full power. Then the third, and the fourth, each one a juggernaut of thirty and more tons rushing into the blurred mist at the far end of the runway.

Each new takeoff seems to be more difficult. The lead bomber at least began its takeoff in undisturbed air. Now the air at ground level is charged with the slipstream and the wake turbulence of the Fortress that have plunged on through the leaden mists. The pilots fight the controls, muscles responding to the feel of pounding as the bombers rock on their wheels, accept the broadside slip of air, the uneven ocean into which they rush. The bouncing stops, there is the rumble of wheels coming up into their recesses, and then smoother flight.

In the lead bomber exhilaration sweeps over Peaslee. It is a sensation a flyer always feels after having completed a hazardous takeoff—successfully. The two men at the controls grin at one another in the dim light. Abruptly the interphone crackles with a sudden burst of chatter from the crew. They're calling to each other, wisecracking, snapping out jokes, and one man bellows happily in what is supposed to be singing.

The feeling passes quickly, for there is work to do; precise, careful, vital work. At 2,000 feet the outside gray begins to brighten. Operations forecast a cloud layer topping at 2,000 feet but the lead Fortress has climbed to 6,000 before Peaslee and McLaughlin can detect the overcast thinning above them. At 6,500 feet the bomber rushes through the last vestiges of cloud and breaks out into full daylight.

Suddenly they are flying above a vast unending ocean of white that stretches in every direction as far as their eyes can reach. The transition is strange and awesome, no matter how many times experienced. There is no sense of movement, no feeling of rushing through the air.

Peaslee turns cumbersomely in his seat and tries to look back through the side glass. The second bomber is five hundred yards behind, shedding wisps of clouds as it breaks through into clear air. . . . From Peaslee's ship bright signal flares rush into the air, a call for Fortresses far from the splasher to slide in, to join in V's, the triangular-shaped elements of bombers in the sky. . . .

Well before the time when the Fortress of Mission 115 entered enemy territory, the powerful air armada had suffered a serious depletion of its numbers. The sixty B-24s intended to carry out a diversionary strike formed with less than half their intended number. Wisely, the commander of the twenty-nine Liberators airborne refuses to commit his weakened force to the wolves awaiting him in German air. The sixty four-engined Liberators assigned to Mission 115 are cut immediately from the strike.

Several of the Fortresses have also aborted. Because of rough engines, runaway superchargers, tachometer oscillation, leaking oxygen regulators, sluggish superchargers, generator malfunctions, weak brakes, insufficient oxygen supply, engine oil leaks, engine instrument failures, oil cooler failures, creeping flaps, cracked exhaust stacks, cracked air ducts, flat tail wheels, propeller governor failures, overboosted engines, leaking fuel tanks, inoperative fuel pumps, and plain rotten weather, thirty-three Fortresses dropped out of the mission.

Of the original force of 383 heavy bombers, the remainder—291—breached the defense line in the sky. That number soon would be depleted even more.

Thunderbolts escorted the Fortresses to the maximum reach of the fighters' range. To its limit the escort proved to be extraordinarily effective. Wherever they sighted German fighters, the American pilots rushed in to attack, giving no quarter, accepting whatever odds might be encountered. In the brief, swirling melees, one Thunderbolt went down—at a cost of thirteen German fighter planes. But then the big American fighters reached their point of no return. It was either leave the bombers—or be guaranteed a crash landing in the English Channel. With a sad parting of hand waves or rocking of wings the Thunderbolts turned for home.

The Germans struck. It was that quick. No sooner did the American escorts swing into their turns to leave than the Messerschmitts and Focke-Wulfs and Junkers and Dorniers and Heinkels plunge to the attack. The last sight the Thunderbolt pilots had of the Fortresses was two great bombers spinning earthward in flames.

The B-17s thundered into Germany in precise formation, stacked into defensive positions. Each combat box—a staggering of three squadrons—was so positioned that the formation had the maximum mutual protective fire of the bombers' guns. From top to bottom a combat box extended 750 feet. It was an intricate living thing, squadrons fitted into groups, the groups into wings, the wings into air divisions. The vertical wedge of a combat wing stretched 3,000 feet from top to bottom and it was made up of three separate combat boxes with the lead combat box in the center, flanked by one higher and the other lower. No matter how a fighter came in to attack, the airplane had to pass before the crisscrossing fire of the defending guns.

"A long time ago I should have known Chicago like a book. But when I walked around to find an address, I had to ask a dozen people where the hell I was going.

"Now we're moving directly to an address in a city none of us have probably ever seen before. You don't ask anybody down there about it, and you're coming in without knocking on the door. Instead, you're going to blow it in, with the walls and everything else.

"The pilot makes a routine check of positions. . . . Like everyone else, you glance at your oxygen indicator, and in turn add your 'okay' to the comments passing back through the bomber.

"From this high, Germany is beautiful. Greens and browns. Peaceful and serene. You think about it, when suddenly someone cries: 'Fighters at eleven o'clock!'

"The whole airplane begins to shudder and shake through its length. Tracers spill through the air like crimson fireballs, arcing lazily, hiding the hidden four bullets between each flashing blur. You kick out some short bursts, leading a black-nosed shape swinging in fast from the three-quarter stern position. They're Focke-Wulfs; one screams in from above, a beautiful swing through the air, and just as his wings and nose blink brilliantly, you squeeze and hold down for a long burst. The guns shake and shudder, hammering sounds, the wind tearing in at you . . . and goddammit, but your bullets smash into the cockpit! She whips over crazily, starting a cartwheel, and your bullets keep at him until suddenly flame appears, the stress of the wild tumble tears a wing off and the fighter disappears in a flash.

"Then, suddenly the Fortress shudders, a quiet groan, but louder than the motors and the calls on the interphone and the hammering guns. A groan, and magically, a jagged tear appears in the left wing. And you're scared; oh, God, how you're scared. . . ."

DIARY OF A B-17 GUNNER, 384TH BOMB
GROUP, MISSION 115

" 'Bogies at six o'clock climbing.'

"Those were the first warning words McLaughlin and I heard of the German fighters closing in.

" 'Bogies!' It was the tail gunner, calling again. 'Many, all climbing on our tail. My God, I count sixty of them, some twin engine!'

"The interphone exploded in bedlam. Everyone in the crew was seeing German fighters—they were coming in from all directions, from all points of the compass, from high and from low. Everyone was trying to report at the same time. This was the moment when the initial flush of the combat about to detonate swept the men in their excitement, when the words babbled from their lips, and they shouted freely of the approaching fighters.

"The moment there was a lull in the shouting and I could make myself heard, I cursed the crew, I cursed them emphatically and with every choice bit of profanity I could jam into several seconds, for their breach of discipline. I gave them hell and admonished them to keep calm, to break their silence only when necessary. Efficiency and discipline in a Fortress are indispensable to survival.

"Let me tell this as it happened, as it was happening; it's easier to turn back the clock that way. . . .

"There are enemy fighters on both flanks and at the rear now—how many I don't know, but many. So far they have made no hostile move. We sit in dread, for we know there will be unlucky ones among us when they start their play. I happen to be looking dead ahead when the first break comes. Suddenly out in front appear flashes resembling continuous photography multiplied a hundred times. I recognize it instantly—I have seen it before. Just as quickly I make out the approaching silhouette of the fighters—and flashes are coming from their 20-mm cannon.

"The opening play is a line plunge through center. The fighters whip through our formation, for our closing rate exceeds five hundred miles per hour. Another group of flashes replaces the first, and this is repeated five times as six formations of Messerschmitt Me-109s charge us. As each group of flashes appears our nose guns break into sound and the vibration shakes the bomber. The tail guns join in occasionally as the gunner takes a quick shot at the fading targets.

"The shock of the first attack is over, and I start to get scared. How the planes ever miss collision is a mystery. It depends on the enemy fighters alone, for we are unable to dodge. That is probably our salvation. If we were able to, we might possibly dodge into their paths, and the results would be sensational. There are few things more spectacular than a head-on collision of bomber and fighter.

"As soon as I get a grip on myself again, I strain to find out what has happened to our formation. It seems a miracle. As far as I can see, all are in position. I call the tail gunner. He reports the aircraft to the rear still in position, but two are smoking—one badly—and another appears to be drifting back. More damage than that has been done, I know—inside our bombers there are dead and dying. The gunner adds one bit of cheerful news—a trail of smoke far to the rear arcs away toward the ground. It is not much to be cheerful about . . . the sky is absolutely filled with German planes.

"I yell into the throat mike—I curse the long machine-gun bursts. I condemn the crew for wasting ammunition. We have hundreds of miles to go yet—if we are among the lucky. Even as I yell, my earphones become bedlam once more.

" 'Here they come! Fighters attacking! Fighters at nine o'clock high! Fighters at four o'clock low! Fighters at six o'clock!'

"I try to look simultaneously in all directions. I can see the fighters on my side. They've half-turned and are diving toward us in a continuous string, their paths marked in the bright sunlight by fine lines of light-colored smoke as they fire short bursts. It is a coordinated attack, the finest I have ever seen. Their timing is perfect, their technique masterly.

" 'B-17 going down in flames,' the tail gunner reports. 'No parachutes. We have two aircraft lagging badly—back about three hundred yards.'

"The damage is beginning to show. The tail gunner continues: 'Form ations of twin engines approaching seven o'clock high. They're back about six hundred yards. My God, they've fired rockets!'

"I look back, my face against the ice-cold side window, and barely see them as they dive away in a turn. When I face front again several great black blobs of smoke appear, and we fly through the smoke almost instantly. There is a slight jar. That was close. Fleetingly I wonder how those rockets were able to strain through our formation without hitting anyone. The whole procedure is repeated a few seconds later, and this time I see it all—the bursts are only fifty feet off our left wing. They are big—about four times as big as ordinary flak, with angry, shapeless blobs of dirty red flame in the centers. I hear them over the roar of the motors, and they sound like someone throwing a handful of heavy stones against a tin roof—*hard!*

"Now we have fighters above us, below us, and to our flanks, all attacking or climbing back into position to attack again. Their coordination, however, is gone. Momentarily I am aware of our own guns. The bursts have become short, but the sound is almost continuous as it bounces at me from the various gun positions. Our gunners are finally aiming, not using their guns like garden hoses.

"As the rocket attacks go on, the action around us continues at such a pace that I see only fragments of it from the corners of my eyes. I try to look everywhere at once to absorb reports from the gunners. For the most part they have fallen silent. There is little use in reporting fighters that are everywhere. There is no way of counting them.

"I feel McLaughlin's hand on my arm. It's a hard grip and I see he is looking down and ahead. I lean over, craning my neck, following his eyes. A few hundred feet in front of us a bomber has been hit by a rocket. I catch sight of it just as the right wing starts to fold upward. The fuselage opens like an eggshell, and a man dressed in a flying suit spins clear out in front. I see the pilot still at the controls, then the plane is swept with flame. The right wing breaks free, and with the two engines still spinning it drifts to the rear, flaming at the ragged end. The shattered mess disappears under our left wing, and the sky is clean again. It all happens instantaneously, but to me it is like a slow-motion movie scene.

"As I look around again I notice our right-wing man, my deputy formation commander, is out of position. He has drifted back a few feet but I can still see him in the cockpit. I call him on our wing channel. There is no reply. I know he is not out of position voluntarily, and I have a premonition that he is not going to be with us long. Our formation has become ragged. Many gaps are left by missing bombers, and our gunfire suffers.

"Captain McLaughlin glances at me. In spite of his concentration on keeping our formation in position, little has escaped him.

" 'Colonel, I don't think we're going to make it.'

"His words are incredibly calm; a matter-of-fact statement. They are nonetheless grim and biting. I agree, of course, but I refuse to commit my thoughts to words, and as our eyes meet above the oxygen masks, I just nod.

"I get a report from my tail gunner. One of our aircraft has pulled out of formation and is turning back. I take a look. I know that if the pilot is trying to reach England he is condemned. Fighters will pick off his aircraft like a sitting duck. There will be a patrol out looking for such as he. I cannot guess the reason for his action, since the plane appears to be in good shape, but he may have a ruptured fuel tank, or wounded aboard who could not survive the full mission. Or he may have become mentally unbalanced by this fight. Whatever it is, he is lost.

"My deputy has drifted farther back, now he has lost the protection of our massed guns. The fighters jump him, but he plugs ahead by himself—he is trying to make the bomb-release line, if no more. That is pure guts.

"Another bomber leaves us. He is smoking and his wheels are starting down, a signal that he is going to land.

" 'My God, please take some evasive action!' someone in the crew begs over the interphone. Yet he knows as well as I do that evasive action in formation is futile—less than futile. 'Jinking' is all we can possibly do—moving suddenly a few feet up or down. Even that serves only to disturb the aim of our gunners, and we are just as apt to jink into a burst as to avoid it. Its only accomplishment is to give some mental relief to the crew. The men feel we are at least doing *something.*

"I suppose this feeling of being caught in a hopeless situation is far from new. Men must have always experienced it. I think of the Middle Ages. I see myself strolling across an open plain with a group of friends. Suddenly we are beset by many scoundrels on horseback. They come from every direction, shooting their arrows. We defend ourselves as best we can with slings and swords, and crouch behind our leather shields. We cannot run, we cannot dodge, we cannot hide—the plain has no growth, no rocks, no holes. And it seems endless. There is no way out—then, or now.

"I have been studying the tactics of the rocket attackers. They make the same approach each time and fire from the same range. I can tell within a few seconds when they are going to fire. I decide maybe there is something that can be done—that I can contribute a little to this fight. There is nothing so useless as being an air commander in an air battle. You just sit there and watch what goes on, for command is lost in the fog of battle and all depends on the training of your crews.

"We will try an experiment. I talk to McLaughlin. As the next rocket formation approaches the firing point, we will start a shallow turn to the right—almost a drift. It will give the enemy an increased deflection shot and will not disturb the formation. As soon as the rockets have been launched we will slide back to our former position.

"I see the rocket planes coming into position. Now! I give the signal. The maneuver works—or maybe it's just luck, or just poor shooting. Anyway, the bursts are to our left. We continue the practice. The bursts still miss.

"We are approaching the Initial Point, the point at which we commit ourselves directly to the bomb run on the target. Schweinfurt, here we come! As we turn, I take a hasty reading on our formation. I have eight aircraft left and my other group has been reduced to six. Fourteen planes left, and we still have so many miles to go! I call the captain leading the other bombers and tell him to close in on me and to drop on my command, 'Bombs Away.' He does not respond, but his formation moves in near to ours as we start the sighting run. The fighters know what our intentions are and they come at us like tigers. . . ."

INTERVIEW BETWEEN THE WRITER AND
COLONEL BUDD J. PEASLEE, 1959

"When a cannon shell smashes into a Fortress, the way it sounds depends upon where you are. If you're not too close, it's a kind of metallic *whoof!* like a small bark from a big dog—and you feel a jar that shakes the whole ship. It is a tremor, it reaches and leaves you quickly. But if the shell explodes nearby, then there is nothing gentle or distant about what happens, and it sure as hell isn't a momentary tremor.

"It sounds like some giant smashing his cupped hand down on the surface of still water. A double sound, really—the first from the impact and the sound when the shell explodes. CRAA-AASH! Like that. Like firing a shotgun into a bucket, so that the sound and the blast all come exploding back up into your face, shaking you up and stunning your mind. For the moment you're not scared, because your senses are knocked silly, and you don't know how to be scared or anything else. Your bowels seem weak and watery and your stomach shrivels up until you know how much damage has been done.

"And this happens all the time through the fight; *all* the time, if they pick your airplane and they find the range . . ."

COMMENTS OF A B-17 PILOT,
MISSION 115

The gunner was not injured by a broadside of exploding cannon shell, but his best friend, a buddy of many years, suffered a tremendous blast in the face. He fell to the belly of the bomber, writhing, hands clasping a bloody, mangled mess that a moment before had been a normal face. The other gunner, hurrying to his aid, slipped, and fell nearby. He glanced down, and in horror noted the crushed eyeball that had been gouged by the explosion from his friend.

The flight surgeon marked the unharmed gunner as unfit for duty for several weeks to come. . . .

*. . . The men in accompanying bombers watch, helpless to assist, as a tongue of flame licks hungrily from a tear in a wing, feeds on fuel streaming backward, gathers strength, and throws itself through the rest of the airplane.*

"These are the sights that tried our souls the most," a pilot explained. "To watch from your own bomber as a sister ship flames and begins to fall off in her death throes. You know what's going on in that plane and the men are your friends and buddies, and maybe you know the pilot's wife well, and know the kids, too.

"It involves more than the men. You don't fly a Fortress for months and years without coming to know that gallant lady in the most intimate respects. You know her, and you place in her sturdy construction, the manner in which she flies, in everything about her, not only your life, and those of your crew, but all the life to come—if we survive this stinking war, that is.

"But one more thing I'll tell you. A Queen dies hard. She doesn't want to go, no more than any man inside her. You may not believe this. If you don't, it's only because you haven't been up there, and you haven't watched combat-hardened men cry as a ship goes down; cry as much for the machine as for the men. Because, you see, when ten men claimed her for their own, she was no longer just a machine. She was *their* bomber. That made her special, and made her come alive."

B-17 PILOT, POST-MISSION
BRIEFING, MISSION 115

"It is past time now for the fighters to leave us, but they do not. They stay with us, fighting in their own flak. This is very strange. Their orders must have been to defend Schweinfurt at all costs.

"I have never seen braver men than these fighter pilots, our mortal enemies. If I were the German in command of men and machines like these, I believe I could stop the daylight bombing of Germany—at least up to this point. But Hermann Goering is their commander, and he has chosen to violate a simple principle of war. He should have ordered total annihilation of the first formation of each attack force. Our commanders live in fear that he may one day do so. Today he has come the nearest to achieving that principle, for his guns allow only a few of our leading aircraft to escape. But he does not know—and at the moment neither do I—that soon the Mustangs will come, the fighters that can cover us anywhere in Germany. Thank God for Hermann—he is our friend.

"The determination to keep us from reaching the target

has been futile, but they have made us pay a terrible price, a price that we cannot afford to pay. The stakes in this game have been terrific for both sides, and the devil took the pot. Below us Schweinfurt is rapidly going to hell as the bomb strings ahead of ours walk through the city. Its dead will outnumber our own by fantastic figures, and the machinery that has made the ball bearings is literally beginning to fly apart.

"The bomb run is good in spite of the fighters and the flak—the kind we refer to as 'flak you can walk on.' It seems as though our aircraft will never reach the bomb-release line—the seconds drag by. Finally, just as we are thinking the bombs must be hung, we feel the bomber lighten in regular little jerks and we know the halfway point has been passed.

" 'Bombs away,' the bombardier reports.

"McLaughlin releases the controls from the bomb sight, and we swing into a right turn toward France. It's a slow turn for reassembly, but there is little need to reassemble. Those left of us are already huddling close.

" '*Primary bombed.*' The strike message flashes back to England. It is a simple statement, nothing more.

"As our right wing dips in the turn, it reveals our approach route, both on the ground and in the air. At our level I can see the rear formations approaching Schweinfurt. They look ragged and are under intense attack. The fighters have left the empty planes for the time being to charge those still carrying bombs toward the city. Our formations do not waver as they crawl across the sky. It is as though they were being pulled by an invisible chain into the thresher of flak over the city, and there they will disgorge their heads of grain, the thousand-pounders.

"Far below them on the ground I see part of our ante to the devil's pot. Our course is plainly marked by rising columns of smoke. I know what those columns mean and I count them—nine, ten, eleven. They represent eleven bombers, with 110 men aboard, punctuating the line from the Initial Point to the target.

"Behind our dipped right wing I can see the city, and it is smudged with smoke in the sunlight. As I watch, and as more bombs splash down, the smudge is renewed and thickened. From now until long after the war is over there will be no windows in this city, and the cold winter winds will sweep unchecked through the homes—all the homes, rich and poor alike, for there will be no window glass at any price.

"We are pulling away from the target toward the French border when there is an unexplainable occurrence. One of our bombers climbs out of formation. He does not appear to be damaged and has plenty of power left in his engines. There are no fighters near us at the moment, and I wonder what his object can be. I broadcast an order for him to return to formation, but there is no acknowledgment. Then parachutes begin to blossom behind and below him. They come at regular intervals until there are ten—the full crew.

"What in hell is this? I will never know. The bomber continues momentarily to fly beside us, then slowly noses over and, gaining speed, disappears below. I cannot fathom it. Did the crew hold a caucus—decide there was no future in this business, decide to quit the war? I wonder.

" 'Well,' McLaughlin tells me over the interphone, 'we have done our flying for Uncle Sam for the day. Now we fly for *us.*' "

INTERVIEW BETWEEN THE WRITER AND
COLONEL BUDD J. PEASLEE, 1959

The total force of bombers that penetrated German airspace for Mission 115 came to 257 Flying Fortresses.

Before the target was reached, German fighters and flak cut twenty-eight bombers from the formations.

During the return flight from Schweinfurt, another thirty-one Fortresses went down.

One battle-ripped Fortress ditched in the English Channel.

Five Fortresses that returned to England were unable to land because of battle damage or fields closed by fog. The crews of three B-17s bailed out; the other two bombers crashed.

That made sixty-five B-17s lost.

Another seventeen Fortresses suffered Category E battle damage—beyond economical repair, they never flew again.

Of the 257 Fortresses that penetrated German airspace—eighty-two were stricken from the aircraft roster of VIII Bomber Command.

Five hundred and ninety-four men are "missing" over Europe. In the bombers that return are five dead men. Ten others are so critically wounded that survival is questionable. Another thirty-three suffer wounds of varying severity.

## EPILOGUE

Sixteen Fortresses took off from Chelveston Airdrome, home of the 305th Group. One aborted, returning early with mechanical difficulties. Fifteen Fortresses went on.

Two bombers returned on schedule to land at Chelveston. Where are the others? Have they landed elsewhere? Where are they?

*There are no others.* Of the fifteen Fortresses that flew

to Germany, twelve fell in flames before the crews ever saw Schweinfurt. Another made its bombing run and was then ripped apart by a rocket salvo.

The 305th Group is virtually wiped out. One hundred and thirty men! The men in thirteen ground crews stare at each other in stunned disbelief. It cannot be; *it just cannot be.*

But it is. Thirteen crews, 130 men. Men for whom they have worked, waved good-bye to, shouted greetings to on their landings.

The concrete, stained with oil and grease where the big bombers have stood, is empty, a terrible, aching void. The ground crewmen scuff their feet aimlessly, walk off. Every man looks as if he has lost his brother.

Mission 115 is over.

# CHAPTER 26

# ASSAULT

The fact was that the Eighth Air Force had for the time being lost air superiority over Germany. And it was obvious that superiority could not be regained until sufficient long-range escort became available. Fighter escort was clearly the answer to the German counterattack, especially to the rocket-firing fighters which, lacking somewhat in mobility, were peculiarly vulnerable to attacks by other fighters. . . . The Eighth Air Force made no more deep penetrations in clear weather into Germany for the rest of the year. That failure was, prior to December, the result of a command decision based on the lack of escort and the need for recuperating the bomber force after its losses on 14 October. After the early part of December the decision was forced by weather, although the Eighth still lacked long-range escort sufficient to make deep penetrations anything but costly affairs, justifiable only on grounds of decisive results. Weather has been bad for visual bombing during the last two weeks of October and it did not improve greatly during November, although the Eighth found it possible to run a number of missions to targets in occupied territory and to conduct a few blind-bombing operations over Germany.... Attack on such distant centers as Leipzig, Oschersleben, Gotha, Halberstadt, Bernberg, Schkopau, and Stuttgart was being planned during November as a coordinated attack by the Eighth and the newly established Fifteenth Air Force in Italy. And the operation was initially scheduled for a date early in December. It so happened that a long enough stretch of fine weather and one prevailing over a wide enough area to permit accurate bombing by such a coordinated force did not occur until late in February 1944."

OFFICIAL APPRAISAL OF THE COMBINED
BOMBER OFFENSIVE AFTER THE MISSION
OF 14TH OCTOBER 1943[68]

THE INVASION OF EUROPE was set for the period of May/June 1944. The initial problem of that invasion—OVERLORD—was stated simply. The AAF historical studies summed it up:

Before that operation could safely be attempted the Allied strategic air forces would have to gain air superiority over western Europe. That meant substantially defeating the fighter force upon which the enemy depended for the protection of the homeland and upon which he had lavished—belatedly—the best of his intellectual and material resources. Now in the fall of the year, with OVERLORD scheduled for the following May, it was a matter of the utmost concern to Allied planners to determine the exact status of the strategic air war.

\* \* \*

Thus began what might be termed the first steps in the final phase of the air bombardment of Germany. As the Eighth regained strength and built up its once-battered heavy bomber units, official attitudes changed. Appraisal had brought reappraisal, and the air reduction of the German Air Force and its industry from England was brought into new focus. It was not enough. Out of the organization that already existed came the United States Strategic Air Forces, capable of heavy aerial bombardment from the Eighth in England down to the Fifteenth in Italy. Massive air attacks carried out across the length and breadth of the Reich—and carried out in simultaneous strikes—would be part of the answer to the bristling German defenses. No longer would bad weather in England bring a complete halt to bomber operations: the bombers would fly from Italy. If the Fifteenth were grounded and the skies clear over England, the Eighth would strike. Whenever weather permitted, the Royal Air Force would continue its massive pounding of German cities and industry. In late July 1943 the RAF devastated the city of Hamburg. In three tremendous attacks, capped off with a "lightweight" night raid and a daylight strike by B-17s, the British set several firestorms in the hapless city. They were the first known in history—on one night, a single fire covered an area greater than six square miles, sucked in air from surrounding countryside at inward speeds of 150 miles per hour. Fifteen hundred yards from the edge of the fire, temperature reached 1,278° F! while flames rose three miles above the city. When the destruction of Hamburg—Operation Gomorrah—ended, more than 120,000 people had been burned or blasted to death, and the great industrial port was an ash-heaped slag-pile.

But despite the damage inflicted on the German war

machine by precision bombing, how quickly were results being achieved in respect to the "strategic timetable"?

"It was not enough," states a secret study of the bombardment effort, "to determine how much damage had been inflicted in relation to the effort expended. The important thing was to determine how near the operation was to achieving its assigned objective within the time allotted. . . ." The invasion of Europe had been set tentatively for 1st May 1944. The invasion could not be carried out—at least not without disastrous losses—so long as the German Air Force could mass in full strength over the invasion areas. The question then was how long that invasion might be delayed before the Allied air forces could destroy German fighting strength in the air.

The chances for success within the time specified appeared slim. The British went so far as to state flatly that the programed timetable for the destruction of German airpower was a full three months behind schedule.

Meanwhile, the Eighth worked day and night to acquire the long-range escort fighters needed so desperately. On the 15th October, just one day after the debacle of Schweinfurt, the first groups of P-38 fighters went on operational service. It would take time to build up this strength, to acquire not only more P-38s and P-47s, but especially to build up the strength of P-51s, the single-engine fighters that could best anything flown by the Luftwaffe and carry the battle to any part of Germany from their English bases.

And there was the need for many hundreds of Fortresses and Liberators. In the United States production was still rising. From the giant new factories, still far from their peak, came an increasing flow of the four-engined heavies, and as fast as the bombers went through their flight tests they were rushed to their new bases in England

and in Italy. Many of the Liberators went to the Pacific. Europe had first priority for the Flying Fortress.

But an airplane superior even to the B-17F was already in the air—and performing far beyond the intentions of its designers. The new airplane would be designated the B-17G.

In July of 1943, scheduling carefully so as not to interfere with the day-and-night production of the Fortress, Boeing introduced the B-17G onto its production lines. By now the numbers of airplanes being manufactured had reached epic proportions. A total of 8,680 B-17G models would be built on the combined production lines of Boeing, Douglas and Vega. The number becomes more meaningful when we see that twice as many B-17G variants were manufactured *as all other B-17 models combined.*

The B-17G was the answer to the insistent clamor for improved firepower against the lethal head-on attacks of German fighters. When Boeing produced its YB-40 "gunship," one solution to this problem had been the installation of a chin turret—a power turret mounted beneath the nose, sighted and fired remotely by a gunner in the nose position. This gave the Fortress a brace of two heavy machine guns which, being power operated, could be aimed through a wide arc of fire, and into the wind which formerly had made firing forward extremely difficult. The Bendix power turret had proved so effective in encounters between the YB-40 and German fighters that the system was approved for the B-17G. Another armament change was in the waist positions which, in the G model, were for the first time enclosed permanently. The guns were mounted within a plexiglas window, providing protection for the gunners against the icy winds of high-altitude flying. (The demand was so great for the chin turret that a batch of turrets were shipped to England and Italy, where they were fitted to B-17F models that were used in lead positions.)

The B-17G, which began to arrive in Europe late in 1943, carried the same armament—thirteen heavy machine guns—as the B-17F, but with far more efficient firepower than its predecessor. The chin turret carried 365 rounds of ammunition, and the "cheek" guns in the nose were supplied with an additional 610 rounds for both weapons. In the B-17F the waist guns were provided with 300 rounds per gun; the B-17G models doubled this ordnance to 600 rounds per waist gun. As changes were made in the B-17G design, starting with the B-17G-90-BO (and the B-17G-50-DL and B-17G-55-VE), the tail position underwent a major modification. A "Cheyenne" tail gun mount provided the airplane with an improved field of fire as well as greater accuracy; a reflector gunsight replaced the earlier ring-and-bead sighting. Total ordnance for defensive B-17G firepower came to 5,770 rounds of ammunition.

There were many other "invisible" modifications and improvements in the B-17G series. The bomb control system, "electric and manual" in the B-17F was changed to an all-electric system for the G. Instead of oil-regulated controls for the turbosuperchargers as in the F, the G model featured electronic controls. The new waist windows were not only fixed but their positions were staggered to provide the gunners with greater freedom of movement. Extensive changes were made in instruments and gauges. The new B-22 turbosupercharger through greater speed raised the service ceiling of the fully loaded G model to 35,000 feet. The entrance to the tail gunner's compartment, covered in the B-17F by a canvas sheet and therefore subject to "ventilation," was modified in the G variant by a complete metal enclosure. Among the other modifications was a change dear to all combat pilots—the engine oil tanks were equipped with standpipes holding an emergency oil supply. If an engine-propeller system was shot out and its oil supply lost, lack of propeller control and wind-milling often resulted. The standpipe supply in the B-17G enabled pilots to feather the propeller blades knife-edge into the wind, to reduce drag, even with the normal oil supply depleted.

Because of equipment modifications, as we have stated before, it is not possible to establish a fixed standard of performance. Performance data established by manufacturer and AAF flight tests describe the "standard B-17G aircraft," as an airplane with an empty weight of 32,720 pounds, an equipped weight of 38,000 pounds, a normal loaded weight of 55,000 pounds, and a maximum overloaded weight of 72,000 pounds.

Under maximum weight for combat conditions the B-17G had a maximum speed of 300 miles per hour at 30,000 feet. More important in evaluating the aircraft capabilities was the maximum continuous speed. Improved engines and paddle-bladed propellers gave the B-17G a "maximum continuous speed of 263 miles per hour at 25,000 feet." It should be noted that on combat missions, especially those in formation and for long range, the cruising speed was less than 200 miles per hour. Fully loaded, the B-17G had an initial rate of climb of 900 feet per minute. With a 4,000-pound bomb load the G could range 1,850 miles in 8.7 hours—this was with a weight of 63,500 pounds flown at 25,000 feet. For this range mission with the two-ton bomb load the fuel totaled 2,810 gallons.

Production of the Fortress would not reach its peak until July of 1944 when the combined industrial team produced a record number of 578 B-17G models in one month. After that, production began its slide downward—

the AAF wanted Boeing to concentrate (with other companies in another industrial team) on the new giant, the B-29 Superfortress.

The AAF reached its peak inventory of Fortresses in August of 1944, when its records showed 4,574 of the bombers "on status."

The bombers could do the job. No one in target planning denied that. But if they were to carry out their missions without crippling losses, fighter escort was essential.

Seven groups of P-47s were operational by mid-October 1943, but their radius of action—only 340 miles—hampered their effectiveness. Certainly they could not carry out deep-penetration escort. On the 15th October the 55th Fighter Group (P-38s) went operational with the VIII Fighter Command—extending escort to 520 miles from the bases in England. On the 3rd November, during a mission to Wilhelmshaven, P-38s "proved especially valuable during the farthest leg of the journey and made the escort virtually continuous throughout the bomber route." The big Lightnings shot down three German fighters without loss to themselves. In fact, they "could probably have destroyed more but remained, according to the strict orders then governing their tactics, in close support of the bombers, warding off attacks and refusing to be drawn off in independent combat."

On the 13th November P-38s and P-47s accompanied the bombers on a mission to Bremen. With their fuel dangerously low the P-47s turned for home, leaving the P-38s alone. Only forty-seven of the twin-engined fighters remained to shepherd the bombers. German fighters, outnumbering the P-38s five to one, tore into the hard-pressed American escorts. In the ensuing melee the P-38s were badly mauled. Surprisingly only two were known to have been shot down although, for causes unknown, five more failed to return to their bases. One P-38 flew back from Bremen with one engine dead and the propeller feathered; the fighter had been hit by more than one hundred bullets and five cannon shells, yet managed to fly all the way to England. Although they shot down few German fighters the P-38s carried out their mission, "holding bomber losses in the target area to a supportable level; and it could reasonably be hoped that a larger force could do the job still more effectively and with relatively less cost to the escort itself."

The AAF history notes that the "P-38 was clearly a most effective fighter, and the Germans honored it with an increasing share of attention. But it was also the easiest of the Allied fighters for the enemy to identify and therefore attack. It was becoming evident that the P-51 could be developed into a more maneuverable fighter and, even more important, into one of longer range. . . . For the rest of the year the P-51 remained linked in American air plans with the P-38 as essential to the long-range escort problem."

By early December the P-51s of the 354th Group escorted bombers to Paris. On the 13th December the Mustangs were part of a fighter escort for a massive bomber attack against Kiel—710 heavy bombers took off to attack the German city in the greatest force dispatched by Eighth Bomber Command up to that time. P-38s joined the P-51s in the escort mission. But to the frustration of the fighter pilots, German interception "proved exceptionally weak."

On 20th December, however, the Luftwaffe rose in strength. The bombers were protected during the trip to Bremen by only forty-four P-51s and thirty-five P-38s. Despite their lesser number the American escorts again and again broke up the attempts of the German fighters to salvo their rockets into the bomber formations. The P-51s, concentrating on bomber protection rather than dogfights, shot down three German fighters while losing three of their own number.

From this point on the P-51s would be rushed into operations with the Eighth Air Force. They would extend their range to more than 800 miles from England—fanning out to cover every part of Germany and beyond. Eventually the strategic fighter escort would be exclusively the job of the P-51, superior for this mission because of speed, range, and maneuverability. The P-38s and P-47s would go to the Ninth Air Force, where they were superior to the P-51 for fighter-bomber and ground-support sweeps.

Even in their initial missions the escort fighters were proving their worth. The statistics tell the story, but nothing tells it better than the words of the gunners who had been through the savage air fighting of October. On the mission of 3rd November to Bremen, when 539 bombers attacked the city, four were shot down by flak—and an astonishingly low number of only three bombers by German fighters. The sky was overcast that day and the German pilots climbing through the clouds were in for a shock when they encountered the American fighters waiting for them. As different gunners stated their feelings:

"This was my twenty-fifth mission, and for me it turned out to be the milk-run of all milk-runs."

"Not a fighter could be seen up there today except our own."

"We'll have a milk bottle instead of a bomb pasted on our ship for this mission. Enemy fighters came up, took a look at us, and went home."

The weather for most of December discouraged major attempts at visual bombing. Most of the heavy bombers flew over thick clouds, found their targets by radar, and then bombed through the overcast. But in spite of poor weather the Fortresses and Liberators unloaded a record 13,142 tons of bombs on their targets.

The Eighth Air Force was coming full stride. For the first time the Army Air Forces in one month exceeded the tonnage hurled against the enemy by the Royal Air Force Bomber Command.

The armadas were rapidly increasing in size.

On the 3rd November 566 four-engined raiders were dispatched from their fields in England.

By 26th November the number rose to 633.

On the 13th December a record 710 bombers were sent off.

On Christmas Eve the new record was set when 722 Fortresses and Liberators took off, of which 670 raiders attacked their targets.

Radar bombing was more damaging than no bombing at all, yet by the close of 1943 "it was becoming clear that radar aids had not worked, and were not likely to work, miracles of accuracy.... The weather continued to be a faithful Nazi collaborator, and there was nothing to do but wait and, meanwhile, maintain a constant pressure on the German war economy by radar bombing. From 4 January to 15 February the heavy bombers of the Eighth Air Force flew combat missions on twenty-one days...."

On the 11th January there came a brief interval of clearer skies. Immediately the Eighth sent out 663 bombers to hit important targets of the German aircraft industry. But the weather was not good enough to permit the kind of bombing operation for which everyone had been waiting. Formations were broken up by storms, many rendezvous attempts failed, fighter escort was diminished by clouds and faulty time schedules. The AAF historians note that "this mission gave proof, if proof were needed, of the extremely complicated factors involved in such an operation; and it helps to explain why more frequent attacks were not made against aircraft industry targets during the winter months." Many strikes were recalled—and sometimes such recall signals were missed by smaller formations that pressed on, unfortunately into the teeth of massive fighter defenses. To the Germans it appeared as if Berlin were the target, and their pilots responded with a ferocity not seen since 14th October 1943. It didn't seem possible but the Germans had improved their technique. With belly tanks fitted to their fighters they cruised just out of range until the escorts turned for home. Then, "dropping their tanks, the enemy planes pressed home large and coordinated attacks on the relatively unprotected AAF formations. In instances where the bomber formation was as tight as was required for mass protection against single-engine fighters, the German twin-engine fighters made use of the opportunity to lob rockets into it from a point beyond normal gun range, often with deadly effect. If on the other hand the formation became spread out enough to make rocket attack relatively harmless, its elements fell prey to mass attack by single-engine fighters."

Where the Mustangs could stay with the bombers they broke up the rocket attacks, warded off other fighters, and fought brilliantly against the enemy. Without loss to themselves the P-51 pilots shot down thirteen German fighters. Where the Mustangs were absent the Germans scored with brutal success. Before the day ended sixty heavy bombers went down.

The weather closed in for two weeks, restricting the bombers to short-range penetrations. Then, on the 29th January, the Eighth again struck in massive force. More than eight hundred heavy bombers, aiming by radar, hit key targets in Frankfurt am Main. The next day another force of heavies battered Brunswick, again bombing through the clouds. On the 3rd and 4th February the Eighth was back again, tearing up targets at Wilhelmshaven, Emden, and Frankfurt. Then once more bad weather imposed a delay in the juggernaut raids against the German aircraft industry.

The break in the weather came on the 19th February 1944, and air planners hurried to put into effect their long-delayed Project ARGUMENT, "a series of coordinated precision attacks by the Eighth and Fifteenth Air Forces against the highest-priority objectives, most of which by February 1944 were situated in central and southern Germany. The RAF agreed to make its night area attacks coincide with the daylight missions both in time and place." The first assault was scheduled for the 20th February.

That morning sixteen combat wings of heavy bombers rose like gigantic locusts over England and assembled into strike formations. More than one thousand heavy bombers took off, of which 941 arrived over their targets. The RAF provided short-range escort with sixteen squadrons of Spitfires and Mustangs, while seventeen groups of American fighters—thirteen P-47, two P-38 and two P-51—flew with the bombers. Fighter escort for maximum range went to the bombers that would strike targets in central Germany, normally those most heavily defended. In all, the heavy bombers blasted no less than twelve targets critical to the aircraft industry of the Reich. The preparations were carried out with exhaustive care. The night before the big raid the British slammed Leipzig with a roaring assault, not only tearing up great parts of the city but also wearing out much of the night fighter force that would have been available to hit the Fortresses and Liberators. The routes were carefully chosen, the fighter escort assigned studiously, so that those fighters of shortest range were able to return to England, refuel, and take off at once to provide withdrawal escort for the returning bombers.

The mission proved to be an outstanding success. On 14th October 1943, against Schweinfurt, sixty bombers out of 257 were shot down. On 11th January 1944, out of 651 bombers carrying out sorties against multiple targets, another sixty bombers went down. Now, on the 20th February, attacking many of the same targets, a force of almost one thousand bombers suffered losses of twenty-one heavies—barely two percent of the attackers. Even more cheering was the confirmation that a staggering blow, accomplished through excellent and accurate bombing, had been dealt the production capabilities of Germany's aircraft industry.

This was the opening blow of a massive strategic operation that gained fame as the Big Week. The Eighth had been prepared to accept losses as high as two hundred bombers for the first mission of 20th February—and lost but a tenth of that number in return for spectacularly effective results of the bombings.

The next day another mighty force rose from England. Hopes for multiple blows, with the Fifteenth and Ninth Air Forces adding their weight to that of the Eighth, were thwarted by weather. On the night of 20/21 February the British came through with a terrifying strike by six hundred heavies against Stuttgart. The morning of the 21st, despite the severe weather, the Eighth went out again in strength of nearly a thousand bombers. The weather frustrated the hopes for another decisive blow against the Reich; crews took solace by plastering secondary targets with high bomb concentrations.

For the 22nd the Eighth was assigned six major cities as targets, while the Fifteenth would go after Regensburg. One major part of the B-17 force from England ran into trouble immediately. So severe was the weather over their fields that rendezvous and assembly of formations became impossible, and when several bombers collided in the air the bombers were ordered back to their fields. Many Fortress formations on that day were decreased from their planned sizes because of weather. The Liberators were strung out badly. The Fortresses from Italy found themselves facing German fighter forces much stronger than had been expected—mainly because the planned heavy strikes to the north had been so weak. The fighter escort had its own devil of a time trying to provide cover to bombers that had made a mockery of assembly points and of timetables.

The result was bitter fighting. In a long running battle the German fighters shot down forty-one bombers out of the 430 heavies of the Eighth that were credited with combat sorties. The Fifteenth lost another fourteen bombers, bringing the German score for the day to fifty-five. But the American fighters, for their part, "had a field day." For a loss of eleven American fighters, they shot down at least sixty of the enemy.

On the 24th excellent fighter protection showed its worth in quality but lacking in quality but lacking in quantity. Mustering all its available strength ("The Luftwaffe had all their planes up but their trainers," a gunner reported afterward) the German Air Force struck with furious intensity against the many formations hitting widely dispersed targets throughout Germany. The task force of eighty-seven Fortresses that hit Steyr lost seventeen bombers. The B-24s that raided Gotha lost thirty-three of their number. The bombers raiding Schweinfurt lost eleven. Sixty-one bombers had gone down in battle. The fighters, often outnumbered by the enemy, lost ten of their own and shot down thirty-seven German fighters; bomber gunners had claimed 108 kills. And, once again, there was no way of knowing how many fighters had been shot down by the bombers that were lost.

On the 25th the Eighth and Fifteenth put up some 1,300 bombers, plus fighters sent out with the Eighth from England. Making the longest penetrations of the Big Week, they ran into heavy opposition despite strong fighter escort. The Fifteenth sent out 400 bombers, of which 176 made the deep penetrations to the Regensburg area. This force took a beating with thirty-three bombers—nearly twenty percent of the strike force—shot down. The Eighth had 738 bombers credited with sorties and lost thirty-one of their number, a percentage more to the liking of those who flew the mission.

The 25th February was the end of the Big Week. The next day the weather closed in over most of the bomber bases. It would remain bad for another month. In the meantime the crews rested and the strategic forces built up their strength.

A study of the Big Week produced impressive and satisfying figures. Most of these have been derived from German as well as American sources. First, the Eighth on these five missions sent up more than 3,300 bombers, and the Fifteenth put up another 500.

The 3,800 bombers that hit their main targets dropped a tonnage roughly equal to the total bomb tonnage dropped by the Eighth Air Force in its entire first year of operations—approximately 10,000 tons of bombs. Planners had expected losses to be very heavy; they were considerably less than anticipated. The Eighth lost 137 bombers and the Fifteenth another eighty-nine, producing an overall loss ratio of about six percent of the strike armadas. Fighters from the Eighth, Ninth and Fifteenth Air Force flew, respectively, 2,548, 712 and 413 escort missions. Twenty-eight fighters were shot down. Approximately 2,600 men were lost—taking into account killed, missing and seriously wounded.

Added to the totals produced by these five heavy raids, the British during this same period sortied 2,351 of the giant RAF night bombers and dropped 9,198 (U.S.) tons of bombs. Their losses were 157 heavy bombers—about 6.6 percent of the attack forces. "This figure," notes the AAF, "slightly higher than that of American losses, is most interesting in the light of earlier estimates of the relative costs of day and night bombing."

What were the results?

The U.S. Strategic Bombing Survey, after ransacking German sources, estimated that the 4,000-odd tons of bombs dropped on targets in the aircraft industrial system alone damaged or destroyed 75 percent of the buildings in plants that at the time accounted for 90 percent of the total German production of aircraft. The immediate reaction in the industry was one of consternation, we are told. The German authorities, whose plans had hitherto rested on unduly optimistic foundations, now apparently for the first time showed signs of desperation. As a result of the bombing, the aircraft industry received in late February a formal order to disperse its plants. . . . Also the bombings helped to precipitate a crisis in the overall organization of aircraft production which culminated in the shifting of responsibility from Goering's Air Ministry to a special agency operating within the Ministry of Armaments and Munitions headed by Albert Speer. . . . The February campaign would have paid off even if its only effect would have been to force the enemy into an intensive program of dispersal. For that program not only accounted indirectly for much wasted effort and production loss; it also left the industry vulnerable to any serious disruption in transportation. The dispersal policy did, in fact, defeat itself when Allied bombers subsequently turned to an intensive strategic attack on transportation. . . . There is reason to believe that the large and fiercely fought air battles of those six February days had more effect in establishing the air superiority on which Allied plans so largely depended than did the bombing of industrial plants. Total USSTAF claims of enemy aircraft destroyed amounted to well above 600, with more than a third of these victories credited to the fighter escort and roughly another third to the bombers of the Fifteenth Air Force, which enjoyed no long-range escort.[69]

The Big Week had also produced a name that was to be in the archives of the VIII Bomber Command. William R. Lawley, Jr., flew a Fortress on the 20th February in the strike against Leipzig. The mission had gone uneventfully until the moment of bomb drop—then bombardier Harry G. Mason gave the pilot the distressing news that their bombs had hung up. The timing was, to say the least, unfortunate. No sooner had Mason made his report when a swarm of German fighters hit their formation, concentrating fire on their bomber. Almost at once the Fortress was battered from nose to tail.

A cannon shell exploding in the cockpit killed the copilot instantly and sent steel fragments tearing through Lawley's body. At the same moment an engine exploded in flames. The body of the dead copilot slumped forward against the control yoke. Still stunned by the blast from the exploding shell, Lawley regained his senses slowly—to discover that one engine was on fire, the B-17 was in a howling dive, and he couldn't see outside the airplane. The cannon shell in killing the copilot had splashed blood all across the windshield, blotting out the outside world. Lawley snapped his eyes to the instruments. To his dismay, these also were splattered with blood and could not be read.

Mason, during this time, was struggling to salvo the bombs. Without their heavy weight, control of the Fortress would be easier. No one in the crew was aware of the dead copilot or the struggle going on in the cockpit, where the wounded Lawley was straining with ebbing strength to regain control. Desperate, convinced they were finished, he shouted on the intercom for the crew to bail out. The replies that came back were not reassuring. Eight men of the crew of ten, including himself, were wounded. Two men were in serious condition. Bailing out was unthinkable; they would never survive the jump. There was no other way—Lawley fought with renewed determination to save the ship. He punched the extinguisher system to kill the burning engine—only to have another wave of attacking fighters set another engine blazing. Despite their wounds, most of the gunners fought back. Lawley smothered the second fire. Abruptly he felt some of the control pressure easing; Mason had salvoed their bombs. Elated at their success, Mason climbed upward into the cockpit where he faced the gory scene of the dead copilot, the wounded and bleeding Lawley, and the blood-sprayed windshield and instrument panel. Lawley took one look at Mason, accepted that help was there, and passed out.

The bombardier, although not a pilot, had flying training behind him. The crew helped in removing the body of the dead copilot and Mason climbed into the right seat, from where he held course for England. There were no further attacks and Mason started a long descent. The moment he sighted an airfield, the bombardier managed to revive Lawley. Despite his terrible pain, Lawley took over the controls and started the landing approach.

An engine sputtered—out of fuel. The ground came up toward them. Another engine exploded into flames. The gear refused to budge. Lawley knew he couldn't hang on much longer. He bellied in the bomber, sending sparks scraping back for hundreds of feet. It was spectacular but, after what they had been through, harmless.

Bill Lawley received the Medal of Honor for his part in the opening play of the Big Week.

When Mission 115 ended late in the day of 14th October 1943, few leaders of the Eighth Air Force doubted but that the Germans had seized a firm grip on air superiority over the Reich. When the Big Week ended late in February 1944, it was becoming just as evident that the Germans had lost what they struggled so tenaciously to attain. That became evident when the Luftwaffe switched its old tactics and adopted a new plan that had *caution* stamped all over it. The Germans could, when they made the effort, put up an intense and effective defense. They could batter a bombing force with deadly results. But they could *not* do so, not any longer, whenever they so wanted. They could not do so as a matter of policy.

The Germans, in effect, were defending their homeland on a partial basis, defending the most important war plants, abandoning other cities and industries to destruction by the massed Fortresses and Liberators. There were, and there would be, occasions when they would concentrate every plane available against a major raid. Other times the thousands of men in the bombers, and their escorting fighter pilots, would see only token defenders in the sky. Gunners one day might be forced to fight savagely for their lives—then for several missions they enjoyed the increasingly frequent milk runs. No one could predict when the Germans would explode in furious defense. But it was evident that the occasions were becoming increasingly rarer.

"In short," noted the AAF, "the policy was one of conservation of strength and it conceded to the Allies the vital point of air superiority."

By now the men who planned the air assault against Germany were more than primed to take every advantage of the sudden weakness in German defenses. Now they wanted the German to fight and they bent every opportunity to force the Luftwaffe into defending the Reich and its cities. The air strategists threw away their long-standing plans of protecting the bombers. Where they had planned missions to avoid the fighters, now they did their best to goad the Luftwaffe into battle. The AAF history notes that "fighter escort, which hitherto had been held down to close support of the bombers, now was increasingly cut loose from strictly defensive assignments with orders to seek out and destroy the foe. And as the role of escort became thus primarily an offensive one, the extension of fighter range made it possible to send great fleets of escorted bombers all the way to Berlin."

This was the city that the Germans meant to defend. This was the target for which they would fight, in maximum number, with unbridled fury. Those who sent out the men in the Fortresses and the Liberators knew that their policy of forcing the fight could produce severe casualties among the heavy bombers. They reckoned that the losses would be worth the damage inflicted on the enemy in the air. The invasion date was nearing and "it became correspondingly more important to force a higher rate of attrition on the German Air Force in being."

The first attack on "Big B" came on 4th March. Severe weather limited results. Two days later the weather improved and Eighth Air Force headquarters laid on the big strike. Six hundred and sixty heavies made it to Berlin to drop over 1,600 tons of bombs. The men who flew the mission knew it was going to be rough. More fighters than usual would be in the air to contest their presence; for several nights the RAF had failed to visit targets over central Germany.

The event justified their fears; the bombers "ran into exceedingly bitter and effective opposition." Intense anti-aircraft claimed its share—and before the day ended no less than sixty-nine heavy bombers went down, along with eleven escorting fighters. Those bombers that returned claimed ninety-seven kills. The fighters, with gun-camera records to back up their claims, racked up eighty-two German fighters shot down in battle. There was no way of knowing the kills scored by the sixty-nine bombers and eleven fighters that were lost.

Was the mission overly costly? Sixty-nine bombers could not be shrugged off. Yet the loss ratio, for a mission of such importance and range from England, could be accepted. It was "just such air fights that the American commanders hoped to provoke, confident as they were in the ability of their airmen to impose a ruinous wastage upon the enemy." The moments when such fierce resistance could be offered would become even rarer than before.

Two days later 462 heavies again raided Berlin. A screen of 174 Mustang fighters escorted them to, over, and away from the target. The number of German fighters in the air was much less than on the 6th, a fact not at all helped by the heavy American escort which, including P-38s and P-47s, came to a record 1,015 sorties flown. During the day, 590 heavy bombers flew credit sorties. Flak and fighters claimed thirty-seven of these.

Once again, the Luftwaffe had suffered a battering. Losing seventeen of their own number, the escorts shot down nearly ninety German fighters.

On the 22nd March a force of 669 heavy bombers returned to Berlin. Despite excellent weather for interception few Luftwaffe fighters were up. Flak shot down ten bombers. One bomber went down from noncombat causes. Total scored to German fighters: one bomber.

And that was over the capital of the Reich. At the close of March the Eighth Air Force noted that the Luftwaffe "could still hit, and hit hard; but it was no longer capable of that sustained counterattack which had at one time so nearly frustrated the entire Combined Bomber Offensive. From this point on, the rate of loss to enemy aircraft suffered by the Eighth Air Force tended sharply to decrease."

In respect to its original goals, the Combined Bomber Offensive "reached its legal end" on the 1st April 1944. Control of the strategic air forces of the AAF reverted from the British to the supreme Allied commander. The new phase of air war was ready—the massed bomber fleets were now prepared to attempt to wreck the German petroleum industry and to paralyze the country's transportation system.

How best to judge the effect of the program to destroy the ability of Germany to fight in the air? It is not the intention of this book to review the matter in all its complex detail, but the conclusion is undeniably clear. After February the Luftwaffe could no longer properly defend the Reich. But the program to destroy Germany's fighting strength in the air had another goal—to permit the invasion of Europe without molestation from the Luftwaffe.

On the 6th June 1944, General Dwight D. Eisenhower

made a statement to the invasion forces he was committing
to the assault on German Europe—

*"If you see fighting aircraft over you, they will be ours."*
He was right.

# CHAPTER 27

# JUGGERNAUT

THE AIR WAR HAD changed. Now there was no question that the bombers would get through to their targets, and would continue to do so, day after day, no matter how intense the fight offered by the Luftwaffe. To lose sixty or seventy bombers on a single mission was a staggering blow, but in respect to the "big picture," that view of the war from the highest level of strategy so soundly cursed by every GI, sixty bombers out of more than a thousand was a blow well enough absorbed. Especially when the strategists who ordered out the bombers knew that the ability of the enemy to repeat his victory had been reduced to such an extent that reoccurrences would be rare—and costlier to the defenders than to those who attacked.

But it still took men to fly, and men to die. And every so often from the thousands who flew and courted death there emerged the pilot or the crewman who would distinguish himself by his actions in a situation where normal courage and normal skills could never have prevailed. On such occasions the Eighth took special pains to assure that those who were involved were singled out for their valor and their performance. In this respect these men functioned as symbols.

No one ever knew what sacrifices were made, or what gallantry and valor went unknown and unrewarded in the many bombers that never came home. The medals for the living were a reminder of the heroism of the men who never returned.

One of those who returned from the 21st April 1944 mission into German air was Lt. Edward S. Michael, B-17 pilot. His deeds on that mission brought him the Medal of Honor. . . .

Michael's bomber was singled out for concentrated attack by German fighters. The Focke-Wulfs whipped past the guns of the escort fighters, flew through their own flak. In less than thirty seconds the B-17 was out of control, plunging away from the formation, starting to roll over on her back. In the cockpit Michael and his copilot fought desperately to regain control of the runaway Fortress. They were winning their life-or-death struggle when they heard a drumming noise, growing louder swiftly. In the next instant a volcano erupted directly before Michael's face as a cannon shell exploded in the cockpit. The blast, along with fragments of jagged metal, ripped open the body of the copilot and smashed him unconscious.

For several seconds Michael was blind. Slowly his vision returned. He looked into the face of death. The wind howled through the shattered remains of the side window. The instrument panel had vanished, replaced with a jagged tangle of torn metal and broken glass. Abruptly Michael forgot all that, forgot everything but the pain that started in his leg and stabbed through his body. Only then did he discover that a long silver of metal, barbed and white-hot, had slashed into his right thigh. He glanced down to watch the blood welling from his torn clothing. The pain seemed like fire eating into his flesh.

If his Fortress had been crippled before, now it was virtually helpless. More cannon shells had hit, exploding against and within the airplane. A severed hydraulic line sent fluid spurting outward as if from an artery. Whipped by the wind it smeared an opaque mask across the windscreen.

The B-17 careened out of control for more than three thousand feet. Despite the pain, flying almost wholly by instinct, Michael brought the stricken Fortress back to an even keel.

Throughout the period when the airplane had plunged out of control Michael had heard the uproar from his headphones. His crewmen, wondering what was going on, trying to find out if they still had pilots, if they should jump . . . Michael reassured and calmed down his crew. The intercom went silent. Then he heard the strained voice of his radio operator. Under other circumstances he might have marveled at the man's seeming detachment as he reported: "Sir, the bomb bay is on fire."

The new catastrophe overshadowed everything else. In precise terms the radio operator explained that three cannon shells had exploded within the bays and *had ignited the tons of incendiaries* jammed tightly in their racks. The entire bay area, concluded the crewman, was now blazing.

Michael yanked hard on the emergency bomb release lever to discharge the lethal cargo. The bombardier, who had listened wide-eyed to the exchange, was also at his emergency release. The bombs stayed with the ship; the release mechanism had been jammed by enemy bullets. They were stuck with their prize. If they remained much longer with the stricken Fortress they would disappear in the explosion that now was inevitable.

Michael ordered the crew to bail out immediately. Through the ship the escape hatches banged open or were whisked away in the howling wind. The men tumbled and leaped from the Fortress. With the wounded copilot Michael prepared to follow the crew.

Then he glanced down into the nose and saw the bombardier, fists wrapped around the handles of a machine gun, blazing away at attacking German fighters. Michael shouted at the man to get the hell out of the airplane. The bombardier grabbed for his chest pack. He stared in dismay at the shredded pack in his hands. He looked up blankly at his pilot.

For a long moment Michael looked back at the bombardier and at his useless parachute. Every second of delay brought him that much closer to a flaming death in the bomber. Michael sighed, a tremor that went through his body, and climbed back into the pilot's seat. He ordered the copilot to jump. The wounded man grinned bleakly at Michael and told him where he could go.

Thus Michael committed himself—with a helpless bombardier and a wounded copilot, wounded himself, in a battered, flaming airplane. The only chance for survival, he felt, was a crash landing.

Wisely he kept the bomb bay doors open. The blazing incendiaries dripped flaming globules downward through the open bays. At least they had that much going for them. . . .

A string of explosions startled the men. For the moment they had been unaware of the German fighters following the crippled airplane, wolves yammering for the kill. With only the bombardier to man their guns they were dead meat.

For forty-five minutes the wounded pilot flew his battered machine, skidding and slipping through wild evasive maneuvers. For forty-five minutes the three men and the Flying Fortress took everything the Germans had to dish out. The fighters attacking them ran out of ammunition. Others joined the fray, charging after the airplane that slowly was coming apart in the sky. At last, he dove the crippled Fortress into a cloud bank toward which he had been racing desperately. The respite was briefer than they had hoped. Patches of sky began to appear and finally the clouds were behind them. The fighters were gone.

But they had eliminated one danger only to be faced with another. Less than thirty seconds after emerging from the clouds the ground below came alive with sparkling flashes. At once the flak bursts hammered at the Fortress. Michael shoved the yoke forward to dive the airplane. For interminable moments the flak barrage tore at them and, finally, the black bursts in the air fell behind.

Down to low altitude they continued to struggle toward England. The open bomb bays imposed a severe drag on the Fortress. Again and again German gunners took advantage of the bomber lumbering through the air. Streams of tracers marked their course homeward. Sometimes the blazing coals found their mark and the Fortress took more punishment. They didn't know how the bomber stayed in the air. Everywhere they looked the airplane was full of holes. The incendiaries still smouldered in the bomb bays, still dripped their lethal rain downward.

They passed over the flak towers along the German border to cross into France. Michael could take no more.

Slowly he slumped forward and lapsed into unconsciousness. The copilot took over. Bandaged by the bombardier, some of his strength regained, he flew the airplane while the bombardier tended to the unconscious Michael. They kept on, across France, across the wind-whipped Channel, and finally the coast of England came into view.

Michael came to shortly after the copilot started down toward a British airfield just inland from the coast. The pilot struggled to remain erect in his seat. He found a hidden reservoir of strength, took over the controls.

The landing seemed impossible. The undercarriage was useless. The big tires had been shot into useless bags of rubber. The hydraulic system to lower the gear was shot away. They couldn't communicate with the ground; their radio equipment was so much wreckage. Several control cables had been severed; the bomber flew in a logy, sloppy manner.

A belly landing was easier said than done. The bomb bay doors jutted downward like great clamshells which could slam into the ground and crack the Fortress in half. The ball turret was jammed in the down position and both machine gun barrels pointed straight down, another warning that they would slew wildly when they touched. The instruments were useless—Michael had no altimeter, no airspeed indicator. The windscreen was smeared and vision was extremely poor. Michael called for flaps. They were shot out; they wouldn't come down.

The wounded pilot had no choice. He brought the Fortress to earth at better than 110 miles per hour, belly torn open, incendiary bombs shaking and burning more fiercely. The bomb doors and ball turret gouged a huge furrow in the asphalt. Dust, smoke, sparks and then flames trailed behind them. Finally the crippled machine lurched to a halt. British rescue crews were in the bomber almost at once, helping the bombardier remove the two wounded pilots.

Mission ended.

Following the assault against the German aircraft industry, the Eighth Air Force turned its attention to the petroleum resources of the Reich. The new campaign had been delayed for months while the bombers hit German missile sites and the Channel defenses of the German army. But if ever Germany had an Achilles heel, then petroleum—the oil production centers and the synthetic oil production plants—was that weakness. There were eighty-one "critical" targets—fifty-eight oil refineries and twenty-three synthetic oil plants. Destroy those facilities and the German war machine would be stopped, on the ground and in the air.

The Luftwaffe had become a wait-and-see defensive force. It rose to battle only when its leaders felt the need was critical. As far as General Spaatz was concerned the cardinal issue was to draw the German fighter into battle. In the coming raids, the heavy bombers, with fighter escort, would accomplish the dual purpose of smashing the oil supplies and wiping out irreplaceable German strength in fighter planes and experienced pilots.

The opening blow and its meaning are reviewed by the historians of the AAF:

Not until 12 May were conditions suitable for the great experimental attack, one which the Germans had been dreading almost above everything. They had foolishly grouped their main synthetic oil plants together, and by now they had no strong Luftwaffe to defend them. Their shortsightedness proved painful on the 12 May mission and during the numerous attacks which followed. On this occasion, fifteen combat wings involving 935 heavy bombers, escorted by Eighth and Ninth Air Force and RAF fighters, took off for what was to prove a historic operation. The aircraft proceeded to a point south of the Ruhr, skirting the highly defended sites in that area and around Hannover and Brunswick, and then flew east and northwest toward the target area. Near Frankfurt the German Air Force rose to intercept the leading combat wings, and the enemy pilots exhibited their usual aggressiveness once they were off the ground. Between 150 and 200 enemy aircraft attacked, mostly in mass, using saturation tactics. In some cases thirty German fighters came in abreast, firing savagely *and even ramming the B-17s* [italics added]. One of the combat wings lost half its bombers and became thoroughly disorganized. Before further harm was done, escorting P-47s and P-51s came to the réscue and the bombers proceeded to their targets. Most antiaircraft fire was of moderate intensity. More than 800 heavies attacked, dropping 1,718 tons on the synthetic oil plants at Zwickau, Merseburg-Leuna, Brux, Lutzkendorf, Bohlen, and other cities. The targets were slightly obscured by low clouds and ground haze. During the withdrawal phase a force of fifty German twin-engine fighters pressed determined attacks against the bombers for almost a half-hour and smaller groups of single-engine fighters attempted interception. In all, the Eighth Air Force lost forty-six heavy bombers on this mission, and ten Allied fighters failed to return. Bomber crews claimed 115 enemy aircraft and fighter pilots seventy-five. Certainly the professed objective of the mission was attained: the German Air Force had reacted vigorously to the attacks on oil plants and had suffered severe losses. More important in the long run was the fact that all of the targets were damaged, some of them very heavily. . . . It was an excellent mission, despite the heavy loss of bombers, and an auspicious opening of the Eighth Air Force campaign to deny the Germans oil.[70]

How reliable were these claims of kills by gunners of the bombers? We have noted several times in any listing of enemy planes shot down that it is impossible to include the kills that may have been attained by those bombers and fighters that failed to return from missions—a figure that at times must have been high. But of those that did return, the question is raised again and again of their accuracy in German fighters destroyed. No doubt that there were duplications; at times it was impossible to avoid duplications, especially when the gunners of a dozen planes might have been shooting, all at the same time, at one fighter that exploded in the air. But the discrepancies between claims and German admissions have never been reconciled. Nor can they be here. However, the writer wishes to add some light to this matter—and it may reflect on the alleged German accuracy in their bookkeeping. The word *alleged* is emphasized, for the conditions that existed in Germany bred padded records of every nature and description.

The Germans insist that their records—especially their secret records—were absolutely accurate. This is most interesting in the light of the mission of 12th May. We claimed 190 fighters shot down that day; the Germans admitted to a loss of sixty. But what of the other records of this same battle?

Secret and official records—*not* public announcements—credit German fighter pilots involved in the 12th May mission as having *definitely* shot down eighty-one American fighter planes, and probably shooting down another ten.

Note that these are confirmed claims. German pilots were credited with having shot down eighty-one American fighters. Those kills went on the record books and added to individual pilot claims for ace status.

The records of the Eighth Air Force—right down to the serial numbers of the planes and the names of the pilots—show conclusively that ten American fighters were lost on the 12th May.

German pilots are therefore credited with seventy-one planes that landed safely in England.

Let the reader decide for himself.

Despite the avowed priority for the campaign against Germany's petroleum industry, the Eighth Air Force found itself required to divert a force of bombers for special combat tests that had long held high favor in Washington. The tests involved the first mass attack of guided missiles in World War II—an honor, for whatever it was worth, that fell to the Flying Fortress. In view of German concentration on missile weapons in the latter part of the war, the role played by the B-17 in guided missile strikes is especially interesting. It is one of the lesser known sidelights to the air effort against Germany.

The missile weapon was the GB-1—Glide Bomb Model One. It was not, contrary to widespread belief, a robot device rushed into being to offset the heavy losses sustained in the bomber offensive against Germany. Tests of GB-1 components had begun as early as June of 1941. By year's end experimental models of the new missile had completed flight tests. They were something less than satisfactory in that accuracy left much to be desired.

The GB-1 was essentially a 2,000-pound bomb with a simple, high-wing structure with twin booms and a tail surface. It resembled a small airplane in flight. It was one of the "gravity powered" missiles in that it fell freely from the airplane and glided on the lift provided by its wing structure. In 1942 AAF engineers claimed it would be possible in GB-1 strikes "to place one hundred percent of them inside a city the size of Dayton, Ohio, from any altitude up to thirty thousand feet, and ... from altitudes up to five thousand feet, the greater percentage of them could be placed inside a large factory area." In October 1942 the AAF ordered quantity production of the GB-1, and directed also that a group of B-17s be trained in the use of the missile, and be ready to use them in combat before the end of the year. In its optimism this last directive ignored the realities of the air war, and it did not take long for the AAF to alter the time of attacks against German cities to 1943. Further delays were experienced, but on the morning of 25th May 1944 the "missile group" was ready to go.

The Eighth wanted nothing to do with the GB-1. Its method of use meant acceptance of area bombing, which the Eighth's leaders were loath to do. They did not believe the attack would produce results commensurate with the effort. Official Washington, eyeing with unhappy eyes the massive antiaircraft defenses of German cities, felt missile attack from thirty miles away might greatly reduce the number of bombers lost and damaged.

On the 25th May, fifty-eight Fortresses approached the German city of Cologne. On a signal from the leader the bombardiers tripped their missile-release switches. From each B-17 two winged robots fell away and sped toward the city. One hundred and sixteen missiles ...

Not one struck Cologne. Instead, upset by air currents and turbulence, controlled by an inadequate preset guidance system, the GB-1s wandered all over the countryside. Astonished German antiaircraft gunners thought they had achieved a sudden spectacular increase in accuracy, for airplanes were plunging out of the sky in every direction. Explosions boomed across the countryside and the suburbs of Cologne. Overjoyed by their success the flak gunners put in claims that day for more than ninety Fortresses shot down.

Disgusted with the performance of their missiles, the Fortress crews went home. They were informed shortly after that the GB-1 program had been canceled.

Several months later the Eighth went back into Germany with new missile weapons, improvements over the simple GB-1. The GB-4 combined remote radio control and visual observation. The bombardier after release of the GB-4 missile kept his eye on a dazzling flare burning on the tail of the weapon, directing it toward a distant target. It proved inefficient, to say the least. The next weapons test came with the GB-8, a marked technological improvement over previous weapons. The same radio control system was used, but instead of watching a burning flare, the bombardier peered into a small television screen. The transmitter was in the nose of the missile and what the missile "saw" as it rushed towards its target, the bombardier also saw from the Fortress. It was a form of "remote suicide dive." The system had great possibilities, but was riddled with technical problems that bedeviled its users more than it hurt the enemy.

The programs were canceled.

The oil campaign, in the brief time allotted to it before the invasion of Europe, struck hard at key industrial sites. The mission of 12th May started the ball rolling, and the Fifteenth Air Force threw its weight into the new program. The latter had already struck hard, on the 5th May, with a force of 500 bombers against the Ploesti oil fields, which produced fully one fourth of all Germany's petroleum. On the 18th May another heavy attack was launched against Ploesti, but severe weather kept the attack force down to some 300 bombers. On the 31st May, another 460 heavy bombers carried out a destructive attack. Six days later 300 Liberators slammed Ploesti with a "highly successful attack." The RAF supported the campaign by filling the Danube with mines "to interfere with barge shipments of oil to the Reich. These Danube mining operations proved more effective than the Allies apparently realized."

On the 28th May the Eighth went back to its new priority targets, smashing with more than 400 bombers at five major oil centers still suffering badly from the 12th May strikes.

The next day 224 heavy bombers wrecked most of the industrial facilities of the Politz synthetic oil plant.

The May attacks were disappointing in bomb tonnage to the air leaders—only 5,166 tons of bombs for the entire month. But the *results* were staggering. German production of petroleum products fell by fifty percent, and in June the German war machine received only half the supplies it predicted three months earlier. "It was only the beginning," notes an AAF study, "and both the Allies and the Germans knew it. U.S. Strategic Air Forces was, of course, jubilant at the effectiveness of these first attacks. Eisenhower was convinced, and the British were won over to the oil campaign by the last of May."

Clearly the days were numbered for the oil industry of the Reich. The Germans placed more than twelve thousand antiaircraft guns around their critical oil targets. The Luftwaffe was goaded into violent defense of the oil plants. All to no avail. The strategic bombers were a juggernaut that could not be stopped. In single-day strikes as many as 1,500 Fortresses and Liberators, covered with swarms of fighters, hammered at the jugular vein of the Reich. The AAF history reviews the critical stage in the air war:

> During the summer of 1944, most of the bombing effort expended by the heavies went into so-called tactical operations for the benefit of the ground forces: attacks on marshaling yards, bridges, airfield installations, and supply dumps behind German lines, as well as the spectacular saturation of enemy positions at Caen on 18 July and near St. Lo on 25 July. Also, they were called upon for extensive CROSSBOW [missile site] operations, and late in the summer some of the strategic bombers were converted into transports in order to remedy the supply emergency brought about by Patton's brilliant drive across France. Even the most staunch proponents of strategic air warfare usually appreciated the necessity of furnishing direct assistance to the land forces, and the praise of ground force commanders was gratifying. But it was clear that the offensive against German war production suffered whenever the heavy bombers devoted their tonnages to tactical targets. As the strategic air commanders judged the situation, they were now for the first time in a position to implement a truly systematic campaign directed at Germany's war-making capacity. They possessed sufficient forces for such an undertaking, they ruled the air, and they had amply fulfilled their commitments to blast the way for a successful D-Day. However greatly the strategic bomber could contribute to the success of the land campaign, its primary role was to weaken and destroy the enemy's ability and willingness to wage war.[71]

That destruction went ahead with renewed determination and stunning strength. On the 20th June the Eighth Air Force alone sent out a record armada of 1,361 bombers and 729 fighter escorts to pound six vital oil-production centers.

As if to reaffirm its tremendous striking power, on the very next day the Eighth laid on an attack against Berlin with twenty combat wings of heavy bombers and twenty-three groups of fighters. Nearly 2,500 planes carried out the battering assault against the German capital with "exceedingly accurate bombing." The two days of operations, involving nearly 4,600 bombers and fighters, had cost the Eighth heavily; massive flak concentrations and one of the rarer appearances in strength of the Luftwaffe cost the Eighth forty-eight bombers on the 20th, and another forty-four bombers on the day following. It was one of the rare periods of "temporary air superiority" for the combined German defenses, and intense concentrations of flak were claiming a much greater percentage of bombers downed than in prior missions.

The blows inflicted by the Fortresses and Liberators (and the RAF at night) grew even more severe, came closer together, until it seemed to the Germans that hardly a day passed without another massive thunderbolt hurled against their country. On the 29th June the Eighth sent out a thousand heavy bombers and many hundreds of fighters to hit oil and aircraft targets. For the first week in July tactical targets took a terrible beating from as many as 1,400 heavy bombers of the Eighth, as well as the thousands of fighters, fighter-bombers and medium bombers of the Eighth and Ninth Air Forces, the Royal Air Force, and the Fifteenth from Italy. On the 7th July the Eighth went back to strategic operations; 1,103 heavy bombers ripped up oil plants. More raids followed throughout France on the 8th and 9th. On the 11th more than a thousand bombers smashed Munich and Augsburg with 2,353 tons delivered on target. The next day 1,117 bombers pounded Munich and Saarbrucken. Another massive raid took place on the 13th.

But these figures represented only the attacks of the Eighth and they fall short of indicating the terrible punishment being meted out to the Reich. On the 7th July the Eighth dispatched 1,103 bombers—on the same day the Fifteenth struck its targets with more than a thousand bombers. On this one day alone the Germans faced the withering bombing of over 2,100 heavy bombers and more than a thousand fighters on daylight strategic operations— thousands of other warplanes also were tearing at Germany's vitals.

On the 19th July, 1,250 heavy bombers and every available fighter of the Eighth blasted targets all across Germany. The next day the Eighth and Fifteenth again coordinated their strikes to put more than two thousand heavy bombers over enemy objectives—plus a vast umbrella of fighters. On the 21st, 1,068 heavies went out. On the 23rd, every available heavy bomber lifted from England to smash German airfields in France; the next day Allied ground armies were to attempt a breakthrough, to sweep aside German ground defenses. On the 24th and 25th, the blows became even greater. Flying over short range and increasing appreciably their bomb loads, 1,600 heavy bombers *on each day* spread terrifying bomb carpets through the German forces. Then the bombers went back, day after day, to mangle German industrial centers. Almost every major attack saw between 800 and 1,300 heavy bombers on their way to destroy the industrial sinew of the Reich.

The Eighth Air Force—and this excludes the Ninth and the Fifteenth, as well as the Royal Air Force—in May 1944 dropped against enemy targets the staggering total of 36,000 tons of bombs. In June the Eighth unleashed 60,000 tons; in July another 45,000 tons; in August, 49,000 tons; and in September, 40,000 tons.

The Big League was demanding the best, and air leaders were listening to crews and noting the results of attacks. In July 1944, because "theater opinion strongly favored the B-17 over the B-24 . . . five groups of heavy bombers in the Eighth Air Force exchanged Liberators for Fortresses by September. . . ."

The fall of 1944 brought with it a studied appraisal of the war with an interesting and unexpected viewpoint:

If the period extending from early September 1944 to the end of that year brought disappointment not untouched by tragedy to the cause of the western Allies, these months also witnessed notable progress. The valuable port of Antwerp fell into Allied hands and Aachen, in the Reich itself, was taken. Hitler's seizure of the initiative as he sent his forces plunging through the Ardennes in December brought dismay to the Allied world and set back the timetable for projected operations by at least six weeks, but this desperate gamble would end with the Allies having managed to drain the reserves of genuine vitality from what remained of Hitler's western forces. And finally, the stragetic air forces during the last quarter of 1944 achieved their long-sought objective of undermining the sources of Germany's war power. In the grim aftermath of the Battle of the Bulge not even the air commanders themselves realized how much they had accomplished, but it soon would be apparent that their strategic offensives had been much more successful than in January 1945 they seemed to have been. The bottom was about to drop out of Germany's war effort.[72]

Rising like a phoenix from its own ashes, the Luftwaffe in the last quarter of 1944 astounded air planners of the strategic bombing campaign with a wholly unexpected resurgence of strength. The number of fighters thrown into the campaign to beat down American and British bomber attacks went up with alarming speed. In September 1944 the Germans had 1,260 single-engine fighters in the west; by mid-November that strength rose to 2,040 planes. In September they had 675 twin-engine fighters; by mid-November, twin-engine strength rose to 855. The cause of that unexpected increase in strength could be found in different areas. The Germans had been thrown out of airfields in France, Belgium and the Balkans. The geographical contraction produced an abrupt increase of strength. There were other causes, among them the concentration of 85 per cent of all single-engine fighters from all combat fronts for bomber attacks. This strength increase may have satisfied German civilians, but not the German Army. "By late September," notes the AAF history, "the Luftwaffe had almost abandoned the Wermacht to devote such fighting power as it had left to the Allied bomber fleets. Practically all pretense at maintaining a bomber force was gone, and bomber pilots now flew fighters. Deployed from west to east for hundreds of miles, Luftwaffe fighters could engage the Allies for almost the whole width of the Reich whenever their commanders chose to consume their scanty gasoline supplies in this fashion, as sometimes they did."

The turn of events, as might be imagined, was unexpected and unsettling. For months pilots and crews had been reporting a sweet refrain: "No enemy air opposition encountered."

Now all hell might again break loose.

Enemy production also seemed inexplicable, until it was discovered that the Germans had spread out single-engine fighter production from twenty-seven main plants to 729 small production facilities, "some of which were located in quarries, caves, mines, forests, or just in villages. . . . In the long run, the effort defeated itself, particularly when the transportation chaos of early 1945 paralyzed so much of the Reich, but the immediate effects were spectacular. . . ."

On the 27th and 28th September the Eighth lost a total of sixty-four aircraft. The Germans lost approximately ninety fighters by the American airplanes that were shot down. B-17s heading for Berlin took a beating on 6th October, and again the next day. On the latter missions the Eighth lost a total of forty-one bombers and fighters to the Luftwaffe.

Then came the sudden, almost complete period of inactivity. *"For more than three weeks the Eighth's fliers seldom saw a German fighter and made no claims whatsoever."* The Germans were hoarding their precious and still-diminishing fuel supplies. When enough was at hand, after sitting on the ground for three weeks while the heavy bombers tore German targets to shreds, the Luftwaffe again rose to do battle. Such tactics could hurt but could hardly be expected to stem the bomber raids on German cities and factories.

On the 2nd November 1944 four hundred German fighters took to the air. It was the greatest show of strength in nearly five months, and the Germans ripped hell-for-leather into the Fortresses. One German group of sixty fighters eluded the Mustang escorts to maul a B-17 formation before being driven off by American fighters. Losses for the day came to twenty-six Fortresses.

The long spells of avoiding combat contributed to the total number of fighters available. Damaged fighters were repaired and put back into action and new fighters rushed to combat units while, during this period, refusal to contest the bombers or fighters battering Germany permitted the

Luftwaffe to increase its strength. Then, with the fuel accumulated, a horde of interceptors would take to the air with the potential of doing enormous damage to the bomber fleets. Another advantage to the Germans was that while the bomber strength of the Eighth Air Force had risen steadily "there had been no corresponding rise in the number of fighter escorts." Thus the escorts were spread thin and it appeared inevitable that the Germans might hurl their massed strength at unprotected formations.

The Germans themselves expressed the conviction that the large and concentrated air fights they hoped to create in this manner might bring down, during a single mission, as many as four hundred or more bombers of the Eighth Air Force. Fighter leaders said they had the means to do so. Hermann Goering demanded such stupendous victories, although his means of addressing his pilots was certainly strange enough. After each massive assault against a German city Goering raged wildly at his fighter commanders, accused them of cowardice and threatened to ship the whole pack of them off to the infantry.

The pattern of a huge and savage air battle, followed by a long period without fighter interception, became accepted. When the Germans did rise to fight it was in a strength that our own air leaders had good cause to fear. On the 2nd November, as noted, 400 fighters shot down twenty-six Fortresses. Then for three weeks the Germans hid in their bomb shelters and amassed fuel. On the 21st November they reappeared, again in a strength of some 400 fighters. But many of their best pilots were no longer in their ranks. The Germans failed to assemble properly and wasted their strength. Mustangs slashed their formations and by day's end, despite the powerful intercepting force, the Germans had managed to down but five B-17s. Five days later, on the 26th, no less than 550 German fighters assaulted more than a thousand Fortresses and Liberators. Twenty-five heavies went down near Hannover.

It was the following day that shook the bomber commanders; 750 German fighters prepared to tear apart a huge armada of Fortresses and Liberators. "But luck was with the Americans," notes the AAF history. "The Germans stupidly mistook a huge force of P-51s for bombers and tangled with the Mustangs, after which it was too late to rectify their error. In the ensuing air battles the Mustangs lost only eleven aircraft and claimed ninety-eight Nazis. Meanwhile, the bombers proceeded to Bingen and Offenburg *without sighting a single enemy airplane.*" (Italics added.)

Three days later, on the 30th November, twelve hundred heavy bombers flew from England to deep within Germany and encountered only "sporadic German opposition." On the 2nd December, 150 enemy fighters managed to shoot down eight B-24s—a number far below what normally would have been expected without the escorting Mustangs. On 5th December a force of 300 German fighters rose to defend Berlin. Once again losses were held to the absolute minimum. Four bombers went down—at a cost of some ninety German fighters destroyed.

For the next two weeks the Eighth's great bomber fleets roamed Germany without a single interception. Not even the all-time record force of 1,467 bombers on the 11th December could provoke the Luftwaffe to do battle.

On the 23rd December the greatest single pack of German fighters—800 strong—did their best to break up attacks against railheads and transportation centers. Escorting fighters screened the bombers so effectively that most of the German attacks were blunted before they reached the Fortresses and Liberators. Then came the 24th December with the Eighth, taking advantage of excellent weather, dispatching a record aerial armada of 1,900 bombers and a great escort fighter screen. Eight hundred German fighters rallied against the bombers—only to run into the pursuing, harrying, maddening Mustangs. Those that got past the American fighters ran into withering defensive firepower from the bombers. The Germans took a beating. Most of the heavy bombers never received so much as a shot fired at them.

In three days of fighting—with their greatest strength assembled at one time in the air—the Germans shot down only thirteen heavy bombers. For their pains they lost 220 of their own fighters, and a crippling loss in skilled pilots. Goering resumed his tirades against his fighter commanders. Plainly, the German Air Force had failed again, and for the next five days it licked its wounds.

A brief statement tells the story. From the AAF history— "Eighth Air Force mission reports for most of January show enormous numbers of heavy bombers, sometimes as many as 1,500, going out day after day to bomb targets whose neutralization would benefit Allied ground forces. . . . Some 147 rail and road targets—rail centers, marshaling yards, repair shops, junctions, bridges, and traffic bottlenecks—received USSTAF raids during the month. . . . Transportation bombings in behalf of the ground forces helped wreck Germany and were by no means wasted even from the most extreme strategic point of view. Meanwhile, the Fifteenth Air Force was prosecuting its long campaign against railways in Yugoslavia, Austria, Hungary, and Italy."

But the strategic air leaders, despite their willingness to do everything possible to pave the way for ground forces, still chafed at the bit to resume their primary purpose of heavy bombardment against the most critical targets of the

Reich. For two months Berlin had escaped a major bombardment and the Eighth was eager to hit the key objectives in and about that city. On the eve of the Yalta Conference, Intelligence determined that the Sixth Panzer Army was moving through Berlin on its way to the Russian front. That alone made a massive raid worthwhile. Then, if the bombers could demonstrate their ability to attack whenever Allied headquarters decided to do so, there "was the possibility of demoralizing the Nazi government with a smashing bombardment."

The 3rd February 1945 was the day. Four hundred Liberators went after railway and oil targets around Magdeburg. The big blow for the day was carried out by a force of one thousand Flying Fortresses. The thunder of B-17 engines shook the ground wherever the great train of bombers, thousands of feet wide and many miles long, passed overhead. On they came, pounding through the sky, escorted by a huge swarm of fleet Mustangs spoiling for a fight. But the Luftwaffe stayed on the ground, willing to sacrifice Berlin.

The Fortresses thundered over the German capital without interference from a single enemy fighter. Most of the city lay exposed; there were only scattered clouds. The flak was "murderous" and it accounted for all twenty-one bombers shot down that day. Those fighters that rose belatedly to the defense of Berlin never made it past the Mustangs. Throughout the entire Berlin area the Fortresses bombed with outstanding accuracy, ripping up marshaling yards and railway stations. Most of the key government buildings of the Nazi party took a severe beating.

Still the bombs rained down. The German fighters had been so thoroughly whipped in their feeble interception tries that the commanders of the fighter escort "turned most of the Mustangs loose." Berliners were astounded and terrified as the Mustangs screamed in at rooftop level where "with spectacular success" they shot up locomotives and strafed railway cars.

Twenty-five thousand Germans died in the raid of 3rd February. "... Swedish newspaper accounts were full of lurid details about the horror in Berlin."

The attacks increased in their intensity. Many raids took place upon request of the Soviet government; the Fortresses and Liberators were "attacking transportation facilities inside cities in missions which the Russians had requested and seemed to appreciate.... The RAF and Eighth Air Force were carrying out extensive and shattering attacks against railway junctions in Dresden, Cottbus, Magdeburg and Chemnitz which resulted in widespread ruin to surrounding areas and tragedy to thousands of German civilians."

During February 1945 the Eighth and the RAF again increased the pressure and "destroyed any serious possibility that Germany might unduly protract the war. The heavy bombers expended their greatest efforts since June 1944.... The enemy's economy became paralyzed and his armies fatally restricted."

There was a new side to the catastrophe tearing through Germany. With so many attacks under way at one time, with so many fighters screening the bombers, with the Luftwaffe strangling on its lack of fuel, great fleets of RAF heavy bombers took to the air in daylight, during which they "continued to pile ruin upon ruin in German cities, immobilizing millions of workers and extinguishing economic life. By the end of February Nazi Germany was no longer an industrial nation."

Robert H. Hodges was a heavy bomber pilot who arrived in Europe late in 1944 and came into an air war totally different from the life-and-death struggle that had characterized the fall of just thirteen months before. This was the period of the Sunday Punch, what the pilots termed the "haymaker," the final ten months when the bombers delivered 72 percent of the total bomb tonnage dropped on Germany during the entire war.

Prior to combat assignment, Hodges, after pilot commissioning as a bomber pilot, went through six months of training in different models of the B-24, during which time he accumulated 222.25 flying hours in that airplane. But before he arrived for combat duty five groups had shifted from B-24s to the B-17 and Hodges found himself in a B-17 group, the 486th Bomb Group at ETO Station 174, Sudbury, England. He walked into the middle of the massive raids against Germany when the Eighth was putting on all the force it could muster. "I arrived relatively late," Hodges recalls. "There was in November and December of 1944 a rush and a ratrace going on, and I managed to get just under twenty-five hours transition time in the B-17 before my first combat mission."

Less than seventy-five hours later Hodges was leading a squadron from the pilot's seat with a total B-17 time of 99:30 hours. He was on the go "with missions being flown one after the other." Rather quaintly, he said, "I was a second lieutenant in January, a first lieutenant in February, and a captain in March."

Assigned to fly a tour of thirty missions, he flew twenty-seven before ending his combat career. His first mission was on the 26th December 1944, his final and twenty-seventh on the 21st April 1945; during this period he accumulated 208:20 hours combat time. Hodges was anxious to complete his required combat tour of missions; he had been promised a Mustang fighter where he would fly an additional twenty-five missions. "That was what I wanted most of all," he said, "but obviously the wrapping up of the war took care of *that*."

What was the B-17G—the late-model Fortress flown by Hodges—like to handle? Hodges relates:

My first reaction to the B-17G, after having been a month away from the B-24, was that it obviously was going to be easier to handle, especially in formations. Less physical effort was demanded of the B-17 pilot when flying manually, since the B-24 demanded considerable leg and shoulder effort in formation flying. Moving out of straight-and-level with a B-24 required a bit more effort and muscle on the yoke and rudder pedals than did the B-17.

In combat formation, natural air turbulence, propwash from planes leading your own, flak, or the combination of these could require considerable physical effort through the hours of a mission. In my case the elapsed time of the mission tour varied from a low five hours forty minutes to a high of ten hours. When a mission of long duration included propwash or turbulence, the effort and resultant fatigue were considerable. This, in spite of learning every technique, the tricks and subtleties, that a pilot acquired, such as the manner of sighting on the element lead, fingertip use of throttles, physical relaxation techniques, anticipating attitude, power and position changes, trim settings and adjustments. But fate put me into the lead slots and my combat tour was characterized by instrument flying—the key aspect of group or squadron lead piloting, rather than fighting the effects of all those machines in front of me.

The relative stability of the Fort with one or more engines out was confirmed on the twentieth mission, to Berlin on the 18th March. Flak knocked out engines one and two. Number one lost oil so rapidly we couldn't feather it in time and it "windmilled" all the way back to England. Since number four also had been hit, in the rear accessory section and turbosupercharger, and wouldn't pull full power, it was impossible to maintain high altitude after the Rally Point. We relinquished lead to the number two aircraft.

Considering that we had lost two engines on the same side, the Fortress trimmed up as well as could be expected, but obviously required continuous application of some degree of right rudder on a shared basis between the two pilots for the rest of the trip back to base. This mission also proved that the B-17G could maintain low altitude—about 1,500 feet—on only one and two-thirds engines.

I'm one of those people who feel that credit must be given, in the success of the Fortress, to the Wright engines. In the "war emergency" power setting of the B-17G I flew we could put out 1,350 horsepower at fifty-one inches manifold pressure and 2,500 RPM. During startup they sounded like threshing machines as their crankshaft counterweights slapped back and forth in their slots. But it was the kind of sound you liked. They were great engines and above all else they were *reliable* engines. They brought us home with our beating our good engines to death—and they never faltered.[73]

*Still* the Eighth applied the vise and the hammer. Reconnaissance planes brought back photographs of Nurenburg "crammed with supply trains." On the 20th February the Eighth ripped up the marshaling yards of the Nazi shrine city with 2,000 tons of bombs. The Fortresses went back the next day to add another 1,800 tons to the smoking shambles of the Nurenburg rail system.

The day following the double-smash at Nurenburg, Operation CLARION went into effect. This was a "plan of long standing designed to utilize all available Anglo-American airpower in a blow at German communications which

would affect both economic life and the tactical situation."
To increase their effect the heavy bombers would go after
their targets from 10,000 feet rather than their customary
bombing altitudes of 20,000 to 25,000 feet. The Eighth and
Fifteenth Air Forces alone put up 2,200 heavy bombers escorted by many hundreds of fighters which, because of
meager and ineffectual German opposition, were "turned
loose" after ground targets in deadly strafing attacks. On
the 23rd the Allied forces repeated the blow. The Eighth
sent 1,193 bombers over target to drop 3,327 tons of
bombs.

It was difficult to believe the minimal loss figures. One
bomber ditched in the North Sea, and the crew of a second
bomber bailed out from their crippled plane—in friendly
territory.

On the 24th February a force of 1,090 bombers left
England. Flak shot down two bombers. Those were the
only losses.

The next day 1,177 heavy bombers struck across Germany. Flak proved to be "murderous" and a surprising
number of fighters rose to do battle. Despite the massive
force, the flak and fighters claimed only five heavy
bombers and five escort fighters.

On the 26th, smashing steadily at German targets, 1,102
heavy bombers of the Eighth appeared over Berlin. They
dropped 2,879 tons of bombs on the city. The official
records show that "as anticipated, no enemy fighter were
encountered."

The 27th February provided no letup in the punishment. Nearly 1,100 heavy bombers and fifteen fighter
groups of the Eighth tore up targets across Germany. On
the 28th the giant armadas went out again to repeat their
hammer blows.

All through this time the Fifteenth carried on its own

sledgehammer strikes, with missions numbering from 400 to 1,000 bombers and escorting fighters.

By March 1945 the tenor of the air war was best summed up in this brief quote from the official AAF study of the strategic air campaign: "The 1 March 1945 mission of the Eighth Air Force required dispatching 1,219 heavies, *a normal effort by this date of the war*, to southern Germany."

The next day 1,210 bombers with fifteen fighter groups as escort appeared in German air. Seventy-five fighters intercepted. One main air battle cost the Eighth Air Force six Fortresses. The German losses were much higher—nearly forty fighters were shot out of the sky, and "results of other engagements in the air made the attempted interceptions disastrous for the Germans."

*3rd March:* 1,048 heavy bombers of the Eighth hit widely scattered targets. German jets intercepted, shooting down six Mustangs and three bombers.

*4th March:* Nearly a thousand bombers sortied; unfavorable weather forced most of the heavies to strike targets of opportunity. No losses.

*5th March:* 500 heavy bombers went into Germany. There were no reported interceptions. The crews were astonished when they received no antiaircraft fire over the Ruhr. "The enemy was at last feeling severe shortages in flak."

*6th March:* Weather "impossible"; the bombers were grounded.

*7th March:* 926 heavy bombers hit German targets.

*8th March:* 1,340 Fortresses and Liberators struck different targets. No losses to fighters; no losses to flak.

*9th March:* More than 1,000 bombers "finished off the great tank plant at Kassel, which was abandoned after the mission. . . ."

*10th March:* 1,358 heavy bombers hit "numerous transportation targets." No losses to fighters; no losses to flak.

*11th March:* More than a thousand bombers were over Germany. . . .

*12th March:* Meeting a Russian request, 671 Fortresses smashed Swinemunde, only fifteen miles from Russian lines. (On this same date, 744 heavies of the Fifteenth hit other targets. . . . )

*14th March:* 1,246 Eighth Air Force heavies went out. . . .

*15th March:* More than 1,340 heavy bombers with fifteen fighter groups left England.

*18th March:* 1,250 heavy bombers and fourteen groups of P-51s struck Berlin. More than 3,000 tons of bombs were dropped in the heaviest daylight attack of the war on the German capital. After two weeks of quiet, the Luftwaffe rose to do battle. Swarms of Messerschmitt Me-262 jet fighters, attacking in formations of up to thirty-six aircraft, hammered at the bombers. Twenty-four bombers and five fighters were lost to the German jets and flak; *the latter damaged 700 bombers.*

*19th March:* Nearly 1,000 heavy bombers and fourteen fighter groups. . . .

*20th March:* Bad weather; 415 heavy bombers attacked Germany. Jets shot down two bombers.

*21st March:* 1,254 heavies attacked. . . .

*22nd March:* More than 1,200 heavies bombed. . . .

*23rd March:* 1,240 heavy bombers of the Eighth went out. . . .

*24th March:* More than a thousand Fortresses and Liberators. . . . That was the way it went.

On the 7th April the Germans rose in strength to strike at the massed American formations. More than 130 conventional fighters and more than fifty twin-engine jets rushed the four-engine bombers. Crews were startled to hear martial music blared into the receivers of the German fighters, and when they saw single-engine fighters ramming several bombers, it was shockingly clear what was happening. Mixed in with the experienced pilots, late-arrival German fliers were slashing at the Fortresses and Liberators in do-or-die attempts. Even the official report transcends its normal aloofness: *"The Germans were expending their last remaining pilots in a suicidal, frenzied effort. Exhortations over the radio were desperate and yet somehow pathetic."*

The Mustangs did a spectacular job. The furious German assault resulted in the loss of only seven bombers.

The Mustangs and guns of the bombers shot down more than one hundred German fighters.

Early in April the British warned that "further destruction of German cities would magnify the problems of the occupying forces. . . ." The Royal Air Force ceased all area bombing.

On the 13th April the strategic bombers were given a prime mission of direct assistance to the army in its ground campaign.

The committee code-named JOCKEY, which had directed the campaign against the aircraft industry of Germany, sent out its last signal: *"Jockey has unsaddled and weighed in. Sic transit gloria Tuesday."*

On the 16th April 1945 General Spaatz dispatched this message:

"The advances of our ground forces have brought to a close the strategic air war waged by the United States Strategic Air Force and the Royal Air Force Bomber Command.

"It has been won with a decisiveness becoming increasingly evident as our armies overrun Germany.

"From now onward our Strategic Air Forces must operate with our Tactical Air Forces in close cooperation with our armies. . . ."

The strategic air war was ended. Germany lay paralyzed, strangled, choked, in ruins.

On the 1st May the mission boards of the Eighth Air Force remained blank. There were no further combat assignments.

Eight days later all ground fighting ended.

There are many ways, many expressions, which might be a fitting close to this chapter. Since the 8th May 1945, when war in Europe ground to a halt, there have been reams of statistics, an avalanche of charts, a torrent of conclusive statements.

To this writer the next "missions" of the Flying Fortress tell it best of all.

Day after day, at the air bases in England, long lines of men waited to board the Fortresses. Day after day, until more than thirty thousand men climbed into the airplanes—with pilots grinning at their passengers.

The thirty thousand men were the ground personnel of the Eighth Air Force who had kept the bombers in the air, who had serviced, armed, bombed-up, fueled, and kept in the best possible condition the bombers they watched go off to war.

Thirty thousand men were taken on aerial sightseeing flights over Germany at one thousand feet. It was quite a tour.

They went to see with their own eyes the mission they had made possible.

\*     \*     \*

The writer knows of no man more deserving, more fitting, better able, than my good friend, Budd J. Peaslee, Col., USAF, Ret., to write the words that follow:

The tumult and the shouting have died away. The B-17s and B-24s will never again assemble into strike formation in the bitter cold of embattled skies. Never again will the musical thunder of their passage cause the very earth to tremble, the source of sound lost in infinity and seeming to emanate from all things, visible and invisible. The great deep-throated engines are forever silent, replaced by the flat, toneless roar of the jets and the rockets. But, on bleak and lonely winter nights in the English Midlands, ghost squadrons take off silently in the swirling mist of the North Sea from the ancient weed-choked runways, and wing away toward the east, never to return. On other nights the deserted woodlands ring with unheard laughter and gay voices of young men and young women who once passed that way. Recollections of all these fade a little with each passing year until at last there will finally remain only the indelible records of the all-seeing Master of the Universe to recall the deeds of valor excelled by no other nation, arm or service. These sacred scrolls will forever remain the heritage of the free and untrampled people of this earth.

# IV

# OPEN LEDGER

# CHAPTER 28

# OPEN LEDGER

WITH THE COMPLETION OF the final combat mission of the Flying Fortress in Europe, a great cycle closed.

The early history of this airplane, well before Model 299 was rolled out from the old Boeing factory, was clearly a struggle for the existence of a realistic and meaningful airpower. The working doctrine of strategic airpower, no matter what its flaws, was only so much meaningless eloquence without the hardware to give it substance.

Strategic airpower came into being with the Fortress. Not with Model 299, not the early YIB-17, not the first Fortresses that went into limited service with the test-and-trial missions flown from Langley Field in 1937. The doctrine of airpower took on flesh and substance when there were sufficient airplanes on hand, when adequate production was assured, when crews became experienced, when more bombers loomed over the horizon of industrial facilities. Not until the B-17 was available in quantity, not until there was, in the words of General Arnold, "airpower you can touch," did doctrine become reality.

The record stands clear. It was the B-17, more than any other single weapon expressing the strength of this nation, that made possible all that you have read in this volume.

There is a temptation to complete this story with the findings and conclusions that were made available after the war in the studies of the United States Strategic Bombing Survey. Perhaps more words attended the aftermath of the conflict than accompanied its existence. But the final results of all the struggle to bring forth the B-17 are provided in the rubble that was Germany.

Certain statistics are important. It is significant that of all the bombs hurled against the Reich in World War II, only *half* of that tonnage fell on Germany proper. And of that half, only a distressingly small percentage hit the industrial targets our air leaders chose as the primary objective of the B-17. But there were other targets which the exigencies of the moment demanded—trucks, airfields, ships, harbors, armies in the field, bridges, railways and marshaling yards, *ad infinitum*. It is important to note, as well, that the strategic air attack against Germany did not attain its full power until the latter part of 1944. Most of the bomb damage to Germany came in the final eight months of the war.

These statistics are germane to the B-17. During World War II, the B-24 dropped on European targets a total of 452,508 tons of bombs. The B-17 released the staggering weight of 640,036 tons. The magnitude of this effort may better be appreciated when we see that another 463,544 tons of bombs were dropped by *all other aircraft*. It is sobering to recall the weight of the powerful night attacks of the British, and then to study the preceding figures.

During operations in Europe the Fortresses flew a total of 291,508 combat sorties.

Certain statistics provide interesting comparisons. Per each raid of a thousand aircraft (statistically) the Fortresses amassed an average of twenty-three enemy aircraft shot down in combat. This may be compared to the B-24's eleven enemy planes shot down per thousand-plane raid; the escorting fighters at eleven; and the medium bombers at three.

During World War II, in all combat theaters around the world, the AAF lost approximately 4,750 B-17s due to enemy action.

It would be impossible to review all the different uses to which the Fortresses were put, aside from their primary combat role, since there has never been a comprehensive attempt to catalogue such activities. Since our primary interest centers on the B-17, the reader may be interested in some of these various modifications and special missions.

Unquestionably the most "colorful" of all B-17s was the FAS—the Formation Assembly Ship as it was employed in England. A Fortress that had since seen its best days in combat was removed from the active list for further missions. Mechanics removed the machine guns, turrets, armor plating, and all weight not essential to the new FAS assignment. The airplane was then painted with ten-foot-wide alternating strips of white and bright red, covering the wings, fuselage, and the tail. Twenty-four high-intensity flashing red lights were then placed about the aircraft. Every twelve seconds the lights flashed the code letter C. Bombers taking off for combat missions would seek out the brilliantly-flashing FAS for their formation assembly.

During 1943, a B-17F produced by Boeing was modified to the XB-40 configuration—the "Gunship" with additional turrets and a heavy ammunition load. After tests with the XB-40, an additional thirteen B-17F-10-VE bombers were converted to YB-40 and sent to Europe for combat tests of the airplane as an escort (beyond fighter range) for the B-17F bomber. As we have noted, these tests proved unsuccessful but they yielded an unexpected dividend in the sorely needed chin turret for the B-17G series.

The British made wider use of the Fortress than is commonly realized. Their first bombers were, of course, the twenty B-17C variants which were modified for use by the RAF as the Fortress I, an airplane employed improperly and which left a sour taste among those involved in its combat operations. In mid-1942 the British received forty-five B-17E models. Most of these were operated by Coastal Command as the Fortress IIA on anti-submarine search and attack missions. Several Fortress IIA aircraft also served on special missions with Bomber Command, operating in daylight and at night.

Nineteen B-17F aircraft went into British service. Again, most of these were operated by Coastal Command for submarine search, training, meteorological reconnaissance missions, and other duties. The single greatest Fortress shipment to England was of the B-17G, of which eighty-five aircraft, known as the Fortress III, were delivered. Several of these bombers went to Coastal Command. Another batch went to No. 100 Group on special missions, using elaborate radio countermeasures to jam and to confuse German radar. They also flew clandestine missions, dropping agents by parachute behind German lines. Others were used as decoys on night bombing missions.

One of the most interesting British variants was a special test model of a B-17E. The British mounted in the nose of this airplane a Bristol turret with a 40-mm Vickers cannon, which was to be used against surface submarines. Conventional attack apparently proved more useful, for the Vickers project was abandoned.

Several Fortresses went into service with the AAF as cargo and transport aircraft. These specially modified bombers were rare since there was so much demand for the Fortress as a combat aircraft. One B-17E was modified extensively into the XC-108; this aircraft became famous as the *Bataan*, the personal transport for General Douglas MacArthur. Modified in this manner the XC-108 had extra windows, office and living space, and airliner type seats. Carrying thirty-eight people, the XC-108 fully fueled weighed 48,726 pounds.

One B-17E was converted to YC-108 configuration as a cargo transport. Loading difficulties with this model produced another B-17E conversion into the XC-108A, with a large cargo door installed on the left side of the airplane. The final modification in this series was a B-17F converted into the XC-108B, with fuel cells installed within the fuselage so that the airplane could serve as a fast fuel tanker. The most capacious fuselage and longer range (at that time) of the B-24 brought the AAF to concentrate on the latter airplane as a cargo/tanker conversion—a move that pleased all those commanders demanding more and more Fortresses as bombers.

B-17E Serial Number 41-2401 became the XB-38 when it was modified to take four Allison V-1710-89 inline engines each rated at 1,425 horsepower for takeoff. This airplane first flew on the 19th May 1943 and with its more powerful engines had a top speed of 327 miles per hour. On the 16th June 1943 a fire destroyed the prototype, and since the Allison engines were in great demand for the P-38 and other fighters, two more XB-38 variants were canceled and the project abandoned.

Sixteen B-17F models were converted to F-9 aircraft for long-range photographic reconnaissance missions. Tri-metragon cameras were installed in the nose and other cameras placed in the bomb bay and in the rear fuselage. A total of sixty-one B-17Fs were modified in the F-9 series; the F-9A and F-9B models were distinguished only by different camera arrangements. Ten B-17G aircraft were modified to F-9C configuration.

One B-17F was transferred to the U.S. Navy; the airplane did not receive a USN designation.

Forty B-17Gs also went to the Navy and after refitting with massive external radomes and extensive interior equipment for early-warning and anti-submarine duties, were redesignated the PB-1W. Of these forty aircraft, sixteen were reassigned to the U.S. Coast Guard where they were designated PB-1G for patrol and search missions.

During World War II, seven B-17s that had made forced landings in Sweden were stripped of turrets and armament and modified extensively to serve as civil transports. They remained in use for some years after the war.

The Luftwaffe made extensive use of the Fortresses that were captured after forced landings by wounded crews. The Rosarius Flying Circus was perhaps best known for its use of the B-17; the bombers were flown to German fighter units for demonstrations to pilots who practiced firing runs on the Fortresses. Less known was the B-17's role with the Luftwaffe unit known as I/K.G. 200 which used its captured Fortresses in secret missions. Known on the Luftwaffe roster as Dornier Do 200s these Fortresses were used for ferrying and parachuting agents in airspace under Allied control. Most of the bombers were repainted with German insignia. I/K.G. 200 used the B-17s especially for long-range missions. In 1944 they were used in the Western Desert for secret agent drops and resupply, and in October

1944 several German Fortresses parachuted agents into Jordan. Similar use was made of these airplanes throughout the Continent. The German B-17s were also used, as we have noted earlier, for flying with B-17 formations to radio to German defenses the flight details of the missions.

A bizarre use of the B-17 as a robot bomb was made during the period June 1944 to January 1945 by the Eighth Air Force; this operation was carried out under the code names CASTOR and APHRODITE. The Fortresses employed in these tests were "war-wearies," B-17s worn out or damaged severely in operational missions. Mostly they were old B-17E and F models which were stripped of all useful equipment. They were then redesignated as the BQ-7, fitted with radio-control equipment for remote control from a "mother" airplane, and crammed with ten tons of Torpex, a British explosive some fifty percent more powerful than amatol.

In operational use the BQ-7 was taken off the ground by a pilot and radio operator. Once well into the air and en route to its target, control was passed to the accompanying airplane and the pilot and radio operator bailed out, leaving the radio-controlled bomber without a crew. The mother airplane was usually another Fortress, although tests were also made with P-38 fighters and British Mosquito bombers. The idea was for the mother airplane to dive the explosive-laden and pilotless B-17 into a target.

In August 1944 the project was renamed by its unhappy participants as Project PERILOUS. After the crew bailed out, one BQ-7 went out of control and plunged—fortunately—into a woods. The crater resulting from the spectacular dive was greater than one hundred feet in diameter. Another BQ-7 that "ran away" kept a British industrial area on its toes when the uncontrolled Fortress circled aimlessly overhead "for some time" before, to the immense relief of all those watching it warily, it wandered off to sea where finally it crashed.

CASTOR and APHRODITE were canceled soon after.

When World War II ended the AAF found itself with several thousand Flying Fortresses for which it had little or no use. Hundreds of the airplanes were kept on flying status but for the greater number were superseded by the B-29 which had taken over the primary strategic bombardment mission for the AAF against Japan—"another airplane and another war." Most Fortresses in Europe were stripped of their heavy equipment and flown back to the United States, carrying as many men as could safely be jammed aboard. Once this ferry mission had been accomplished the bombers were flown to storage centers in the United States where they were declared surplus. Many were sold to private dealers but the majority were finally broken up and melted for their scrap value. Buying a Flying Fortress was an enticing enterprise and the price was certainly right— anywhere from ten to twenty percent of its original cost— but how many people could afford to operate a four-engine bomber? As a transport the B-17 was uneconomical; bombers, after all are not made to fly with economical efficiency. From an accountant's viewpoint the airplane, as a passenger plane, was a money loser. Its fuselage, built for strength and for carrying bombs and guns, was rugged but cramped and the operating costs were brutal.

The military, however, still had use for its Fortresses. We saw how the B-17 was used as a missile launcher with the GB-1, GB-4 and GB-8 series. In the postwar period dozens of B-17s went into service as missile carriers, launching many different types of air-to-air and air-to-ground missiles. The more interesting of these tests included launch operations—two missiles to one B-17—of the

American version of the German FZG-76 better known to the public as the infamous V-1.

Radio-controlled versions of the Fortress, mostly as the QB-17, were flown through the radioactive clouds of nuclear bomb tests for radiation monitoring missions. Other B-17s, with full equipment and in excellent condition, were used on the ground as targets during nuclear explosions.

There were CB-17 and VB-17 transport models, RB-17s for reconnaissance and SB-17s for search missions. QB-17 and DB-17 modifications have been used as targets for missiles. One B-17G with all guns and turrets mounted and the airplane kept in its combat status, was flown by the All Weather Flying Center at Wright Field, Ohio, for storm research. An ETB-17G, with elaborate equipment installed in the airplane, was used for extensive electronics experiments.

During the Korean War there were still some of the old Fortresses around for search and rescue missions. Immediately after World War II the Air Force converted approximately 130 B-17G aircraft into the B-17H and TB-17H variant. Beneath these airplanes was a large lifeboat, complete with engine, fuel, emergency provisions, radio equipment, and the necessities for survival at sea. Several of these airplanes were in service in Japan in 1950 and were pressed into action. One other Fortress became well known for its Korean War duties. *Hi Penny* served as the personal transport for Lt. General Matthew B. Ridgway.

The last Fortress in use with the United States Air Force survived well into the age of new robot weapons. A DB-17 which had endured many years of service on the Air Force Missile Test Range in both piloted and radio-control missions, and became the final on-duty B-17, was slated for a dramatic end. The airplane was flown downrange of Cape

Canaveral during the launching of a Boeing IM-99 Bomarc, a three-engine (one rocket and two ramjets) pilotless interceptor. Far out over the Atlantic the silver-and-blue Bomarc whipped at supersonic speed into its pilotless victim.

It seemed ironic to those involved in the test. What Boeing had started, Boeing finished.

No one person knows to what extent the Flying Fortress saw military service after World War II with air forces other than the United States, simply because the diversity of that use—and a deliberate absence of information—has cloaked such activities. One of the better known, of course, is the combat assignment of the Fortress with the Israeli Air Force which used the B-17 to bomb Cairo and other Egyptian targets. That air war was a parody of reversed roles. Israeli pilots—many of them Americans—flew Messerschmitt Me-109F fighters in escort of the B-17s, which were intercepted and attacked by Egyptian Spitfires. . . .

The Flying Fortress remains on active operation duty with different national air forces today. The B-17s may be seen in the colors of the Portuguese Air Force, operating out of Portugal and different air bases in the Azores. Eleven Fortresses went into service with the Forca Aerea Brasileira, and it is of interest to note that this service *began* in *1951*. With the passing of years after World War II it became more and more evident that the B-17 could outperform, with lower investment and running cost, many of the other military airplanes available to different nations. The first Brazilian Fortress was B-17G Number 5400 which went on duty on the 4th May 1951 and was joined later by ten more Fortresses. By October 1966 B-17G Number 5402 had logged—entirely in Brazilian service—no less than 5,596 hours, which must be added to the flight time accumulated prior to 1951. Since their duty assignment with Brazil, five members of the Fortress fleet have been retired and their parts and assemblies used to maintain the six airplanes still on duty.

Several B-17G models have been and still remain on duty with the French; they have for years carried out special high-altitude assignments with the *French Institut Geographique National.*

One of the more surprising aspects of B-17 service is that while their number has decreased steadily because of attrition and a lack of resupply, they are coming more and more into demand. John Hawke, and international dealer in used aircraft, spent months during 1967 combing the United States and other countries for available B-17s; he had two customers—South American governments—which were extremely anxious to purchase the Fortresses for their air forces.

Hawke found a number of Fortresses, but couldn't make any deals.

Nobody wanted to sell the airplanes.

Those of us who have been in aviation for several decades would never have believed that the Flying Fortress would continue in demand or could have been pressed into such extensive service as the airplane has seen. Once again it is impossible to not *all* the uses to which this airplane had been put, simply because there hasn't been anyone around to keep such records. The reader should understand, then, that the cases that follow are only representative of a use much wider than is recorded here.

Perhaps the most unusual of the postwar Fortresses has been the *Flying Fish.* An enterprising dealer in rare tropical fish bought a B-17 and rebuilt the airplane with several pressurized compartments within the fuselage—in which he placed water tanks containing rare and experimental fish. These were picked up at various collection points outside the United States and, safe in pressurized conditions, were flown into this country with a minimum loss of the delicate and perishable cargo.

Enterprising best denotes one pilot who showed up at Ryan Field in Tucson, Arizona, to pay hard cash for a war surplus B-17G. He found the airplane weary but in excellent condition, and paid cash on the line to have wide cargo doors and windows placed in the fuselage. The same pilot, usually flying solo, then closed contracts with cucumber farmers. The contracts were to deliver the cucumbers swiftly and at prices competitive with normal means of pickup and delivery. Our commercial adventurer flew the Fortress right into the fields where the cucumbers had been collected; they were loaded by chute into the airplane. The moment the ship was filled—and a heavy load was carried—the pilot took off and flew directly to the delivery point. As quickly as the airplane was unloaded he was on the way back for another pickup.

At the end of two seasons the same pilot reappeared at Ryan Field with the same airplane—ready to dispose of his pickle bomber. He sold the ship for approximately half its purchase price, grinning broadly as he accepted his money. The reason for his pleasure was evident—he had made, clear, five times the purchase cost, and all expenses, of his Fortress.

That same airplane was sold again—and is still in use.

One Canadian Fortress has now been in active service—going on fifteen years—as an electronic-equipped airplane carrying out radio propagation and other scientific studies in the far north. Most of its flights take place north of the Arctic Circle.

For years the Curtiss-Wright Corporation flew one of the rarer Fortresses to be seen in the air—a five-engined model. Engineers rebuilt the nose and installed a huge turboprop engine for flight tests. That single engine pulled so much power that the Fortress could often be seen with all four Cyclones shut down and the propellers feathered—all power being supplied by the giant turboprop in the nose. After years of flight testing the airplane was returned to normal configuration and sold—for considerably more than the original purchase price.

Easily the most luxurious Fortress seen in the air was the airplane converted by an industrialist into a private transport. From nose to tail the interior was thickly padded with leather-surfaced cushioning. It was equipped with desks and working space, sleeping bunks, radio-telephones, elaborate galley and bar. Best of all, however, was the nose. A beautifully molded sheet of curving plexiglas replaced the former bomber nose. The compartment, which had housed the bombardier and navigator, was thickly insulated and fitted out with elaborate cushions. Directly before the plexiglas nose, to provide a spectacular panorama of flight, was placed a luxury couch.

For two.

More prosaic, but equally important, use of the Fortress has been made in the agricultural field. The states of Georgia and Florida have an entire fleet of Fortresses, which have been equipped as spray planes, dusting crops, or pressed into service to meet special needs. The two states have combined their efforts with their Fortress fleet to carry out a war against hordes of fire ants. Low-altitude (treetop) flying with spray equipment is one of the flight tricks the Fortress can perform better than any other aircraft in the business.

Other Fortresses have served as water and borate-bombers in aerial firefighting.

One B-17 on the west coast of the United States is something of an aerial ham. The Fortress plays itself in a television series on the Fortress in World War II.

The nose, tail and other gun positions of the Fortress have endeared it to film makers as one of the best aerial camera ships ever to leave the ground. Those readers who saw the film *Dr. Strangelove* undoubtedly will recall the spectacular low-altitude flying across Canada and the ice-littered ocean off the coastline. That was no B-52—the pictures were filmed from a B-17. Its commercial number was N9563Z. It was the same plane in which this writer was to have some wild misadventures of his own.

My own flights in a Flying Fortress took place in the fall of 1961. Three airplanes—all ex-B-17G models—were involved, and the "mission" was to find three Fortresses, rebuild them to flight status, and then fly the airplanes (complete with gun turrets and other combat equipment) to England, where they would be repainted and fitted out for starring roles in the motion picture, *The War Lover*. The star of this episode was a spectacularly gifted pilot, Gregory R. Board, who cut his flying teeth on Buffalo fighters in Singapore back in 1941, twenty years before he and his team resurrected three beaten-up, long-abandoned Fortresses.

Greg Board is a man not given to visible emotion, but even he shook his head sadly as he surveyed the wrecks he was to bring back to life. He was looking at three great air-planes that scarcely revealed their pride of years past. Three of the famed Fortresses. Queens that had been re-duced to tattered rags, to metal blotched and splashed with disuse and years of neglect. The once-shiny plexiglas was shattered into splinters that jutted dangerously from gun hatches, windows and turrets. The tires were flat and rotted. The fabric that once covered the control surfaces had vanished completely, victim of time and weather. The first time Board climbed into one of the airplanes he did so with extreme caution, and when he brushed aside the thick cobwebs to move through the Fortress he did so carefully. For the airplane was inhabited, as Board knew it would be. The new denizens were snakes, some of them poisonous, and they had been here for years. They did not like intruders.

As he studied all three airplanes the situation looked worse and worse. The more he inspected the Fortresses the more neglect and damage he found. Thunderstorms, hailstones, torrential rains and other weapons of the weather had done their best to destroy the machines. What nature left unharmed crowds of vandals had tried to wreck with stones, hammers, and metal bars. Kids and adults with a blind penchant for destruction had smashed instruments— anything and everything that could be bent, broken or splintered. One airplane especially seemed totally beyond repair. It was sunk into the ground so deeply the wheel axles were covered. The massive tires were so badly deteriorated that a man could place several fingers into the split rubber. Grass reached completely above the wheels and when Greg Board pried open a fuselage hatch he was met with an onslaught of shrill cries and shrieks. *Hundreds* of birds flew frantically from the Fortress . . .

Greg Board's handpicked team from his outfit, Aero Associates, went to work. In the ensuing days, crowds of disbelievers gathered in increasingly greater numbers to watch the resurrection. All bets on the airfield had it that those airplanes were fit only for junk, and here were lunatics spending perfectly good money on old wreckage. The jeers faded slowly and the watching chins hung just a bit lower as the bombers went through their Cinderella process. Before too many days passed the hangars across the field resounded to the crashing echoes of Wright Cyclones in rising and falling thunder as the mechanics nursed them back into life.

Fourteen days after they started the mechanics were through. On the morning of the fifteenth Day Greg Board, somewhat tired (he had never before flown a B-17 and spent several hours that night reading the manual), climbed into the pilot's seat of the first airplane. He closed the hatch behind him. He was alone.

He fired up the Fortress (that hadn't flown for years), gunned it down the runway and lifted smoothly into the air. Board pulled back the throttles to climb power, adjusted propeller pitch and cowl flaps, brought up the flaps, retracted the gear, and did the several dozen small things a crew usually does in flying a four-engine bomber. Over the mountains near Tucson he nosed down, set up a pattern for Ryan Airfield. From his altitude the runway resembled a small and wretched postage stamp.

Ryan is four thousand feet long. It is several thousand feet above sea level, it is hot (*very* hot), and has turbulence enough to make strong pilots weep. Board came in on a long, flat approach and slapped the wheels down on the edge of the runway. He tramped brakes and handled the rudder gingerly (none of this modern stuff like reversing props and other handy gimmicks). Two thousand feet down the runway the Fortress groaned to a halt. Board taxied off to the parking ramp.

By that afternoon Greg Board had ferried the other two Fortress to Ryan Field, racking up three solo takeoffs and landings on the first day he had ever taken the pilot's seat of the B-17. . . .

Some time later a group of us were flying those old

Fortresses from Arizona to England where they were to go before motion picture cameras. We left in the wake of our twelve whirling propellers (when they were all turning, that is) a mixture of incredulity and, in some instances, anger.

It was a flight replete with minor but maddening mechanical failures. We arrived finally in England despite the dire forebodings of our fellows in the aviation community—predictions abetted by several engine fires that at times threatened to disturb our peace of mind. The weather was consistently opposite to the forecasts; instead of predicted clear skies, we encountered howling storms in which the strength of the B-17 was again tested severely.

Our flight began as nothing more adventurous or exciting than a delivery of three airplanes from the United States to England. On the face of it, this was the mission. But the more you examined it, the more impossible it seemed. For our airplanes were ancient derelicts which had been written off years before as worthless junk. In such machines we were to span the Atlantic, in formation, at a time of year when the ocean is notorious for its generally terrible flying weather and violent storms. The men who would fly the airplanes, for the most part, had never even been *in* a B-17. But there is a saying among the flying community that a great airplane can always be made to fly again, and any really good pilot can fly it.

The British aviation press, not known for unseemly enthusiasm, described our flight as "an operation which was not without its epic quality, with weather difficulties and engine troubles." That is in some ways a grand understatement but nevertheless one in which all of us who were involved can concur.

After the British press visited with us at Gatwick, where we landed, the stories enlarged somewhat, the reporters now having a firmer grasp on the details. Our delivery flight had become "aviation history ... with the safe arrival, despite many vicissitudes, of three B-17 Flying Fortresses at Gatwick ... Literally taken from the scrapheaps, the reconditioned planes made an inspiring sight, landing from formation at Gatwick, each plane touching down within a matter of minutes."

Before we took off from the United States, we brought along with us on a brief flight a man who hadn't seen a B-17 since 1944. That was when they carried his inert form tenderly from the debris of a Queen that had become a flying wreck, riddled by enemy guns, long before it reached its home field.

This man, this friend of mine, crawled all through the resurrected bomber. Quietly, without a word, he went from turret position to position, from the bombardier's station in the nose all the way back to the turret in the tail where a man had knelt on his knees and defended his airplane with two heavy machine guns.

Then he sat before the waist gunner's window and stared out, and he went back in time seventeen years, when a Fortress had brought him home. He will never know exactly what happened, because he was bloody and slashed with steel and unconscious, but neither will he ever forget that day. Because when he regained consciousness several days later in the hospital and asked about the other men of his crew, no one seemed able to give him an answer. Not for a while, anyway.

You see, the bombardier was dead. So was the ball turret gunner, and one of the waist gunners.

And when the medics squeezed into the cockpit, splattered from ceiling to floor to side walls and windows with blood, they stared in awe at what they found.

Both pilots were . . . dead.

So the Queen is many things to many people, and nobody said anything or mentioned aloud that we had seen tears on the face of the man staring out that waist window. For him, the clock had turned all the way back for the full seventeen years.

This, then, was the airplane . . . the *Queen* herself, that our small group would bring back to England. And this is why, wherever we landed, wherever we went, we couldn't keep the people away from those wonderful, old, weary, derelict and glorious airplanes.

When we took the Fortresses back into the skies information, the song those engines gave out wasn't just the thunder of pistons ramming up and down and of propellers thrashing mightily at the air. The old Fort hurls forth a cry that is singularly hers. No other airplane anywhere has quite that deep-throated and distinctive sound. And there isn't another airplane in the world that looks quite like the B-17, that is as beautiful in the sky as seen from a sister ship in formation. The lines of the Fortress don't begin to flow until she sings her song of flight in the elements for which she was designed.

To the writer, no other airplane ever built can fly like the Queen. She had a touch with her controls that defies description; she was a big and a husky airplane, but as sweet and true in her handling characteristics as any pilot could ask. When you took the yoke in your hands and planted your feet on the rudder pedals, she was *yours*, and no mistake about it.

She was all these things, and more. There was something else that was terribly real and important in our flight. It is obvious that we were turning back the clock for many years in our mission across the Atlantic. Perhaps ours was the final, the last formation flight across the ocean that the Fortress will ever know, and there is a touch of sadness in writing this kind of *finis* to the Grand Old Lady.

It seems that when we flew the Atlantic, whether we cruised above enormous sweeping banks of clouds, or drifted like tiny spores between canyon walls of thunderheads that sailed out of sight above us, or when we rushed scant feet above the wind-whipped waves ... no matter where we were, or where we flew, we had passengers with us. You couldn't see them; you had to feel, or sense, their presence, but it did seem as though we had ghostly visitors in those airplanes.

If you listened carefully, very carefully, through the roar of the engines and the creaking of the airplane and the cry of the wind ... you could hear the whisper of all those who had come and gone. In the deep, shadowy gloom of the fuselage, with the airplane swaying and rocking gently in the wind, you might almost see the forms of the men. Then, drifting timelessly from wherever it is that the great battles of the air are remembered, the ghosts would come alive.

In that half-light and gloom the turrets would seem to move and men to bend to their guns. When sunlight speared the gloom and illuminated the dust motes, you could, by squinting carefully, see behind the dust the floating wisps of smoke from the guns and see the flash of the empty shell casings as they whirled to the floor of the airplane.

If you believed, and you tried, really tried ... well, it all depends upon what the Fortress means to you.

That kind of ledge will never be closed.

# Sources/References

1 *Famous Bombers of the Second World War*, by William Green: Hanover House

2 *The Army Air Forces in World War II*, edited by W. P. Craven and J. L. Tate: University of Chicago Press

3 Taped interviews with Walter A. Krell, 1963; with Martin Caidin and Edward Hymoff

4 *Vision—The Story of Boeing*, by Harold Mansfield: Meredith Press

5 *The Development of Air Doctrine in the Army Air Arm, 1917–1941*, by the Air University: USAF Historical Studies No. 89

6 *Ibid:* reference #4

7 *Ibid:* reference #4

8 *Ibid:* reference #2

9 *Ibid:* reference #2

10 *Ibid:* reference #2

11 *Ibid:* reference #2

12 *Ibid:* reference #2

13 *Ibid:* reference #2

14 *Ibid:* reference #5

15 *Ibid:* reference #4

16 *Ibid:* reference #2

17 *Ibid:* reference #5

18 *Australia in the War of 1939–1945*, Series Three, Volume 1

19 *United States Army in World War II:* Department of the Army

20 *Ibid:* reference #2

21 *Ibid:* reference #2

22 *Ibid:* reference #2

23 *Ibid:* reference #2

24 *Ibid:* reference #2

25 *Ibid:* reference #2

26 *Ibid:* reference #2

27 *Ibid:* reference #2

28 *Ibid:* reference #2

29 *Ibid:* reference #2

30 *Ibid:* reference #2

31 *Ibid:* reference #4

32 The material for the action of December 10, 1941, has been adapted from *The Ragged, Rugged Warriors*, by Martin Caidin: E.P. Dutton

33 *Ibid:* reference #2

34 *Ibid:* reference #4

35 *Ibid:* reference #2

36 *Ibid:* reference #18

37 *Samurai!*, by Saburo Sakai, with Martin Caidin and Fred Saito: E.P. Dutton

38 *Ibid:* reference #2

39 *Ibid:* reference #2

40 *Ibid:* reference #18

41 *Ibid:* reference #18

42 *Target: Germany, the Official Record of the VII Bomber Command*

43 *Ibid:* reference #2

44 *Ibid:* reference #42

45 *Ibid:* reference #2

46 *Ibid:* reference #2

47 *Royal Air Force 1939–45:* Her Majesty's Stationery Office

48 *Ibid:* reference #2

49 *Ibid:* reference #2

50 *Ibid:* reference #2

51 *Ibid:* reference #42

52 *Ibid:* reference #2

53 *Ibid:* reference #2

54 *Ibid:* reference #4

55 *Ibid:* reference #42

56 *Ibid:* reference #42

57 *Ibid:* reference #42

58 *Ibid:* reference #2

59 *Ibid:* reference #2

60 *Ibid:* reference #2

61 *Ibid:* reference #2

62 *Heritage of Valor*, by Colonel Budd J. Peaslee, USAF (Ret): J. B. Lippincott

63 *Ibid:* reference #42

64 *Ibid:* reference #2

65 *Ibid:* reference #62

66 *Black Thursday*, by Martin Caidin: E.P. Dutton

67 Adapted from *Black Thursday*

68 *Ibid:* reference #2

69 *Ibid:* reference #2

70 *Ibid:* reference #2

71 *Ibid:* reference #2

72 *Ibid:* reference #2

73 Interview between the author and Robert H. Hodges, Major, USAFR; Kennedy Space Center: October 1967